Foundations of Cognitive Psychology

Fernand Gobet, Philippe Chassy and Merim Bilalić

The **McGraw·Hill** Companies

London Boston Burr Ridge, IL Dubuque, IA Madison, WI New York San Francisco
St. Louis Bangkok Bogotá Caracas Kuala Lumpur Lisbon Madrid Mexico City
Milan Montreal New Delhi Santiago Seoul Singapore Sydney Taipei Toronto

Foundations of Cognitive Psychology
Fernand Gobet, Philippe Chassy and Merim Bilalić
ISBN-13 9-78-00-7711908-9
ISBN-10 0-07-711908-8

McGraw-Hill
Higher Education

Published by McGraw-Hill Education
Shoppenhangers Road
Maidenhead
Berkshire
SL6 2QL
Telephone: 44 (0) 1628 502 500
Fax: 44 (0) 1628 770 224
Website: www.mcgraw-hill.co.uk

British Library Cataloguing in Publication Data
A catalogue record for this book is available from the British Library

Library of Congress Cataloguing in Publication Data
The Library of Congress data for this book has been applied for from the Library of Congress

Acquisitions Editor: Natalie Jacobs
Development Editor: Jennifer Rotherham
Marketing Manager: Kevin Watt
Production Editor: Alison Davis

Text design by Hard Lines
Cover design by Adam Renvoize
Printed and bound in Italy by Rotolito Lombarda, Italy

ISBN-13 978-00-7711908-9
ISBN-10 0-07-711908-8

Dedication

To Chananda, FG
To Anne, PC
To my parents Živadinka and Midhat, MB

Brief table of contents

Detailed table of contents

Preface

Cognitive psychology is an exciting but also complex topic. The fascinating questions it addresses about consciousness, problem solving and memory, to take just a few examples, require the use of sophisticated methods for collecting data and developing theories. Moreover, cognitive psychology has become increasingly interdisciplinary. In particular, the last two decades have seen a close collaboration between cognitive psychology and neuroscience in what is often called *cognitive neuroscience.*

Cognitive psychology is a very active area, with intensive research being carried out to address both basic and applied questions. Given the rapid developments taking place, there is an abundance of ideas, concepts and techniques. The number and variety of methods used in cognitive psychology (e.g. behavioural experiments, brain imaging, cognitive neuropsychology, computer modelling) can be overwhelming and confusing for the student.

Rather than providing an encyclopaedic treatment, we have written this textbook as a first introduction to cognitive psychology. To achieve this goal, we obviously had to be selective with respect to the material covered. In general, we have aimed to strike a balance between discussing classic studies and presenting cutting-edge research. In doing so, we have tried to keep the sense of excitement and discovery that is palpable in the field, but also to provide material that is suitable at the early stages of learning. Thus, we offer a fairly simple introduction that is technically correct and that provides a solid foundation for further study.

The intended book audience is primarily first-year and second-year psychology undergraduates taking a first course in cognitive psychology. The audience also includes students majoring in other fields taking cognitive psychology as an elective. The book can also be used for self-study.

While the structure of the book is standard (starting from low-level mechanisms such as neural transmission and perception, and moving to higher-level functions such as creativity and expertise), its originality is in using a unique theoretical framework that organises and integrates the material in all chapters. More advanced topics (e.g. consciousness or computer modelling) are not ignored, but they are dealt with in detail only after the basics of cognitive psychology have been fully introduced.

The book is organised around four main sections:

- Part 1 introduces the topic, offers some historical pointers and provides a brief introduction to neuroscience.
- Part 2 covers basic cognitive processes, such as perception and learning; these processes are to some extent shared by other animals.
- Part 3 discusses higher-level cognitive functions, such as language and thinking; these functions tend to be uniquely human.
- Part 4 deals with advanced topics, such as the neuroscience of visual perception, and computational modelling. The goal is not to provide an extensive coverage of these topics, which is beyond the scope of this book, but rather to show how they link with the topics discussed in the first three sections of the book.

The framework used in this textbook is loosely based on theories and computational models developed to explain, amongst other phenomena, expert perception, learning, memory and problem solving (Gobet *et al.*, 2001; Gobet and Simon, 2000; Richman *et al.*, 1995). Following the principle that the building blocks of knowledge should be taught first, we will not present our framework in detail here or even in the next chapter, but rather we will build it gradually in the first three sections of the book. The final chapter, 'Putting it all together', will bind the various strands together and show how all aspects of cognition – most notably perception, memory, learning, decision making and problem solving – hang together closely. At this stage, it is sufficient to point out that this framework can summarise a large amount of knowledge by a series of propositions that are accepted by most cognitive psychologists, and that together can explain a surprisingly large number of phenomena. As previously mentioned, the statements will be introduced incrementally as the empirical evidence is presented in the respective chapters. A few examples will suffice at this stage:

- The brain and the mind are organised hierarchically.
- Perception is strongly parallel.
- Attention is limited and is essentially serial.
- Short-term memory is limited in capacity.
- Rationality is limited.

While such statements can be found in most textbooks, the originality of our book is that they will be used systematically to build connections between chapters, and thus to facilitate learning. Using this framework provides a coherent and integrative structure that will help counteract the fragmented impression often given by cognitive psychology. Anchoring information in a single framework does not mean that we will ignore the main competing theories. On the contrary, a fair amount of text will be devoted to such theories.

CHAPTER PREVIEW

☑ Cognitive psychology is the scientific study
the interdisciplinary study of the mind.

☑ Cognitive psychologists answer theoretical
dependent variables are the percentage of c
errors, and verbal protocols. Brain-imaging

☑ Besides healthy adult humans, cognitive ps
patients suffering from brain damage.

☑ Theories enable scientists to summarise an
Computer models make it possible to deve
that can address complex phenomena.

☑ Cognitive psychology consists of numerous
applied questions.

☑ Research has shown that being active durin
and retention of the material, and cognitiv
studying efficiently.

Chapter Preview

As an introductory overview, learning
objectives help you quickly identify the
essentials you will learn in each chapter.

Glossary

ological loss of the
member, either
ormation has been
ecause one is
trieve it. Amnesia
the loss of past
etrograde amnesia)
ity to store new
anterograde
ormal loss of
in long-term
eferred to as

almond-shaped
clei located at the
the base of the
e. It is part of the
m, and is
n emotion (in

approach (symbolic approach):
The school of cognitive
psychology which considers
that cognition consists of the
manipulation of symbols and
which uses the computer
analogy of the mind.

argument: In Kintsch and van
Dijk's theory, the meaning of a
word.

arousal: Level of activity of the
automatic nervous system.

artefact category: A category
consisting of human-made
objects.

attention: Basic cognitive process
that enables us to focus on a
particular stimulus at the
expense of others.

Key Terms and Glossary

Key terms are highlighted in the chapters and
defined in the glossary at the end of the book.
An ideal tool for last-minute revision or to
check definitions as you read.

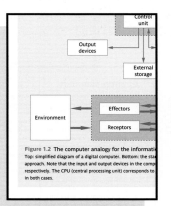

Figure 1.2 The computer analogy for the informatic
Top: simplified diagram of a digital computer. Bottom: the sta
approach. Note that the input and output devices in the comp
respectively. The CPU (central processing unit) corresponds to
in both cases.

Figures and Tables

Each chapter provides a number of figures,
illustrations and photos to help you to
visualise the key theories and studies of
cognitive psychology.

nonsense syllables, adjectives unrelated to the s
nyms. In addition, a control group just rested so
that could be compared to the groups who had s
clear pattern. The resting group performed bette
task. Among these groups, the best performance v
and the worse by the group that learned synon
semantic proximity – that is, if words are semant
interferences distort the original memory traces.

Stop and Think Why chatting is detrimental
Considering what you know about memory traces an
effects that enter into play when someone chats durin
taking place with the person talking, the person listeni

Recent models of working me

Short-term memory has been a very influentia
Several information-processing models were dev
ing the empirical data better than its predecessor
on the information-processing aspects of short-t
term memory is now increasingly called *working*
influential theories of working memory. Badd

Stop and Think

These questions have been designed to
challenge you to think critically in evaluating
themes in cognitive psychology and its
relevance to your own life.

Box 5.2 EVERYDAY APPLICATION: Atten

The scenario at the start of this chapter is what o
a cognitive psychologist and hobby magician.
lighter trick in front of participants while record
2005; Tatler and Kuhn, 2007). It turned out th
unaware of the trick spotted the cigarette drop.
informed about the nature of the experiment as,
spotted the cigarette drop. All participants fixate
cian's face or his right shoulder. Yet, when the t
ants who had initially failed to spot the cigarette
done. Surprisingly enough, only one-quarter of
dropped the lighter, while the other three-quarter
the lighter, the right shoulder) as in the first trial
trick.
    A similar pattern was observed in another ex
case, it was a ball that disappeared. The magician
times and suddenly the ball was not in the air! (T
the normal condition, the magician used all sc
attention – he looked at the ball when it was in
was supposedly in the air. When the tape was sh
that they saw the ball move up and leave the s

Everyday Applications

Drawing on examples from everyday life, including film and literature, these examples are used to illustrate how cognitive psychology can be applied in the world around us.

Box 14.4 IN FOCUS: Love

Surprisingly, love has not been the focus of
been neglected: for the thousands of studies
find only a handful about love. This is astonish
behaviour. Even the law acknowledges the ve
sideration when setting the tariff in murder c
not enough of an emotion or that it is too com
tal paradigm.
    According to Sternberg (1986), love can ta
can be romantic or companionate. To accoun
proposed that love is the result of the interact
sion is intimacy, the second passion (referri
decision making. 'Intimacy' describes all the
person and to generate the warm security th
does not include physical attraction, which
passion component encapsulates all the stron
the decision-making component reflects the
loved one.

In Focus

These boxes encourage you to take a more detailed look at some of cognitive psychology's key theories and challenge you to think critically about the issues presented.

Box 6.1 RESEARCH CLOSE-UP: The free

Although free recall is one of the oldest method
most popular. The typical experiment has three
presented with the material to remember. Tw
information. First, there is the nature of the ma
there is the rate of presentation. Whether an it
further processing. The second phase is the reten
presentation of the items and their recall. The
participants are allowed to rehearse information
kept busy by completing another task such as co
chosen three-digit number. The load imposed by
cipants to rehearse. The last phase is recall, whe
tion interval and the beginning of the participan
and accuracy. (Response time or latency is the p
    The following example illustrates the three phas
You are presented with a list of monosyllabic wo
'BALL, LIFT, GRANT, WAR, BOLD'. Then, for 30 se
Finally, you have to recall the list. How long was th

Research Close Up and Classic Experiments

These features offer you a detailed understanding of how cognitive psychologists use various research methods to explore fascinating questions such as 'how do we remember things?

Chapter summary

This chapter has barely scratched the surface
echoing the conclusions of Chapter 10 on boun
As a consequence of strict limitations in attentic
ties, we are severely constrained in our cognitiv
tics. When making social judgements and decis
as attractiveness, and spontaneously generalise
effect). We also simplify our lives by judging c
effect) and by using schemas when making soc
they are fast, often work, and do not necessitat
have costs: they can lead us to use stereotypes, t
ing the behaviour of others, and to fall prey of
supporting evidence and neglecting evidence t
These biases might have benign consequences
lecturer or to decide whether to invite somebo
benign when they affect children's education o
crises made by political leaders – political leade
ties but also, or even mainly, because of the wa

Chapter Summary

The detailed chapter summaries help you to remember key concepts and issues. They also serve as an excellent study and revision guide.

occurs when these instances are heavily biased
events. The representativeness heuristic correspo
or only a few instances characteristic of a whole g
    While Kahneman and Tversky paint a rather
and others take a more positive stance. Heuristi
strated by the example of the recognition heuristi
ased' by using appropriate internal representatio
biases in thinking and decision making as well a
rence. Errors and biases give us additional insig
instances without errors do not offer.

Further reading

Markman and Gentner (2001) provide a useful
higher-level cognition. The classical papers by Ka
1973a; Tversky and Kahneman, 1974) should no
gist. Gigerenzer's entertaining book *Reckoning*
familiar with his counterattack on the Kahneman
the two popular books by Sutherland (2007) an
relevant everyday examples of the theories prese
read that it is impossible not to recommend then

Further Reading

At the end of each chapter you'll find a further reading section to help you research and read around the subject in more depth.

Technology to enhance learning and teaching

Visit **www.mcgraw-hill.co.uk/textbooks/gobet** today.

Online Learning Centre (OLC)

After completing each chapter, log on to the supporting Online Learning Centre website. Take advantage of the study tools offered to reinforce the material you have read in the text, and to develop your knowledge of cognitive psychology in a fun and effective way.

Resources for students include:

- *Self-test multiple-choice questions*

Also available for lecturers:

- *PowerPoint presentations*
- *Seminar material*
- *Test bank*

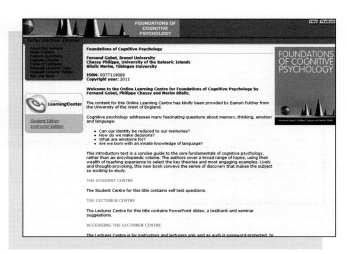

Custom publishing solutions

Let us help make our content your solution

At McGraw-Hill Education our aim is to help lecturers to find the most suitable content for their needs delivered to their students in the most appropriate way. Our **custom publishing solutions** offer the ideal combination of content delivered in the way that best suits lecturer and students.

Our custom publishing programme offers lecturers the opportunity to select just the chapters or sections of material they wish to deliver to their students from a database called CREATE™ at

www.mcgrawhillcreate.com

CREATE™ contains over two million pages of content from:

- textbooks
- professional books
- case books – Harvard Articles, Insead, Ivey, Darden, Thunderbird and BusinessWeek
- Taking Sides – debate materials

across the following imprints:

- McGraw-Hill Education
- Open University Press
- Harvard Business Publishing
- US and European material

There is also the option to include additional material authored by lecturers in the custom product – this does not necessarily have to be in English.

We will take care of everything from start to finish in the process of developing and delivering a custom product, to ensure that lecturers and students receive exactly the material needed in the most suitable way.

With a custom publishing solution, students enjoy the best selection of material deemed to be the most suitable for learning everything they need for their courses – something of real value to support their learning. Teachers are able to use exactly the material they want, in the way they want, to support their teaching on the course.

Please contact your local McGraw-Hill representative with any questions or alternatively contact Warren Eels e: *warren_eels@mcgraw-hill.com.*

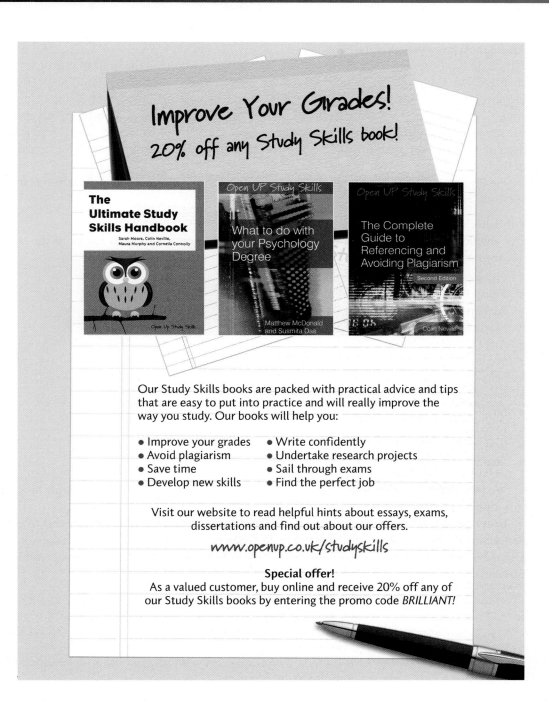

Acknowledgements

Author's Acknowledgements

This book has benefited from the comments of colleagues who read the draft of one or several chapters: Stan Gaines (Brunel University), Andy Parton (Brunel University), Sena Quaye (Buckinghamshire New University), Yvan Russell (Oxford University), Maria Uther (Brunel University), Chris Vincent (University College London) and Omar Yousaf (Cambridge University). We are particularly grateful to Anastasia Giannakopolou (Brunel University), who read a first draft of most chapters, and Lynda Shaw (Brunel University), who commented on the final draft of the book.

Finally, we would like to thank our editor Jennifer Rotherham and the production team at McGraw-Hill for their support and guidance.

Publisher's Acknowledgements

Our thanks go to the following reviewers for their comments at various stages in the text's development:

- Phil Beaman, University of Reading
- Philip Fine, University of Buckingham
- Barbara Kingsley, Roehampton University
- Maria Kontogianni, Nottingham Trent University
- Ard Lazonder, Universiteit Twente
- Michele Pisani, Buckinghamshire New University
- Sena Quaye, Buckinghamshire New University
- Jane Redshaw, Leeds Metropolitan University
- Ian Robertson, University of Bedfordshire
- Jo Saunders, University of Swansea
- Eric Soetens, University of Brussels
- Stephan van der Stigchel, Universiteit Utrecht

We would also like to thank Eamon Fulcher, University of the West of England, for his contribution to our online resource package.

Every effort has been made to trace and acknowledge ownership of copyright and to clear permission for material reproduced in this book. The publishers will be pleased to make suitable arrangements to clear permission with any copyright holders whom it has not been possible to contact.

Fernand Gobet is Professor of Cognitive Psychology and Director of the Centre for the Study of Expertise at Brunel University, West London. Previously, he held research and teaching positions at the University of Fribourg (Switzerland), Carnegie Mellon University (Pittsburgh, USA) and the University of Nottingham (UK). He has published extensively on the psychology of expertise, language acquisition and computational modelling. He is the main architect behind the CHREST project (Chunk Hierarchy and REtrieval STructures), one of the few cognitive architectures in the world. CHREST currently provides state-of-the-art models in multiple psychological domains including expert behaviour, vocabulary development and syntactic development. He has authored five books, including *Perception and Memory in Chess* (with Adriaan de Groot) and *Moves in Mind: The Psychology of Board Games* (with Alex de Voogt and Jean Retschitzki).

Philippe Chassy was awarded a PhD in Psychology in 2007 at Brunel University, West London, for his work highlighting the dynamics that make emotions regulators of cognition. He then worked for two and a half years at the University of Toulouse, both in the laboratory of psychology and the laboratory of artificial intelligence. He spent a year at University Hospital Tübingen to perfect his knowledge of neuroscience and neuroimaging. Following this training, he joined the Institute of Health Sciences Research (IUNICS) at the University of the Balearic Islands. His research has addressed expert behaviour, numerical cognition and reasoning, using a variety of techniques including behavioural experiments, neuroimaging and computer modelling.

Merim Bilalić is a research fellow at Tübingen University (Germany). He received his DPhil in Experimental Psychology from Oxford University (England), and has subsequently held research and teaching positions at Brunel University (London, England) and Humboldt University (Berlin, Germany). His research on the *Einstellung* (mental set) effect won the Award for the Outstanding Doctoral Research Contributions to Psychology by the British Psychological Society in 2008. His interests include expertise, skill acquisition, problem solving and brain imaging techniques. His research has been published in *Cognitive Psychology, Journal of Experimental Psychology: General, Cognition, Proceedings of the Royal Society B: Biological Sciences, Current Directions in Psychological Science, Intelligence* and other psychological journals.

Abbreviations and acronyms

ACT-R	Adaptive Control of Thought – Rational
AD	Alzheimer's disease
AI	artificial intelligence
ANS	autonomous nervous system
CHREST	Chunk Hierarchy and REtrieval STructures
cm	centimetre
DNA	deoxyribonucleic acid
EEG	electroencephalography
fMRI	functional Magnetic Resonance Imaging
GABA	gamma-aminobutyric acid
IT	inferior temporal cortex
km	kilometre
LTM	long-term memory
LTP	long-term potentiation
m	metre
MEG	magnetoencephalography
M cells	magnocellular cells
MRI	magnetic resonance imaging
ms	millisecond
MT	medial-temporal cortex
NP	noun-phrase
PET	Positron Emission Tomography
P cells	parvocellular cells
s	second
S	sentence
SAS	supervisory attentional system
SQ3R	survey, question, read, recite and review
STM	short-term memory
UTC	unified theory of cognition
VP	verb-phrase
V1	visual area 1
V2	visual area 2
V4	visual area 4
VSSP	visuospatial sketchpad (also known as the visuospatial scratchpad)

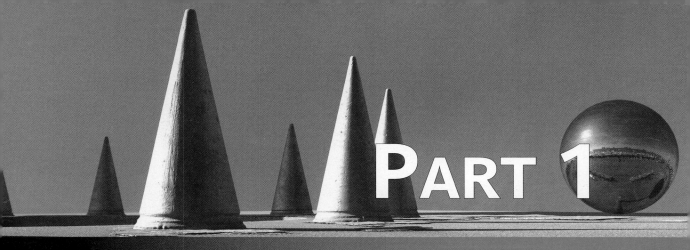

PART 1

Introduction

Part contents

Chapter 1

Introduction to cognitive psychology

CHAPTER PREVIEW

- ☑ Cognitive psychology is the scientific study of mental processes. Cognitive science is the interdisciplinary study of the mind.

- ☑ Cognitive psychologists answer theoretical questions by running experiments. Typical dependent variables are the percentage of correct answers, response times, types of errors, and verbal protocols. Brain-imaging data are increasingly used.

- ☑ Besides healthy adult humans, cognitive psychology also studies children, animals and patients suffering from brain damage.

- ☑ Theories enable scientists to summarise and explain data, and to make predictions. Computer models make it possible to develop theories that are highly specified and that can address complex phenomena.

- ☑ Cognitive psychology consists of numerous subfields that address both basic and applied questions.

- ☑ Research has shown that being active during learning leads to better understanding and retention of the material, and cognitive psychology has developed methods for studying efficiently.

Introduction

How does the mind work? What is the link between brain and mind? Why do we forget? Does strong emotion help or hinder memory? What is the nature of consciousness? How do we think? These questions – some of the most difficult that humans have ever tackled – are the subject matter of cognitive psychology. As you can see, you are about to engage in an exciting voyage of discovery!

Cognitive psychology is the scientific study of mental processes – that is, processes that allow us to perceive our environment, memorise information, use language to communicate, and make decisions. It also covers topics such as **attention** and **consciousness**. Most of these processes occur automatically, without us even noticing they have happened. In spite of this, every waking minute is filled with events that are studied by cognitive psychology.

The difficulty of the questions cognitive psychology aims to answer, as well as the interdisciplinary nature of its research, has a two-fold consequence. On the one hand, it is a very exciting field, in which new discoveries are made almost daily. On the other hand, it is a fairly complex field: ideas from different sciences (cognitive psychology has often teamed up with other fields, such as neuroscience and computer science; see Box 1.1) must be assimilated and combined; many topics are covered; students must have at least elementary knowledge of different types of experimental methods; and, perhaps more than in any other field of psychology, the sometimes complex interplay between data collection and theory development must be understood.

Box 1.1 IN FOCUS: **Cognitive psychology and cognitive science**

Cognitive psychologists study a staggering number of topics: they are interested in the way people perceive, learn, speak, read, make decisions, do mathematics, play chess, and even develop new scientific theories! Given this range of interest, it is not surprising that they often carry out interdisciplinary research. For instance, an understanding of language comprehension may require collaboration with linguists, and the study of consciousness may put together a group of cognitive psychologists, computer scientists and philosophers. The boundaries between disciplines sometimes become fuzzy, and the interdisciplinary study of how the mind works has become a scientific field in itself: **cognitive science**. Cognitive science can be seen as the intersection of several fields including psychology, anthropology, artificial intelligence, computer science, neuroscience, linguistics and philosophy.

The experimental methods of cognitive psychology

Cognitive psychology is first of all an experimental science. A theoretical question is addressed by running an **experiment** in which the **independent variable** of interest is manipulated, and the effect of the manipulation is assessed by measuring **dependent variables** (see Box 1.2). The dependent variables most often used are response times, the percentage of responses that are correct, and the type of errors made. Eye-movement recordings are sometimes used, as the duration and location of fixations provide useful information about where the focus of attention is directed. When studying high-level functions such as problem solving and decision making, cognitive psychologists often ask participants to think aloud. The **verbal protocols** that are obtained can then be analysed at different levels of granularity: for example, to look at the speed with which participants carry out mental processes, or, at a higher level of analysis, to identify the strategies that are being used.

Stop and Think Sternberg

Sternberg (1966) concluded that his data supported the hypothesis of a serial and exhaustive mechanism. Can you think of other ways he may have interpreted the data, for example explanations using parallel scanning?

For many years cognitive psychologists have been interested in how cognition is implemented in the brain. However, breakthroughs in **brain imaging** technology in the past 20 years, combined with the broad availability of high-speed computers, have brought about a revolution in the way cognitive psychologists collect data. As we will see in Chapter 3, it is now possible to observe brain activation in real time when participants carry out experimental tasks.

Box 1.2 CLASSIC EXPERIMENT: **Sternberg's experiment**

Saul Sternberg (1966) carried out one of the most famous experiments in cognitive psychology, and, although we will cover short-term memory in detail in Chapter 6, it is instructive to describe this experiment here. Sternberg was interested in how we access the contents of our short-term memory. Is it done serially, one item after the other, or can we access all the items simultaneously? For example, if you memorise a list of numbers, say 7 3 9 2, and are asked to say whether 9 was a member of the list, do you have to mentally go through 7 and 3 to finally reach 9, or can you access 9 as rapidly as any of the other numbers?

The task we have just described actually closely follows Sternberg's procedure. He presented a list of digits (which he called the 'memory set') and then a probe digit, and the task of the participants was to press either a YES button or a NO button as rapidly as possible to indicate whether the probe was, or was not, part of the memory set. The independent variables that Sternberg manipulated were the size of the memory set, from 1 digit to 6 digits, and whether the probe was, or was not, part of the memory set. The dependent variable was the time taken to press the YES or NO button. Sternberg wanted to answer two questions. We have already mentioned the first one: is the access to short-term memory serial or parallel? If short-term memory is accessed serially, then it should take longer to respond with a large memory set, say five items, than with a small memory set, say two items. If short-term memory is accessed in parallel, there should not be any difference. With his second question, Sternberg wanted to know whether search is exhaustive or not. That is, after having found the target, does the search stop, as one would expect intuitively, or does it continue to the end of the list? To return to the example above, does search stop after reaching 9, or is 2 considered as well? Note that, with NO answers, the search is expected to be exhaustive: the entire list has to be scanned if one wants to be sure that the probe is absent. For each memory size, half the required answers were YES and half were NO. With the YES trials, the position of the target in the list was changed with equal probability.

▶

Participants were very accurate, with only 1.3 per cent of their responses being incorrect. As shown in Figure 1.1, response time increased as a function of the size of the memory set, and there was little difference between the YES and the NO answers. The results are very well fitted by a straight line, and the slope of the line indicates that every additional digit increases scanning time by 37.9 milliseconds (ms). Sternberg considered that his results gave a clear answer to his two questions. First, search is serial, as larger memory sets incur longer scanning times. Second, scanning does not stop when a target is found and thus search is exhaustive: this is indicated by the fact that the YES answers take as long as the NO answers.

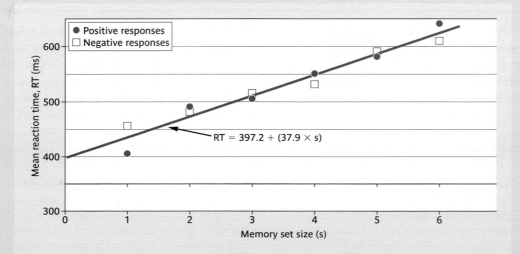

Figure 1.1 Results of Sternberg's experiment
The graph shows the mean response latency as a function of the number of symbols in memory, as well as the best-fitting linear regression line.
Source: Adapted from Sternberg (1966)

Cognitive psychologists run experiments with different types of population. The default is to use healthy adult participants – typically psychology students – who are naïve about the question being studied. In the field of expertise, the performance of experts is contrasted with that of intermediates or novices. In **neuropsychology**, the comparison is between patients suffering from a brain lesion and healthy participants, and the question of interest is the extent to which brain damage affects cognition. Developmental aspects are studied with children and even infants. Some questions can be addressed by studying animals, typically non-human primates. In all cases, experiments are designed that both address specific theoretical questions and are ethically appropriate to the population under study.

Developing theories that explain the data

Once data have been collected, cognitive psychologists develop **theories** to explain them. Without good theories, even the best data are of little use (see Box 1.3). In addition, theories are also a powerful way to generate new predictions and thus new ideas for future experiments, which enables a better understanding of the phenomena under study.

In general, the more precise a theory, the better it is – that is, we should prefer theories that are explicit about the structures and the mechanisms involved to theories that leave many details unspecified. One way to do this is to use **mathematical models**. For example, the rate of forgetting can be expressed mathematically (see Chapter 7). However, these models make assumptions that are often not met by the type of data collected in cognitive psychology, and they also force more simplifications than is desirable. As we will see in the next chapter, on the history of cognitive psychology, one of the great contributions of the 'cognitive revolution' is the idea that computers can be used to implement scientific theories in psychology. This idea really has two meanings, which you should clearly distinguish.

The first meaning is that, at some level of abstraction, human cognition is roughly similar to a digital computer (see Figure 1.2); in particular, both include input and output mechanisms, programs, different types of memory, serial processing (i.e. only one operation is carried out at a time), and so on. This meaning, which is the one used by the **information-processing approach**, is best illustrated by Newell and Simon's (1972) work on how humans solve problems in domains such as logic and chess. This work will play a central role in Chapter 11.

Box 1.3 IN FOCUS: **Why do we need theories?**

A large number of theories have been developed in cognitive psychology, and this book will discuss a fair number of them. But why bother with theories, in particular if one is more interested in applications (e.g. in applying cognitive therapies to help depressed people, or in improving financial decision making in a business)? Why not simply collect data?

Well, thousands of experiments are carried out every year on different aspects of cognition, and it would be impractical, if not impossible, to survey even a subset of them when developing a specific application. The initial relevance of theories is thus to *summarise* data. In some cases, this can be done to the point where **scientific laws** can be derived (see the power law of learning in Chapter 7). But we can go one step further. Theories can *explain* data: that is, they can highlight the causal mechanisms that underlie a phenomenon. Finally, theories make it possible to *predict* future behaviours.

It is essential to realise that theories are important for applied science. If you want to construct a plane, you'd better know about theoretical physics. If you want to develop medicines, you'd better know about theoretical biochemistry. The same applies with (cognitive) psychology. If you want to develop better educational techniques, improve on the current cognitive therapies, or provide better environments for the elderly, you need to use and understand the current theories in your specific field of interest.

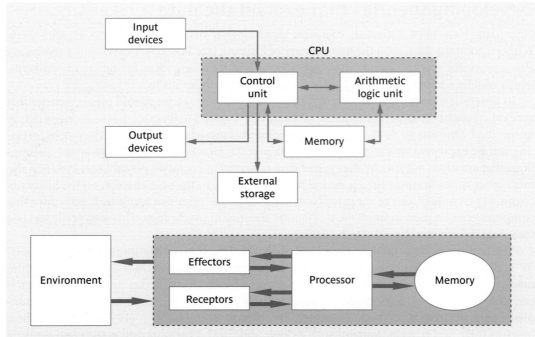

Figure 1.2 The computer analogy for the information-processing approach
Top: simplified diagram of a digital computer. Bottom: the standard view of cognition in the information-processing approach. Note that the input and output devices in the computer correspond to the receptors and effectors, respectively. The CPU (central processing unit) corresponds to the processor. The final component, memory, is present in both cases.

Stop and Think The computer analogy
The analogy between computer and cognition has had a considerable influence on cognitive psychology, and is still often used today. For example, researchers in cognitive neuroscience use concepts such as input, output or processing of information. Identify the aspects of this analogy that are particularly strong, and those that are weak.

The second meaning is that the computer can be used as a modelling tool to simulate cognitive behaviour, without necessarily accepting the first meaning. Just like other sciences such as physics or chemistry, cognitive psychology can use **computer modelling** to understand complex systems that evolve as a function of time (Figure 1.3 illustrates the idea). Weather forecasting is possible because scientists have a sufficiently detailed understanding of the physical laws that are implicated. (A **scientific law** is a verbal or mathematical statement that describes a relation between two or more empirical variables.) These laws can be expressed as mathematical equations, which in turn can be implemented as computer programs. If you want to predict the weather in London for the next day, you can run such computer programs together with data about the previous days' conditions (e.g. temperature and air pressure) at numerous spots in and around London. Given the amount of data to process and the complexity of the computations to carry out, serious predictions cannot be made without using powerful computers. Human cognition is more complex than the weather in London – which is rather predictable and usually not very enjoyable – and computer modelling is a crucial tool for understanding psychological phenomena at different levels of abstraction. Figure 1.3 illustrates this with an example of social cognition. A group of business people meet to make an important decision. We can measure the knowledge of these individuals, their goals and their emotional state. Together with our understanding of cognition and emotion, which can be stated as laws and used to develop a computer program, we can make predictions about the likely outcome of the meeting – for example, that the chief executive will be put in a defensive position and react angrily in order to convince the other members of the board. This example illustrates the use of computational modelling with high-level cognition. Computer models can also be developed to explain low-level aspects of cognition (e.g. the perceptual mechanisms used to discriminate between two different letters), and they can also be used to simulate phenomena at the brain level (e.g. how the connection between two neurons can be strengthened by the simultaneous presentation of two stimuli).

Stop and Think Computer modelling
What is harder – to simulate yesterday's weather, or to simulate the results of Sternberg's (1966) experiment (see Box 1.2)?

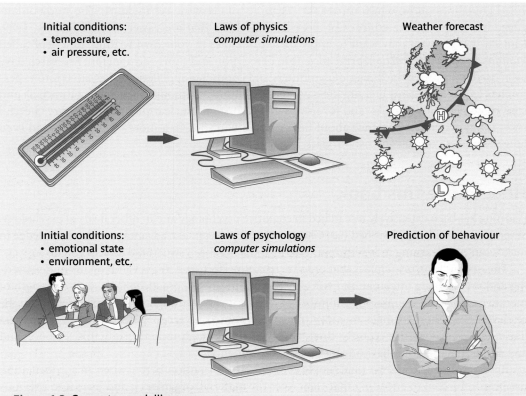

Figure 1.3 Computer modelling
Computer modelling in weather forecasting and in psychology. In both cases, initial conditions combined with laws make it possible to derive predictions.

The subfields and applications of cognitive psychology

Cognitive psychology is not a homogeneous field, but consists of a number of subfields. This organisation is apparent in the type of scientific journals where research is published or the type of conferences that are organised to disseminate results. The subfields can be identified either using the type of behaviour they study (e.g. psychology of perception, psychology of reading) or the type of experimental technique they used (e.g. eye movements, brain imaging). These fields can also be grouped as doing either basic research (e.g. statistical properties of reaction times) or applied research (e.g. cognitive design, psychology of driving, educational psychology).

As we shall see in the next chapter, one of the reasons behind the birth of cognitive psychology was the need to answer very practical questions, such as how to keep the vigilance level of radar operators high. The field has maintained this interest for practical issues, and the scientific principles it has uncovered have generated countless real-life applications (e.g. Pezdek *et al.*, 2006). We will discuss many of these applications in this book, but here is a small sample. Research into attention has clearly shown the dangers of using cell phones when driving. Work on long-term memory and learning has led to new methods for instructing new drivers, training technicians in industrial settings, and teaching mathematics to children; this last application includes the development of intelligent computer-tutoring systems. This work has also provided guidelines on how to improve the reliability of eyewitnesses in court. The study of language has led to advice concerning how to write texts that are easier to read (Hayes, 1989; Kintsch, 1998) – you may want to apply these principles in your own writing. In a field called *human–computer interaction*, principles from perception and short-term memory research have been used to improve the design of computers and computer applications. Research into expertise has led to novel and literally life-saving applications: methods for training physicians and land mine detection experts, and for improving security in nuclear plants. On a more cheerful note, it has generated guidance about how to train your dog in a more efficient way and even how to protect yourself against burglars.

How to use this book

Learning has been extensively researched in cognitive psychology and in other fields of psychology. Several laws have been identified (see Chapter 7) and you can take advantage of this knowledge to make your own learning more efficient. This textbook has been structured to help you do so.

The overarching principle is that practice makes perfect, and this is valid too for understanding and memorising information from a textbook. In general, practice increases the strength of memory traces and increases the number of different ways through which information can be retrieved. Together, stronger memory traces and numerous access paths make forgetting less likely. However, practice requires time. Give yourself enough time to study this textbook and any additional material that your instructor recommends.

Research has also shown that people remember information better when this information has been subjected to encoding that elaborates the material, organises it and links it to previous knowledge. A particularly powerful way to make sure you memorise and understand material is to force yourself to recall or otherwise generate (e.g. by answering questions) the information you have learned. Among other things, generating material creates additional retrieval cues and leads to the creation of new links in your knowledge base. In a nutshell: when you learn, do not read passively, but be active!

The validity of these study principles has been tested experimentally, and it has been repeatedly found that students who follow them learn better than those who do not. (If you want to find more about this research, you can check Anderson, 1990.) In addition, a variety of techniques have been developed to help students develop efficient learning habits. The SQ3R method (Tadlock, 1978) is a particularly efficient one, the efficacy of which has been confirmed by research. The acronym stands for Survey, Question, Read, Recall and Review. When studying a chapter, first *survey* its contents, by reading the preview section at the beginning of the chapter and skimming its contents. Then, think about the types of *question* you would like the chapter to answer. When you *read* the chapter, regularly go back to these questions, and also try to link the material to what you already know about the topic. Also, read critically, and do not hesitate to question the material. At the end of each section of a chapter, force yourself to *recall* the essential points of what you have learned. Finally, after finishing a chapter, *review* it regularly, and try to link its contents to the preceding and following chapters. This method is certainly more time consuming than reading the chapters once whilst daydreaming, but it will also ensure a much better understanding and memory of the material.

This textbook has been written to encourage you to be active when reading, and indeed to make use of the SQ3R method. In each chapter, the *Learning Objectives* at the beginning enable you to survey the chapter (you can also use the *Chapter Summary* at the end of each chapter for this purpose). In the body of each chapter, *Thought Questions* and connections with the other chapters will force you to think deeply about the issues. Reviewing is made easier by the presence of a *Chapter Summary*. *Further Reading* will direct you to more advanced material that will allow you an even deeper processing of the information.

Stop and Think SQ3R

When studying in the past, have you used techniques, including self-developed techniques, for improving your concentration and learning? How do these techniques differ from SQ3R? If you have never used such techniques, study one chapter of this book the way you normally study, and another chapter using SQ3R. Can you observe a difference?

Chapter summary

Cognitive psychology is the scientific study of mental processes. The chapter has provided an overview of the research questions addressed by cognitive psychology, and the kind of methods that are used to answer them. Cognitive psychology is first of all an experimental science, although the development of theories, often realised as computer programs, plays an important role as well. A central message of this chapter is that theories are essential not only for the development of fundamental knowledge, but also for devising applications – for example, instructional methods.

The next chapter, which provides a brief history of cognitive psychology, also expands on some of the topics we have just covered. A good understanding of cognition requires some knowledge of the biophysical medium in which it is implemented – the brain – and a full chapter (Chapter 3) will be devoted to the basics of neuroscience.

Further reading

The four-volume collection edited by Pashler (2002) provides extensive coverage of the experimental methods used in cognitive psychology. Newell (1990) contains an interesting discussion about the link between data and theory, and how this affects the development of theories. Among the many journals that publish general research on cognitive psychology and cognitive science, the most important are *Cognitive Psychology, Cognitive Science, Cognition,* the *European Journal of Cognitive Psychology, Journal of Experimental Psychology: Learning, Memory, and Cognition, Memory & Cognition, Psychological Review* and *Trends in Cognitive Science. Applied Cognitive Psychology* contains papers on how cognition relates to everyday life.

2

A brief history of cognitive psychology

CHAPTER PREVIEW

- ☑ The German Wilhelm Wundt opened the first laboratory of psychology in 1879, and other scientists started studying psychology experimentally around the same time. In 1890 the American William James published a textbook of psychology that anticipated many of the questions that were later addressed by cognitive psychologists.

- ☑ While psychologists were actively researching cognition in Europe during the first half of the twentieth century, in the USA behaviourism proscribed the study of mental processes and directed attention to learning behaviours in animals.

- ☑ The Second World War put an end to the Gestalt and Würzburg schools in Germany, which were both interested in cognition, but also alerted psychologists to the importance of attention and vigilance in human behaviour. The war effort speeded up the development of the digital computer, which was essential in the birth of modern cognitive psychology.

- ☑ The cognitive revolution happened over several years, but 1956 is often seen as its foundation date. Three key factors led to this revolution: the computer analogy developed by Broadbent in the UK and Newell and Simon in USA; the development of new linguistic theories by Noam Chomsky; and the use of information theory to explain psychological phenomena.

- ☑ Cognitive psychology has split into numerous subfields and has increasingly influenced other scientific fields.

☑ In the 1980s cognitive psychologists started using models inspired by the biology of the brain (connectionist models). Critical developments in brain-imaging techniques in the early 1990s led to the growth of cognitive neuroscience, which uses knowledge from biology to explain the way the mind works.

☑ Unified theories of cognition, which are embodied as computer programs, aim to provide a single theory explaining every aspect of cognition.

Introduction

Humans have been interested in their mental processes at least since the Ancient Greeks. For example, Aristotle proposed that our memory is like a clay tablet on which information can be written, and Socrates thought that knowledge is innate: one can recollect it, but not acquire it. However, we had to wait until the end of the nineteenth century to see philosophical speculations replaced by truly scientific investigations. In 1879 Wilhelm Wundt opened a psychology laboratory at the University of Leipzig, in Germany. At about the same time, a number of scientists were carrying out experiments on cognitive processes. The French academic Alfred Binet was investigating the strategies used by mental calculators, using measures that are now standard in the field (such as reaction times and errors), and the German Hermann Ebbinghaus designed nonsense verbal stimuli (such as BOF, GIF or ZID) to study memory and learning.

Wundt (1874) himself used a rich repertoire of methods, of which **introspection** is of special interest. This method consisted in training participants to report and analyse their own perceptions and sensations. This method was anchored in **structuralism**, a school of thought that assumed that the contents of consciousness can be broken down in elementary parts, just like a chemical compounds can be broken down into atoms. Unfortunately, this method was riddled with problems. For example, as we shall see in this book, most mental processes occur unconsciously and thus are simply not reportable. The problems plaguing introspection quickly became apparent as participants in different laboratories were reporting different elementary processes. It is now clear that the participants' introspections were influenced by the theoretical preconceptions of the experimenters.

In 1890 the American William James wrote a textbook, *Principles of Psychology*, that became particularly influential. While Wundt was interested in the *structure* of consciousness, James was interested in its *function*: that is, he wanted to know how the mind enables adaptation to the environment. His approach was non-experimental and rather speculative, but he anticipated some of the questions that would later occupy cognitive psychologists for decades. For example, as we shall see in Chapter 6, current research is still busy studying James's distinction between **primary memory** (the content of which is immediately available to consciousness) and **secondary memory** (which is much larger and can be seen as the repository of previous experiences).

The study of cognitive processes in the USA was stalled almost at its inception by the advent of **behaviourism**, which had started just before the turn of the century. The weaknesses of introspection as a method and structuralism as a framework offered an easy target at which experimental psychologists lashed out. A particularly clear statement of the aims of behaviourism was given in John Watson's (1913) article, 'Psychology as the behaviorist views it', which is often seen as the behaviourist manifesto. Watson argued forcefully that, being a branch of the natural sciences, psychology should strive to gather objective and experimental data. Scientific laws in psychology should quantify the relation between observable behaviour and observable stimuli in the environment, the so-called 'stimulus–reaction (S–R) bond'. These laws are the same for animals and humans. Thus, there is no place for ill-defined concepts such as mental processes, consciousness and mind.

For more than half a century (roughly from 1900 to 1960), most experimental research in America focused on animal learning, as this made possible the close control of both stimuli and responses. Little research was carried out by psychologists on issues such as decision making, thinking and memory, which all had to presuppose more complex mechanisms than stimulus–response bonds. It should be pointed out that, during this American 'cognitive winter', the study of mental processes was active in Europe. For example, in the Soviet Union Alexander Luria was investigating phenomena ranging from **aphasia** (impairment of language production and comprehension due to brain damage) to the processes involved in lying, and in Switzerland Jean Piaget was working on a general theory of cognitive development. Research was particularly active in Germany. **Gestalt psychologists** were studying perception and problem solving (see Chapters 4 and 11), and the members of the **Würzburg School** examined in great detail the processes underpinning high-level thinking such as arguing philosophical questions.

The cognitive revolution

The Second World War had two opposite effects on the development of cognitive psychology. On the one hand, it slowed down the vigorous research that was carried out in Germany. Several of the researchers of the Gestalt and Würzburg schools were persecuted under the Nazis and had to escape Germany. On the other hand, the war effort in the USA and the UK encouraged psychologists to study factors such as attention and fatigue. For example, radar operators had to stay vigilant for hours in conditions where nothing happened for most of the time, but where one second of inattention could mean missing an enemy plane and could have disastrous consequences. This was clearly a topic for which cognitive psychology could provide important insight. As we shall see in Chapter 5, a substantial amount has been learned about attention from this research.

By accelerating the technological advances in engineering that led to the construction of computers, the Second World War provided another critical thrust for the development of cognitive psychology. In England, just after the war, Donald Broadbent proposed the **computer–mind analogy**: both have receptors dealing with inputs and effectors dealing with outputs. In addition, both are characterised by a fairly small **short-term memory** and channels of limited capacity, which has the consequence that a fair amount of processing is carried out serially (i.e. only one thing is done at a time).

One the other side of the Atlantic, Newell and Simon went a step further. They noted that both computers and humans manipulate **symbols** (i.e. physical patterns standing for something else). If both carry out the same type of information processing – at some level of abstraction – then one should be able to develop computer programs that simulate aspects of human cognition, or even that could think. This insight was not only the motivation behind an important approach in cognitive psychology – **the information-processing approach**, also called the

Box 2.1 IN FOCUS: **The influence of engineering on cognitive psychology**

Several fields of engineering had a direct impact on the birth of modern cognitive psychology, and their influence is still detectable in some of the terms cognitive psychologists use routinely today. *Information theory* (a branch of engineering interested in measuring information: for example, the amount of information that is exchanged during a phone conversation) has given us several terms. These include input, output, channel capacity (the largest amount of information that can reliably be transmitted on a channel), redundancy (the idea that the components of a system or a message are duplicated in order to augment reliability), **code** (a specific type of representation) and **encoding** (the process by which information in one type of representation is converted in a different type of representation). From *computer science* we have terms such as **buffer** (a memory store that keeps information for a limited duration only), **production** (a rule consisting of a condition and an action) and **algorithm** (a set of instructions). Computer science has also provided cognitive psychology with diagrams called **flowcharts** (charts that show the path of data through an information-processing system and the operations performed on the data; see Figure 1.2 in Chapter 1, and almost any chapter of this book), and the programming techniques and languages used for developing computational models. These techniques have turned out to be highly useful in enabling cognitive psychologists to state theories unambiguously, which enables them to simulate complex phenomena and make quantitative predictions (e.g. the number of errors a child will make when learning multi-column subtraction). Computers have also been tremendously important for collecting and analysing data – think of their use nowadays for processing the huge data sets produced by brain-imaging techniques such as event-related potentials and fMRI.

symbolic approach – but also led to the creation of the field of artificial intelligence (AI). Whereas cognitive psychologists use computer modelling to understand cognitive processes, AI researchers are interested in producing computer programs or robots that behave intelligently, even if this entails mechanisms that are unlike those characterising animal and human cognition (see Box 2.1).

Another critical development consisted in a … book review! As noted above, behaviourism was rampant, and Skinner, one of its leaders, published a book called *Verbal Behaviour* (1957), where he argued that the simple mechanisms identified by the research on animal **classical conditioning** could explain language, a capacity that is uniquely human. Two years later, a young linguist named Noam Chomsky destroyed Skinner's argument in an article that must count as the most influential book review ever written in science (Chomsky, 1959). Written in a surprisingly aggressive tone by today's standards, Chomsky essentially accused Skinner of scientific incompetence at best and dishonesty at worst, and argued that the mechanisms proposed by Skinner simply could not explain even simple aspects of human language. Chomsky based his virulent attack not on empirical data, but on an abstract analysis of the properties of human language. As we will see in Chapter 9, this preference for abstract considerations over empirical data has remained a characteristic feature of **linguistics**. It is fair to say that Chomsky's article dealt a serious blow to Skinner's enterprise, and to almost any attempts to explain language using simple associative mechanisms such as S–R bonds. The field would have to wait nearly three decades and for the advent of connectionism to finally witness a serious attempt to do so (see below).

Stop and Think Behaviourism
Behaviourism denied the existence of mental states, which seem to be the subject matter of psychology. In spite of this, behaviourism was more successful than any other approach in the history of psychology, dominating the field for more than 50 years. Why do you think this was the case?

The year 1956 is often taken as the starting point of both (modern) cognitive psychology and artificial intelligence. Two epoch-making conferences took place that year, which were attended by many of the researchers we have mentioned. The Dartmouth conference brought together researchers writing the first AI programs, and the Symposium of Information Theory that was held at the Massachusetts Institute of Technology saw talks by Newell, Simon, Chomsky and others on communication, language and problem solving. The year 1956 also saw the publication of highly influential papers and books. Miller (1956) published his 'magical number seven' paper in which he argued that the capacity of short-term memory, as well as other aspects of human cognition, was limited to seven items. Miller also introduced the important notion of **chunking**: that grouping items together as units helps obviate the limits of short-term memory. For example, while it is difficult to memorise the sequence of letters 'T H I S S E N T E N C E I S E A S Y T O M E M O R I S E', it is much easier to memorise the following sequence where letters are grouped in meaningful

Box 2.2 IN FOCUS: **The different meanings of the term 'theory'**

We have so far used the term **theory** as if it were referring to a single 'thing'. However, the term is used with different meanings depending on the context, and it is useful to be explicit about these meanings. Three meanings are apparent in many sciences, including cognitive psychology (Newell, 1990). Theories referring to loose collections of concepts and mechanisms are known as **frameworks**. For example, information-processing psychology assumes that human cognition is similar, at some level of abstraction, to the digital computer: both can be characterised by the presence of inputs and outputs, a central processor and memories. Frameworks are not specified enough to enable any clear-cut predictions, and their validity is judged in terms of the success of the theories (in the strict sense) they generate.

With **theories** (in the strict sense), the relations between concepts and mechanisms are specified, and qualitative predictions can be made. However, various parameters are left unspecified, which makes quantitative prediction difficult. For example, within the framework of information-processing psychology, a theory could specify that memory is divided into two stores (short-term memory and long-term memory), the capacity of short-term memory is limited, and the time to encode information in long-term memory is fairly long. Such a theory would predict that people are not particularly good at memorising a sequence of 20 digits, but could not make precise predictions about the number of digits that can be memorised and the type and number of errors made. Additional details are necessary for this, which are provided by **models**. With models, detailed mechanisms are proposed and all parameters are specified, which makes it possible for quantitative predictions to be made. In our example of memory for digits, such a model would have to specify, among other things, the capacity of short-term memory, the probability of making an error, and the rate of transferring information from short-term to long-term memory. A number of such models have been developed, amongst which the most influential has been the model proposed by Atkinson and Shiffrin (1968) (see Chapter 6).

units (chunks): 'THIS SENTENCE IS EASY TO MEMORISE'. Another important publication was the book published by Bruner *et al.* (1956), which systematically investigated how people form concepts, and highlighted the role of strategies in thinking.

Stop and Think Cognitive revolution

The events taking place in 1956 are often taken as indicating the beginning of the 'cognitive revolution'. However, we have also seen that much research had been done on cognition before that, in particular in Europe. Is the idea of a 'cognitive revolution' just hype fuelled by American psychologists blinded by half a century of behaviourism? Or was something genuinely new?

Cognitive psychology comes of age

The developments we have just described clearly jolted psychologists. But one had to wait until nearly ten years after the seminal Dartmouth and MIT conferences to see the new ideas firmly crystallised, with the publication of the first textbook on cognitive psychology by Ulrich Neisser (1967). Reflecting the interests of psychology at the time, Neisser's book focused on perception and attention, and devoted relatively little space to memory, language and thinking. It is also interesting to note that Neisser, although using an information-framework approach, was fairly critical about the possibility of simulating mental processes with computer programs, as he argued that mental processes were too complex to be explained by simple mechanisms. This attitude is still widespread and many cognitive psychologists, while paying lip service to the information-processing framework, are more reluctant when it comes to using computer programs as models of specific phenomena (Ericsson and Kintsch, 2000). Indeed, it is fair to say that the majority of cognitive psychologists would define their field as the use of elegant and sophisticated experimental paradigms to answer specific questions about the mind and/or brain, rather than the development of theories implemented as computer programs.

Since the early 1960s cognitive psychology has flourished. Numerous experimental paradigms have been created, and numerous theories have been developed to explain the large amount of empirical data collected. The field has rapidly divided into several subfields (see Chapter 1), to the extent that today a cognitive psychologist interested in language hardly speaks to a colleague interested in, say, visual perception. Cognitive psychology has also increasingly influenced other fields of psychology. For example, the concept of a **schema**, which was developed to explain phenomena in memory and language, started being used to explain depression in clinical psychology (Beck, 1975), stereotypes in social psychology (Brewer and Hewstone, 2004; see also Chapter 18), and the way schoolchildren learn in educational psychology (Siegler, 1986).

Cognitive neuropsychology has become an important subfield of cognitive psychology. Here, patients with brain lesions are studied with the hope that the pattern of cognitive deficits they display will shed light on normal cognitive mechanisms. (We will consider examples of cognitive neuropsychology in Chapters 6 and 9.)

On the theoretical side, two concepts have been highly popular: semantic networks and production systems. With **semantic networks**, knowledge is represented as a network of nodes connected by links. The nodes stand for concepts, and the links stand for relationships between concepts. The links are labelled, which means that the type of relationship is explicitly represented (see Figure 2.1). Semantic networks nicely capture several aspects of memory. One of

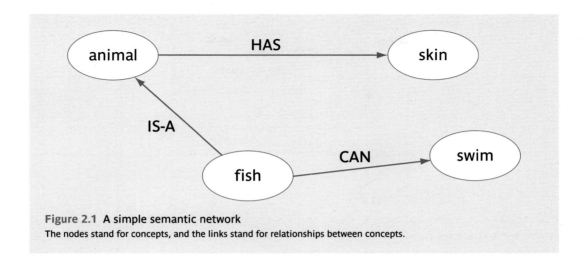

Figure 2.1 A simple semantic network
The nodes stand for concepts, and the links stand for relationships between concepts.

them is **priming**. As we shall see in Chapter 7, one important property of memory is that it is associative. Thus, when one node in memory is activated, this activation tends to spread to other nodes (see Box 2.3).

Production systems consist of rules called 'productions', which are stored in **long-term memory**. A *production* has two parts: a *condition* (the IF-statement) and an *action* (the THEN-statement). Whenever the condition is satisfied, the action is executed. A simple example of a production is: 'IF the light is red, THEN stop.' Figure 2.3 shows a more complicated example. The content of **working memory** (another word for short-term memory) is used to select productions. This basic explanation omits a number of complications: for example, what happens when the conditions of several productions are satisfied (see Klahr *et al.*, 1987, for details).

Box 2.3 CLASSIC EXPERIMENT: **Priming experiment**

A nice example of the idea that activation flows between nodes in a semantic network is provided by priming experiments. In a typical priming experiment, strings of letters are briefly presented on a computer screen, and participants have to decide whether they form a word (e.g. 'fish') or not (e.g. 'xbyp'), by pressing one of two keys as rapidly as possible. (This task is called a *lexical decision task*.) The target word is preceded by the very rapid presentation of another word, called a **prime**, which might or might not relate to the second word (see Figure 2.2, top). Numerous experiments have shown that the decision is faster when a related word is presented first (e.g. 'animal' before 'fish', rather than 'chair' before 'fish'). This can be explained by the idea that when the prime ('animal', in our example) appears on the screen, its representation in memory is activated, and activation then spreads to concepts that are related to it ('fish' and 'skin' in Figure 2.2, bottom). Given that the activation of the node 'fish' is higher than normal when the word is presented on the screen, the time to make a decision is faster (see Meyer and Schvaneveldt, 1971, for an example of the application of this paradigm).

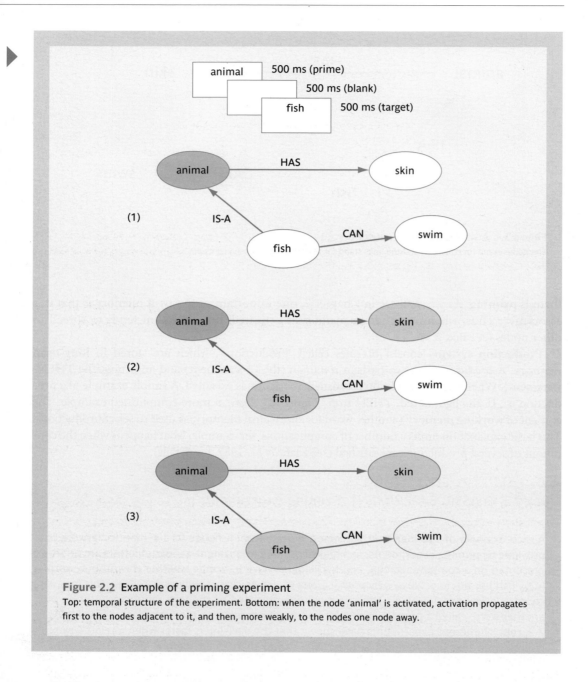

Figure 2.2 Example of a priming experiment
Top: temporal structure of the experiment. Bottom: when the node 'animal' is activated, activation propagates first to the nodes adjacent to it, and then, more weakly, to the nodes one node away.

Production systems capture some important aspects of cognition, and we will meet several of them in this book. One useful property of productions is that they are modular – that is, one can add or delete a production without affecting other productions, although the overall behaviour of the system may change. Production systems capture rule-like behaviour, and have for instance been used for simulating the errors that children make when learning about

IF

    expression has variable term on right side

THEN

    subtract variable term from both sides, and simplify

$$2x + 4 = x + 2$$

$$2x + 4 = x + 2 \qquad - x$$

$$x + 4 = 2$$

Figure 2.3 Production

Top: example of a production used for solving algebra problems. Bottom: example of the application of this production. The equation in the first line has a variable on the right side. Therefore, the production is applied (second line). The third line shows the outcome after simplification.

subtraction (Young and O'Shea, 1981). In general, they have produced good models of learning, including how people acquire **procedural knowledge** (i.e. knowledge about rules).

Stop and Think High school
Select two topics that you studied in high school. To what extent can a production system and a semantic network describe what you have learned?

Stop and Think Semantic networks vs production systems
What are the differences between semantic networks and production systems? What are their respective advantages and disadvantages?

Connectionism strikes

The computational models we have considered so far have used fairly high-level representations, such as productions, to simulate cognition. Why not develop models using our knowledge of the brain, in particular the fact that a large number of **neurons** 'work' in parallel (see Chapter 3)? In fact, a stream of research has attempted to do so. For example, Rosenblatt (1958) carried out a number of experiments where kinds of neural net known as *perceptrons* learned to recognise patterns (e.g. letters; see Box 2.4). This type of research was brought to an abrupt end by Minsky and Papert (1969), who showed that there were serious limitations to what could be learned by perceptrons. Connectionists had to wait until the 1980s to see the development of models that overcome these limitations. The magic bullet was a learning algorithm called *backpropagation* (Rumelhart *et al.*, 1986), which was more sophisticated than that used by the perceptron. The presence of an algorithm powerful enough to carry out in principle any type of learning led to a resurgence of connectionism, which has since been used to simulate phenomena in many domains, including perception and the acquisition of language. This has also led to sometimes heated debates (e.g. Pinker and Mehler, 1988) as to what is the best way to model cognition – Newell and Simon's symbolic approach or connectionism? Increasingly, researchers have come to the conclusion that both approaches are useful in different ways: the symbolic

Box 2.4 RESEARCH CLOSE-UP: **Connectionist networks**

Connectionist networks, also called *artificial neural networks*, take as an analogy the way neurons transmit information in the brain. (We will consider biological neurons in the next chapter, where it will become apparent that artificial neural networks are much simpler than biological neural networks.) A connectionist network consists of nodes (also called *units* or *neurons*), connected by links. Nodes have activation levels, and links have weights, which will determine how strongly activation will propagate to the next node. The weights of the links can be changed by learning mechanisms, of which back-propagation is one of the most successful.

Figure 2.4 illustrates a simple connectionist network, of the type that was used by Rosenblatt (1958) in his seminal study. The input layer receives activation from the input, which is often coded as binary numbers (i.e. using only 0s and 1s). The input layer then sends information to the output layer; here, it is important to note that the level of activation of the input nodes is modulated by the weights of the links between the input and output nodes. The level of activation of the output nodes is then computed: for example, by taking the sum of the activations they receive. Then, a rule is used to transform the activation level of the output nodes into an output. For example, in Figure 2.4 the output node with the highest

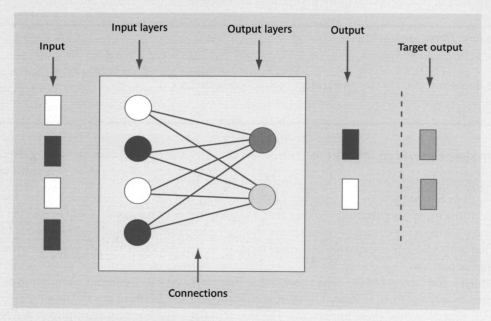

Figure 2.4 Illustration of a perceptron

The input, coded in a binary fashion, reaches the input layer. Activation propagates from this layer to the output layer, depending on the activation of the input nodes and the weight of the links between the input and output layers. The node in the output layer with the highest activation determines the output. The perceptron then compares the output with the target output, and if they are different, the weights of the links between the nodes in the input layer and those in the output layer are modified.

activation wins and the output to which the node is attached is selected. More complex networks have sets of nodes between input and output nodes. These nodes are called 'hidden units' and considerably increase the kinds of behaviour the network can simulate.

With many learning algorithms, the output selected by the network is compared with the correct output. If it is not the correct one, some weights in the network are changed so that the correct output is more likely to be selected in the future. The details of the learning algorithms rapidly become complicated, and you are referred to more advanced texts, such as those mentioned in the Further reading section, for more information.

approach to explain high-level aspects of cognition such as problem solving, and connectionism to explain lower aspects of cognition such as perception. Connectionism, with its emphasis on neuron-like processing, paved the way to the next upheaval in cognitive psychology and cognitive science: cognitive neuroscience.

The ascent of cognitive neuroscience

While connectionism questioned the theoretical foundations of cognitive research, **cognitive neuroscience** brought about crucial changes in the way empirical data are collected to study cognition. Until the early 1990s cognitive psychologists' main measures were reaction times, percentages of correct answers, eye movements, types of errors, and verbal protocols. It is true that data about the brain were used in cognitive neuropsychology, and that some experimentalists were using **event-related potentials**. However, data about the brain and its activation were not seen as mainstream by the majority of cognitive psychologists. All this has changed dramatically in the past two decades. Staggering technical breakthroughs enabled the development of several **brain-imaging** techniques that make it possible to look at changes in brain activity in real time (see Chapter 3). First, Positron Emission Tomography (**PET**), next, functional Magnetic Resonance Imaging (**fMRI**), and then a number of other techniques have mushroomed, to the point that the use of brain-imaging data has now become routine when running experiments in cognitive psychology. (Electroencephalography (**EEG**) and **event-related potentials**, which had been around for more than 50 years, have also enjoyed renewed interest recently due to the wide availability of computers powerful enough to analyse the huge amount of data recorded.) The new brain-imaging techniques have also empowered cognitive neuropsychology, as it is now possible to measure the extent of brain lesions precisely without having to wait for the patient's death to carry out a *post-mortem* analysis.

Stop and Think Link between cognitive psychology and technology
We have seen many examples of how new developments in engineering and technology have pushed forward the field of cognitive psychology, most notably the advent of the digital computer and brain-imaging methods. Is it a good or bad thing? What technology will bring the next 'revolution' in cognitive psychology?

In spite of these impressive technological advances and the large quantity of experiments that have been carried out on cognition using these techniques, the impact on cognitive theories has been less clear. The dream of cognitive neuroscience is to realise a double integration (see Figure 2.5): *horizontally*, between the different types of cognitive functions (perception, memory,

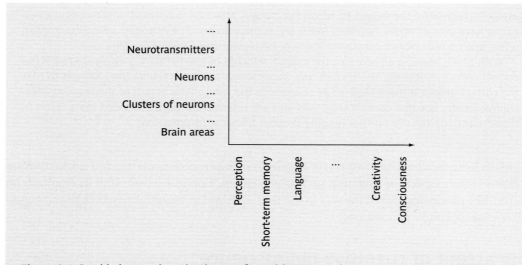

Figure 2.5 Double integration, the dream of cognitive neuroscience
A general theory should explain both our diverse cognitive abilities (horizontal axis) and the way these abilities are implemented in the brain, not only at the level of broad regions, but also at finer levels of granularity (neurons and neurotransmitters).

language, thinking and so on) and the brain areas they engage; and *vertically*, by linking processes at the neuronal level (or even the levels below) to high-level processes such as recognising a Picasso or understanding language. It is likely that such integration will require much more powerful theories and computational models than those that are currently available. This issue of integration will be taken up in Chapter 3.

The search for unified theories of cognition

One possible way forward to address the issue of large-scale theoretical integration is offered by the idea of **unified theories of cognition** (UTC), originally proposed by Newell (1990). As you can see in Box 2.5, one important property of good theories is that they can be refuted by experiments. Newell noted that cognitive psychologists have focused on falsification, by designing experiments aimed at refuting current theories, and, unlike physicists, have not put much emphasis on building theories that account for a large amount of data. This has resulted in a large number of small-scale theories, which sometimes explain only the results of a specific experimental paradigm. For example, a theory might be developed to explain how boys (as opposed to girls) learn to read in Chinese (as opposed to English). Newell argued that cognitive psychologists should try to construct more ambitious theories that account for a large number of phenomena. Anomalous data not explained by the theory should be used as cues suggesting how to improve it. Newell's central insight was that, as a theory explains an increasingly larger number of phenomena, these phenomena offer so many constraints that the theorist is almost forced to develop a correct theory. Given the large amount of data to simulate, and presumably the complexity of the processes involved, such a theory must be implemented as a computer program.

Box 2.5 IN FOCUS: **What is a good theory?**

Scientists generally agree that a number of properties should be met for a theory to be considered as viable. First, a theory should be *testable*, or 'falsifiable' (Popper, 1959) – that is, experiments should exist that in principle could lead to results showing that the theory is incorrect. Second, a theory should be *internally consistent* – it should not contain any contradictory statements. As an example of theory that is not consistent, consider a theory claiming both that (a) short-term memory is limited to seven items, and (b) short-term memory is not limited in its capacity. The problem is that an inconsistent theory can generate any prediction and its opposite, which makes it in fact non-testable. Third, a theory should be fully specified: that is, all key terms and processes should be defined. When this requirement is not satisfied, it is too easy – but scientifically unproductive – to explain any data inconsistent with the predictions by adding **ad hoc hypotheses**, which in fact means, again, that the theory cannot be tested. Now, the bad news is that most theories in (cognitive) psychology are informal and rather vague, and thus flout this third requirement. The final requirement is that a theory should be *generalisable*, and thus should be applicable beyond a specific set of experiments. A weakness of cognitive psychology is that numerous theories cannot really be generalised, as they aim to explain only the results of a narrow set of experiments (Newell, 1990).

Stop and Think Good theory
(a) Take your favourite theory in science (not necessarily psychology), and evaluate to what extent it satisfies the criteria of testability, consistency, specification and generalisability.
(b) To what extent does astrology satisfy these criteria?

Let us consider an example. A first researcher develops a theory of memory, and manages to estimate two parameters: the capacity of working memory, and the time to create a new node in long-term memory. A second researcher develops a theory of problem solving in arithmetic. Although she uses a parameter for the capacity of working memory, she is not aware of the work of the first researcher, and can essentially freely vary the value of this parameter to fit the data. Now, consider a third researcher, who is following the UTC approach, and who is interested in both domains. Once the capacity of working memory has been estimated with the simulations on memory, it is not a **free parameter** any more when doing the simulations on arithmetic. If the first simulations have shown that the capacity of working memory is seven, then this value should be used in the simulations about arithmetic, and indeed in all subsequent simulations.

This is a powerful idea, but not an easy one to carry out in practice. At the moment, there are just half a dozen UTCs, and we briefly review three of them. Newell (1990) developed a program called *Soar*, where cognition is essentially seen as problem solving. Soar is implemented as a production system, and has simulated numerous phenomena about learning, problem solving, categorisation and natural language understanding. CHREST (Gobet *et al.*, 2001) emphasises the role of perception in cognition; knowledge is implemented as the growth of a network of perceptual chunks, which are linked to possible actions. Simulations include how people become experts in chess and physics, and how children acquire their first language. The most sophisticated UTC is currently ACT-R, developed by Anderson and his group (Anderson *et al.*, 2004;

Anderson and Lebière, 1998). ACT-R is a production system, and the essential aspects of cognition are seen as the activation of production rules and declarative elements in long-term memory. The simulated phenomena range from simple perceptual and memory tasks to solving algebra problems and driving a car. A particularly interesting feature of Anderson's work is that, while Soar and CHREST have mostly simulated data about performance, errors and response times, ACT-R has also simulated brain-imaging data, thus building a fascinating link with cognitive neuroscience.

Chapter summary

While psychology as a scientific field was founded in 1879, modern cognitive psychology was founded in 1956. It is now a mature field of research, and there is no doubt that it can boast tremendous achievements. Sophisticated experimental techniques have been developed, and key cognitive concepts, such as production systems and semantic networks, have been identified. Powerful theories have been developed, such as Anderson's ACT-R, which can make detailed predictions about behaviour in numerous domains. Finally, cognitive psychology has led to the development of practical applications in fields such as education and even psychotherapy.

In recent years, there has been a trend towards an increased partnership between cognitive psychology and neuroscience, as exemplified by simulations using artificial neural networks and the use of brain-imaging techniques. As is perhaps typical of mature sciences, cognitive psychology has split into numerous subfields. Interestingly, certain issues have shown little progress. In spite of several attempts, cognitive psychology still lacks a unified theory, and some very old questions are still debated today. These include the distinction between primary and secondary memory, originally proposed by James in 1890, and the nature of consciousness, to which Wundt devoted considerable attention in 1874.

Further reading

Gardner (1987) provides a lively history of the cognitive revolution. Broadbent (1958) wrote one of the first books where the computer analogy is used systematically. Classic books on the standard information processing approach include Newell and Simon (1972) and Lachman *et al.* (1979). The standard source for the connectionist approach is offered by the two volumes edited by McClelland and Rumelhart (McClelland and Rumelhart, 1986; Rumelhart and McClelland, 1986). Bechtel and Abrahamsen (1991) and McLeod, Plunkett and Rolls (1998) provide a non-technical introduction. The recent developments in cognitive neuroscience are covered by Bear *et al.* (2007) and Gazzaniga *et al.* (2009). Newell (1990) is the key reference about the idea of unified theories of cognition. Christopher Green's *Classics in the History of Psychology* (http://psychclassics.yorku.ca/index.htm) contains many of the early works mentioned in this chapter.

3

A brief introduction to neuroscience

CHAPTER PREVIEW

☑ There are two main types of cell in the brain: neurons and glial cells. Neurons process and transmit information, and glial cells provide support for the neurons.

☑ Within neurons, information is transmitted electrically, through action potentials. Between neurons, information is transmitted chemically by releasing neurotransmitters in synapses, the small gaps separating neurons.

☑ The two hemispheres of the brain comprise three main parts: the brain stem, the midbrain and the forebrain. These parts are further divided into smaller structures.

☑ The cerebral cortex, a component of the forebrain, is the place where most high-level functions take place. It consists of four lobes: the frontal lobe, the temporal lobe, the parietal lobe and the occipital lobe.

☑ While its explanations must respect the constraints offered by biology, cognitive psychology studies mental behaviour at a specific level – the cognitive band – which has its own laws and principles.

Introduction

The brain is one of the most complex objects in the known universe. It has 100 billion neurons, and each neuron is on average connected to 7000 other neurons – that makes a stunning 700 trillion connections! These numbers are staggering, but a moment's thought will convince you that all this complexity is needed. Not only is the brain at the basis of essential low-level biological functions, such as monitoring heart rate, respiration and feeding, it is also required for behaviours key for survival, such as perceiving, learning and making rapid decisions. It is also the organ underpinning the abilities that are (perhaps) unique to humans: thinking, emotions, consciousness and love. Given all this, it is not surprising that the brain is extremely demanding with respect to energy: whilst accounting for only 2 per cent of body weight, the brain consumes about 20 per cent of the glucose used by the body.

The 1990s were designated the decade of the brain by former US president George H. W. Bush, which was recognition of the incredible advances that had been made in our understanding of the brain and the potential for future progress. Converging efforts from biochemistry, biology, neuroscience and psychology, among other sciences, have led to stunning discoveries about the workings of the brain and the mind. This has been made possible by numerous technological breakthroughs, most notably with computers, microscopy and brain imaging.

Cognitive psychologists want to understand the mechanisms underpinning mental processes, and some of the answers inevitably lie in the brain. It is, therefore, important to have at least some knowledge of the biology of the brain in order to understand how the mind works. This is becoming increasingly necessary as the gap between cognitive psychology and neuroscience is diminishing, as witnessed by the new discipline of cognitive neuroscience. This chapter provides a brief introduction to neuroscience, with an emphasis on themes that are important for the study of cognition.

The complexity of the brain not only resides in the number of neurons and the intricate biochemical mechanisms that allow them to function, but also in how these neurons are organised in clusters, these clusters are organised in yet larger clusters, and so forth. It is probably the case that, while the different levels of this hierarchy are fairly well understood, we still barely know the mechanisms that relate the various levels together. In this chapter, we consider two important levels in the hierarchical architecture of the brain: the cell level at the microscopic level, and the structural level describing the main regions of the brain at the macroscopic level. (A more advance treatment of vision will be provided in Chapter 16.)

The neuron

There are two main types of cell in the brain: glial cells and neurons. **Glial cells**, which include astrocytes and oligodendrocytes, have a number of functions: they supply nutrition to neurons, repair them, provide structural support, help maintain homeostasis, produce myelin (see below), and facilitate signal transmission within and between neurons. Glial cells constitute about 90 per cent of the cells in the human brain, while neurons make the remaining 10 per cent.

Neurons come in several types, depending on their structure and their function. Among many others, one can distinguish between sensory, motor and pyramidal neurons (see Figure 3.1). In spite of their variety, all neurons have the same overall function: to process and transmit information. As shown in Figure 3.2, which depicts the structure of the typical human neuron, most neurons have three main components: body, dendrites and axons.

The *body*, also called *soma*, is between 5 and 100 microns in diameter. (A micron is one-thousandth of a millimetre.) It is surrounded by a membrane and contains the cytoplasm, the nucleus and a number of organelles. The *cytoplasm* is a jelly-like substance that is in continuous movement. The *nucleus* contains the genetic code of the neuron, which is used for protein synthesis. The *organelles* are essential for the metabolism of the neuron: they carry out chemical

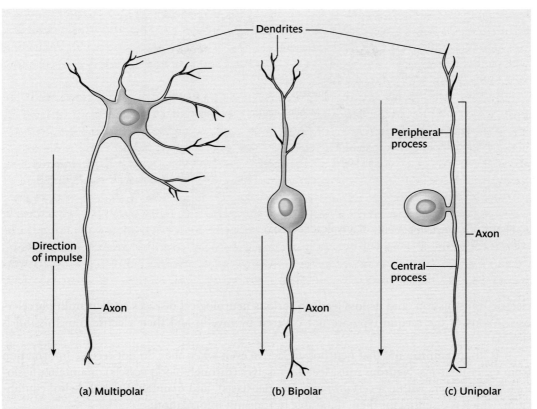

Figure 3.1 Different types of neuron
(a) Multipolar neurons have many extensions from their body: one axon and several dendrites. Most neurons in the brain are multipolar. (b) Bipolar neurons have two extensions: one consisting of dendrites and one axon. They are typical of specialised sensory pathways (e.g. vision, smell, sight and hearing). (c) Unipolar cells have a single extension (an axon) from their body. Many somatosensory (touch, pain, temperature) neurons are unipolar.
Source: Shier, Butler and Lewis, 2010.

synthesis, generate and store energy, and provide the structural support (a sort of 'skeleton') for the neuron.

Dendrites are branching structures that receive information from other neurons. Note that dendrites only receive information from other neurons and cannot transmit any information to them. Instead, they propagate information to the soma, which in turn propagates information to the axon.

Axons, which can be from a few millimetres to 1 metre long, transmit information from the soma to other neurons. They end with *terminal buttons*, which store chemicals that are used for inter-neuron communication, as we shall see below. There are two types of axon. Axons of the first type – *myelinated axons* – are covered by a fatty, white substance called **myelin**. Crucially, as we shall see in the next section, there are gaps in the sheath of myelin at places called the **nodes of Ranvier**. Myelin insulates the axon from its environment, and therefore makes electric transmission more efficient and faster. With this kind of axon, myelin is essential for proper

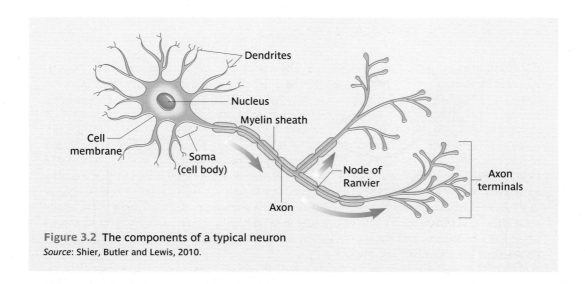

Figure 3.2 The components of a typical neuron
Source: Shier, Butler and Lewis, 2010.

electric transmission, and its loss leads to serious neurological diseases such as multiple sclerosis. Axons of the second type are not covered by myelin and their electric transmission is slower.

It is important to note that neurons are active even when they do not receive information from other neurons. Neurons must feed themselves (through blood vessels), maintain physiological parameters within a certain range (homeostasis), and maintain their electrical equilibrium, which is essential for them to be able to transmit information.

Communication within and between neurons

Within-neuron electrical communication

Electric signals are used for transmitting information from the soma to the end of the axon. The **action potential**, also known as *nerve impulse* or *spike*, is a brief electrical impulse that moves along the membrane of an axon. It is initiated at the place where the axon leaves the soma, called the 'axon hillock'. The potential of a neuron membrane is normally at −70 millivolts. Signal transmission is achieved by changing this potential. By altering the equilibrium of chemicals (mostly sodium and potassium) within and outside the membrane, there is first a depolarisation, where the voltage is increased. This is followed by a hyperpolarisation, where the potential is more negative than normal, and then a return to the −70 millivolts resting potential. This sequence lasts about 2 milliseconds.

With myelinated axons, the action potential travels continuously down the axon once started, until it reaches a node of Ranvier. Then, the sequence of depolarisation, hyperpolarisation and back to resting potential starts again, initiating a new impulse. The electrical impulse is thus propagated through the myelin from one node of Ranvier to the next one. Given that transmission 'jumps' from one node of Ranvier to the next one, this method of conduction is called 'saltatory conduction' (from the Latin *saltare*, to hop).

Box 3.1 IN FOCUS: **Reticularists vs neuronists**

The idea that neurons are the building blocks of the brain and that they communicate through synapses is now so well known that it may come as a surprise that it took decades of research and bitter arguments to reach this conclusion. Two competing views were advanced during the nineteenth century. The 'reticularists' (*reticulum* in Latin means network) proposed that neurons formed a continuous network and were fused together by their neurites (axons and dendrites). The analogy was the blood-circulation system, in which arteries and veins form a continuous network. This was seen as an important exception to the cell theory proposed in 1838, which saw cells as distinct elements. By contrast, the 'neuronists' argued that neurons were indeed distinct functional units, and that there were gaps between them. It was difficult to reach a clear-cut conclusion, as the then-available microscopes did not have the necessary resolution. In addition, neural tissues appear as a whitish, jelly-like substance when placed under the microscope, and it was not possible to decide with any degree of certainty whether there were gaps or not between neurons.

Critical progress was made by the development of stains – substances that colour different parts of the neural tissue differently. One of the key contributions was made by the Italian Camillo Golgi. The stain he developed, which is still used nowadays and appropriately bears his name, enabled histologists (biologists specialising in the microscopic analysis of cells and tissues) to clearly see the two main components of neurons: the soma and the neurites. But the key data were collected by the Spanish histologist Santiago Ramón y Cajal, who patiently used Golgi stain for over 25 years to identify different types of neurons and how neurons were connected, bringing considerable evidence for the presence of gaps between them. This conclusion was later unambiguously supported by electron microscopy in the 1950s. Golgi and Ramón y Cajal shared the Nobel prize in physiology or medicine in 1906, but the irony is that, while of course Ramón y Cajal supported the neurone doctrine, Golgi remained during his entire life a champion of the reticular hypothesis. (For detail about this controversy, see Bear, Connors and Paradiso, 2007.)

With myelinated axons, transmission can reach 100 metres per second, and there is little decay in the strength of the signal. In non-myelinated axons, the transmission loses its strength due to interferences and leaks, and is also relatively slow. Note that the signal (impulse) is either on or off; therefore, what is being used to transmit information is not the strength of the signal, but the rate of firing. Neurons typically can fire up to 100 impulses per second, although some can fire up to 500 impulses per second.

Between-neuron communication

The gap between the end of the axon of a neuron and the dendrites of another neuron is called the **synapse**, or *synaptic cleft*. It is about 10–50 nanometres wide. (A nanometre is one-millionth of a millimetre.) Once the action potential reaches the end of an axon, it releases chemical substances called 'neurotransmitters' in the synaptic cleft. **Neurotransmitters** can either *excite* the postsynaptic neuron (i.e. they increase the likelihood that this neuron generates an action potential) or *inhibit* it (i.e. they decrease this likelihood). By extension, synapses can be either excitatory or inhibitory. There are over 100 different types of neurotransmitter, which belong to three main categories: amino acids, peptides and monoamines.

Two particularly important *amino acids* are glutamate and GABA (gamma-aminobutyric acid). Glutamate modulates the threshold of excitation of neurons, and is implicated in learning and memory. GABA inhibits action at receptors. The human brain uses about 100 different types of *peptides*. *Endogenous opioids*, an important class of peptides, have two main functions: they reduce pain and are implicated in reward/reinforcement mechanisms, which of course are essential for learning. Note that drugs from the opiate family, such as opium, morphine and heroin, stimulate endogenous opioids receptors, with the double effect that they act as analgesics and lead to dependence due to their strong effect on reward systems.

Some *monoamines* are particularly important for cognition. *Dopamine* modulates attention, learning and movement. *Serotonin* affects arousal. Finally, *adrenalin* and *noradrenalin* (also known as epinephrine and norepinephrine, respectively) play a role in alertness. Other neurotransmitters do not fit into the categories of amino acids, peptides and monoamines. An important example is *acetylcholine*, which plays an excitatory role in the brain, and is linked to arousal, reward and learning.

Learning is thought to result from changes in the synapses between neurons, by a mechanism called **long-term potentiation (LTP)**. The chemical details are complex, but LTP is essentially the strengthening of the connection between two neurons by changing the chemicals in the synapse. A key principle for LTP is *Hebbian learning*: 'neurons that fire together, wire together' (Hebb, 1949). Recent studies also suggest that some learning is underpinned by the growth of new synapses.

Stop and Think Brain design

Imagine a (perhaps not too) distant future, where it is possible to develop 'smart drugs' – drugs that improve learning, memory and thinking. You are the chief scientist of a company designing such drugs. What kind of approach do you choose: (a) drugs that increase the myelinisation of axons; (b) drugs that increase the size of neurons; (c) drugs that increase the number of neurons; or (d) drugs that affect the quantity of specific neurotransmitters? Defend your choice(s) using what you have learned in this chapter.

Brain anatomy

The brain consists of two hemispheres separated by the longitudinal fissure and connected by the *corpus callosum*, a large bundle of more than 250 million axons. It can be further divided into three broad parts: the brain stem, the midbrain and the forebrain. In turn, each part can be divided into subparts, which again can be analysed more finely, and so on until one reaches the level of fairly small networks of neurons, called *nuclei*. Indeed, a quick look at an advanced textbook on brain anatomy will reveal a dazzling number of structures and substructures. We will not go into such detail here, but rather present a simplified roadmap to the brain (see Figures 3.4 and 3.5 for a quick overview of the structures of the brain). When reading the subsequent pages, keep in mind the following property of the brain: in general, the left part of the brain is linked to the right part of the body and vice versa. So, for example, if you suffer damage to the part of the *left* brain dealing with finger movements, you might lose control of the fingers of the *right* hand.

Box 3.2 RESEARCH CLOSE-UP: **Brain-imaging techniques**

In the following chapters, we will occasionally come across experiments where imaging methods are used for studying what parts of the brain implement specific cognitive functions, or how rapidly the brain processes information. It might therefore be useful to give a brief introduction to these techniques here.

Electroencephalography (EEG), invented in 1929, has been used since the 1960s for studying cognitive processes (Luck, 2005). Electrodes are placed on the scalp and record the sum of all the electrical activity of the millions of neurons located on the other side of the skull. A variation of EEG, called event-related potentials (ERP), measures electrical activity while stimuli are repeatedly presented. ERPs are useful for psychologists as they produce more reliable data than EEG alone. Finally, there is a long tradition of research in neuroscience where electrodes are inserted in the brain of animals for measuring the activity of a single neuron – a technique called single unit recording (Huettel *et al.*, 2004).

Functional Magnetic Resonance Imaging (fMRI) is used in psychology and cognitive neurosciences to measure blood-related responses to neural activity in the brain. Because neurons need energy to work properly, we can measure blood activity, which itself reflects the supply of sugar and oxygen to neurons, to know which neurons are active.

Positron Emission Tomography (PET) is a technique based on the detection of a radioactive tracer (positron-emitting particle), which constructs a three-dimensional image of the level of activity for the tracer. The tracer is a biologically active molecule that emits gamma rays for a brief period of time. The molecule is selected with the aim of targeting a specific physiological function. The advantage of this technique is that we can see where a specific molecule acts in the body and pinpoint the extent to which a particular location is active.

Magnetoencephalography (MEG) is the magnetic equivalent of EEG. While EEG records electrical activity on the surface of the scalp, MEG records the magnetic fields around the scalp.

Figure 3.3 shows the spatial and temporal resolution of the four techniques we have described. You can see for instance that fMRI has a very good spatial resolution (less than

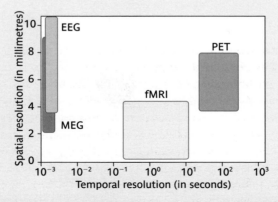

Figure 3.3 Temporal and spatial resolution of common brain-imaging techniques
The horizontal axis shows the temporal resolution in seconds, and the vertical axis shows the spatial resolution in millimetres.

4 mm) compared to the other techniques, and thus is the best if one is interested in locating cognitive functions. On the other hand, EEG and MEG have good temporal resolution, even though they lack special precision.

Researchers have recently developed methods to use EEG and fMRI simultaneously, and so take advantage of the high temporal resolution of EEG and the high spatial resolution of fMRI.

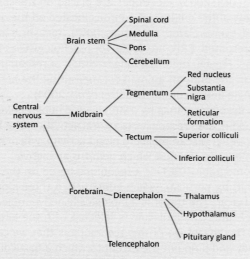

Figure 3.4 The main components of the central nervous system
See Figure 3.5 for the details of the telencephalon.

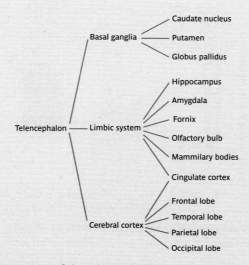

Figure 3.5 The main components of the telencephalon (or cerebrum)

The brain stem

As its name indicates, the **brain stem** is located at the bottom of the brain (see Figure 3.6). It connects other parts of the brain with the *spinal cord*, which sends motor commands to the body, and receives internal and external sensory information from it. Moving up, the next structure is the *medulla*, which relays information from and to the spinal cord, and is in charge of vital autonomic functions such as respiration and swallowing. The *pons* relays messages from the medulla further up in the brain, and controls sleep and arousal. It also serves to transmit information between the cerebellum and other parts of the brain. The **cerebellum** is a large structure (about 10 per cent of the volume of the brain) that contains about half of the neurons in the brain. Its role is to integrate various types of information, and it is in particularly implicated in classical conditioning (a simple form of learning; see Chapter 7), motor control and coordination, as well as language production.

The midbrain

The **midbrain**, also known as *mesencephalon*, consists of two main structures – the tegmentum and the tectum – together with a number of smaller structures. The *tegmentum* comprises three main parts. The *red nucleus* and the *substantia nigra* fulfil important functions in the motor system. The *reticular formation* regulates arousal, attention and sleep. Damage to the reticular formation leads to coma. The *tectum* consists of two main structures. The *superior colliculi* play a role in reflexive eye movements to sudden visual changes, and the *inferior colliculi* play a role in auditory reflexes.

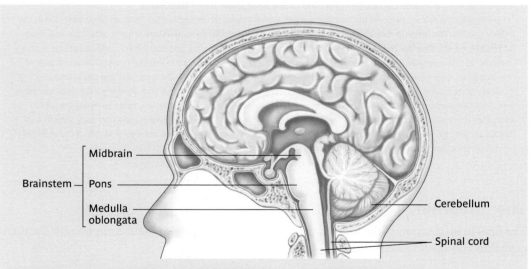

Figure 3.6 The major components of the brain stem, with their main functions
The *spinal cord* transmits sensory-motor information between the brain and the body. The *medulla* is a relay station between the brain and the spinal cord, and is responsible for respiration and swallowing. The *pons* is in charge of sleep and arousal, and is a relay station between the cerebellum and other parts of the brain. The *cerebellum* plays an important role in classical conditioning, motor control and coordination, and language production.
Source: Shier, Butler and Lewis, 2010.

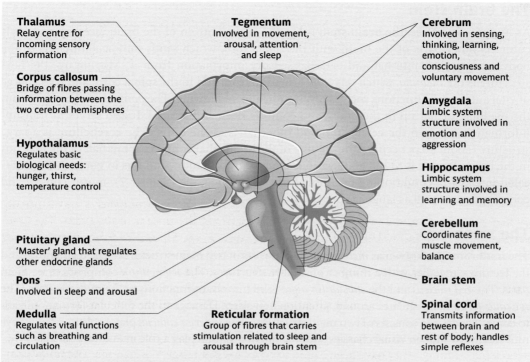

Thalamus
Relay centre for incoming sensory information

Corpus callosum
Bridge of fibres passing information between the two cerebral hemispheres

Hypothalamus
Regulates basic biological needs: hunger, thirst, temperature control

Pituitary gland
'Master' gland that regulates other endocrine glands

Pons
Involved in sleep and arousal

Medulla
Regulates vital functions such as breathing and circulation

Tegmentum
Involved in movement, arousal, attention and sleep

Reticular formation
Group of fibres that carries stimulation related to sleep and arousal through brain stem

Cerebrum
Involved in sensing, thinking, learning, emotion, consciousness and voluntary movement

Amygdala
Limbic system structure involved in emotion and aggression

Hippocampus
Limbic system structure involved in learning and memory

Cerebellum
Coordinates fine muscle movement, balance

Brain stem

Spinal cord
Transmits information between brain and rest of body; handles simple reflexes

Figure 3.7 The major components of the brain with their main functions

1) Midbrain. The *red nucleus* and the *substantia nigra*, which belong to the *tegmentum*, play an important role in the motor system. The *reticular formation*, which also belongs to the *tegmentum*, monitors arousal, attention and sleep. In the *tectum*, the *superior colliculi* are one of the centres of eye movements, and the *inferior colliculi* control auditory reflexes. **2) Diencephalon.** The *thalamus* integrates and relays sensory information to the cerebral cortex. A part of the thalamus, the *medial geniculate nucleus*, relays neural information between the inner ear and the primary auditory cortex. Another part of the thalamus, the *lateral geniculate nucleus*, relays neural information between the eyes and the primary visual cortex. The *hypothalamus* monitors feeding, aggression, sex, body temperature and circadian rhythms; it also plays a role in reinforcement and learning. The *pituitary gland* monitors body growth and sexual physiology, and controls the other endocrine glands in the body. For a more detailed diagram of the midbrain and diencephalon please log on to www.mcgraw-hill.co.uk/textbooks/gobet

The forebrain

The final main division of the brain is the forebrain, which has two main components: the diencephalon and the telencephalon.

The diencephalon

The *diencephalon* is located above the mesencephalon. Its largest components are the two lobes of the thalamus. The **thalamus** is a central structure of the brain, not only spatially but also in the sense that it is the integration centre through which passes most of the neural information sent to the cerebral cortex. Among the numerous nuclei of the thalamus, one can mention the *medial geniculate nucleus*, an intermediate structure between the inner ear and the primary auditory cortex, and the **lateral geniculate nucleus**, an important relay between the eyes and the primary visual cortex. (We will say more about the lateral geniculate nucleus in Chapter 16.) Below the thalamus we find the *hypothalamus*, which in spite of its small size (more or less the size of an almond) is important for monitoring and adjusting the body's basic physiological responses through the autonomic nervous and the endocrine systems. The hypothalamus controls vital behaviours such as feeding, aggression and sex. It is also linked to the control of body temperature and circadian rhythms, and is implicated in reinforcement and thus learning. The hypothalamus connects to the *pituitary gland*, which monitors several hormones important for a number of functions including body growth and sexual physiology. The pituitary gland is also in control of the other endocrine glands in the body.

The telencephalon

The *telencephalon* (or **cerebrum**) occupies most of the two brain hemispheres and is usually divided into three components. The cerebral cortex lies at the surface of the brain. The basal ganglia and the limbic system, called subcortical regions, are located beneath it. In terms of evolution, the telencephalon is more recent than the structures we have reviewed so far.

The **basal ganglia** are a group of nuclei on the side and on the top of the thalamus. They consist mostly of the *caudate nucleus*, the *putamen* and the *globus pallidus*. They are essential for learning skills and habits, and for regulating movement. Dysfunction of the basal ganglia leads to diseases such as Parkinson's.

The **limbic system** comprises several structures originally thought to be linked to emotional processing, although they have been found to cover a wider range of functions. The **hippocampus** is a structure central to the creation of new memories and to spatial navigation and memory, and the **amygdala** is linked to the processing of fear. The *fornix* and the *mammilary bodies* are also thought to be involved with memory. The *olfactory bulb* deals with the processing of odours. Finally, some structures technically belonging to the cortex are also included in the limbic system, most notably the **cingulate cortex** (thought to be engaged in a wide range of functions including detection of conflict, anticipation of reward and emotions).

We have now reached the last station of our journey through the brain structures and have reached the **cerebral cortex**, also called the *neocortex*, a 3-mm layer on the surface of the brain. 'Cortex' means bark in Latin, and this name is used to indicate that, just as bark covers the trunk of a tree, the cerebral cortex covers the two hemispheres of the brain. The cerebral cortex is mostly made of cell bodies and glials, which gives it its greyish appearance. This is also known as the *grey matter*. The bundles of axons connecting neurons in the grey matter to other parts of the brain have a whitish appearance due to the presence of myelin, and form what is known as the *white matter*.

The human neocortex is the most recent brain structure from an evolutionary point of view, and one of its striking features, compared to that of other mammals, is that it is heavily wrinkled. The presence of a larger number of folds essentially increases the surface of the cortex: when unfolded, the typical human cortex covers a surface of about 0.75 m^2, which is about three times more than the actual surface of the brain (0.25 m^2). Increasing the surface of the cortex makes it possible to pack in a surprisingly large number of neurons (about 25 billion) and axons (a total length of more than 100 000 km!). The grooves on the cortex are called **sulci** (singular: sulcus) and the bulges are called **gyri** (singular: gyrus).

The neocortex is divided into four lobes – frontal lobe, temporal lobe, parietal lobe and occipital lobe – which are defined by the bone divisions of the skull. Three sulci (or fissures), particularly visible, help delimit these lobes: the central sulcus separates the frontal from the parietal lobe; the lateral fissure (also known as the Sylvian fissure) separates the temporal from the frontal lobe; and the parieto-occipital fissure delimits, as its name indicates, the parietal and occipital lobes.

These four lobes deal with fairly well-defined processes. The **occipital lobe** is involved with vision, and specific sub-areas are critical for particular visual properties such as shape, colour or motion (see Chapter 16). The **parietal lobe** processes spatial information and is involved in working memory and attention. The region close to the central sulcus, called the *somato-sensory cortex*, processes sensory information from the body; different parts of the body map into specific parts of this cortex, and highly sensitive parts, such as the fingers, occupy a much larger region than less sensitive parts, such as the legs. The *primary motor cortex*, the region on the other side of the central sulcus and belonging to the **frontal lobe,** has a similar organisa-tion, and encodes information related to motor commands (Figure 3.10). Other parts of the frontal cortex are involved in planning, working memory, decision making and emotions. One

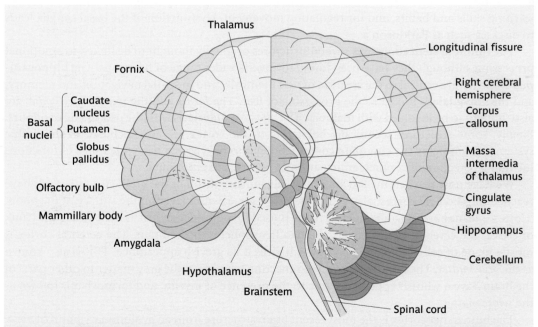

Figure 3.8 The major components of the *basal ganglia* and the *limbic system*, with their main functions

1) Basal ganglia. The *caudate nucleus*, putamen and *globus pallidus* play a key role in monitoring movement as well as acquiring skills and habits. **2) The limbic system.** The *hippocampus* is essential for the creation of new memories and for spatial processing. The *amygdala* is important for information processing, in particular fear. The *fornix* and the *mammilary bodies* are implicated in memory formation. The *olfactory bulb* processes odours. The **cingulate cortex** is implicated in emotions, detection of conflict and anticipation of reward.

particular area in the left frontal lobe, called **Broca's area**, plays an important role in speech production. Finally, the **temporal lobe** contains cortical areas essential in the storage of perceptual information and in the creation of new memories. For example, regions of the *fusiform gyrus*, located at the bottom of the temporal lobe, deal with face recognition and written-word recognition. Sensory information from the ears is processed in the *auditory cortex*, located below the lateral sulcus; given the presence of auditory input you could expect that the temporal lobe also contains centres dealing with language, and this is indeed the case. In particular, **Wernicke's area**, located in the posterior part of the left temporal lobe, is associated with language comprehension.

For students, one confusing and frustrating aspect of learning neuroanatomy is that there are different systems for labelling cortical structures, and that different authors use different variants of these systems. The systems typically adopt one of three approaches for labelling brain regions: (a) using the pattern of sulci and gyri; (b) using the types of neuron that populate a given part of the cortex (e.g. in 1909 Korbinian Brodmann identified 52 areas that still bear his name); and (c) using the functions thought to be implemented by cortical areas (e.g. visual cortex for the cortex of the occipital lobe).

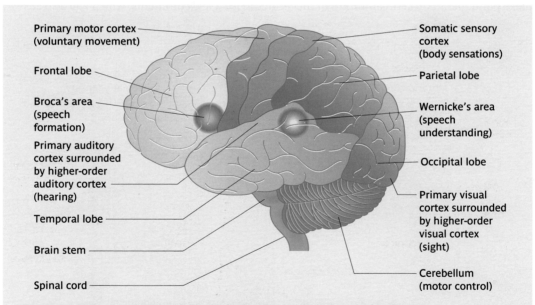

Figure 3.9 Main components of the cerebral cortex, with their main functions

The *occipital lobe* processes visual information. The *parietal lobe* is involved with spatial information processing, working memory and attention. The *somato-sensory cortex* (anterior part of the parietal lobe) processes sensory information coming from the body. The *frontal lobe* plays a key role in planning, working memory, decision making and emotions. Its posterior part, the *primary motor cortex*, processes motor commands. Broca's area is important for speech production. The *temporal lobe* creates new memories and stores perceptual information (e.g. face recognition and written-word recognition are in part carried out by the *fusiform gyrus*). The *auditory cortex* processes auditory information coming from the ears. Wernicke's area plays a key role in language comprehension.

Source: Shier, Butler and Lewis, 2010.

Stop and Think Brain plasticity

There is considerable evidence that the brain is highly plastic. This of course does not mean that the brain is made of plastic. Rather, it means that the brain can (in part) rewire itself during life. For example, children suffering from lesions affecting brain areas devoted to language typically see their brain recruit new regions for processing language. How is brain plasticity consistent with the general picture of the brain given in this chapter?

Conclusions: from biology to psychology

Some striking properties of the human brain are apparent from this brief introduction to neuroscience. First, the human brain is obviously complex. Second, many things occur in parallel, as all the structures we have described are active most of the time during waking hours. Third, the brain has a fair degree of redundancy, in the sense that similar functions are carried out by different parts of the brain (for example, we have seen that learning implicates the cerebellum, the hypothalamus, the basal ganglia and the hippocampus, among other brain structures). Finally, the brain has a strong hierarchical organisation, starting from neurotransmitter molecules to neurons, and then, after skipping a few levels, to broad regions such as the frontal lobe. The complexity and hierarchical organisation of the brain call for a few comments, which will also answer

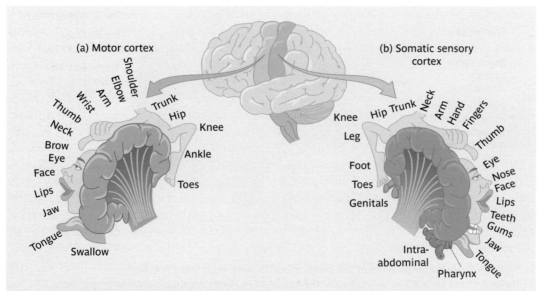

Figure 3.10 The motor and sensory homunculi

(a) *The motor homunculus.* This frontal section represents how the different anatomical divisions of the primary motor cortex encode motor information. Importantly, the areas are proportional to the complexity of the movements that body parts carry out, not to their size.

(b) *The sensory homunculus.* Frontal section of the primary somatosensory cortex. The areas are proportional to the quantity and importance of somatosensory input from a region of the body.

Source: Shier, Butler and Lewis, 2010.

a question you might have been asking yourself for a while: what is the role of cognitive psychology in all this? Can a discussion of mental processes be replaced by a description of the activity of neurons, as proposed by philosophers such as Patricia and Paul Churchland (1998)?

In his classic essay on the 'Architecture of complexity', Simon (1996) noted that hierarchies are ubiquitous in natural systems. Consider physics, for example, and in particular the way elementary particles form atoms, atoms form molecules, and molecules form more complex entities such as rocks. Or, to take a more mundane example, consider the way a book is organised: letters, words, sentences, paragraphs, sections and finally chapters. As noted earlier, the same kind of hierarchical structure can be found in biological systems, and in particular in the way the brain is organised. Simon convincingly argues that, in order to evolve, complex systems must have some degree of stability, and that a hierarchical organisation precisely enables such stability. The idea is that hierarchical systems typically have some degree of redundancy – that is, similar functions are carried out by different components – and if one component fails, the system is only marginally affected because the function can still be performed to some extent by other components. Systems that lack a hierarchical organisation also lack this degree of flexibility. The conclusion is that a system as complex as the brain must have a strong hierarchical organisation, or it would not have been able to evolve in the first place.

A key insight of Simon's analysis is that scientists should actually be very grateful to nature for the presence of hierarchies, because they make it easier to understand the mechanisms involved. This can be done by focusing on one specific level rather than having to understand phenomena in all their complexity, and this is possible because each level has its own laws and principles. At a first approximation, what happens at the levels below can simply be averaged without taking into account all the details, and what happens at the levels above can be considered as constant. To take a specific example, when Darwin formulated his theory of evolution, he did not have to worry about the structure of DNA – which was, of course, discovered nearly 70 years after Darwin's death – and he did not have to consider the way the Earth came to exist. What he did was to focus on an intermediate level in the hierarchy of natural phenomena: how species evolved over time. This example also illustrates an important point in this analysis: the levels below and above provide constraints that can be useful in understanding the processes involved at the level we are interested in. What happens at the low levels (e.g. the biochemical level) and what happens at high levels (e.g. the cosmological level) limit how species evolve; if the biochemistry of life had somehow been disrupted, and if Earth did not provide the type of environment that made life possible, evolution simply would not have happened. Of course, as science progresses, links are made between these different levels of explanation. We now know that DNA is essential at the biochemical level for the transmission of the heredity traits postulated by Darwin. Even so, it is important to note that the theory of evolution has not been replaced by molecular biology. Although linked in strong and important ways, both theories explain different phenomena at different levels.

This analysis also applies to the relationship between cognitive psychology and neuroscience. In the large hierarchy spanning from molecular events in the neuron to what happens in human societies, cognitive psychology studies a level that is near the top end: the way human beings perceive, think and make decisions, what Newell (1990) calls the *cognitive band*. Behaviour at this level is constrained by the levels below. For example, deficiency in the neurotransmitter dopamine will affect learning. But behaviour is also constrained by the levels above. What society deems important will influence what will be taught at school and, as a consequence, what children learn. While these constraints are significant, it is important to realise that there are plenty of laws and principles that can be, and have been, discovered at the cognitive band, essentially ignoring the other bands. The remainder of this book will present the most important of these discoveries, but one example might be useful at this stage.

We have seen in the previous chapters that considerable research has been carried out on short-term memory, and we will of course discuss this work in more detail in Chapter 6. This research has shown that a substantial amount of data can be explained using mechanisms that are essentially at the psychological level. Among these mechanisms one can mention that old items tend to disappear from short-term memory because its capacity is limited; items that can easily be grouped because they have already occurred together in the past are easier to memorise than disconnected items (the principle of chunking); and that the kind of strategies people use drastically affects their recall performance. These three mechanisms can be the starting point of more sophisticated theories that can make precise predictions (e.g. about the number of items recalled, the type of errors made and the exact influence of familiarity of the material to recall). Again these predictions are made at the psychological level only, ignoring other levels including the biological one. It is obviously interesting to know how the brain implements the mechanisms postulated at the psychological level, but the point is that useful scientific theories can be developed at this level to explain phenomena about short-term memory.

To conclude, it is important to realise that the effect of constraints goes not only from neuroscience to cognitive psychology, but in the opposite direction as well. Ignoring psychology is not a good idea for neuroscience! To go back to the example of memory, ignoring the kind of strategies people use (e.g. mere rehearsal as opposed to organising the material), as is often the case in current research in neuroscience, is likely to yield incorrect conclusions about the brain mechanisms underpinning memory.

Stop and Think Mental disorders

Many mental disorders have a biological basis (think of Alzheimer's or schizophrenia). To what extent can psychotherapies – which are therapies not using any medication – help patients suffering from these diseases? Use the idea of hierarchies of mechanisms to answer this question.

Stop and Think Reductionism

Recall that Patricia and Paul Churchland proposed that an explanation at the neuronal level should provide a sufficient explanation of what happens at the psychological level. Discuss the pros and cons of this view.

Chapter summary

Although this book is mostly concerned with what happens at the psychological level, it is important that you have some minimal knowledge about the biological basis of cognition. This is because the biology of the brain imposes constraints on cognition, such as how rapidly information can be learned. When reading this chapter, you no doubt have been impressed by the complexity of the brain. In fact, in spite of nearly two centuries of research and the tremendous speed with which new data are currently collected, we have only started to understand the way the brain implements the mind. The individual levels of the hierarchy – neurotransmitters, neurons, clusters of neurons, clusters of clusters of neurons, and so on up to brain areas – are fairly well understood, but what is lacking is an appreciation of how these levels are connected to produce mental states and behaviour. When reading the remainder of this book, keep in mind the complexity of the biological apparatus making cognition possible.

Further reading

More thorough treatment of the biology of the brain can be found in standard textbooks such as Shepherd (1994), Kandel, Schwartz and Jessell (2000), Bear, Connors and Paradiso (2007) or Carlson (2007). Eichenbaum (2008) focuses on the neuroscience of learning and memory. The current interest in brain imaging has spawned numerous books, among which we recommend Luck (2005), who discusses the technique of event-related potentials, and Huettel, Song and McCarthy (2004), who focus on functional Magnetic Resonance Imaging (fMRI). The question of complexity in hierarchical systems, including the brain, is discussed in Simon (1996) and Newell (1990).

PART 2
Basic processes

Part contents

Chapter 4

Perception

CHAPTER PREVIEW

☑ Perception is the process by which the cognitive system constructs an internal representation of the outside world. To do so, it uses simple input data from the environment (sensations) and processes these data with rules.

☑ Perception does not produce a copy of reality. Instead, it is an active process that allows us to make sense of the world around us.

☑ Perception does not always provide a veridical rendition of reality: we can see things that are present, we can see objects that are physically impossible, and we can see two different animals in one single drawing. Studying visual illusions is an important way to understand human perception.

☑ Although the image on the retina is two-dimensional, the brain is able to construct three-dimensional representations of scenes, by using monocular and binocular cues.

☑ According to Marr's and Biederman's theories, human perception uses basic three-dimensional shapes to recognise objects.

☑ The brain uses different areas for recognising faces than for recognising other objects.

Introduction

Released in March 1999, the movie *The Matrix*, directed by Andy and Larry Wachowski, became an instant hit. The plot was simple yet amazing. By deceiving our perceptual system, computers take control of our minds and rule mankind. The matrix is the program and interface imposing a non-existent reality to our senses. It makes us believe that we are living in a free world; in fact, the virtual reality is just a mere simulation that keeps us in psychological prisons. Humans are used as batteries. The question posed by the movie is whether we can escape our own perception.

Perception is the only way to know the world around us. If perception fails and does not account for what is going on outside, are we going to notice it? The answer provided by the Wachowski brothers is 'no'. In the matrix, the hero Neo (Keanu Reeves) is shown the way out of the matrix by people who are not under the control of virtual reality. The movie can be understood metaphorically. Do we perceive what is in there? To what extent are we deceived by our senses? Is there anything to do to correct the mistakes that perception sometimes commits in capturing the world? All these questions, implicit in the movie, are addressed explicitly in this chapter.

We start by showing that the aim of the perceptual system is to inform the mind about reality. Then, we describe the senses that serve this purpose. By analysing the processes that create percepts, we show why perception is not a mirror of reality but is a reconstructed representation, much like a painting, with its beauties and flaws. The relationship between the objective intensity of physical stimuli and their perceived intensity constitutes the field of psychophysics, which is presented in the second part of this chapter. From this section onwards, we focus on visual perception. Visual perception is the kind of perception we rely on most often. Evolution has shaped what was at the beginning a mere light detector to a remarkably complex perceptual system. Focusing on vision will allow us to demonstrate the key characteristics of perception in a pictorial and intuitive way.

The third part details the basic mechanisms that our perceptual system uses to group together meaningful pieces of information so as to form basic chunks of information. We will see that these laws, known as the Gestalt laws of perception, are applied automatically to the bottom-up processing of perceived objects.

The fourth part shows how our cognitive apparatus builds a three-dimensional view of the world by analysing the two-dimensional images provided by the retina. In the remainder of the chapter, we show how visual illusions highlight some specific aspects of the perceptual system by pointing to its weaknesses. We also present two central theories aiming to explain visual recognition. Marr (1982) proposed a stage view of object recognition, and Biederman (1987) proposed a theory emphasising that our perceptions are the result of binding together basic visual shapes. Finally, we consider face perception. Faces are the most common visual objects that we meet in our everyday life. The study of face perception provides an insight about how we perceive objects with complex, changing visual features.

What is perception?

Sensing the world

Our environment changes continuously and rapidly. Although most of the events are of no relevance, a few are potentially either harmful or beneficial. Our species has evolved perceptual mechanisms to select such relevant information, mechanisms that are shared to a considerable extent with those used by non-human primates. We do not have direct access to what is happening in the environment – rather, we collect cues that are used to build an internal representation of the external world. This chapter is concerned with how we figure out what is going on in the outside world.

Consider Doolittle's painting 'Pintos' (1979), shown in Figure 4.1. How many horses are hiding in this painting? The painting is interesting in that both the horses and the background are

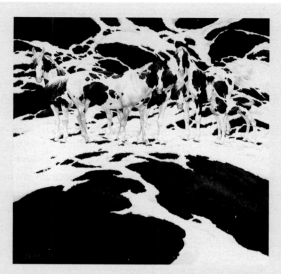

Figure 4.1 Pintos, © Bev Doolittle, courtesy of The Greenwich Workshop®, Inc.

white and brown. It is likely that you needed time to find out that five horses are embedded in the image. The fact that you needed some time illustrates that perception is an active, complex process, and not just a passive system registering the external world. It might fail to organise percepts correctly, so that you do not perceive a visual scene as it is in reality. For instance, in Doolittle's painting, one might see only four horses instead of five. One crucial point, to which we shall return in this chapter, is that **representations** of reality are not the same as reality: a page of this book is obviously too small to host five horses! We can see something that does not exist (horses) and we can fail to see something that in fact exists (a drawing on a page of paper).

Doolittle's painting illustrates what visual perception is all about. Obviously, our perception of the world is not limited to visual input. Many other types of input, such as sounds and odours, provide useful information. This relates to what is known as 'sensory modalities'. A **sensory modality** is a dedicated subset of the nervous system that responds to specific physical inputs. For instance, audition is the detection and interpretation of air motions or vibrations, and balance detects the direction of gravity and corrects the body posture accordingly so that we can keep upright. Sensory systems inform us not only about many aspects of the world around us (**exteroception**), but also about what happens inside our body (**proprioception**). There are important limits to what the senses can detect. Consider for instance the fact that lights that are too intense force us to close our eyes or that motions that are too slow cannot be perceived. These limits imposed upon our ability to capture the physical aspects of the outside world narrow the window of the portion of reality we are sensitive to (see Box 4.1). For this reason, sensory systems are said to be 'bounded'. These boundaries, in turn, force the perceptual system to make some assumptions about how events are connected in order to build a representation of the outside world. Unfortunately, the assumptions can be proven wrong in some circumstances, leading to perception being deceived by the senses (see the section on illusions

Box 4.1 RESEARCH CLOSE-UP: **Oscillatory processes**

An oscillatory process is determined by the following equation $y = A \sin(k2\pi)$. A stands for amplitude (how far from zero the oscillations go). For example, sea waves may range from a few millimetres to dozens of metres, and this would be indicated by different values of A. The coefficient k stands for the number of oscillations per second; it is called frequency and is noted in hertz (Hz). The inverse of k is $p = 1/k$, and is the wavelength. Another parameter which does not appear in the above equation is wave speed. On the sea, the waves may travel more or less fast. As for electromagnetic radiations (including visible light), the speed is around 300 000 km/s!

Electromagnetic radiations are classified according to their wavelength. Visible lights are radiations of wavelength in the range between 470 and 700 nanometres (nm; a nanometre is one-millionth of a millimetre). Thus, the eye perceives only a fraction of the radiation range. It is worth having a brief look at the other wavelengths; Table 4.1 shows the relationship between wavelength and type of electromagnetic radiation.

What does this table mean? That most of the electromagnetic reality is out of the reach of our perceptual system. For example, we need complex devices to detect X-rays, a more intense form of 'light'. We also need a device to capture infrared rays. Our perceptual system captures a narrow window within the range of electromagnetic radiations. As this is the fraction of light we are sensitive to, our senses make us believe that this is reality. For example, you perceive your pen as red because it reflects the light mostly in the frequency corresponding to red. But you are unable to see whether your pen is hot (since you touched it an instant ago) or whether it is cold. If you were sensitive to frequencies indicating heating radiations, you could know whether your pen is hotter that the objects around it just by looking at it. If your eyes were sensitive to much shorter wavelengths than they are in reality, you could see X-rays and thus scan inside everyone's body!

Table 4.1 The spectrum of electromagnetic radiations

Wavelength (in metres)	Class	Visible
10^{-12} m	Gamma rays	No
10^{-10} m	X-rays	No
$400 - 700 \; 10^{-9}$ m	Light	Yes
10^{-6} m	Infrared	No
10^{-3} m	Radar	No
10^{-0} m	FM radio	No

below). Table 4.2 lists the most common human senses and the type of physical entities they detect. (The exact number of sensory modalities is debated.)

Each physical property is captured by specific sensory neurons, which are called **sensors** or **receptors**. For instance, photoreceptors are neurons sensitive to light. The role of the sensors is to translate physical stimulation into signals that are interpretable by the brain, a process that is called **transduction**. After transduction has taken place, the brain interprets the neural signals to build a representation. The percepts built up by neural analysis are not necessarily related to the outside world. While most of the senses presented in Table 4.2 are concerned with events occurring outside the body, many senses, such as those related to arterial pressure and heart rhythm, are concerned with events occurring inside the body. Such senses, which are grouped in the category of proprioception, are less accessible to consciousness. Still, through automatic controls, they play a key role in the regulation of the body. The senses related to the outside world are the focus of this chapter, since they concern how we understand and interact with our environment, including other people through social interactions.

Sensory systems receive information from their dedicated sets of receptors. The role of the receptors is to bring into the system the basic elements of perception that combine to form a **percept** (i.e. the mental representation of what is perceived). These basic elements are referred to as **sensations**, while more elaborated material is referred to as **perceptions**. Neither sensations nor perceptions can exist on their own. Both processes are entangled, and it is sometimes difficult to determine where sensations end and perceptions begin. It is important to realise that multiple specialised sensory systems participate in constructing an internal representation of reality.

Bottom-up and top-down processes in perception

Our brain processes the information collected by our senses in order to construct percepts. If this processing were perfect, we would just capture an exact copy of the external world. However, this is not the case. Information can be ambiguous, and often the brain uses previous knowledge to remove ambiguity. For example, try to read the words presented in Figure 4.2 as fast as possible.

It is likely that you read the words 'the cat'. Have you noticed that the same symbol was used to represent an A and an H? Somehow, your brain managed to decide that it was an A in one case and an H in the other, and not vice versa. The visual features constituting the letters were captured by the visual receptors. To interpret the signals, they were then forwarded to

Table 4.2 Senses. The most common human senses

Vision	The ability to detect electromagnetic radiations within a narrow band of frequencies (visible light)
Audition	The perception of air vibrations
Taste	The detection of various chemical compounds in food and liquids, by a variety of receptors. Each receptor is in charge of detecting the presence of specific molecules
Smell	Similar to taste, but detects chemical compounds in the air
Touch	The perception of pressure on skin
Equilibrioception	The perception of balance; it is based on the detection of the direction of gravity
Thermoception	The perception of temperature
Nociception	The perception of pain. Yes! This is an independent sense served by its own specific set of receptors

increasingly complex levels of processing (see Chapter 16 for details). This kind of information processing, starting from basic sensory information up to more conceptual information, is called **bottom-up processing** or **stimulus-driven processing**.

Another mode of processing – called **top-down processing** or **concept-driven processing** – is also at work: high levels of cognition control and regulate events affecting lower levels of cognition. In the example of Figure 4.2, high-level cognition and the knowledge that 'the' and 'cat' are words helped perception to decide which word was read. Another interesting example of top-down processing is offered by the 'word-superiority effect', which we will describe in Chapter 9. In a nutshell, the effect shows that it is easier to recognise a letter when it is part of a word than when it is presented individually. As a final example of top-down processing, consider search, where higher levels of cognition direct perception through attention (see Chapter 5). When you are looking for a pen, you process objects one after another until an object matches your target.

Top-down processes may use context, expectations and knowledge to structure the information sent by bottom-up processes. You will see in the next chapter how knowledge influences attentional processes. Here, we focus on the bottom-up processing aspect of perception – that is, how the basic sensory building blocks are put together to make a percept. You should be aware that the influence of top-down processes is limited in that they cannot correct some assumptions made by bottom-up processes. For example, as we live in a three-dimensional world, our visual system has been designed by evolution to process a three-dimensional space; as a consequence, it automatically interprets ambiguous data in a way that satisfies the constraints of a three-dimensional world, and there is not much that top-down processes can do to change this interpretation.

Consider the Ponzo illusion in Figure 4.3. The top horizontal segment seems longer than the bottom one, but in fact the two segments are of equal length. One standard way to explain this illusion is to consider it as a normal interpretation in a three-dimensional world. Imagine that you are standing on the tracks of a railway, looking at objects placed at different distances. If an object closer to you has the same apparent size than another object located farther away, this implies that the object located farther away is bigger. This interpretation is automatically generated by the perceptual system without any possibility to influence it. Even though you *know* that the top segment has the same length as the bottom segment, you cannot correct your perception that it is bigger. This is clear evidence that the process of reconstructing reality is under the influence of knowledge. The perceptual system uses a set of assumptions to interpret data; when one or several of these assumptions are incorrect, an illusion occurs. The fact that the perceptual

Figure 4.2 Word recognition

When reading this, did you notice that the H and A had the same symbol?

system makes assumptions or hypotheses about what to expect in the environment is a crucial aspect of the cognitive system (Gregory, 1980). Perception is not an isolated process but is under the influence of knowledge.

The psychophysics approach

As we have seen, perception is the product of intertwined processes. Figure 4.4 illustrates how these processes influence the final percept. Which one of the two squares in the middle of the two large squares is brighter?

Figure 4.3 The Ponzo illusion

On a scale from 1 (white) to 10 (black), try to estimate the level of grey for these two squares.

In fact, the two squares have the same intensity of grey. (If you are not convinced, cut a piece of paper so that you can see only the two central squares). This illusion is a startling example that perception does not mirror reality. It actually distorts it. Psychophysicists – psychologists interested in the relationship between physical stimuli and their perception – have addressed three central questions about how perception captures reality.

The first question has been to determine the **detection threshold** of the receptors. In other words, what is the minimal strength of a stimulation so that we can notice its presence? This minimum value is called the *absolute threshold* of the receptor. Each class of receptor is characterised by a different absolute threshold. For example, consider the sensation of pressure on the skin. What is the lowest-intensity stimulus that can be detected at a given location? Below the absolute threshold, our sensors are unable to detect the presence of a physical stimulus. Sensors also have a maximum level of detection. For example, we cannot hear sounds of very high frequency (ultrasounds). Thus, sensors have windows of responsiveness (i.e. windows between minimum and maximum levels of detection).

The second question concerns the minimal difference in amplitude that can be detected between two stimuli. Of particular interest is the issue of **just noticeable difference**. How sensitive are the receptors to variations in magnitude? For example, you apply pressure on your skin. How much additional pressure should you apply to notice a difference? Such a difference relates to what is known as the *relative threshold*. In general, receptors are not sensitive to any variation but only to variations within a certain range.

Figure 4.4 Two dark squares
Pay attention to the squares in the middle. Which one is brighter than the other?

The last question – the so-called question of **scaling** – is about quantifying the relationship between stimulus intensity and subjective perception. Here, the questions are of the following kind: how much must the magnitude of a physical stimulus increase so that you have the subjective impression that the stimulus is twice as strong in intensity? The relationship between physical intensity and subjective intensity is not linear. Perception does not merely reproduce the external world: a light twice as intense (i.e. the physical amplitude is doubled) does not lead to the subjective perception of a light twice as bright (i.e. subjective perception). (See Box 4.2 for more detail about scaling.)

Reality, therefore, can be deformed when captured by our sensory modalities. How did humans manage to survive and even dominate earth using such (apparently) limited information? To address this issue, we need to have a closer look at the visual system. This will illustrate how a sensory modality, by picking up only a few samples of the external world, is nevertheless able to inform us about key events. In the next section we briefly survey the rules used by the cognitive system to organise two-dimensional information.

Two-dimensional visual information (Gestalt theory)

As we have seen in Chapter 2, Gestalt psychology emerged at the beginning of the twentieth century. Its leaders, such as Wertheimer, Köhler and Koffka, viewed perception as the process by which object form is reached after self-organisation of basic elements – 'the whole is more than the sum of its parts'. By emphasising self-organisation, Gestalt psychology was in opposition to the traditional **reductionist** approach that science normally uses to understand phenomena. It is mainly known for developing the so-called 'Gestalt laws of perception' (see Figure 4.6), which describe how the mind coordinates the perception of several basic parts to generate a whole percept.

For Gestalt psychologists, perceptual organisation may be reduced to the *principle of Prägnanz* (*Prägnanz* means conciseness or simplicity in German). This principle states that we organise the perceptual input so that we perceive the simplest and most stable forms. However vague this definition, this principle is the central assumption of the Gestalt theorists and the starting point for several laws. The *law of proximity* states that perception clusters objects according to their proximity (Figure 4.6, Panel A). Thus, if a set of objects are close to each other and separated from other objects, they will be perceived as an autonomous group. The *law of similarity* states that similar visual elements will be grouped together. In Panel B, we see the circles and triangles as forming four horizontal rows in the first drawing, and four vertical columns in the second drawing. The *law of closure*, illustrated in Panel C, states that perception completes visual elements. Although the large circle made up of small circles has gaps, we tend to see it as a full circle.

The *law of symmetry* states that we tend to perceive objects as organised around symmetrical axes or centres (Panel D). The *law of continuity* says that we tend to perceive objects as forming smooth continuous patterns. Consider the drawing in Panel E. It is likely that you perceive a horizontal bar hiding two oblique lines. Your mind automatically interprets the two separated chunks of the oblique lines as being part of the same object. Yet, if you take a ruler and extend any of the two line segments, you will realise that they actually do not match. The rule of continuity tricked your perception! Objects presented in spatial sequences are clustered together to

Box 4.2 RESEARCH CLOSE-UP: **Stevens's law**

Fechner (1860/1966) was among the first to address the question of scaling, which really boils down to studying how much distortion our senses impose on physical stimulations. He showed that, when the magnitude of the stimulus increases multiplicatively, psychological impression increases only linearly. Fechner's law is not precise and is also not valid for some sensory modalities. However, the fact that perceived intensity increases less rapidly than physical intensity is an important result. Stevens (1957) estimated that the relationship linking the brightness of light (stimulus intensity) to perceived brightness (perceived intensity) is characterised by a proportional increase with a ratio between 0.3 and 0.5 (see Figure 4.5).

The dashed line shows what a linear relation between intensity and perception would look like. The bold line plots the physical – psychological relationship as determined by Stevens's equation; note that the difference between two perceived intensities is not the same as the difference between two physical magnitudes, as it is with the linear function. Let us consider the four points A, B, C and D in the graph. The points are located at equal distance on the scale of intensity (the physical stimulus). However, the progression of the perceived brightness is different: at each step, the difference in perceived brightness diminishes. Stevens's law is a powerful demonstration that perception applies transformations to the stimuli from their very detection.

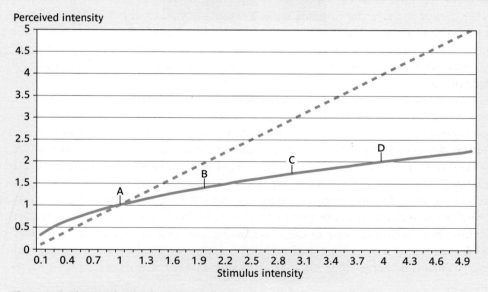

Figure 4.5 The Psychophysics of brightness

Steven's law links stimulus intensity to perceived intensity. The law links stimulus intensity (here in arbitrary units) to perceived intensity (also in arbitrary units). The bold line shows that perceived intensity increases only as a power function of stimulus intensity, and not as a linear function (showed by the dashed line). Thus, perception departs from a mirror image of reality.

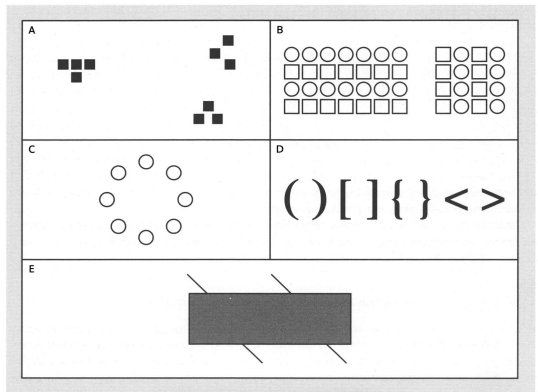

Figure 4.6 Gestalt laws

Drawings showing how the Gestalt laws organise perception. Panel A shows the law of proximity. Panel B shows how similarity affects perception. Panel C offers an illustration of the law of closure. Panel D shows how symmetry influences grouping of perceptual elements. Panel E illustrates the law of good continuity. Finally, the drawing at the bottom shows an artistic use of law of figure-ground segregation.

Source (of the drawing): M.C. Escher's "Sky and Water I"

form lines. The law of continuity highlights the fact that we use contours of objects to form perceptual units.

Finally, the *law of figure–ground segregation* states that perception tends to structure the visual field into two parts: a figure and a ground. The bottom panel in Figure 4.6 illustrates figure–ground segregation. Whether you are looking at the birds or the fish, the figure is the focus of attention and the ground recedes to the back of perception and attention. What is striking in Escher's drawing is that you can focus on either the birds or the fish in the air–water frontier. However, if you follow the figure from top to bottom, the perception is forced to see birds at the top, then either birds or fish in the middle, and finally fish as you reach the bottom. It is very difficult to force perception to see the birds between the last rows of fish. Another standard example of figure–ground segregation is offered by **bistable percepts** – stimuli that can be perceived as two different objects. In the Rubin illusion (see Figure 4.10 below), you can switch at will between the perception of a vase or of two faces.

Gestalt theory has been very good in describing the organising principles that guide perceptual processes. However, little or no explanation has been put forward to explain the existence of these laws (see Box 4.3).

The third dimension: depth

The Gestalt laws illustrate how we organise simple visual patterns into larger perceptual structures. However, they do not address the question of how we localise these percepts in our three-dimensional world. To realise the importance of three-dimensional representations, imagine trying to assess the distance of the cars coming into a junction, or finding your way in a new building. The perception of the third dimension is crucial, for the obvious reason that we live in a three-dimensional world. Because the eyes occupy different locations in space, they have two

Box 4.3 RESEARCH CLOSE-UP: **The advance of science**

Science is a difficult subject matter. Before they come to the correct conclusion, scientists are often mistaken. For example, it took centuries to have a basic understanding of the laws of gravity. It had also been a long journey before scientists came to understand the basic brain processes that underlie perception. The French philosopher Descartes was one of the first to give it a try. Unfortunately, the science and technology of the seventeenth century did not allow him to untie this knot. Three centuries later, the Gestalt School, so successful at the time in explaining two-dimensional perception, also attempted to explain perception with neural mechanisms. Wolfgang Köhler postulated that percepts emerge from the electrical field generated by our neurons. The pattern of electrical activity was supposed to mirror the topological features of the percept. If this explanation was correct, then disturbing the electrical field – for example, by placing metallic implants in the brain – should perturb the electrical activity and thus impair perception. This hypothesis was put to the test by Karl Lashley and colleagues (Lashley *et al.*, 1951) in an experiment using monkeys. The results showed that the metallic implants did not alter performance. The conclusion is that percepts are not the result of a patterned field of electrical activity.

different images of a scene, and these images are two-dimensional. The question is then to understand how we perceive the world in three dimensions using two two-dimensional images.

To perceive depth, our visual system uses both monocular cues (i.e. cues from one eye) and binocular cues (i.e. cues from both eyes). Three types of monocular cues are of particular importance with respect to the relative distance between objects. **Occlusion** refers to the fact that an object partly hidden by another object must be behind it. **Texture gradient** refers to the fact that objects, such as walls, have a specific texture that changes with distance. **Motion parallax** refers to the fact that, when you are moving, objects that are closer seem to move faster than objects that are far away. Next time you travel by car or train, notice how the objects close to the road or the railway seem to pass by very quickly, while the buildings at the horizon seem almost motionless.

Two binocular cues are particularly important: **binocular disparity** and **convergence**. The eyes have a slightly different view of the world. The difference between the images is called disparity (see Figure 4.7). To have an idea of how much retinal images are affected by disparity, try the following. Position a finger at 30 cm from your nose. Look at the finger with your left eye only and then with your right eye only. You will notice that, depending on which eye is open, the finger is in front of a different part of the visual scene – the so-called *shift in the image*. The difference between the two retinal images provides information about distance and thus about depth: the farther away the object, the smaller the shift. The other cue that is used to estimate depth is convergence, which is the coordinated and inward movement made by the two eyes to focus on a near object. The information provided by convergence is independent of the image on the retina: the brain is informed of the gaze direction of each eye by the muscles controlling the position of the eyes.

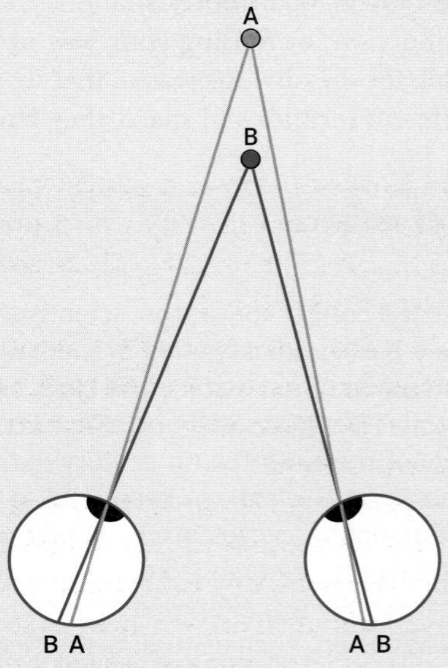

Figure 4.7 Binocular disparity
Here the eyes are focusing on two different objects, A and B. A is located farther away than B. You can see that the image of both objects in one retina will mirror the image of the other retina.

Stop and Think Is one eye enough?
Considering the fact that binocular cues are employed to reconstruct the third dimension used by two-eyed people to navigate in their environment, how would you explain the fact that people with vision in only one eye can navigate safely in a three-dimensional world?

When the visual system is deceived: visual illusions

Our visual system has been shaped by evolution to rapidly detect potential threats or opportunities. Although it is well adapted to the kinds of natural environments in which it has evolved, it can be confused surprisingly easily. **Visual illusions** are physical stimuli that deceive our perception. It is useful to

Box 4.4 IN FOCUS: **Watching the ghost**

If people report seeing a ghost, you are likely to think they are drunk or under the influence of drugs. Yet it is possible to see things that do not exist. The mind sometimes plays little tricks on us and makes us believe that we see something while there is actually nothing there in reality. From today on, you can tell your friends that you can see things that do not exist, and that you can even show them these things if they do not believe you! Consider Figure 4.8. You can clearly see a light blue equilateral triangle, which is brighter than the background. Please, feel free to follow the contours of the triangle. By doing so, you will notice that the triangle has actually no contours and, in fact, does not exist. The illusion occurs because of the way information is processed bottom-up and cannot be corrected by top-down processes; in this case, the brain tends to complete disconnected visual elements so that they form a whole (Gestalt law of closure). Although you now know that this is an illusion, you still perceive the light blue triangle!

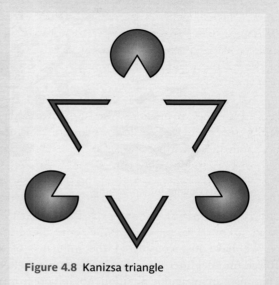

Figure 4.8 Kanizsa triangle

study visual illusions because they provide clues about how our cognitive system processes information. By understanding how stimuli cause illusions, we can identify which processes have failed, and why they have failed. Let us have a look at several famous visual illusions that illustrate some aspects of our cognitive system particularly well (see Box 4.4).

The conclusion from the Kanizsa illusion (Figure 4.8) is that those who report having seen things that are impossible should not automatically be considered as drunk or on speed; rather, they may just have been tricked by their perceptual system. They have really experienced something that is not there, just as you can see a triangle that is not drawn!

A striking example of the influence of knowledge on perception is provided by Figure 4.9. Something is hiding in this figure. What could it be? Take a few seconds and try to find out.

What is hiding in the picture is a Dalmatian dog. If you have not found it, have a second look. It is likely that you will find it now. Knowing that there is a Dalmatian in there helps you to find it. As another example of the influence of knowledge on our understanding of the environment, consider watching the North Pole star. Knowing that it marks the direction of the North Pole (as it is approximately aligned with the Earth's axis of rotation), you can now 'see' where north is and thus by inference where east, west and south are. If you see the same star without knowing that it is the North Pole star, you just see a pale dot in the sky. What a change in the perception of the whole environment is made by just adding a piece of knowledge to a star!

Figure 4.9 Looking for something?

We have just considered the influence of knowledge on the perception of a known object. Another interesting case is where one single visual stimulus can elicit two different percepts. This raises an intriguing question, not remote from science fiction: can we control whether we can perceive the same stimulus as one or another object? A positive answer would be evidence for a clear influence of our knowledge and control processes on how the perceptual system organises information. Look at the left panel of Figure 4.10 for a few seconds.

Do you see a rabbit or a duck? If you see the rabbit, try to see the duck. Once you can see both, you can train yourself to switch your perception from the duck to the rabbit and vice versa. You can control what you see! As already mentioned, that kind of stimulus is called a **bistable percept**. It is interesting to note that, in the Rubin illusion (right panel of Figure 4.10), the switch in perception between the vase and the face can be identified by neural recordings (Hasson *et al.*, 2001). Two more important points about the pictures in Figure 4.10. First, you initially saw either the rabbit or the duck. The reason why you see one rather than the other is unknown. Second, you cannot see the two animals at the same time, even though the visual features necessary for imagining them together are present. Once a visual feature is considered to be part of one animal, it cannot be part of the other, and this precludes any simultaneous perception. Perception has to make a choice!

Visual illusions shed light on some interesting features of perception. So far, we have considered illusions related to objects that actually exist in our environment (for example, Rubin's vase illusion). But we can also see objects that are physically impossible, as shown by Figure 4.11. These examples illustrate the extent to which our perception is automatic and how conditioned we are by our senses. Just like in the movie *The Matrix*, we are limited by our ability to capture meaningful events in the external world. We are bounded by our perceptual system to such an extent that it is actually surprising that we can see beyond our noses.

Figure 4.10 Two examples of perception switch: the rabbit–duck figure and the Rubin illusion

---

Stop and Think Four-dimensional objects

We have seen that it was possible to trick the mind so that it perceives impossible three-dimensional objects. Is it possible to perceive four-dimensional objects?

Perceptual illusions have sometimes led to curious debates in popular science. A famous example, which illustrates how defiant we should be with respect to our own perception, is the case of the *Face on Mars*, discussed by the astronomer Carl Sagan (1996). When the Viking orbiter was approaching the planet Mars in 1976, it took many photographs among which one was quite disconcerting (see Figure 4.12(a)). As you can see, one of the rocks really looks like a face. Unsurprisingly, but also unfortunately, this rock has been interpreted by some as a sign of extraterrestrial intelligence. Since then, astronomers have had a hard time making people understand that this was not proof of intelligent life on Mars. In his book, Sagan hoped that a new and closer photograph would disprove this speculation. It actually took more than 20 years before a better photograph, much closer to the surface, could be taken. It clearly showed that the face was just an effect of shadows (see Figure 4.12(b)).

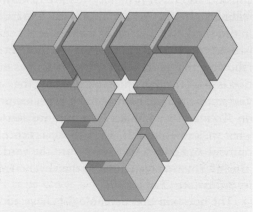

Figure 4.11 Tricking the mind: an impossible object (by Escher)

Stop and Think UFOs

Many people have reported seeing UFOs (unidentified flying objects). Assuming that these people did not hallucinate, use what you have learned in this chapter to account for these reports.

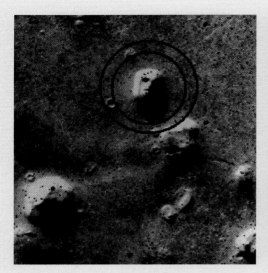 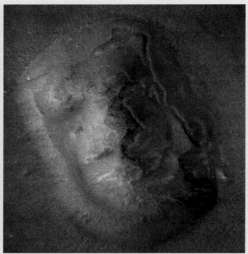

Figure 4.12(a) Surface of Mars from afar
The black rings indicate the rock that looks like a face.
Source: Courtesy NASA.

Figure 4.12(b) Region of interest on the suface of Mars
Where has the face gone?
Source: Courtesy NASA.

Perception is cognition

The purpose of perception is to recognise objects so that actions can be selected and carried out. In most cases, to recognise an object is to check whether or not we know the object under consideration. For instance, we have to know Paul to recognise him as Paul. Another example will illustrate that recognition is not a mere bottom-up perceptual process. Let us travel back in time and ask a person of the thirteenth century to identify a computer and to tell us what it is used for. It is likely that we will not get any answer. The person does see the computer (showing that perception works) but does not know what it is. The process of object recognition is at work all the time: recognising the computer with which you work, the chair on which you sit, the remote control to change channels, the letters in the book you are reading, and so on. To identify an object is to put into consciousness not only the recognised object but also what we know about it. The process is central in that it retrieves information about the environment and allows us to structure the world as sets of potentially useful or harmful objects. The information recognised is then evaluated with respect to the task at hand in order to assess its utility (see Chapter 10).

The question that psychologists have addressed is how the recognition of complex objects can be made so quickly. We now describe two theories that were developed to account for object recognition in general. Later, when we talk about face recognition, we consider more specific theories that are limited to only one class of objects – in that case, faces.

Marr's theory

Marr's (1982) objective was to develop a computer model of object recognition. As we have seen in Chapter 1 and will discuss further in Chapter 15, developing computer models helps us understand the consequences of theories. Marr's model describes the process of object recognition in four bottom-up stages. In the first stage, the visual information is used to generate an image of the scene in the outside world. The image represents the contours of objects. The contours are derived from averaging the light intensity of small regions. Such a representation is called a *grey-scale representation*. The contours are used to identify the edges and surfaces belonging to objects. The process determines which edges go together. Following the rules put forward by the Gestalt school, edges are grouped together to form *tokens*. As a result of this process, the representation consists of sets of tokens. This representation is known as the *full primal sketch*. Two more steps have to be carried out before recognition is completed. The first step is to incorporate the third dimension. This is done by adding a range map to the full primal sketch. The *range map* adds information about distance to every point of the two-dimensional (2D) representation. It is assumed that the perceiver uses the depth cues we described earlier to allocate a given distance and angle to each object. Distance and angle are measured from the point of view of the perceiver. This representation of the world (called **egocentric representation**) is dependent on the perceiver. If the perceiver moves, the visual angle changes and so does the representation. At this stage of processing, the representation is called the *2½ dimensional sketch*. The last step is to match the target object with an internal representation. To do so, the perceptual system has to move from view-dependent to view-independent perception (also called **allocentric perception**). Figure 4.13 illustrates these steps.

The four panels of the figure are a rough approximation of the result of each processing stage in Marr's theory. The top-left panel shows the input on the retina. The image has been reformatted using larger pixels to simulate the fact that the retina has a very high, but limited, number of cells for encoding a visual scene. This first image is the raw material from which the perceptual system will extract the meaningful information and eventually recognise a plush rabbit. The top-right image shows the primal sketch. This grouping of visual elements is done in a 2D representation – that is, it is impossible to distinguish in this image what is figure (the rabbit) from what is ground (the rose on the wall). The third image, bottom-left panel, corresponds to the state of processing when the image is set in 2½ dimensions. In this image we can see which tokens belong to which objects and also how the surfaces relate to each other. Now we can see that the drawing of the rose is behind the rabbit. The last image, bottom right, shows the result of the processing. A full three-dimensional image (even though on a 2D paper!) which clearly shows the relationships between the various elements of the image, providing instantaneous information about the size and distance of each and every part of the visual scene.

Among the key ideas put forward by Marr, the idea of using primitives to represent objects has proved very valuable. Marr proposed that these primitives are *cylinders*. Accordingly, objects are perceived as aggregates of cylinders (see Figure 4.14). This idea of coding objects as a set of primitives has been used to develop a second important model of object recognition, which we will consider next.

Figure 4.13 A plush rabbit illustration of Marr's theory
Photo: Philippe Chassy.

Recognition by component theory

The recognition-by-component theory, developed by Irving Biederman (1987), posits the existence of 36 basic three-dimensional geometric shapes that constitute a visual alphabet used to represent objects. Biederman introduced the term **geon** (standing for geometric ion) to refer to such basic shapes. Geons are a simplified representation of perceived objects as they code only for their gross features.

Figure 4.15 illustrates how geons (left panel) combine to code objects (right panel). According to Biederman, objects can be coded with a set of well-chosen geons, regardless of their complexity. The fact that we can recognise the objects presented in the right panel supports Biederman's view, to some extent. Indeed, if we could not recognise geons, we would not recognise the objects represented in these drawings!

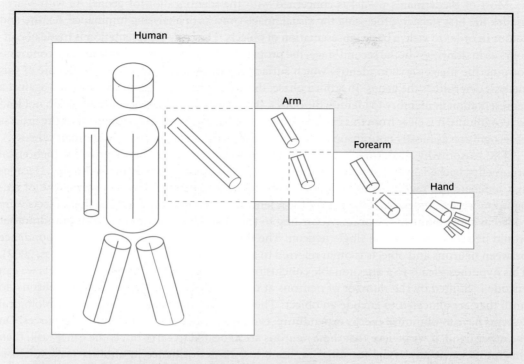

Figure 4.14 A computational view of Marr's recognition theory
Source: Adapted from Marr, 1982.

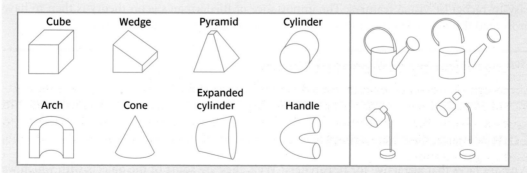

Figure 4.15 Geons and objects made of geons
Adapted from a cyberbook, 'avian visual cognition', edited by Robert J. Cook, which is available at http://www.pigeon.psy.tufts.edu/avc/toc.htm. The images are an adaptation of the pages of Kimberly Kirkpatrick section object recognition at http://www.pigeon.psy.tufts.edu/avc/kirkpatrick/default.htm

Most of Biederman's model is concerned with the identification of geons. As with Marr's model, the first stage in processing the visual image consists of analysing luminance, texture and colour in order to yield a basic representation of objects. The basic representation is made of contours as in drawings. In the second stage, the properties of the regions (as delineated by contours) forming the image serve to identify which surface is part of which object. The outcome of this analysis determines the geons. In a third phase, the arrangements of geons are matched against a representation in memory to identify the object. Partial matches might occur but they do not lead to recognition. It is clear from this cascade of events and analyses that Biederman views the process of recognition as mostly bottom-up. (See Box 4.5 for empirical support for Biederman's theory.)

The reason why Biederman's model has been so important is that it provides theoretical arguments, backed up with empirical evidence, to solve a classic problem in psychology. Decades ago, a debate was raging about how objects are coded in the brain. Two opposite views of recognition were put forward. One part of the scientific community was arguing that objects were coded as single units in the brain. According to this theoretical standpoint, your grandmother would be recognised by one single neuron. The theory positing a one-to-one correspondence between neurons and objects is often referred to as the 'grandmother cell' theory (Gross, 2002). This hypothesis leads to a questionable conclusion: it implies that the number of objects we can encode is limited by the number of neurons at our disposal. But what do the free neurons do until they are allocated to encode an object? They cannot just wait in a queue, since biological systems have to minimise energy expenditure: evolution does not tolerate unused resources. On the other hand, if we believe that these neurons are allocated to carry out some other task, then this implies that any visual learning implies a loss of performance in another task, which is rather improbable.

The second view, which is also the current one, is that objects are coded as sets of visual properties and neurons encode these properties. The same neuron coding for a particular visual shape may be involved in the encoding of several objects insofar as the objects share this shape. Hebb (1949) introduced the concept of a **cell assembly** where neurons code for objects organised as sets of properties. Later, this view was adapted to the visual cortex with theories of recognition such as Marr's and Biederman's, which state that objects are coded as groups of visual, easy-to-recognise visual features. The importance of Biederman's geon theory is then to have promoted this view of perception as the processing of groups of visual features.

Stop and Think Building the perception of new objects

Biederman put forward the theory stating that we recognise known objects by assembling basic geometric items (geons). How can we perceive new objects according to this theory?

Complex objects: faces

Why are faces that attractive for researchers? Well, they are some of the objects with which we interact most often. Moreover, they convey emotions and as such are important for social communication. What is striking is that we can recognise the face of someone we know whatever the angle, lighting and the expression displayed. The variability of traits has little influence on our ability to process a face.

Box 4.5 CLASSIC EXPERIMENT: **Hayworth and Biederman's experiment**

If objects are coded as sets of basic geons, then there should be a stage where geons are identified before being combined to form a recognisable object. Hence, eliminating some of the geons from a 2D drawing should impair recognition. This hypothesis was tested by Hayworth and Biederman (2006).

Hayworth and Biederman designed two classes of probe stimuli and three classes of target stimuli (see Figure 4.16). In the first class of probe stimuli, part of the line drawings of two-dimensional images was deleted (*Local Feature Deleted condition*). The entire image of the object was thus altered but all the geons were still present in the image. For the other probe stimuli, they just deleted one entire fraction of the object (presumably coded by one geon) and thus obtained images where entire parts of the objects were missing (*Parts Deleted condition*). Three conditions were used for the target images. In the identical condition (I condition), the images were a copy of the probe images. In the complement condition (C condition), the images consisted of the missing parts of the probe images. In the different exemplar condition (DE condition), the images consisted of other images that were altered with the same process. Hayworth and Biederman presented participants with target-probe pairs and asked them to tell whether the reference and the target were identical, complementary or different images. It turned out that deleting an entire geon made the task much more difficult, as indicated by accuracy (percentage correct).

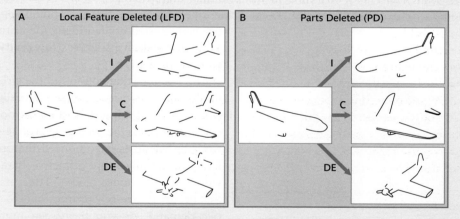

Figure 4.16 Images from Hayworth and Biederman's experiment
A minor alteration of all the geons yields images of the Local Feature Deleted condition. Getting rid of a part of an object (supposedly an entire geon) yields images for the Parts Deleted condition.
Source: Hayworth and Biederman, reprinted with permission.

Face perception involves several stages (Liu *et al.*, 2002). Visual features are assembled according to the processes described in the previous sections. Then, the brain computes features such as gender and provides an estimate of age. Three lines of evidence support the hypothesis that specific processes deal with faces. First, unlike many familiar objects (such as a pair of scissors), faces are more difficult to recognise when they are upside down. Second, photographs of faces are more difficult to recognise than familiar objects when they are presented as negatives. The third line of evidence is offered by data from neuroimaging techniques. Using fMRI, Kanwisher and co-workers have found that a specific region of the brain called the 'fusiform face area' responds preferentially to faces (Kanwisher *et al.*, 1997). Similarly, single-neuron recordings in monkeys suggest that specific neurons respond to faces (Desimone, 1991). It is not to say that one given neuron is associated with one face, but rather that a given neuron preferentially responds to some facial features. Thus, a face is coded by a pattern of activation in the neurons concerned with face processing.

Not everybody agrees with the role of the fusiform face area. According to an alternative view, the fusiform face area is a visual area specialising in the visual processing of objects we are familiar with (Gauthier *et al.*, 1999). Faces are the objects we interact most with, so it makes sense that this part of the fusiform gyrus is activated when recognising faces. Thus, rather than being the product of a specialised part of the cortex, our ability to discriminate faces would be the result of becoming expert in face perception, much like expert chess players discriminate chess positions at a glance (see Chapter 12).

Facial expressions are a very efficient way to diffuse one's feelings socially. A face is also an important factor in a person's attractiveness. A research field in cognitive evolutionary psychology is interested in identifying the features of a face that make it attractive. How pretty is the girl in Figure 4.17?

The odds are that you found the girl in the photograph good-looking. But actually, you will never meet this girl, because she does not exist. This face is the average face of 14 young women. Scientists have noticed that average faces are usually more attractive than individual faces (Rhodes, 2006). Thus, it seems that beauty is inversely proportional to cognitive demand. As you have seen numerous female faces since you were born, you have a template for the typical female face and what it should look like. The closer the percept to a prototype, the simpler the perceptual analysis. Thus, a typical female face imposes a lower cognitive demand and looks pretty.

You can realise the complexity involved in face processing by considering the model developed by Schweinberger and Burton (2003). In this model, no less than a dozen

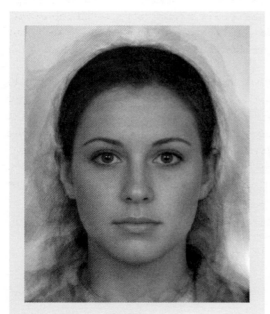

Figure 4.17 A girl's face
Source: © APA

modules are cooperating to complete face recognition. Many of the modules are mapped into anatomical structures. For example, the *Person Identity* module is linked to the anterior temporal cortex, and face recognition units are in the fusiform gyrus. This modularity accounts for the fact that, if a brain region is damaged, the model can predict the type of syndrome that will appear. The model also has a component dealing with changes in skin conductance when recognising a face: that is, the model accounts for the fact that our entire body responds to the presence of a familiar face. This component is often associated with emotions, and its presence makes the point, once more, that the components of cognition are highly connected.

Like other models, Schweinberger and Burton's assumes that the visual features of a face are stored in a different brain region from the semantic features (e.g. who is the person?). Thus, this model makes two important points. First, faces are visually complex objects, as the perceiver should be able to recognise the face despite changes in the exact position of the visual features (e.g. eyebrow position varies with mood). Second, faces mobilise neural networks in different brain centres.

Chapter summary

The main lesson of this chapter is that perception is far from being a passive process. To take the visual system as an example, visual representations prove to be different from photographs of reality. The perceptual system captures aspects of the physical reality and *actively* reconstructs a representation of the world. The representation arises as a result of two streams of information. The first stream, called 'bottom-up', is concerned with reorganising the information brought about by the receptors. Step by step, and following the laws of Gestalt, the visual system links together basic perceptual elements to form basic objects. The second stream, called 'top-down', selects relevant information based on past experiences. As counter-intuitive as it may seem, our perception is under the influence of what we know. Both streams constitute the essence of the dynamics that help us make sense of the world.

Visual illusions demonstrate that the mechanisms used to perceive are not infallible: we do not perceive reality as it is. The most striking case is when perception misinterprets the input data and provides a representation of an otherwise physically impossible object. The end product of perception is the percept: a chunk of information used to make sense of the world. Perceiving a chair or a fork leads to a percept, but so does perceiving a dog or a face. Percepts are representations of reality on which the perceptual system focuses, regardless of their size or features. They are the chunks with which we think. The remainder of this book will explain how we learn chunks and use them when memorising objects or when thinking.

Stop and Think Exobiology, exoperception?

In astronomy, exobiology refers to the possible biological features of animals from other planets. In the movie *Predator*, an extraterrestrial creature has an electronic device that enables it to capture a part of the spectrum of the electromagnetic radiations which is different to what humans use: it can see heat. What are the things that we can perceive but that it cannot perceive? Conversely, what are the things that it can detect but that would escape our perceptual world?

Further reading

Blake and Sekuler (2005) and Shiffman (2002) provide an in-depth discussion of all the aspects of perception we have introduced in this chapter. They add many interesting, but also more complex topics, such as colour perception. These advanced textbooks will be of interest to those who wish to carry out experiments in the field of perception. Tovée (2008) is a good introduction to the neuroscience of vision. It describes the main anatomical features relevant to the psychology of vision and explains how the neural signal is forwarded from the retina to higher regions of the brain, with an explanation of the steps involved. The book might seem technical at first sight but, once you overcome the biological technicalities, it really provides an insight into how the brain reconstructs an internal image of the external world. Arnheim (2004) is particularly interesting because it links basic research with real-world data. It explains the perception of visual art and uncovers part of its mysteries. A very good book, for learning and for fun!

Chapter **5**

Attention

CHAPTER PREVIEW

☑ Attention helps us focus on important aspects in the environment. Focusing on few elements is adaptive, but also leaves us vulnerable to missing some events in the environment. Magic tricks are a good illustration of how limited and selective our attention is.

☑ What happens to the unattended stimuli was one of the major questions at the beginning of attention research. Early selection models assume that unattended stimuli are filtered at the sensory level before being processed for meaning and thus do not influence behaviour. In contrast, late selection models suppose that all stimuli are processed for meaning.

☑ One rather strong assumption of late selection models is that the stimuli we are not aware of will also have an effect on our behaviour. This claim, which is at the basis of some commercials and self-help tapes, has been investigated using the subliminal priming paradigm.

☑ Attention can be seen as a capacity-limited process. If much effort is required, we will have to focus all our attentional capacity on the task at hand. If the task is easy, we will be able to give a share of our attention to other stimuli in the environment.

☑ Sometimes we can do two things at the same time. When a task has been practised for so long that we can do it without much effort, we speak of automaticity. Automaticity enables us to execute the task accurately, quickly and seemingly without much effort. Dangers can arise when we need to adapt to a new situation that requires a different response.

Introduction

Imagine this: you are enjoying a cup of coffee and an interesting conversation with your friend. During the conversation, the friend sitting opposite you reaches for the pack of cigarettes lying on the table and takes out a cigarette. While he is putting the cigarette in his mouth, he looks at the lighter and takes it from the table. He then proceeds to light up the cigarette. Suddenly, strange things start to happen. The cigarette is the wrong way round and will not light up, which baffles your friend. He turns the cigarette the right way round and tries again to light it up. As it turns out, the cigarette cannot be lit – the hand is empty, the lighter has vanished! You and your friend are puzzled looking at the hand that previously held the lighter. Then your friend looks at the other hand which was holding the cigarette to make sure that there is indeed a cigarette and that he is not dreaming. But the cigarette has disappeared as well! Your friend looks amused but you are really shocked – in a matter of seconds the cigarette and the lighter have disappeared from view!

Magicians have long exploited a particular characteristic of our cognitive system – **attention**. While it may seem that we are able to see, feel and hear the stimuli from the world in amazing detail, upon closer reflection we realise that we need to focus on particular details if we want to perceive them fully (see Box 5.1). Magicians use various techniques to (mis)direct our attention and suddenly pull 'a rabbit out of a hat' (see Box 5.2). We have seen in Chapter 2 that experimental research on attention only started in the 1950s; this seems to reflect the long-held belief that the notion of attention is intuitively clear to everybody. William James (1890) captured this idea in his famous quote 'Everybody knows what attention is' (p. 403). As some would cynically observe today, a better definition is yet to be found. William James, however, did go on to describe attention as '. . . the taking possession of the mind, in clear and vivid form, of one out of what seem several simultaneously possible objects or trains of thought. Focalisation, concentration, of consciousness are of its essence' (pp. 403–404). We can thus generally describe attention as the process enabling us to focus on a particular stimulus while at the same time disregarding other stimuli.

Box 5.1 RESEARCH CLOSE-UP: **Attention in perception**

If we look around us we will experience an amazing richness of detail. We just need to close our eyes and ask ourselves what the object on the right side was and what kind of colour it had, to realise the deceptiveness of our visual experience. Unless we deliberately direct our attention to a part of a scene, there is a good chance that we will not notice the details of the objects found there. This characteristic of our visual system is powerfully illustrated in the **change blindness** phenomenon. Imagine that you are required to spot a difference between two pictures. That sounds simple enough – we find similar tests in newspapers where two pictures are printed next to each other. However, imagine a more naturalistic setting: you are looking at a scene, blink and upon opening your eyes again you try to spot the change that occurred within the blink. A blink can be simulated by inserting a brief blank screen between two pictures that are alternatively presented for a short time. If we then try to spot the difference between the two pictures, we will realise that the task is not that easy despite our

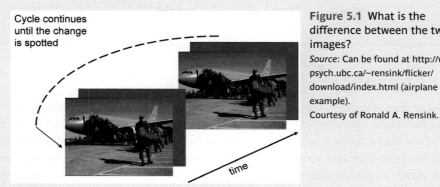

Figure 5.1 What is the difference between the two images?
Source: Can be found at http://www.psych.ubc.ca/~rensink/flicker/download/index.html (airplane example).
Courtesy of Ronald A. Rensink.

impression that we perceive many details. Rensink *et al.* (1997) demonstrated that one needs dozens of alternations between two pictures to spot changes as big as the disappearance of a whole jet engine. Change blindness demonstrates that the feeling of visual richness is false and that we need something else, namely attention, to be aware of things.

A similar phenomenon is **inattentional blindness** where, due to involvement of attentional resources in other tasks, we may miss obvious events. We have all had the experience of a friend passing us by on a street without greeting us, or may have unintentionally ignored a friend thanks to misdirection of our attentional resources. Similarly, if we are in a crowded film theatre looking for a place to sit, we may miss our friends waving at us. In an amusing experiment, Simons and Chabris (1999) demonstrated that these everyday occurrences are not exceptions. The participants watched a video of two basketball teams consisting of three players each, and wearing black and white shirts, respectively. Each team had its own ball that was passed among its own players. The participants' task was to count the number of passes made by the white team. Somewhere in the middle of the tape, which lasted about a minute, a gorilla walked from the right side of the screen, looked at the camera, thumped its chest, and finally walked away. Although the gorilla was present for nine seconds, only half of the participants noticed its presence! If you think that the result of this study is surprising, think about this: Memmert (2006) showed that the participants who did not notice the gorilla actually spent on average about a second looking at it! Counting passes engaged attentional resources in such a way that the walking and thumping gorilla could go unnoticed even if our eyes were momentarily fixed on it.

Figure 5.2 A frame from Simons and Chabris's experiment with the gorilla thumping its chest
Source: Simons and Chabris (1999).
Figure provided by Daniel Simons.

Stop and Think Change blindness
Change blindness and inattentional blindness deal with the characteristics of our visual system and the importance of attention for perception. Despite obvious similarities, the two phenomena are not the same. What are the differences, and how do they relate to attention?

Models of attention

In the 1950s attention became an increasingly popular topic for research. Psychologists were interested in how people choose which stimuli to attend to from the environment and which to ignore. One of the major questions addressed was the level at which information is processed when we decide to pay attention to a stimulus. Another related question was what happens to the stimuli to which we do not attend. One possibility is that we select a stimulus based on its physical properties such as tonality, loudness, brightness and intensity of colours. In this case we process the stimuli only at the level of their physical characteristics before we decide to which stimuli to devote our cognitive resources. Another possibility is that we not only process the physical characteristics but also the meaning of the stimuli. The processed meaning in turn directs our attention. According to these views, there is a selection, a kind of a filter, that lets through only certain stimuli. The disagreement is only about where the selection occurs. While the **early-selection models** of attention propose that the filter selects information at the very beginning of processing, **late-selection models** put the filter much later in processing.

Early-selection models

Imagine you are at a party bursting with people, as parties usually are. You have no problem concentrating on your conversation despite all other people talking at the same time. You also have little difficulty switching your focus from your conversation to another one if needed. This

Figure 5.3 Cocktail Party ... without Cherry
The cocktail party phenomenon.
Source: © pressmaster/fotolia.

particular phenomenon, termed '**cocktail party**', was the focus of investigation of a British engineer, Colin Cherry. Cherry (1953) devised a paradigm called **dichotic listening** where a different auditory message was presented to each ear at the same time. When the voices were the same – i.e. they had the same physical properties – people had difficulty separating the messages using meaning only. Cherry was also interested in how much would be retained from a message that was unattended. To make sure that his participants focused on the message dictated on a specified ear, and did not attend to the other message, Cherry required them to **shadow** the target message – i.e. they had to repeat aloud the words they had just heard. As it turned out, mostly the physical properties (e.g. tonality) of the unattended message were noticed. People did not notice if the voice in the unattended message switched from English to German, or from male to female, or if the message was in reverse speech.

Cherry's (1953) findings were incorporated into Donald Broadbent's **filter model** (1958), which was also the first detailed information-processing model, as we saw in Chapter 2. Broadbent's model sees the cognitive system as a series of channels for processing information. At the beginning, when we perceive information from the environment, various specialised channels (e.g. acoustic or visual channels) operate simultaneously, bringing information into a buffer store. The information in the buffer store is then passed through a filter that chooses the stimuli for further processing. This selection is made based on the physical properties of the stimuli. The chosen stimuli are further processed and become the focus of attention. The other stimuli are completely disregarded.

The filter model comprehensively explains Cherry's cocktail party effect, but appears to lack explanatory power for real-life situations. Regardless of how much we are focused on our conversation, from time to time we will process meaning from other unattended conversations. If our name or the name of our love interest, for example, is mentioned, our focus will shift automatically to the new conversation. This phenomenon of highly familiar stimuli getting beyond the processing of physical characteristics has been confirmed in other research using the dichotic listening task (Moray, 1959; Underwood, 1974).

Anne Treisman (1964) accounted for this finding by offering an alternative model of attention, the **attenuator model**. This model builds on Broadbent's filter model. It introduces a different mechanism for filtering stimuli at each input channel, the so-called 'attenuator'. Attenuators in turn allow processing of the stimuli to a different degree, unlike in the filter model where stimuli are processed in an all-or-nothing fashion. This allows for simultaneous processing of stimuli from different channels. Just like the filter model, the physical properties of the stimuli capture and hold attention. However, the attenuators are also influenced by previously analysed material. It is thus possible that some stimuli, in particular those highly familiar

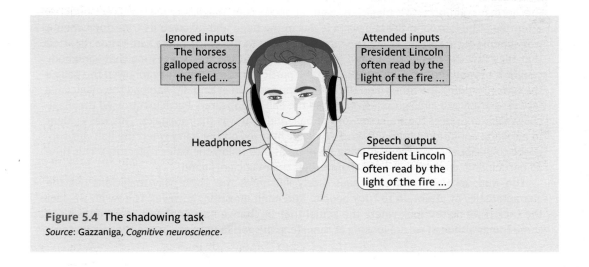

Figure 5.4 The shadowing task
Source: Gazzaniga, *Cognitive neuroscience*.

or semantically relevant in context, reach the semantic level of processing although they do not belong to the initially attended cluster of stimuli.

Both the filter model and the attenuator model specify that selection occurs early, at the level of our senses (sensory memory level). While the filter model assumes that the filter operates in an all-or-nothing fashion, the attenuator model allows graduation of filtering. This modification of filter theory explains why we hear our name mentioned in another conversation during parties, or why the context-relevant stimuli capture our attention although they come from an initially unattended cluster of stimuli. Both models, however, agree that all other unattended information is left to decay in sensory memory. Unattended information has no effect on behaviour: that is, behaviour is influenced only by the information we become aware of.

Box 5.2 EVERYDAY APPLICATION: **Attention in magic**

The scenario at the start of this chapter is what often happens to the friends of Gustav Kuhn, a cognitive psychologist and hobby magician. Kuhn himself performed the cigarette and lighter trick in front of participants while recording their eye movements (Kuhn and Tatler, 2005; Tatler and Kuhn, 2007). It turned out that none of the ten participants who were unaware of the trick spotted the cigarette drop. It did not help much if the participants were informed about the nature of the experiment as, in that case, only two out of ten participants spotted the cigarette drop. All participants fixated on the hand holding the lighter, the magician's face or his right shoulder. Yet, when the trick was performed again to the 18 participants who had initially failed to spot the cigarette drop, they all figured out how the trick was done. Surprisingly enough, only one-quarter of the participants looked at the hand that dropped the lighter, while the other three-quarters looked at the same areas (the hand holding the lighter, the right shoulder) as in the first trial when they could not spot the essence of the trick.

A similar pattern was observed in another experiment by Kuhn and Land (2006). In this case, it was a ball that disappeared. The magician was taped throwing the ball in the air a few times and suddenly the ball was not in the air! (The ball was held in the magician's hand.) In the normal condition, the magician used all social cues magicians use to direct people's attention – he looked at the ball when it was in the hand and followed its trajectory when it was supposedly in the air. When the tape was shown to the participants, two-thirds reported that they saw the ball move up and leave the screen at the top, suggesting that somebody caught it beyond the top screen. Although the participants said that they followed the ball all the time, including the time when the ball disappeared, they actually watched the magician's face very often and almost exclusively when the ball disappeared. Participants used the magician's face to predict the trajectory of the ball, and that was their mistake. This was evident in a second condition where the magician kept his eyes on the hand when the ball was supposed to disappear (instead of moving them up as if to follow the ball's trajectory). This time all participants realised that the ball never left the magician's hand.

The work by Kuhn and colleagues nicely illustrates the skilful way magicians use the characteristics of attention to trick people. The main question, however, is how do we spot the trick if we do not look where the actual trick or change happens? Just as we do not see some things although we are looking at them (e.g. the gorilla from the inattentional blindness

Figure 5.5 Frames from Kuhn's experiment with the eye fixation during the drop of the cigarette

The top-left picture presents a frame when the cigarette drop starts in the first performance. The white dots present the fixations of the uninformed participants who did not know that they were watching a magic trick. The top-right picture presents the fixations, at the moment of the cigarette drop, of the informed participants who were previously told about the trick. The bottom-left picture presents the second viewing of the uninformed participants, while the bottom-right picture shows the fixation of the informed participants in the second viewing. The white arrows indicate eye movements at the time of the drop.

Source: Kuhn and Tatler, 2005. The full video can be obtained at http://www.scienceofmagic.org.

Figure 5.6 Frames from Kuhn's ball vanishing trick with eye fixations

The first picture shows the fixations of participants watching the trick when the magician used social cues. In the second picture, the magician did not use the social cues (he is still looking in the hand instead of pretending to follow the ball). The dots present the fixations of the participants who did not spot the trick, while the x's stand for the fixations of the participants who did. There were no differences in the positions of the fixations of the participants who spotted the trick and those who did not in either condition.

Source: Adapted from Kuhn and Tatler, 2005. The full video can be obtained at http://www.scienceofmagic.org.

▶ experiment), we can perceive things although we are not looking at them directly. In the case of **overt attention**, we are focused on what we fixate on with our eyes without spending resources on other things (e.g. we focus on the instructor during a lecture). **Covert attention** describes the state in which we notice other things within our visual field although we do not directly fixate on them (e.g. noticing our friends fooling around while maintaining the focus on the instructor). Kuhn's studies indicate that covert attention is necessary for finding what lies behind magic tricks.

Stop and Think Covert attention

If covert attention is necessary for finding how magic tricks work, who should magicians be more afraid of – a random bystander who does not pay much attention and nonchalantly follows the trick, or a person who is very keen on finding how the trick works and follows the performance with full attention?

Late-selection models

The attenuator model explains problematic findings for the filter model, but it does this at the cost of loosening the filter concept. It is not clear which particular stimuli should be processed beyond physical properties. If it is necessary to take into account the relevance of the incoming stimuli with the previously processed information, is it not preferable to allow all incoming stimuli to be analysed for meaning before focusing on a particularly relevant cluster of stimuli? The idea that all stimuli are processed for meaning is the crux of the late-selection models of attention.

Unlike early-selection models, which specify that attention operates at the sensory level, late-selection models (Deutsch and Deutsch, 1963; Norman, 1968) assume that selection happens at the level of memory. All stimuli are processed for meaning and are assigned corresponding representations based on previously stored knowledge. Just as in the early-selection models, the problem is then how does attention select from stimuli that activate representations in memory. In addition to physical characteristics, meaning influences the selection of memory representations. For example, when we hear a story about a girl who is in bed and sleeping, we have certain expectations that bias the activation of memory representations. If we hear further that the girl woke up suddenly all in a sweat, we are likely to activate the representation of a nightmare.

Late-selection models of attention were at first based exclusively on theoretical speculations (Deutsch and Deutsch, 1963; Norman, 1968). Empirical investigations produced mixed results (MacKay, 1973; Treisman and Geffen, 1967; Treisman and Riley, 1969). Devising a rational and adequate test of early- and late-selection models was a challenging task for researchers. The logical choice of the paradigm of dichotic listening with shadowing turned out to be unsuitable. Shadowing one message in the dichotic listening task ensures that attention is devoted to just a single stimulus and does not fluctuate between different stimuli. On the other hand, late-selection models require that all stimuli be recognised in order for a suitable action to be chosen. The action in the shadowing task has already been chosen (shadowing itself!), which leaves little space for organising another response for a different stimulus. What would then count as evidence for late models of attention? These models predict that unattended stimuli should have an effect on behaviour despite the fact that people are not aware of the unattended stimuli. This bold prediction has been tested using the **subliminal priming paradigm**.

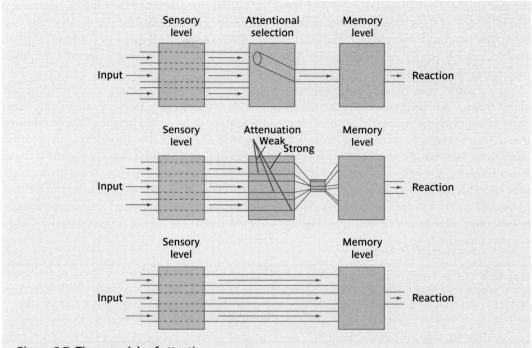

Figure 5.7 Three models of attention
From top to bottom: Broadbent's filter model, Treisman's attenuation model and late-selection model.

Subliminal priming

The film theatres have the annoying habit of bombarding us with numerous commercials that last up to half an hour before allowing us to see the actual film. If we are lucky, popcorn, fizzy drinks, ice creams and other products will interrupt only the commercial session and not the film itself. Would it not be great, from the perspective of the theatres, if they could somehow unconsciously influence people to buy those products? That is exactly what James Vicary, an advertising expert, claimed to do in the late 1950s (Pratkanis, 1992). He flashed short messages such as 'Eat Popcorn' or 'Drink Coke' lasting for a third of a millisecond every five seconds during the same film. Obviously, the audience could not notice the messages, but nevertheless the messages apparently influenced behaviour. According to Vicary, after six weeks of subliminal messaging the sales of Coke increased by 18 per cent and the sales of popcorn by almost 58 per cent. The messages never reached awareness but nevertheless influenced behaviour. This claim stimulated debate about **subliminal persuasion**.

Vicary's claims produced a public uproar and very soon the UK, Australia and most states in the USA banned this kind of advertising. Although Vicary later admitted to having exaggerated the influence of subliminal advertising to help his crumbling marketing company (Pratkanis, 1992), the myth of subliminal persuasion has persisted until today. Probably the most extreme claim for subliminal persuasion, and an example which shows that subliminal persuasion is not restricted to visual stimuli, was made by the parents of two teenagers who committed suicide in the mid-1980s. They alleged that the rock band Judas Priest incorporated the subliminal message 'Do it' in one of their songs, and this message was directly responsible for the death of the two boys. The band was eventually acquitted, but the issue of subliminal messages remains topical, as evidenced by more recent accusations against Walt Disney of having inserted subliminal message in the films *Aladdin* and *The Lion King* (Moore, 1996).

At the same time, there is no empirical evidence that subliminal messages can influence let alone control our behaviour (McConnell *et al.*, 1958; Moore, 1982, 1988). Probably the most compelling evidence against this possibility was the study done at the height of the subliminal persuasion hysteria produced by James Vicary. In 1958 the Canadian Broadcast Corporation flashed the message 'Phone Now' more than 300 times during a popular Sunday night TV show. Not a single person called. When they subsequently asked the viewers to guess what the message was, more than half of viewers who sent their guesses claimed to have experienced the feelings of hunger and thirst during the show. Not a single person correctly guessed the actual subliminal message. It is probable that their feelings were related to the media coverage of the Vicary claims at the time.

Stop and Think Subliminal messages

Many people will swear that tapes containing subliminal messages have helped them to improve certain aspects of their lives (e.g. memory, self-esteem, confidence). Research has confirmed that there is often an improvement after listening to subliminal tapes, but that the effect is usually attributable to something else. What could be the real cause of the improvement?

It is hard to believe that stimuli which are presented for a very short period of time and which circumvent our awareness could motivate our behaviour. Even if they have a motivational effect, it would not be surprising if they were completely overridden by conscious stimuli, which are stronger (because they are conscious!) and more frequent. Nevertheless, subliminal stimuli might influence our cognitive processes in the short term, which would support the late-selection models of attention. If the preceding stimulus makes the processing of the next stimulus easier, we talk about **priming**. In the case where we are not aware of the stimuli that prepared us for the upcoming stimulus, we speak of **subliminal priming**.

Dehaene *et al.* (1998) gave participants the task of deciding as quickly as possible if the presented digit was smaller or larger than 5. Before the presentation of the target digit written in Arabic numbers, another digit written in letters was briefly shown and followed by a random letter-string mask so that the participants could not see it. When the subliminal digit was congruent with the target digit (i.e. they both were larger or smaller than 5), participants were faster than when the subliminal and target digits were incongruent (e.g. target was larger and subliminal was smaller).

Stop and Think Difference in reaction time between subliminally congruent and incongruent stimuli

The typical difference in reaction time between subliminally congruent and incongruent stimuli is between 5 and 10 milliseconds. Although it may look rather small, the effect is very robust and has been found over and over again. What would be its importance in everyday life?

This is one of many convincing studies showing the existence of subliminal perception (e.g. Bar and Biederman, 1998; Debner and Jacoby, 1994; Merikle and Smith, 2005). Despite the fact

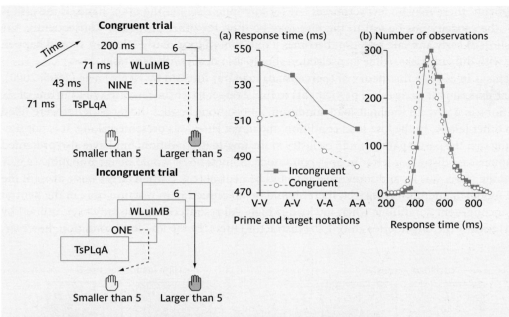

Figure 5.8 Illustration of Dehaene *et al.*'s (1998) procedure and results
In all trials, a written number, the so-called 'subliminal prime', was presented for a short time between two random-letter-string masks. The target number was then presented and the participants had to indicate whether the presented target number was larger or smaller than 5. In the congruent trials, the subliminal prime number and the target number were both larger (or both smaller) than 5. In the incongruent trials, the participants could not use the subliminal prime to predict the category of the target number because they were different (e.g. subliminal prime was smaller and the target larger than 5).
Source: Dehaene *et al.*, 1998.

that the stimuli never reach the level of awareness, they had been processed for meaning, as evidenced by their influence on subsequent behaviour. Both early- and late-selection models agree that there should be no long-term subliminal effect. The effect of unattended stimuli is too weak and short-lived to make a lasting impression. The existence of subliminal perception, however, favours late-selection models of attention. One could argue that it is because of the choice of the paradigm. If the dichotic listening with shadowing was inappropriate for testing late-selection models, so too the subliminal priming paradigm may be unfavourable to early-selection models. This is because it does not allow stringent control of the stimuli the participant attends at the sensory level.

(Perceptual) load model of attention

We all know that some things are more difficult than others. Finding a DVD among other DVDs on a shelf, for example, is more difficult than finding it among videotapes. Instead of seeing attention as a filter located somewhere within the cognitive system, it is possible to see it as a system with limited resources. These resources are required by the demands of the task at hand. The question thus becomes how much of the resources the task will demand. If the task is difficult, there may be few resources left for anything else. On the other hand, if the task is easy, the capacity not bound to the task may be used for other purposes. Consequently, the question of early and late selection becomes a question of load. Early selection should happen only with difficult tasks, while late selection should also occur with easy tasks.

This is in essence the **theory of (perceptual) load** put forward by Neely Lavie (1995; 2000). In one experiment Lavie asked participants to find a target letter (lower-case x or z) in one of six positions in a row. In the high-load condition, all positions besides the target letter were filled with other letters. In the low-load condition, the target letter was presented alone. It is not surprising that the participants should be faster in the low-load condition, but Lavie also presented an upper-case distractor letter in both conditions. Sometimes it would be incompatible (e.g. X when the target was z), and sometimes it would be neutral (e.g. F when target was z or x). If the load model of attention is correct, there should be no reduction in reaction time in the neutral and incongruent conditions when the load is high. All resources have already been utilised by searching for the target letter among the distractor letters. In the low-load condition, however,

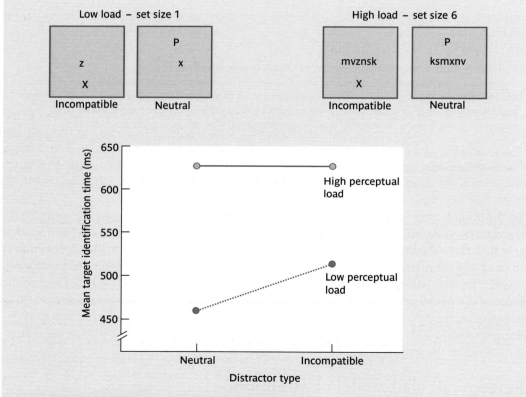

Figure 5.9 Graph plotting Lavie's design and results

When the load was high it did not matter if the distractor letter was neutral or incompatible because participants could not devote attentional resources to it. In the low-load condition, however, incompatible distractor letters slowed down participants.

Source: Laine *et al.*, 2005.

the incongruent condition should capture the remaining resources and slow down the search in comparison with the neutral condition. If you remember the research on change blindness and inattentional blindness, you can correctly predict that only the people in the low-load conditions were affected by the incompatible distractors. Just as we miss our friends at the theatre when looking for free places, we also miss distractors when dealing with a high-load task.

Stop and Think Parking a car

Parking a car is a skill that depends on practice – highly skilled drivers have no problems with it, while it is one of the most difficult things for beginners. Who would be more affected by the comments and questions from a passenger? A beginner or an experienced driver? Give your reasons using the load-theory arguments.

The (perceptual) load theory has been tested mainly with visual stimuli, although it should also explain the early-late selection problems with the auditory selection. While it is not clear what exactly is load or how it should be defined, the load model of attention provides a more flexible framework than the previous early- and late-selection models. It does not focus on the bottleneck in the process of attention but rather on understanding why it occurs. Attention is not a rigid system influenced only by physical stimuli, but it also depends on various factors such as familiarity, practice, age and motivation.

Automaticity

We are all proficient at some things. For example, most of us can drive a car. If we are experienced drivers, we can even have meaningful conversations while driving. This was certainly not the case when we had just started driving and when almost everything unrelated to driving, including conversations, was a big distraction. Over time, we have practised driving so much that most of the actions involved in it do not require extensive effort or attention. When an action does not require attention, we say that it has been **automated**.

Stop and Think Using mobile phones while driving

In the UK and many other countries it is forbidden to use mobile phones, even hands-free, while driving. What do you think are the reasons for such a decision? How would you devise an experiment using the dichotic listening paradigm to check whether the use of mobile phones during driving is dangerous?

Probably the most compelling demonstration of an automated action was shown by Stroop (1935), who developed a task consisting of naming the colour in which a word is written. We can do it without problems if the word is neutral (the word 'RABBIT' printed in red). Similarly, we are very quick to name the colour of a word if the word is congruent with the colour: that is, denotes the colour you need to name (say the word 'RED' written in red). However, try to name the colour if the word is not congruent with the colour: that is, it refers to a different colour (e.g. the word 'GREEN' written in red). Very quickly you will realise it is not so easy! This effect, when the incongruent meaning of the word slows down the naming of the colour of the word, was termed the **Stroop effect** in honour of the researcher who demonstrated it for the first time (for a description of Stroop's classical experiment, see Box 5.3).

Box 5.3 CLASSIC EXPERIMENT: **The Stroop effect**

John Ridley Stroop (1935) showed how incompatible words influence the naming of colours. The manipulated/independent variable was the presence/absence of a written word when a colour was presented. In the experimental condition, there were 100 words printed in ten rows and ten columns on a single card (making it a 10 × 10 stimulus card). Five words were used ('red', 'blue', 'green', 'brown' and 'purple') and they were printed in five colours (red, blue, green, brown and purple). The words, however, did not correspond to the colour in which they were printed. Thus, the word 'red' was never printed in the colour red, 'blue' in blue and so on. Each word appeared twice in each row and column of the stimulus card. The words appeared equally often in each of the four colours (excluding the colours that corresponded to the word). The second stimulus card had the same stimuli, except that they were presented in the reverse order. In the control condition, the two cards had the same ink colours as in the experimental conditions. However, the printed words from the experimental condition were replaced by solid squares. The task of the 100 participants was to name the colour of the stimuli one by one while correcting the errors made. They were first given ten items for practice, after which they proceeded to read the control and experimental cards (the order was counterbalanced). The dependent variable was the time it took the participants to read the experimental and control cards.

If the words are processed automatically, they should have an interference effect on naming the colours, given that the words and colours do not match. Thus, naming the colours from the solid squares should be faster than naming the colours from the incongruent words. It turned out that there was a huge difference between the two conditions. The participants took slightly more than a minute (63 seconds) to name the 200 colour names from the solid squares in the control condition. It took them almost twice as long (110 seconds) to name the colour names from the incongruent words. The Stroop effect proved to be reliable and robust, and has since been used to investigate attention and automaticity. In current research, one often replaces the solid squares in the control condition with the word that corresponds to the colour. While the design may be more elegant because one uses the words (congruent and incongruent) as the background in both conditions, the effect remains the same – it is still much harder to name the colours from the incongruent words.

While there are several explanations for the Stroop effect, they all agree that the reason for the difficulties is that the meaning of the word automatically comes to our mind. We are so familiar with reading words, including colour names, that we recognise them instantly and cannot do much about it. This explanation gains credibility in the light of numerous studies which show that children who are poor readers experience less slowing-down in the Stroop task than children who are good readers (Fournier *et al.*, 1975; Samuels, 1999; Schiller, 1966). Similarly, the Stroop effect is less pronounced when the language in which the words are written is unfamiliar (Dyer, 1971; Mägiste, 1984, 1985).

Schneider and Shiffrin's model of automaticity

Schneider and Shiffrin (1977; Shiffrin and Schneider, 1977) demonstrated important aspects of automatisation. They used a **visual search paradigm** where participants had to remember up to four letters or digits (the memory set). They were then presented with a new set of up to four letters or digits (the display set). Their task was to indicate whether any of the symbols in the display set corresponds to any of the symbols in the memory set. The participants practised the task for a long time in one of two conditions. In the *consistent mapping condition*, only numbers were used in the memory set, and only consonants were used in the display set as distractors (and vice versa). In the *varied mapping condition*, both consonants and numbers could be in the memory set and serve as distractors in the display set. For example, if the memory set consists of four numbers, spotting a single number among the four symbols in the display set would automatically mean that it is present in the memory set. In contrast, if the memory set and display set both contain numbers and letters, one would need to serially match one by one each digit/letter in the display set with the memory set. This means that in the consistent mapping condition there should be no increase in the reaction time, regardless of the size of the memory and display sets. On the other hand, in the varied mapping condition where a serial matching is necessary, there should be a clear increase in the time needed to react depending on the number of digits/letters in the memory and display set. This turned out to be the correct prediction.

Schneider and Shiffrin (1977) explained these results using the notions of two kinds of processing: **controlled processing** and **automatic processing**. While controlled processing is effortful, and usually slow and error prone, automatic processing is effortless, fast, outside awareness and uncontrollable. In the consistent mapping condition, it was possible to develop automatic processing, which was not affected by the set size. Varied mapping, however, prevented development of automaticity and the set size played a role.

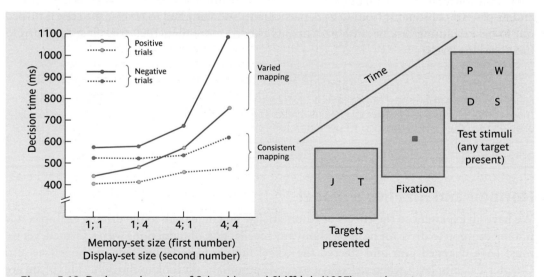

Figure 5.10 Design and results of Schneider and Shiffrin's (1997) experiment
Despite the increasing number of elements in the display and memory sets, the reaction time did not significantly increase in the consistent mapping condition. In the varied mapping condition, on the other hand, the reaction times increased with the increase in the memory and display sets.
Source: Adapted from Shiffrin and Schneider, 1977.

Schneider and Shiffrin's model assumes that automaticity is the product of increased efficiency of processes. An alternative would be to assume that there is a strategy shift in the performance rather than increased efficiency of processes. The **instance theory of automaticity** (Logan, 1988) supposes that automaticity is a transition from a general algorithm used to solve problems to memory retrieval of past solutions. At first, individuals rely on crude, slow and effortful strategies of obtaining the solution to the problem at hand. With each encounter of a stimulus, however, individuals store relevant traces – that is, instances of the stimulus that can later be retrieved when the same stimulus is encountered. Imagine a simple arithmetic problem of multiplying 6×7. At the beginning we would need to sum six seven times to get 42, a laborious process. Later, with experience, we would simply need to retrieve the solution as we had already encountered it numerous times. According to Logan, the performance on a task is determined by two kinds of races. The first race is between specific instances in memory and a general algorithm, while the second is the race between the instances themselves, the number of which grows with each encounter with the stimuli. Instance Theory traces automatisation processes back to memory retrieval: that is, when instances start winning the race against general algorithms. The idea that memory traces help reduce attention load is also present in Simon and Chase's (1973) chunking theory (see Chapter 12).

Whatever the mechanism assumed – process efficiency or strategy shift – it seems that practice is the main ingredient of automaticity. It also appears that automatic processing is difficult to control because it is outside of awareness. Although this is mostly advantageous, what happens in situations that require a different response from the automated one? Shiffrin and Schneider (1977) clearly showed the extent to which automaticity affects flexibility. After participants had over 2000 trials with consistent mapping where the memory sets were consonants from B to L and display set consonants from Q to Z, participants suddenly had to reverse the sets. It turned out to be a daunting task because participants needed more than 1000 trials just to return to their baseline levels!

Stop and Think Schneider and Shiffrin

Schneider and Shiffrin used a simple task to illustrate the dangers of automaticity. What would happen if more complex tasks such as driving, crossing streets and using a word editor were used? If we suddenly drive on the other side of the road, or use a new text editor where the functions are inverted in comparison with the previous (e.g. *insert* is now *delete*), would experienced drivers and users of a text editor have more problems than new ones? Give reasons for your answer.

Norman and Shallice's model

We have all experienced the effects of automaticity. To come back to the driving example, it is not uncommon to drive for hours without any recollection of the actions we performed, yet we must have changed gear and steered the wheel hundreds and hundreds of times (see also Chapter 11). Similarly, when we cross a street we automatically look to the right side (if you are from the UK), pass half the street and then look again to the left before crossing the remaining part of the street. We have done it numerous times and we really do not think about it any more. We simply execute the action if the setting in the environment requires it. Some parts of driving and street crossing must surely be highly automated and beyond conscious control. However, we are very good at adapting to new situations that require different responses.

Figure 5.11 Crossing a street in London
Source: © c/fotolia

When people from the UK go to the continent, they hardly have any problems in getting used to crossing streets. Only a few unlucky ones do not manage to suppress the common reaction (looking right first) and most have no problems with looking in the right direction (the left side). Although these actions are highly automated and executed immediately when people cross streets at home, they can be suppressed and replaced with the appropriate actions if necessary.

Norman and Shallice (1986) proposed a model that deals with our ability to inhibit automated behaviour. Our actions are (a) fully automated, (b) partially automated or (c) under conscious deliberate control. While there is nothing spectacular in this categorisation, Norman and Shallice's model offers a detailed account of conflict resolution among different kinds of action. Automatic actions are triggered by environmental clues and controlled by **schemas**. Schemas are sets of organised plans acquired through experience with many subcomponents that regulate our routine behaviour (schemas are also prominently featured in Chapter 12). For example, upon getting to a street, we will automatically retrieve a set of actions from our (long-term) memory: look at the right side, cross, look at the left side, cross. If two routines clash – for example, a British person crossing the road in Berlin – there is a contention scheduling operation, which assesses the relative importance of different routines in the context and adjusts them accordingly. The central idea of the model, however, is the notion of a

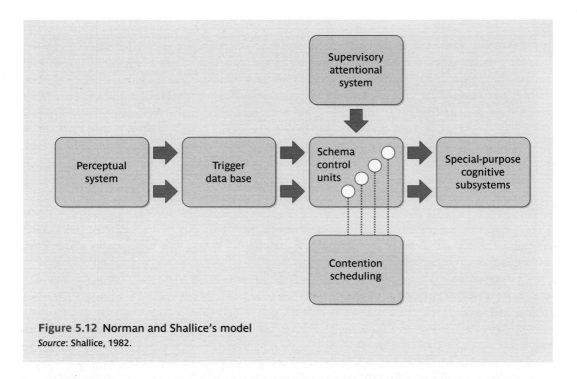

Figure 5.12 Norman and Shallice's model
Source: Shallice, 1982.

supervisory activating system (SAS). Although a good part of our behaviour is more or less automated, sometimes it is necessary to adjust our actions. This is particularly true when we encounter new situations where routine actions may not be appropriate. In such situations, SAS, which can be seen as an attentionally limited controller, becomes active and tries to resolve the conflict.

Unlike the previous theories of automaticity, Norman and Shallice's model is firmly grounded in neuropsychological evidence. Routine behaviour is difficult to inhibit, as we all know, but it is almost impossible if the brain structures in which SAS resides are damaged. Patients with frontal lobe damage have great difficulty changing direction, leaving old routines and choosing new ones, which implies that brain structures in the frontal lobe may play the role of the SAS (Shallice, 1982).

Chapter summary

In a complex and ever-changing environment, it is a small wonder that we are not drowning in the astonishing number of things that are constantly happening around us. Attention is the process that enables us to find a way through the mass of stimuli that bombard us every day. In order to become aware of a stimulus, we must give it our attention. Selectivity and exclusivity are the major characteristics of attention. Consequently, we are not always able to spot changes in the environment, especially when our attention has been engaged with something else. Magic in everyday life, and change blindness and inattentional blindness in laboratory settings, clearly illustrate the characteristics and pitfalls of attention.

Attention was often seen as a filter for sorting out which stimuli we become aware of. The main question at the beginning of this strand of research was the exact placement of the filter. The early-selection models, such as Broadbent's filter model and Treisman's attenuator model, presupposed that the selection happens early in the process, just after the sensory level. Dichotic listening was the preferred paradigm for investigation. The late-selection models, on the other hand, made a claim that stimulus selection happens much later, when all stimuli are analysed at the memory level. It proved challenging to devise a fair test of the two theoretical standpoints. The dichotic listening paradigm prevented all stimuli from being recognised, an assumption necessary if late selection is to occur. The paradigm of subliminal priming in its weaker version provided some evidence for the late-selection models. One could argue that subliminal priming is not suitable for testing the claims of the early-selection models, because it does not offer a way of controlling which stimuli are attended at the sensory level. One way around this blind alley is to see attention as a resource, a capacity or mental power required for the task at hand. Lavie's model of (perceptual) load gives a possible explanation of why it is possible to sometimes have early selection, and late selection at the other times.

We know through experience that it is difficult to focus on two things at the same time, but that it is sometimes possible. Well-practised tasks become automated and do not engage our attentional resources fully. Consequently, sometimes we are able to do two or more things simultaneously. Shiffrin and Schneider (1977) provided evidence that automatic processing is fast, accurate and effortless. Once triggered by familiar stimuli, it is impossible to stop it, because we do not exert control over it. While it is difficult to suppress well-practised responses in some cases, such as the Stroop effect, automaticity in real life is usually not all or nothing as postulated in Shiffrin and Schneider's model. Norman and Shallice's model (1986) is more realistic with its assumptions of a supervisory system, which is responsible for adjusting our well-learned behaviours when necessary. This way we are still able to enjoy the benefits of automaticity without necessarily becoming inflexible in our behaviour.

Further reading

A good introduction to attention in particular and psychology in general is William James's book *The principles of psychology* (1890), from which the famous quote at the beginning of this chapter is taken. The book is available at the excellent Web collection of classical contributions in psychology: http://psychclassics.yorku.ca/. Donald Broadbent's classic, *Perception and communication* (1958), is still remarkably fresh and a good example of the ideas developed in the cognitive revolution. Styles (2006) and Pashler (1998) have both written readable and approachable books focused on attention exclusively.

For more information on change blindness and inattentional blindness, we recommend the original articles by Rensink *et al.* (1997), and Simons and Chabris (1999). A good review of the research is provided by Simons and Rensink (2005), while Rensink (2000) draws similarities and differences between the two phenomena. The change-detection database website (http://viscog.beckman.uiuc.edu/change) has all the video clips described in the text and much more. Video clips of Gustav Kuhn's magic can be found on his website together with the accompanying papers (http://www.scienceofmagic.org/).

A highly readable overview of the research on subliminal persuasion is provided by Pratkanis (1992) available from http://www.csicop.org/si/show/cargo-cult_science_of_subliminal_persuasion. Moore (1996) deals with the Judas Priest trial (http://www.csicop.org/si/9611/judas_priest.html), while Finkbeiner and Forster (2008) provide a recent cross-section of the research on subliminal perception.

Stroop's original paper is also available from the Classics in the History of Psychology website. MacLeod (1991) provides a comprehensive historical and theoretical review of the Stroop effect, while MacLeod and MacDonald (2000) review more recent developments, focusing on fMRI studies. The classic Shiffrin and Schneider paper can be found, together with the complete experiment, at http://step.psy.cmu.edy/scripts/Attention/Schneider1977.html.

Chapter **6**

Short-term memory

CHAPTER PREVIEW

- ☑ Chunks are the atoms of the cognitive system upon which memory operates.

- ☑ The capacity of short-term memory is limited to about seven chunks.

- ☑ Sensory registers are modality-specific memory stores that hold perceptual information for a very brief period of time, beyond conscious control. Part of the information is dismissed as a result of attentional selection and a limited amount is forwarded to short-term memory.

- ☑ Information in short-term memory is normally coded in a verbal format. Memory span for verbal material relates to the time it takes to articulate words. We can also hold and process information in short-term memory using a visuospatial format.

- ☑ The quality of memories depends on how deeply the material to memorise has been processed. Thus, elaborative rehearsal leads to better recall than maintenance rehearsal.

- ☑ Baddeley's theory consists of four components – the central executive, the phonological loop, the visuospatial sketchpad and the episodic buffer. The approximate span of the phonological loop is two seconds, which is the time necessary for the articulatory rehearsal process to go through all the items held in the phonological short-term store.

- ☑ According to Cowan, working memory is a system spanning three activity-defined levels: activated chunks in the focus of attention, chunks activated but not in the focus of attention and inactive elements. In this transversal view, working memory is a unitary process and there is no clear difference between verbal and visuospatial processing.

Introduction

Consider the following scene from Bram Stoker's book *Dracula*, which takes place when Count Dracula meets Jonathan Harker, the hero of the book. The author introduces Dracula to both Harker and the reader. The door opens and...

> Within, stood a tall old man, clean-shaven save for a long white moustache, and clad in black from head to foot, without a single speck of colour about him anywhere. He held in his hand an antique silver lamp, in which the flame burned without chimney or globe of any kind, throwing long, quivering shadows as it flickered in the draught of the open door. (Stoker, 2000, p. 15)

While reading these lines, you build an image of how Dracula appears to Jonathan Harker at their first meeting. Gradually, as the author describes the central character of the story, each sentence adds some details to your inner eye. You are able to visualise him thanks to your ability to work on an internal representation of the character. Should you wish to, you could dress Dracula in blue, red or even pink, even though the new dress would not add anything dark to the threatening character of the Count. This ability to hold and transform internal representations is the essence of memory and the focus of this chapter.

Memory has been at the centre of interest since antiquity. For example, the Greek philosopher Plato played with the idea that memory was like a tablet of wax on which sense impressions could be imprinted. Similarly, for many centuries, memory was conceived as a mere storage system. However, the experimental data collected in the last century, together with neuroimaging data and results from neurobiology, have shown that memory refers to a wide range of processes, serving four important functions: encoding, storage, retrieval and processing of information. To understand memory, one has to have a clear view of what functions it serves. The type of memory presented in this chapter – short-term memory – is the one used when, for example, we need to remember a telephone number for a few seconds before dialling it. This is the type of memory William James (1890) had in mind when talking about primary memory (see Chapter 2). Just to confuse things, authors use different terms to refer to this type of memory. You may read about primary, short-term, immediate or working memory, but remember: you are actually learning about the same concept!

In the following section we distinguish short-term memory from other forms of memory. Then, we spell out the chunking hypothesis, a central hypothesis for this book. To make a long story short, it is the idea that the cognitive system has a way of compressing any reasonable amount of information into a single memory unit. We then see how chunks are handled within the memory architecture proposed by Atkinson and Shiffrin. This will also be the opportunity to learn how memory and perception are related and to make the point that that we should talk about *memory systems* rather than just memory. We then examine how we build memory traces and how these traces fade away with time or interferences. Finally, we present two current theoretical frameworks that account for short-term memory phenomena. By the end of this chapter you will understand why Dracula looks so vivid to you!

Memory types

Have you ever heard one of your friends complaining about their memory? Such a complaint shows that we usually conceive memory as a single function. However, research has demonstrated that this is not the case. Supporting James' insight, research in the late 1950s and the 1960s has clearly shown that there are at least two different memory **systems**: short-term and long-term memory. Support for this division comes both from experimental psychology, neuropsychology and neuroscience. Murdock (1962) ran a **free recall** task (see Box 6.1) in which participants had to remember lists of 10, 15, 20, 30 and 40 words. He also manipulated the presentation rate: items within a list were presented either every second or every two seconds. Participants recalled the list of words immediately after having heard it. When recall performance is plotted as a function of the item position in the list, a clear U-curve is apparent (see Figure 6.1): that is, participants tend to recall the first and particularly the last items better than the items in the middle.

Box 6.1 RESEARCH CLOSE-UP: **The free recall paradigm**

Although free recall is one of the oldest methods for studying memory, it is still one of the most popular. The typical experiment has three phases. In the first phase, participants are presented with the material to remember. Two variables may influence the encoding of information. First, there is the nature of the material (e.g. words, digits or images). Second, there is the rate of presentation. Whether an item is presented for 1 or 2 seconds affects further processing. The second phase is the retention interval, which is the time between the presentation of the items and their recall. The central decision here is whether or not the participants are allowed to rehearse information during this interval. If they are not, they are kept busy by completing another task such as counting backwards by threes from a randomly chosen three-digit number. The load imposed by this second task makes it very hard for participants to rehearse. The last phase is recall, where the experimenter records response time and accuracy. (Response time or latency is the period of time between the end of the retention interval and the beginning of the participant's responses.)

The following example illustrates the three phases of a free recall experiment (see Figure 6.1). You are presented with a list of monosyllabic words (please spend 5 seconds on each word): 'BALL, LIFT, GRANT, WAR, BOLD'. Then, for 30 seconds you have to count backwards from 582. Finally, you have to recall the list. How long was the latency before recalling the first word?

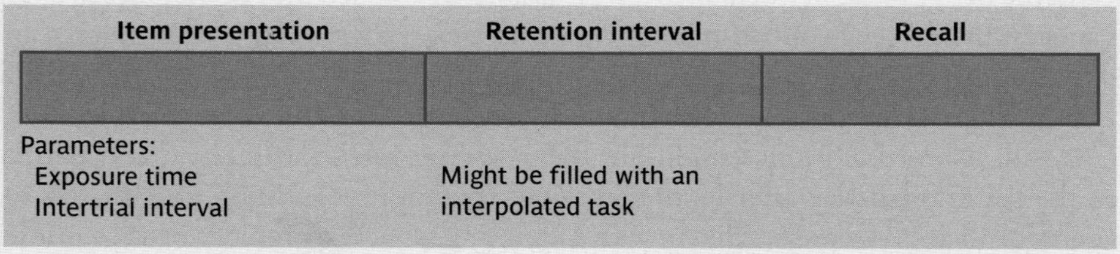

Item presentation	Retention interval	Recall

Parameters:
Exposure time
Intertrial interval

Might be filled with an
interpolated task

Figure 6.1 The three phases of a recall task

> Note that, with free recall, the order in which stimuli are recalled does not matter (in our example, recalling 'WAR, GRANT, LIFT, BOLD, BALL' is just fine. In another related paradigm, called *serial recall*, items have to be recalled in the order they were presented.

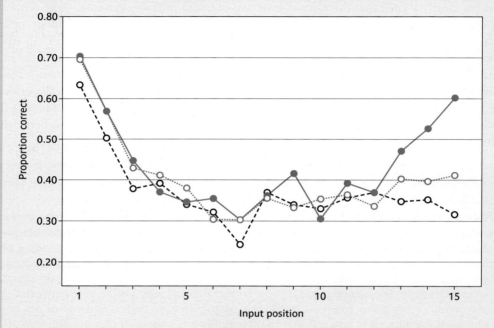

Figure 6.2 Recall performance as a function of serial position and delay interval (0, 10 and 30 seconds)

Source: After Glanzer and Cunitz, 1966.

This curve is called the **serial position curve**, as it relates the position of the words in the list to the amount of recall. The better recall performance for the first items is called the **primacy effect**, and the better recall performance for the last items is called the **recency effect**. These two effects suggest the presence of two memory systems: one related to long-term storage and one related to short-term storage, respectively. Postman and Phillips (1965) were among the first to collect empirical data supporting this hypothesis. They used the free recall paradigm with lists of 10, 20 and 30 words. In one condition, there was no retention interval and participants recalled the list immediately after its presentation. In another condition, the list was recalled after a delay of 15 or 30 seconds, filled in with a counting task. The presence of a retention interval led to the elimination of the recency effect. Hence, keeping the mind busy for a while erases the memory of the last items on the list, which were presumably stored in short-term memory, but has no effect on the first items, which were presumably stored in long-term memory.

Waugh and Norman (1965) conducted an experiment that led to one of the first theoretical attempts to systematise the data on memory. Participants were first shown a list of digits, and were then given a probe, which was one of the digits in the list. Their task was to retrieve the digit that immediately followed the probe in the list. For example, if the list is (9 0 8 5 3) and the probe is 8, then you should answer 5. Compared with the experiments we have described in the previous paragraphs, the difference is that Waugh and Norman asked their participants to focus on the digit currently presented so that they did not pay attention to the entire list. This technique essentially suppresses rehearsal. The results revealed a weak memory for the recall of the items presented last. Thus, suppressing rehearsal eliminates the recency effect. Waugh and Norman put forward a simple but elegant explanation to account for their finding: to avoid forgetting, information is put into short-term memory, where it is constantly rehearsed. If information is rehearsed long enough, it is put in long-term memory. As an example, read the following sentence once: 'The neuron is the fundamental structural and functional element of the brain' (Kandel, 2001, p. 65). If you do not rehearse this sentence, you are likely to forget its exact phrasing, but if you rehearse it long enough, you are likely to remember it exactly as it is.

If we assume that short-term and long-term memory systems are different, we could expect that one form of memory may be damaged while the other remains intact. Such evidence has been collected by Scoville and Milner (1957). HM, a patient suffering from epilepsy, had undergone surgery to relieve his symptoms. The ablation of parts of his right and left medial temporal lobe (including about two-thirds of the hippocampus and amygdala) had a dramatic effect: HM was unable to store new memories in long-term memory. HM would meet a new person one day and forget their existence the next day. In spite of this striking change, HM could perform tasks requiring short-term memory such as recalling a few items for a few seconds or holding a conversation. Supposedly, HM had an intact short-term memory but a damaged long-term memory. The psychological distinction between short and long-term memory has also found support in neurobiology, where it has been demonstrated that the mechanisms in charge of long-term memory differ from those underlying short-term memory (Kandel, 2001). Because memory is made of two components, each serving different functions, we will consider each component separately. We deal with short-term memory in this chapter and with long-term memory in the next.

The atoms of cognition: the chunking hypothesis

As discussed in Chapter 2, the first half of the twentieth century saw the growth of experimental psychology and the associated development of measures for estimating human performance in various memory tasks. An important research question concerned the nature of the basic units of memory – the atoms upon which memory is operating. With computers, it is easy to identify these building blocks: they are 0s and 1s, a simple binary coding scheme (it is either one or the other). With human cognition, things are more complicated. Consider reading. One might propose that the building blocks are the letters of the alphabet, but you might correctly object that, when you read, you do not perceive letters but rather entire words.

The top-left panel of Figure 6.3 displays a sequence of 28 letters. Read this sequence once and try to recall as many letters as possible. In the top-right panel, the same 28 letters are rearranged as groups of seven items. Again, read these letters once and try to recall them as best as you can.

OEUOPCKLDFLALOIKPAFREMSSAOBK	PACKLOADFILLKEEPFOURMASSBOOK
LISTCLADSINKLIKE	HYPNOTICCANNIBALROMANTICSHEPHERD
OEAOIEOEUOEOTBRNTTBTHTISTHQSTN	TOBEORNOTTOBETHATISTHEQUESTION

Figure 6.3 The difference between recalling letters and chunks

It is likely that using groups of letters made it easier to remember the whole sequence. Note that you can probably remember the letters in the correct order. Repeat the same memory task with the two lists of letters in the middle row. Both strings of letters are made of four words. However, the words on the right are twice as long as those on the left. Although this is more difficult with longer words, you should be able to remember both letter strings. In the final part of this demonstration, try to memorise the two strings of letters at the bottom of the table. Both strings have 30 letters, but the letters in the right panel have been rearranged not only in words, but also as a sentence. Compare how difficult it is to memorise the letters in the first string (without organisation) and in the second string (with organisation). It is highly unlikely that you will remember the 30 letters as presented in the left panel and it is highly unlikely that that somebody knowing English is *not* going to remember the letters as presented in the right panel. How is this possible?

The answer was provided in a seminal article by Miller (1956). Miller put forward the hypothesis that the cognitive system fuses together functionally related bits of information, a process termed *chunking*. A **chunk** can be defined as 'a collection of elements having strong associations with one another, but weak associations with elements within other chunks' (Gobet *et al.*, 2001, p. 236). Chunks are long-term memory structures and as such are the result of learning. Words are a good example of chunks. In many languages using an alphabet, a technique for children to learn reading consists of first learning letters before chunking them into words or sequences of words. Interestingly, the technique consisting of directly learning words is less efficient than the one introducing letters, as if chunking letters without learning their function would be counterproductive in the long term (Ehri *et al.*, 2001). Hence, chunking enables the accretion of simple units into groups, which can later be used as units themselves. One important implication of Miller's article is that the capacity of short-term memory (often called **memory span**) should be measured in terms of chunks, and not in terms of more elementary units. Miller suggested that the usual memory span is between five and nine chunks, typically seven.

In a seminal study, Murdock (1961) carried out a clear demonstration of the extent to which chunking can affect performance. Murdock's experiment consisted of four sessions. Each session used a free recall task, but differed with respect to the material to recall. In the first session, participants memorised trigrams (sequences of consonant-vowel-consonant, such as XUW and BAJ). In the second session, they recalled three-letter words (e.g. DOG). The third session was dedicated to the recall of three three-letter words at every trial. In the final session, participants were asked to listen to one three-digit number and then count backwards in threes. The results revealed that recall percentage was similar between the trigrams (three letters) and triads (three words but nine letters). Thus, what matters is the number of chunks, not the number of letters. It was also found that the recall of single words was easier than the recall of trigrams, even though both consisted of three letters. Continuing this line of research, Simon (1974) argued that short-term memory contains between five and seven chunks, and that about five to ten seconds were necessary to learn one chunk in long-term memory.

The impact of working memory span goes beyond memory. Because it specifies the maximum amount of information that can be processed at a time, it has generated much research, and here we present a recent example. Lépine and Barrouillet (2005) showed that measures of working-memory span (e.g. reading span and operation span) correlate positively with measures of academic performance (e.g. literacy and mathematics). They proposed that working-memory span is a fundamental limit and characteristic of the human cognitive system. It makes sense to argue that the maximum number of chunks that one can handle at the same time has a huge influence over the intellectual development of the person; for example this would affect the potential to learn (for similar results, see Chapter 9). On a less academic note, designers of video games have developed the rules of some games (e.g. Tetris) so that their memory demands are consistent with Miller's estimate of memory span.

Atkinson and Shiffrin's multi-component model

The idea that memory is organised around several subcomponents, each in charge of fulfilling a specific function, helps us understand how the mind stores information. Atkinson and Shiffrin (1968) were among the first to formalise memory processing by providing an integrated view of the **cognitive architecture**. Atkinson and Shiffrin's model, which has generated a great deal of research, postulates that memory functions are served by a set of connected components (see Figure 6.4). When interacting with the environment, the cognitive system receives **input**; this input in turn generates cognitive processing, which will ultimately produce some behaviour – the **output** of the system. Each component serves a specific, well-defined set of functions and is represented as a box in Figure 6.4. The flow of information is represented with arrows. As we have seen in Chapter 1 such a representation is referred to as a *flowchart*.

Components of the model

Memory stores are places where information is maintained and processed. The nature of the processing differs from one component to another and depends upon its function within the system. The role of the **sensory registers** is to keep a trace of sensations until the information is forwarded to the short-term store. Sensory registers are memory stores that hold modality-specific information for a few hundred milliseconds. There is a sensory register for holding visual information and another for holding auditory information. This information is not accessible to consciousness. The memory capacity of the sensory register is larger than the span of short-term memory (see below).

The **long-term store** is a space where information is stored permanently. It holds all the information that one has acquired through learning, from the name of one's first pet to the fact

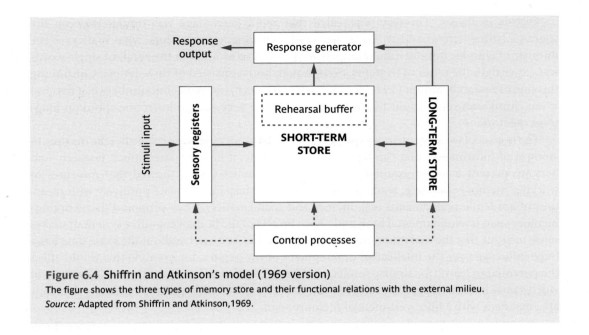

Figure 6.4 Shiffrin and Atkinson's model (1969 version)
The figure shows the three types of memory store and their functional relations with the external milieu.
Source: Adapted from Shiffrin and Atkinson, 1969.

that Moscow is the capital of Russia. Long-term memory is assumed to be infinite in capacity and insensitive to **interferences**.

The **short-term store** is a powerful structure: it serves the functions of holding and processing information in all modalities. It is the turning point of the cognitive system in that it organises information to produce a behavioural response. It contrasts with long-term memory on two dimensions. First, information in the short-term store is sensitive to interferences. As we have seen above, this assumption is supported by the elimination of the recency effect whenever an interpolated task is completed between presentation and recall. Second, the span of short-term memory is limited to about seven items. The items must be rehearsed constantly to avoid forgetting. In Figure 6.4, the box labelled 'control processes' indicates the processes that regulate and control the information flow between the memory components.

Regulation of the information flow

In Figure 6.4, the circuit depicted by the arrows indicates how information is handled within the system. It is apparent that the short-term store plays the central role in this system. It receives information from two different sources: the sensory registers and the long-term store. Information coming from the perceptual system has to go through the sensory registers before entering the short-term store. As the arrows indicate, information travels in one direction only, from sensory registers to short-term store. Only information that is not discarded as a result of attentional inhibition is transferred to the short-term memory store. The other way for the short-term store to get task-relevant information is from the long-term store, which provides the necessary knowledge for carrying out the current task. Finally, the information in the short-term store is processed and an output is produced.

Shiffrin and Atkinson (1969) emphasised that memory processes are in the need of supervision in order to work properly. They postulated a component consisting of *control processes*. One of its key roles is to control the input of the short-term store, which is done in two ways. First, it filters information coming from the sensory registers and so controls the amount and quality of the information. This relates to the filtering mechanisms we have discussed in Chapter 5. Second, it controls how much information and which information is retrieved from the long-term store. Another important role of the short-term store is to select the type of cognitive operations that are applied to the information held in the short-term store; for example, it decides to rehearse this information.

Shiffrin and Atkinson's model has been highly influential, and offers a useful framework for organising the empirical evidence on sensory registers and short-term memory. However, the model also has limits, as three central assumptions have turned out to be incorrect. The first incorrect assumption was that items are encoded in long-term memory as a result of their stay in the short-term store. As we shall see shortly, it turns out that items can be processed frequently in short-term memory without being stored in long-term memory. This raises the question of how long-term memory storage occurs, and we shall also see that what matters is not so much the amount of rehearsing, as the type of rehearsing. The second incorrect assumption was that the short-term store was considered to process unitary information – that is, there are no differences in the type of information used. We will demonstrate that this is an oversimplification, and short-term memory deals with at least two very distinct types of information: verbal information and visuospatial information. The third main incorrect assumption was that the short-term store can be considered as a unit. Assuming a limited amount of resources, which is likely, this implies that the resources engaged by one process are not available to another process. For example, if you are learning a list of words, the simultaneous completion of a visual task should impair performance of word learning. However, this has been shown not to be the case (Baddeley, 1986). Short-term memory thus turns out to be a more complex system than proposed by Shiffrin and Atkinson, and problems with the model have led psychologists to propose other models of human memory. In the next sections, we review the key findings referring to sensory registers and short-term memory. Then, we discuss recent models of short-term memory.

Stop and Think Paradigm shift

Indicate the weaknesses of Atkinson and Shiffrin's theory and explain how these weaknesses were overcome by new theories.

Sensory registers: stealth memory stores

As noted above, the sensory registers in Atkinson and Shiffrin's (1968) model filter information from the perceptual system in a few hundred milliseconds, and then select some of the information for further processing in short-term memory. Sensory registers were one of the first concepts to refer to a form of memory that contains information never accessed by consciousness.

The existence of such short-lasting memories was established by a series of pioneering experiments carried out by Sperling (1960). The task he developed consisted of remembering briefly presented arrays of letters (see Figure 6.5). The participants had first to attend to a fixation cross. Then, a random array of letters appeared for 50 milliseconds. The trial ended with participants attempting to recall the content of the array. In a first experiment, Sperling varied the size of the arrays that were presented. He found that the maximum amount of information recalled is about four items. In a second experiment, Sperling varied the presentation time from 50 to 500 ms. Results showed no improvement in memory performance with an increase in time of exposure. In the third experiment, Sperling kept presentation time constant but asked the participants to recall a specific row. The participants went through two experimental conditions, one with arrays consisting of two rows and one with arrays consisting of three rows. For each condition, the rows contained either three or four items (either letters or digits). After the presentation of the array, a brief tone indicated which row (bottom, middle or top) had to be recalled. Sperling used an atypical measure of performance; he considered that average performance reflects the percentage of letters encoded in memory. For example, if a participant had been correct 90 per cent of the time in reporting three letters in the array of three rows of three letters each, then the measure of average memory for this participant is about eight letters ($.90 \times 9$ letters = 8.1 letters). On the basis of this assumption, Sperling calculated the average performance for each array size and each session. He found that the amount of information retained in the sensory register is quite high (up to 8.64 letters). He also found that the material is kept for only 50 ms on average in the sensory register, and then either dismissed or forwarded to short-term memory. The important conclusion of this study is that much more information is available to the visual sensory register (between eight and nine letters) than to short-term memory (only four letters).

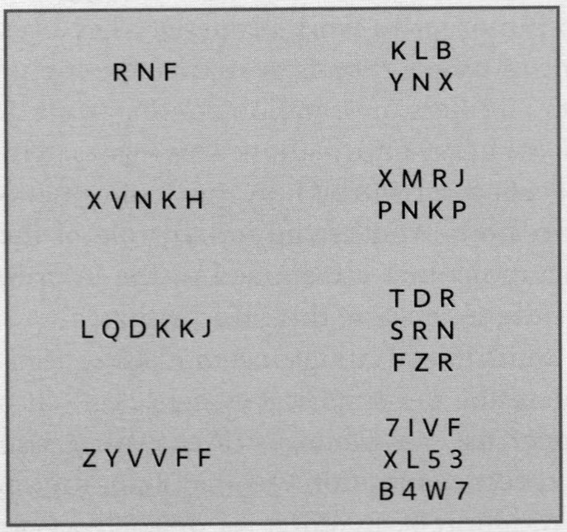

This series of experiments made a strong case for the existence of a memory store that plays the role of a half station toward conscious processing. This memory lasting less than a second has been called **iconic memory** by Neisser (1967). A similar short-lasting, modality-specific memory exists for auditory information (e.g. Darwin *et al.*, 1972), which Neisser (1967) has called **echoic memory**.

Short-lasting memories that are out of the reach of consciousness are not limited to the echoic and iconic stores. Harris *et al.* (2002) have shown that haptic perceptions – perceptions related to the sense of touch – also survive only briefly. Hence, even though most of the research is dedicated to understanding how visual and auditory information is processed, you should keep in mind that other sensory modalities bring continuously new and relevant information to the cognitive system.

Figure 6.5 Examples of arrays
Source: Sperling, 1960.

Stop and Think Evolution of memory
If we assume that evolution makes things more adaptive, how would you explain that the span of memory has not improved over time?

Short-term memory: verbal information

Imagine that you have to remember a new phone number for a while before dialling it. You read it once to store it in short-term memory. Then, you rehearse it in order to refresh information regularly until you reach the telephone. Without rehearsing, it is likely that you would forget the number. The fact that people rehearse verbal information has been established in controlled experiments. This critical result was already an important motivation behind Waugh and Norman's conception of memory in 1965, and has been reused and adapted in numerous models.

Before entering short-term memory, verbal information is processed so as to be coded phonologically. This encoding process can be a source of errors. Two studies by Conrad (1964) showed that the cognitive system is sensitive to surface features. The first experiment consisted in recalling spoken letters. While participants were listening to the experimenter, they were simultaneously submitted to a background noise of varying intensity. The results revealed that spoken letters might be confounded if the background noise is strong enough. Letters are clustered according to their acoustic proximity. That is, listening to letters that present acoustic similarities (e.g. M and N, or B and P) leads to more errors at the perceptual stage than listening to letters that are different. In a second experiment, participants had to recall lists of six-letter strings that were presented visually. The same pattern of results was found as in the first experiment. Conrad put forward the hypothesis that short-term memory rehearses the acoustic code of the letters rather than their visual code. As the phonological encoding into memory might lead to errors, subsequent memory performance might be impaired. The phenomenon is known as **acoustic confusion** and highlights the fact that we encode verbal information as series of sounds, even when it is presented visually. (The acoustic properties of letters will be taken up in Chapter 9.)

How many items can we hold simultaneously in the verbal store? Early studies have argued that the span is around seven chunks, measuring chunks on the basis of visual information (i.e. counting letters, syllables or words). As Conrad's study has shown, words are encoded as sequences of sounds. Are written words equivalent to spoken words? Actually, the difference in terms of memory load between a written word and a spoken word can be significant. For instance 'fill' and 'feel' are both made of four letters arranged in one monosyllabic word, but it takes longer to pronounce the latter than the former. Thus, if memory is bounded by its ability to store sequences of sounds, it should be easier to store monosyllabic words than words made of two or more syllables. The first line of evidence comes from the **word-length effect**. Baddeley *et al.* (1975) asked participants to study words of various lengths (from one to five syllables). The results showed that memory performance is inversely proportional to word length: the longer the word the worse the memory performance. Together with errors due to acoustic confusion, this suggests that the information stored in short-term memory is coded as sounds (sub-vocally spoken words). Another line of evidence comes from studies examining cross-linguistic

Box 6.2 CLASSIC EXPERIMENT: Chinese memory

At this point, you may have noticed that we have surreptitiously switched from a chunk-based measure of the capacity of short-term memory to a time-based measure. Is it possible to reconcile the two accounts, one based on Miller (1956) and the other on Baddeley (1986)? In a study on the memory of native Chinese speakers, Zhang and Simon (1985) proposed just such an integration. Their aim was to assess whether short-term memory capacity can best be measured by either the number of chunks or the number of syllables. Taking advantage of the characteristics of the way Chinese is written (Chinese is a logographic language), they manipulated the number of syllables independently of the number of chunks. More specifically, the lists consisted of characters (one syllable), words (two syllables) or idioms (four syllables). As they are familiar to Chinese speakers, characters, words and idioms can be represented as a single chunk. Lists of characters, words and idioms were presented before the participants underwent the recall phase.

Participants' mean performance is presented in Table 6.1. The interesting result is that the capacity of working memory is not constant either for the number of chunks or for the number of syllables, as predicted by chunking theory and working memory theory, respectively. These results indicate that 'the more syllables in each chunk, the smaller will be the STM [short-term memory] span measured in chunks and the larger will be the STM span measured in syllables' (Zhang and Simon, 1985, p. 199).

Using these and similar results, Zhang and Simon developed a mathematical model which predicted memory span by making three main assumptions: (a) the larger a chunk, the longer it takes to rehearse it; (b) for English words, it takes about 280 ms to bring a chunk into the articulatory mechanism of short-term memory; and (c) it takes about 55 ms to articulate each syllable beyond the first one. (The respective values for Chinese are 310 ms and 120 ms.) The details of the model are beyond the scope of an introductory textbook, but the key message of Zhang and Simon's research is that it is possible to unify the chunk-based and time-based approaches to short-term memory capacity. This research has inspired a successful model of the way children acquire vocabulary (Jones et al., 2007), in which the chunking mechanism helps explain how phonological working memory interacts with long-term memory.

Table 6.1 Chinese memory

Type of item	Number of chunks	Number of syllables	Number of chunks recalled	Number of syllables recalled
character	1	1	6.58	6.58
word	1	2	4.58	9.16
idiom	1	4	3.00	12.00

Source: adapted from Zhang and Simon (1985).

differences. If memory span depends on time, then the rate at which people speak should affect measures of memory span. Languages use different sounds and also different durations for these sounds. For example, digit names in Welsh are comparable to English with respect to the number of syllables, but they are made of longer vowels. On average, articulation rate is 385 ms/digit for Welsh and 321 ms/digit for English (Ellis and Hennelly, 1980) – that is, the pronunciation of an equal number of digits will take more time for a Welsh speaker than an English speaker. Hence, an English speaker can say more digits in two seconds than a Welsh speaker, and thus has more opportunity for rehearsing them. The prediction is that Welsh speakers will perform worse in the digit-span task than English speakers, which is indeed the case. Welsh speakers also perform worse on arithmetic tasks, both with respect to speed and error rate. Could this be explained by different levels of intelligence between the English and the Welsh? No, because the impaired performance in the digit-span task disappears when Welsh-English bilinguals do the task in English. These results show that the span of verbal memory is better measured by time duration than by the number of syllables. The current view is that verbal memory has an approximate time duration of 2 seconds.

Stop and Think   Memory span

As noted in this and previous chapters, the computer analogy is often used in cognitive psychology. How much do you think our performance would improve if our memory span were to double?

Short-term memory: visuospatial information

A question that has long been a focus of attention amongst researchers is the format of information. For many years it had been believed that mental operations in short-term memory are done only in an acoustic format. Accordingly, most of the experiments were run with verbal material. However, a crucial experiment by Roger Shepard and Jacqueline Metzler (1971) showed that information held in short-term memory can be coded in a visuospatial format as well. Participants were presented with pairs of line drawings depicting three-dimensional objects (see Figure 6.6(a)). In half the trials, the object on the right was the same as the object on the left, but was rotated in space. In the other half of the trials, the object on the right was a mirror image of the object on the left, and was also rotated in space. The angle of rotation varied from 0 to 180 degrees by steps of 20 degrees. Participants had to indicate whether the objects were similar or mirror images.

Figure 6.6(b) shows the response time as a function of the angle of rotation. The striking result is that response time is proportional to the rotation angle. Why would this be the case if information were processed in verbal format? However, if we assume that information is processed in a visuospatial format, then the results make sense: the response time reflects the time used by the participants to rotate the object in their mind's eye. The larger the angle of rotation, the longer it takes to process this object. Shepard and Metzler's results were among the first to support the hypothesis that our representation of visuospatial information is **analogue** (i.e. there is a correspondence between the representation in the mind and the external representation) rather than **propositional** (i.e. the relationship between the representation and what is represented is arbitrary, such as in language). Thus, we can see things in the mind's eye and manipulate information in this visuospatial format without any need for verbal processing. The span of visuospatial memory is assumed to be about four items (Gobet and Clarkson, 2004).

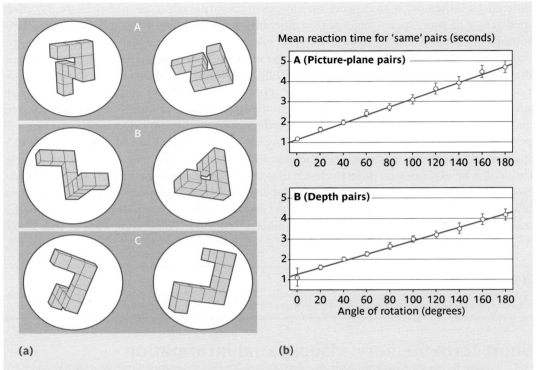

Figure 6.6(a) Shepard and Metzler, three-dimensional stimuli and **Figure 6.6(b)** Shepard and Metzler results

Graph A shows the results with two-dimensional stimuli, and graph B with three-dimensional stimuli.

Source: Shepard and Metzler, 1971.

Box 6.3 CLASSIC EXPERIMENT: **Finding your way on an island**

Our understanding of the mental processes operating upon visual images has much improved in the past 40 years since Shepard and Metzler's seminal experiment. Kosslyn *et al.* (1978) provided another clear demonstration for the existence of visual images. They first asked the participants to learn the map of a fictional island (see Figure 6.7). The map was then removed from view and the participants had to draw it. If the map was not drawn accurately enough, the participants had to redraw it. This procedure was used to check that the participants had correctly learned the location of landmarks and the distances between them.

In the testing phase, participants listened to two words presented in a five-second interval and were asked to scan their mental image of the map; more specifically, they had to mentally move a speck from the location indicated by the first word to the location indicated by the second word. The results revealed that the time necessary to scan the map was proportional to the distance between the two landmarks. This experiment and others with a similar design support the idea that the format of the information in visual short-term memory is analog.

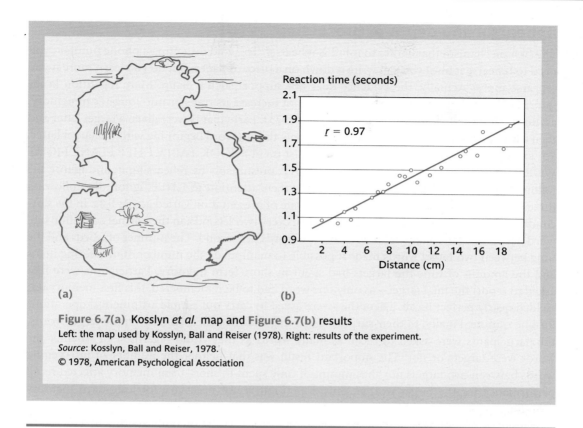

Figure 6.7(a) Kosslyn *et al.* map and **Figure 6.7(b)** results
Left: the map used by Kosslyn, Ball and Reiser (1978). Right: results of the experiment.
Source: Kosslyn, Ball and Reiser, 1978.
© 1978, American Psychological Association

Stop and Think Account for hallucinations
Some individuals claim that they see extraterrestrials or people who have passed away. Use cognitive psychology to pinpoint which elements of working memory are used to generate these hallucinations.

Memory traces

According to Atkinson and Shiffrin's model, information enters the short-term store after having been processed by the sensory registers, provided it has not been discarded by attentional filtering mechanisms (see Chapter 5). This section deals with what happens with this information then, and focuses on the concept of a **memory trace**, which relates to two aspects of psychology with deep practical implications: encoding and forgetting.

Encoding

Encoding depends on the way information is organised and presented to the cognitive system. Several factors have been shown to affect information encoding and, thus, later recall. These factors are central to understanding the mechanisms underlying memory functioning and are therefore part of any model of memory. Also, these factors are of interest to learners as they may help them organise material and thus optimise learning (see the section on How to use this book in Chapter 1).

Rehearsal and depth of processing

The first mechanism that comes to mind is rehearsal. To avoid forgetting a phone number, you need to rehearse it until you can write it down on a piece of paper. But do you learn more if you rehearse more? Actually, the evidence does not support such a claim. Mere repetition keeps information in short-term memory but does not increase its transfer into long-term memory, as illustrated by a study by Craik and Watkins (1973). Participants were given a target letter and then a list; they were instructed to remember only the last word beginning with the target letter. For example, if the target letter is 'C' and the list is CAT BOOK TABLE CHEF PLANE FIGHT WORD, participants would first remember CAT, presumably by rehearsing it, and ignore the following two items. Then, they would switch their attention to CHEF, ignore the following three items, and report CHEF at the end. The rate of presentation varied across lists: in the slow condition, the participants listened to one word every two seconds; in the normal condition one word per second; and in the fast condition two words per second. The number of words and the time between two target words made it possible to manipulate the number of interfering items and the amount of time the targets had spent in short-term memory. Participants were first asked to report the final target – as only one word had to be remembered, this first memory test yielded nearly perfect recall. Then, they were asked to carry out simple arithmetical operations for one minute. Finally, to their surprise given that they had focused only on the target words, the participants were asked to recall as many words as they could regardless of whether the words were targets or not. The important result was that neither the number of intervening words between two targets nor the amount of time spent in short-term memory affected recall performance for the target words. Thus, repetition is not necessary for long-term memory encoding.

This basic result has been replicated many times since, with different experimental methods. For example, Glenberg *et al.* (1977) presented participants with a four-digit number for 2 seconds. Before recall, participants were asked to rehearse the number for 2, 6 or 18 seconds. They underwent this procedure with 64 numbers and thus carried out 64 recalls. Unexpectedly, a recall of all the numbers took place at the end of the experiment. The retention interval, and thus the opportunity to rehearse the numbers, had little effect on recall performance. Just like Craik and Watkins's study, this result shows that the amount of repetition does not correlate with memory performance.

If repetition does not necessarily lead to the creation of memory traces, then what is the mechanism involved? In their *depth of processing theory*, Craik and Lockhart (1972) argued that the strength of memory traces depends on the amount of processing to which stimuli are subjected. The more deeply a stimulus is processed, the stronger the memory trace, and thus the easier it is to recall. They distinguished between **maintenance rehearsal**, where stimuli are simply rehearsed so that they can be held in short-term memory, and **elaborative rehearsal**, where stimuli are subjected to deeper, typically semantic processing that recodes them more efficiently. According to Craik and Lockhart, only elaborative rehearsal leads to long-term learning.

Craik and Lockhart's theory (1972) has received good empirical support. Craik and Tulving (1975) conducted a series of experiments showing that processing material helps encode it better. In one experiment, participants were presented with words such as 'book', and were required to provide judgements for them. There were three different types of judgement, which implemented three different levels of processing. The shallowest level was about visual features: e.g. 'Is the word starting with a capital letter?' The intermediate level was about the phonological structure of words: e.g. 'Does the word rhyme with "Look"?' Finally, the deepest level was about meaning. Participants were asked to tell whether the word could fit in a given sentence: e.g. 'I am going to read this _____'. Participants completed a series of judgements before being submitted to an unexpected **recognition task**, where they had to say whether words had been presented or not during the judgement phase of the experiment. The results, which have been replicated time and again, showed that recall performance correlated with depth of processing (Lockhart and Craik, 1990; Slamecka and Graf, 1978; Sporer, 1991).

Importance of meaning

The results on depth of processing raise the general question of the importance of meaning in long-term memory encoding, and many studies have been carried out to test the possible implication of a semantic code to encode information into memory. Klein (1970) used a recognition task to assess the extent to which acoustic and semantic similarity affects the processing of material in memory. The learning material was made of six words. Words were presented once at a rate of one word every 1.5 seconds. Afterwards, the participants were kept busy by a variety of tasks for 6 s, 20 s, 80 s or 1200 s (i.e. 20 minutes). Finally, participants received a new list of words at a rate of 8 s per word and had to perform a recognition task. The test list consisted of eight words: two words from the learning list, two acoustically similar words, two semantically related words and finally two neutral words. Words in the learning list and the test list were controlled for length (four letters), appearance (capitals only) and frequency. The crucial result of this experiment was that recognition times increased when the words in the test list were semantically related to the words in the learning list, which suggests that semantic information has been encoded in long-term memory.

Forgetting

Information decay refers to the gradual fading over time of a memory trace. The mirror image of decay is retention, which reflects the persistence of a memory trace. As you can imagine, it is much easier to measure something that is still present by asking participants 'What do you remember?', rather than estimating the amount of something that has disappeared. Therefore, retention is often used to infer forgetting. Forgetting is measured as the amount of information that is not retained since the end of learning. The idea of suppressing rehearsal to study memory retention was first used by Brown (1958) and Peterson and Peterson (1959), two of the most influential studies ever carried out in psychology. Participants were presented with a single trigram (e.g. XAJ) immediately followed by a three-digit number. As soon as the digit was spoken, participants had to count backwards by threes at the tick of a metronome until the experimenter gave the signal to recall the trigram. The retention interval during which participants completed the counting task varied between 3, 6, 9, 12, 15 and 18 s. As the word presented at the start of the trial had to be retained over various periods of time, this procedure made it possible to measure how long the content of short-term memory can be held without active rehearsal.

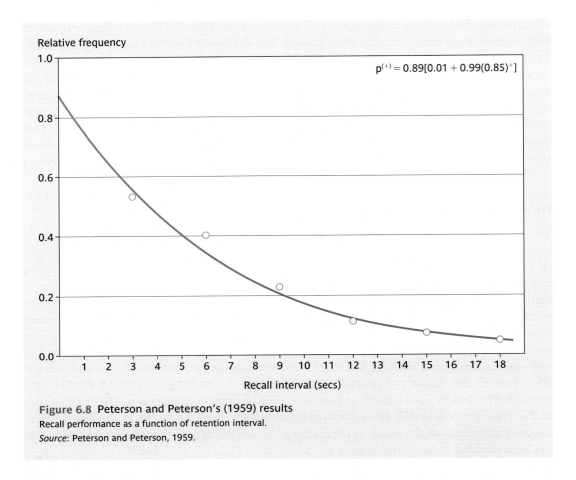

Figure 6.8 Peterson and Peterson's (1959) results
Recall performance as a function of retention interval.
Source: Peterson and Peterson, 1959.

Figure 6.8 illustrates how information fades over time. The shape of the curve shows that the rate of loss decreases as time passes by. This curve reflects the process of normal forgetting when we do not rehearse information. As the data show, after 3 seconds we are likely to have lost about 30 per cent of the information if we do not rehearse it. So, if a friend gives you her phone number, make sure you rehearse it! (Or even better, recode it using the principle of meaning encoding.)

The Brown and Peterson paradigm not only produced important results with respect to memory processing, but also introduced a new technique to study short-term memory that has inspired a large number of studies. In general, the results of these studies support the hypothesis that short-term memory forgetting is due to decay. However, some of these results can also be explained in a different way: forgetting might be due not to decay, but to interferences between the presentation of the items to learn and the material processed when carrying out the distracting task. This view has led researchers to put forward the **interference theory** of forgetting. According to this theory, it is not so much the time passed since learning that affects the quality of memory as the interferences caused by the inevitable neural events that cause noise in the encoding and processing of information. Two types of interferences are distinguished. **Proactive**

interference refers to the influence of previously learned items on the learning of new material. **Retroactive interference** refers to the opposite influence from new items to already learned items.

What does lead to interference? Similarity. If new items are similar to items in memory, for instance phonologically, then interferences are likely to occur. An early example of this was provided by McGeoch and McDonald (1931). Participants had to learn a list of adjectives; after they had reached perfect recall, they were given ten minutes before another recall session. During these ten minutes participants were allocated to one of five different experimental groups, which completed different tasks. The five groups were respectively asked to learn three-digit numbers, nonsense syllables, adjectives unrelated to the study items, antonyms of these items or synonyms. In addition, a control group just rested so that their performance would offer a baseline that could be compared to the groups who had something to learn. The results depict a crystal-clear pattern. The resting group performed better than the groups allocated to a second learning task. Among these groups, the best performance was obtained by the group that learned numbers and the worse by the group that learned synonyms. In general, performance decreased with semantic proximity – that is, if words are semantically close, then their encoding is affected and interferences distort the original memory traces.

Stop and Think Why chatting is detrimental
Considering what you know about memory traces and interferences, make a list of all the psychological effects that enter into play when someone chats during a lecture. Differentiate between the interferences taking place with the person talking, the person listening, and other people nearby.

Recent models of working memory

Short-term memory has been a very influential concept and has generated much research. Several information-processing models were developed in the 1960s and the 1970s, each capturing the empirical data better than its predecessors. In later years the tendency has been to focus on the information-processing aspects of short-term memory rather than on storage, and *short-term memory* is now increasingly called *working memory*. In the next sections we describe two influential theories of working memory. Baddeley's theory has been chosen because of its remarkable impact on the field. Cowan's theory, though less influential, deserves attention as it shows that the same body of empirical evidence can be accounted for by a different set of psychological concepts and mechanisms.

Baddeley's theory of working memory

As we have seen earlier, Atkinson and Shiffrin proposed that the short-term store both retains and processes information, and that resources are distributed between these two functions. In an influential paper, Alan Baddeley and Graham Hitch (1974) questioned not only this assumption, but also the concept of a short-term store in general. Baddeley and Hitch filled participants' short-term memory with material (e.g. a list of numbers) and then asked them to perform a wide range of resource-demanding tasks, such as reasoning. If the short-term store both holds and processes information, then filling it should use up the resources needed to carry out the reasoning task. Hence, the memory load exerted by the first task should markedly impair performance on the second task. The key finding of Baddeley and Hitch was that performance is not affected as much as it should be if the two processes depended on the same memory component. Motivated by these results, Baddeley's theory of working memory was proposed to replace Atkinson and Shiffrin's theory, which it has successfully done.

Baddeley has developed his working memory theory for more than 30 years. While the first version of the theory (Baddeley and Hitch, 1974) included only three components – the central executive, the phonological loop and the visuospatial sketchpad – the current theory (Baddeley, 2000, 2003) consists of four components, an episodic buffer having been added (see Figure 6.9).

The **phonological loop** is dedicated to speech-based information. In order to account for a wide variety of findings (e.g. word length, serial position, acoustic confusion), the phonological loop has been broken down into two subcomponents: the phonological store and the rehearsal process. The **phonological store** holds the items online in a passive way, in either an acoustic or a phonological format. Items are characterised by an activity level that decreases over time. As demonstrated by free recall tasks, information is lost if it is not refreshed. After two seconds on average, the activity of an item is so weak that it cannot be retrieved any more and is forgotten. Activity is set back to its maximum by the **rehearsal process**. This second component refreshes memory item by item and then comes back to the first item to start again the refreshing cycle. (As an analogy, think of the circus performance where a large number of plates are kept spinning on poles without falling off.) Both systems cooperate to keep information for further processing. Given that the material that cannot be rehearsed within two seconds is forgotten, Baddeley and Hitch argued that the most suitable measure of phonological information is duration rather the number of items. As long as the items (whether digits, letters, trigrams or words) can be phonologically encoded within the two-second boundary, they do not exceed the phonological memory span and thus can be recalled.

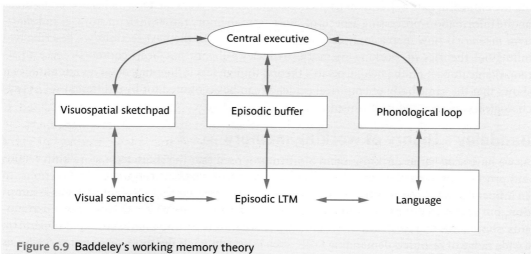

Figure 6.9 Baddeley's working memory theory
Source: Adapted from Baddeley, 2003.

The input of the phonological store can be auditory or visual. Visual input is analysed to detect words that are further recoded into their phonological equivalent by an orthographic to phonological translator. Auditory input passes a phonological detector in charge of detecting words. The output of the system is spoken words.

The **visuospatial sketchpad** (VSSP; also called the 'visuospatial scratchpad') holds and manipulates visuospatial information. Only three or four items can be held simultaneously in the VSSP, and these items are subject to decay. Given such a limit, it is not surprising that people find it difficult to notice differences in complex visual scenes in which one object has been removed (see Box 5.1 in Chapter 5). Logie (1995) has proposed that the visuospatial sketchpad is divided into two subcomponents: the **visual cache** holds visuospatial information, whereas the **inner scribe** carries out cognitive operations on this information (e.g. rotating an object). You have probably noticed a parallel with the functioning of the phonological loop in that a passive system stores information while an active component is in charge of processing it. The VSSP can cope with tasks such as texture discrimination that mobilise its visually related mechanisms. It can also easily deal with tasks that mainly muster mechanisms dedicated to spatial information, such as the Corsi task. (The Corsi task consists of a series of cubes distributed on a board. The experimenter taps the cubes in sequence. Once this is finished, the participant has to tap the sequence in the same order, from memory.) The distinction between visual and spatial functions suggests that the VSSP has separate mechanisms to process information in the visual format when shape, colour and contours are concerned, and to process information in the spatial format when the task requires location coding or path analysis. Measures of visuospatial span are often integrated as a measure of non-verbal intelligence in intelligence tests, for example in the Wechsler Adult Intelligence Scale.

Stop and Think Blind people perceive space

People born blind have an ability to represent space as demonstrated by their ability to navigate in the environment. Some individuals have developed a system based on sound (known as *echolocation*). How would you modify Baddeley's visuospatial sketchpad and phonological loop to better fit blind people's way of representing the world?

The **central executive** is close to Norman and Shallice's supervisory activating system (see Chapter 5). Its purpose is to monitor attentional processes, such as dividing attention, switching attention and focusing attention on task-relevant items. The central executive controls the information flow within and between the phonological loop and the visuospatial sketchpad. It also controls the information arriving from the senses and supervises retrieval from memory. Although the central executive is a key element of Baddeley and Hitch's working memory theory, it has not been the focus of much research. This may be due to the fact that it covers a wide range of processes, so that it is difficult to pinpoint its specific properties.

For many years the working memory theory has proposed that the central executive is in charge of coordinating the various pieces of information stored by the two slave systems. However, Baddeley (2000, 2003) has recently revised his theory and added the **episodic buffer** to account for two phenomena. The first phenomenon is the fact that we perceive things as wholes and not as discrete parts. When you are watching a movie on TV, you perceive the words coming from the people in the movie and not from the TV itself. If a conversation is held, you perceive each character as a unit. According to Baddeley, this integration of information in single percepts is done in the episodic buffer. To serve this function, the episodic buffer combines information from the VSSP (the people you watch on TV) and information held in the phonological store (what they say) into a single representation. In addition, if you know the actors, it is likely that you retrieve information from long-term memory and integrate it with information already in working memory. Because the episodic buffer combines information from the slave systems and long-term memory, it really is the place where the integrated information is held and is available to consciousness. It follows that the span of the episodic buffer reflects the performance of working memory, and that this span may be different from the spans of the phonological loop and the VSSP. By integrating information, the episodic buffer builds new memories and it is thus the place where chunking between different modalities takes place.

Evaluation of Baddeley's theory

Baddeley's theory of working memory has been developed for nearly 40 years. In general, it does better than Atkinson and Shiffrin's model in accounting for the empirical data on short-term memory. However, in spite of the wide range of phenomena it accounts for, and like any scientific theory, it is not perfect. Its main weakness is that it is rather vague on many details. Consider for example the central executive. Although it is a crucial component of the theory, it is underspecified. It is not known how it integrates information from different modalities. The way it monitors information in the slave systems or how it controls the attention focus in the episodic buffer are not specified either. In addition, Jones et al. (2004) have recently challenged the phonological store and the articulation mechanism, which are central in Baddeley's theory to explain the way auditory information is processed. Jones and colleagues collected data showing that the two routes (a direct, auditory route and an indirect, visual route) that enable information to access the phonological loop do not process information as stated by the theory. In spite of these weaknesses, Baddeley's working memory theory has been highly influential, as it offers a useful framework for organising a large amount of empirical data on working memory.

Cowan's theory

Nelson Cowan (1988) has put forward a rather different view of working memory. For him, what is referred to as 'working memory' emerges as the interaction of processes taking place at different levels. Cowan's theory is composed of three main components (see Figure 6.10). (Only a relatively minor role is played by sensory registers, which briefly hold information.) The *central executive* is in charge of allocating attention to task-relevant stimuli and monitors voluntary processing. *Long-term memory*, the central component of the theory, emphasises the dynamic nature of memory. Cowan's view is that memory records have a level of activation that reflects their accessibility to consciousness. Following long-term memory retrieval, memory records are activated. (Memory records may be letters, words or geometric figures.) The set of activated records changes as a function of perceptions and task requirements. This dynamically defined set of memory records forms the third component of the theory, the *short-term store*, which is a set of records available for processing by the central executive. The short-term store is part and

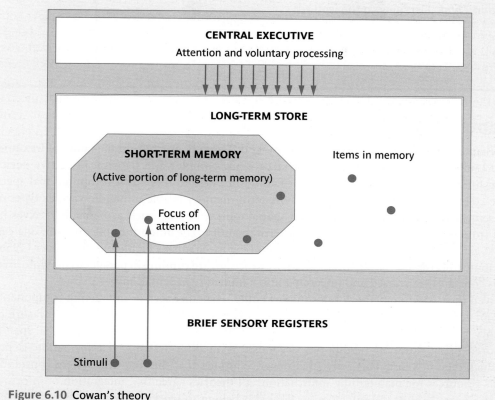

Figure 6.10 Cowan's theory
Cowan's model of short-term memory.

parcel of working memory but does not constitute the essence of it. Information is processed only when it is under the focus of attention. Attention is highly limited: only a few items can be processed at one time.

Hence, we get a three-level view of memory processing. First, there is the set of long-term memory records that do not benefit from activation and as such are outside the scope of central-executive active processes. Second, there is the set of activated memory records that constitute the short-term store but that are not focused upon. Finally, there is the set of items which are the focus of attention and can benefit from cognitive operations.

Let us consider an example of how this model works: the rotation of a cube in space. The first phase is the recognition of the cube by the perceptual system. As a result of this, the memory trace of the object stored in long-term memory is activated. As it is the most relevant item, the central executive directs attention to it. Then, the central executive searches in memory a rule to apply rotation. Finally, the rule is applied to the object and a new image of the cube is generated.

Stop and Think Compare theories
Compare Baddeley's and Cowan's models of short-term memory.

Stop and Think Listening to the lecturer

As many experiments have convincingly demonstrated, understanding the material and thinking over it facilitates not only understanding but also learning. Considering this evidence, it is clear that everything that cuts you from the logical flow of an argument makes it difficult to understand it and thus memorise it. Using either Baddeley's or Cowan's model, account for the many ways in which a disturbance during a lecture might stop students following the flow of the argument.

Chapter summary

This chapter has shown that short-term memory differs very much from the tablet of wax proposed by Plato. Short-term memory is a structurally complex and dynamically active device whose function is not only to hold information, but also to serve as a computational space where cognitive operations take place. Short-term memory is able to handle various types of representation: words, visual objects and spatial representations such as maps. It receives its input from perceptual processes and long-term memory. The amount of information one can hold at a given time is strictly limited. The chunking mechanisms highlighted by Miller (1956) contribute towards alleviating this limit. Many processes are running in parallel so that information is constantly rehearsed and integrated into a unified representation.

Given that working memory is a complex entity – whether seen as interacting components or as an active subset of long-term memory – it is not possible to use one single measure of memory span. Visual span is measured using capacity (about four chunks) and verbal span is measured using duration (about two seconds). With both systems, if information is not refreshed, then it is lost. This active maintenance implies that the cognitive system constantly invests resources for maintaining information. All theories agree that integration of information and regulation of the information flow also belong to working memory. Because many processes are going on simultaneously, information can be hampered by interferences.

Working memory is also the place for simulating the world. The mind's eye is used to process visual information, and carries out cognitive operations such as finding the shortest path on a map. We also use this ability to simulate the world when we read a novel. The meaning of the words is retrieved from long-term memory and integrated in working memory to form a unique scene: the one that makes us feel. Literature, such as the novel *Dracula*, is based on this simulation ability, and it is up to the talent of the writer to assemble words and sentences in such a way that they make us believe that things are real. Memory is actually far from the popular conception of what it is!

Further reading

Baddeley's book *Human memory* (Baddeley, 1997), which discusses at length each component of his theory, will be useful to readers interested in his point of view. The book also provides good coverage of learning. Together with many other publications, Cowan's (1988) seminal paper is available at http://web.missouri.edu/~cowann/pubs.html. Miyake and Shah (1999) present and compare a dozen models of working memory. The biological underpinnings of working memory can be learned from Squire and Kandel (1999).

Long-term memory and learning

CHAPTER PREVIEW

- ☑ Long-term memory is the place where we store all our memories, the hard drive of the mind.

- ☑ Long-term memory covers a wide range of different memory systems, which are defined according to the type of information they store.

- ☑ Facts (e.g. 'Berlin is the capital of Germany') and events (e.g. your first date) are stored in declarative memory.

- ☑ Declarative memory holds different types of memory items, from simple structures such as words or visual objects, to complex structures such as scripts, schemas and concepts.

- ☑ Non-declarative memory is concerned with performance. It holds and displays a variety of types of memory records. Among these, we can distinguish memories that (a) reflect mere reactions to a stimulus, (b) associate the stimulus with a typical response, (c) modulate the importance of any one behaviour in a given context, (d) improve perceptual skills and (e) encode motor skills.

- ☑ Long-term memory systems differ in the way information is processed regarding storage and retrieval.

- ☑ While declarative knowledge needs a halfway station (i.e. the hippocampus) before being definitely consolidated, non-declarative memories seem to be stored more directly within the networks implementing the related performance.

> ☑ There are two main types of memory pathologies. Retrograde amnesia impairs the ability to recall information from the past. Anterograde amnesia impairs the creation of new memories.

Introduction

In the film *The Bourne Identity*, the main character (played by Matt Damon) is found floating in the Mediterranean Sea with two gunshot wounds in his back. He does not remember what he was doing in the sea, who he is, where he was born, not even his name. As the story develops, he displays considerable mastery in advanced martial arts, weapon use and other skills that are useful when one tries to escape the CIA, various national police forces and a number of professional assassins. He also discovers that he is fluent in several languages.

The movie gives a credible account of (total) retrograde **amnesia**, a condition that we will describe later in this chapter. Specifically, it correctly depicts the dissociation between declarative memory (the hero does not remember anything about his personal life) and procedural memory (but he still is able to apply his mortal skills and speaks several languages).

Long-term memory is often referred to as the database where we store all that we know. Presented in this way, long-term memory is a passive store holding just a sample of our life experience. The perceived passivity of this description tends to make us believe that our memories are mere objects. This chapter will show that the variety and the complexity of our memories are underpinned by active processes. Let us start with a little quiz. Try to answer the following three questions as quickly as possible.

1 What is the forename of your cognitive-psychology teacher?

2 What was Alexander the Great's e-mail address?

3 Do you know how to ride a bicycle?

This is a sample of the kind of information that might be stored in your long-term memory, and each question highlights one facet of it. Let us consider the forename question first. It is unlikely that you had to scan all your memories to find the answer. It came immediately, without any cognitive effort and you are confident about the answer provided. How is it that you found the correct answer immediately, considering the numerous forenames and people you know? We need mechanisms to explain how information can be retrieved so rapidly. The second question is similar: you do not need to scan the content of your memory to know that it does not contain this information. How do we know that we do *not* have a given piece of information? In this case, it is because you are aware that Alexander the Great was born a long time before computers were invented. However, we can phrase the question differently, such as 'Can you give the personal mobile phone number of the president of the USA?' It is unlikely that you can, and yet you believe that he has one. Here too, you are aware that you do not have this information. Unlike computer operating systems, humans do not have to scan all memory records to find out that something is not in there.

The last question is about knowing how to ride a bike. If you have answered yes, can you explain how to ride a bike in such a way that other people can learn it? You might explain that riding a bicycle is about keeping balance and pedalling. Will somebody who had never tried cycling before be able to ride a bike straight away with this information? Most likely not. Watching a novice practising bicycle riding will remind you how time-consuming, difficult and sometimes painful learning can be. Becoming skilled at riding a bicycle is a learning process that leads to the creation of memories, even though we cannot describe verbally what has been learned. These memories about performing actions are automatic and do not require much attention and conscious control (see Chapter 5). If you know how to ride a bicycle, you will do it effortlessly to the point that you can chat with a friend at the same time. With a few questions we have shown that long-term memory holds different types of information. Learning shows a high variability in the processes that take place or in the nature of the information that is recorded.

This chapter first reviews the different types of memory that are hosted in our mind. Then, it details the various kinds of information that are stored in the declarative system. We will see that several theoretical frameworks can account for a variety of findings that highlight how memories are stored, retrieved, and sometimes distorted. The section about non-declarative memories will show that behavioural changes and skill acquisition are actually a form of memory.

Long-term memory systems

Long-term memory reflects the variability of learning, as memories are stored in different brain regions, which results in a large variety of storage and retrieval mechanisms. To cope with this complexity and organise the empirical data, scientists have sought to classify memory systems. Larry Squire, a leading scholar in the field of memory, has proposed the following taxonomy of long-term memory, based on the functions of memory systems (taken from Squire, 2004).

As Figure 7.1 shows, long-term memory systems are arranged in a hierarchical way. The first branching point marks the difference between declarative and non-declarative memories. **Declarative memory** refers to knowledge about facts and events. It is recollected consciously and can be verbalised for communication. This is the type of memory referred to when the word 'memory' is used in everyday language. It is also the type of memory that scientists refer to when they talk about **amnesia** (see the section on amnesia at the end of the chapter). Declarative memory holds representations of the world that can be used as models to understand it and predict future events.

Declarative memories are consciously recollected and may be manipulated in short-term memory. These common features do not make all declarative memory records the same. On the basis of empirical evidence, we can distinguish between two subtypes of declarative memory: semantic and episodic memory. **Semantic memory** stores general knowledge about the world, including facts, meanings and **concepts**. Examples of knowledge stored in semantic memory are 'Jupiter is the largest planet of the solar system' or 'The psychologist Jean Piaget was Swiss'. An important characteristic of semantic memory is that it is not related to specific experiences. By contrast, **episodic memory** stores memories of events that are associated with a specific place

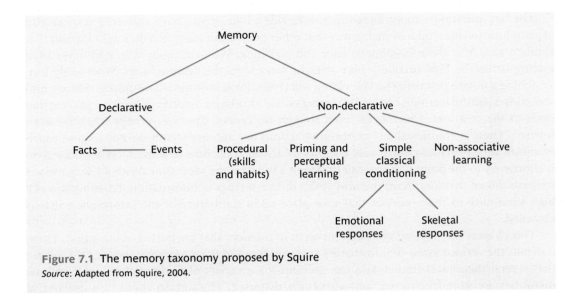

Figure 7.1 The memory taxonomy proposed by Squire
Source: Adapted from Squire, 2004.

and time. Episodic memories use records from semantic memory, but combine them according to a specific event that colours the memory with a particular flavour. The recollection of an episodic memory leads to re-experiencing the original event, though with less intensity. The subset of episodic memory that contains important events in one's own life, such as the first kiss, is called **autobiographical memory**. So, the fact that you had cereal this morning for breakfast is an episodic memory but not an autobiographic memory, unless the cereal led to some food poisoning requiring hospitalisation, in which case it would be considered as autobiographic memory.

Non-declarative memories are very different. They are related to the notion of performance. These memories are often the modification of an existing specialised performance system. For example, when you learned how to ride a bicycle, you had to learn to control your balance on the narrow points of contact made between the two wheels and the ground, by making subtle adjustments in your motor system (i.e. posture and motion). Another example is learning to swim: you actually learn a pattern of coordinated motor movements that makes you float. Thus non-declarative memories are expressed through behaviour rather than recollection. The following sections explain clearly the content and functioning of each memory system, starting with semantic memory.

Stop and Think Yet another taxonomy

Memory systems can be classified according to different criteria. Each set of criteria is going to generate a different tree of relationships between any two memory systems. Try to classify the memories that are under conscious control and those that are not. Do you see any overlap with the classification offered by Squire's taxonomy?

Declarative memories

Semantic memory

Semantic memory holds many different types of knowledge. To begin with, let us consider facts, such as forenames. Facts do not require a long period of learning; for example, if you are told that *Paco* is the Spanish diminutive of *Francisco*, you learn this rapidly. However, with experience, we develop more complex memory structures. These memory structures play the role of models that help us understand the world. For instance, we have constructed an internal model of a *chair*, but also of the more abstract concept of *freedom*. These examples highlight the fact that semantic memory encodes different types of knowledge that vary in complexity. Scientists have identified several ways in which memory can encode complex semantic memories. The most important memory structures used to store complex information are concepts, schemas and scripts. (The SQ3R method presented in Chapter 1 for facilitating learning actually helps with the acquisition of these three types of memory structure.)

Concepts are a central kind of semantic memory; in fact, they are so important that we will devote an entire chapter to them (Chapter 8). For the time being, we can define a concept as a memory structure that encodes a **chunk** of information referring to an object or a category of objects. For example, *pigeon* and *chair* are concepts. To illustrate, please close your eyes and describe what a chair is. Even though not all chairs correspond point to point to your internal model, you are able to recognise them as such. This shows that internal models have some flexibility. To appreciate the variety of semantic memories further, consider the idea of *freedom*. How would you describe freedom? It is likely that such an abstract concept (compared to the concept of *chair*) will lead to a different type of description. The notion of a concept is used to formalise how we understand the world. Chapter 8 will discuss how single concepts are encoded. Here, we focus on other complex memory structures, which are often concerned with how we approach objects and events in our everyday lives.

Schemas are organised memory structures that relate several chunks of information in a task-orientated, context-dependent manner. Schemas are built up out of our past experiences. Their main function is to organise and thus stabilise our perception of the environment. Schemas consist of two parts: a **core** containing constant information, and **slots** containing variable information. For example, the schema for a *room* contains the information that rooms have a floor and a ceiling (as this is true for all rooms, this corresponds to the core of the schema), but also that rooms can have a number of doors and a number of windows (as the exact numbers will change from room to room, this variable information is encoded in the slots of the schema).

How does a schema affect our memory? Brewer and Treyens (1981) asked participants to wait in an office while the experimenter was checking for another participant. Once the experimenter returned, the participants were told to go in another room and were unexpectedly asked to recall the items in the office. As expected, participants recalled all the items that would usually be present in an office. But the surprising result was that some participants recalled having seen books when there were actually no books in the office. This false memory is easy to explain if one assumes that participants did not instantiate their schema of an office with the information that there were no books in it, probably because they did not notice the absence of books. Schemas usually help but they may trick memory as well.

An important kind of schema is the **script**, which was introduced by Schank (1975). Scripts are schemas for sequences of events. The events are linked to each other so that the representation integrates events and cues. The restaurant script, for instance, lists the events that occur when one enters a restaurant as a customer. The beginning of such a script may be a sequence such as the following:

1   Entering the restaurant
2   Reading the menu
3   Choosing the dishes
4   Calling on the waiter
5   Ordering the food
6   Eating
7   Paying
8   Leaving the restaurant.

In this example, each step includes information about how the sequence of events develops; a more complete example would include the conditions that may trigger an event or put an end to it. Scripts are goal-orientated memory structures. They provide information about which events are expected and which are not in a given context. For example, the restaurant script is activated when you enter a restaurant and the doctor script is activated when you go to the doctor. When a script is activated, it is used as a framework to understand the events. Accordingly, it leads to expectations about how the environment is likely to change in the next minutes. A waiter asking you whether you prefer to have chicken or beef for dinner sounds fairly natural, but your doctor asking such questions would be very odd indeed. Scripts are memory structures that allow one to predict future events in the world. They stabilise our perception in that we just pick up the necessary information to understand what is going on. Since they lead to automatic inferences about the environment, scripts are used to understand written stories.

Consider the example put forward by Abelson (1981, p. 715): *'John was feeling very hungry as he entered the restaurant. He settled himself at a table and noticed that the waiter was nearby. Suddenly, however, he realized that he'd forgotten his reading glasses.'* Immediately, we can draw a link between the glasses and the menu and realise the difficulty confronting John. Scripts are developed as a result of the many occasions that put us in a similar situation. You have to go many times to the restaurant to integrate all the events that typically occur and link them to one another. During our life, we come across many typical situations, such as going to a doctor, shopping, and eating in a restaurant. Each of these situations is characterised by a set of features that make it belong to a particular class of situation. Going to the doctor follows a simple script: salutations, description of symptoms, diagnosis and medication. The questions will be different if the doctor is a urologist or a neurologist but the general procedure and thus the main script will remain the same. We can therefore consider that the script encodes a class of situations. Scripts have been widely used in artificial intelligence to program computers so that they can simulate human behaviour or train people to respond correctly to typical situations.

Semantic networks

A very influential model of the structure of semantic memory was put forward by Collins and Quillian (1969), and further revised in Collins and Loftus (1975): the **semantic network**. In Collins and Quillian's model, knowledge is captured in tree-like memory structures. The basic component of memory is the **node**, which encodes objects, living beings, and so on. For example, the concept of a *bird* is coded as single node. Attached to the node are the properties of the object coded. For example, the node coding for *bird* may contain the information that birds have wings, can fly, and have feathers. Similarly, the node coding for *canary* will specify that canaries are yellow and can sing. However, the model is not a mere collection of objects; it also provides mechanisms to explain how we associate objects to one another. Collins and Quillian posited that nodes are hierarchically connected. For example, the concept of a canary is subordinated to that of a bird. Consequently, the node canary inherits the properties of birds: it has wings, can fly and has feathers. The structure of memory can thus be defined as a network where knowledge is arranged in a hierarchical manner. You can find a more extended example in Figure 7.2.

This model provides a means to encode a considerable amount of information in a single node. Consider the 'canary' node, for example. It inherits not only the properties of birds, but also the properties of the animal category (has skin, can move, eats), as birds belong to this category. Hence, a single concept can inherit, and be qualified by, a large number of properties. If memory is really a network as proposed by Collins and Quillian, then moving from one node to another in order to explore the inherited properties of an object should require a small amount of time. Collins and Quillian tested this prediction in a simple experiment. They asked participants to check the veracity of simple sentences. Participants were presented with statements such as 'canaries can fly', 'canaries eat' and 'birds can talk', and had to point out whether the statements were true or false. The results were consistent with Collins and Quillian's theory in

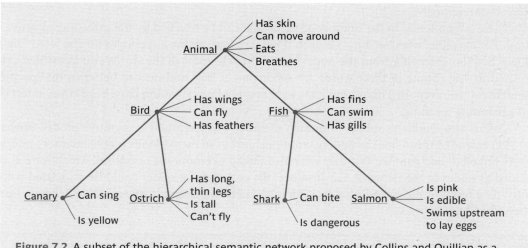

Figure 7.2 A subset of the hierarchical semantic network proposed by Collins and Quillian as a model of semantic memory
Source: Collins and Quillian, 1969.

that the time necessary to confirm that 'canaries are birds', which requires traversing one connection according to their model, is shorter than the time necessary to confirm that 'canaries are animals', which requires traversing two connections.

The model was the focus of intense research in the early 1970s and had to face much criticism. The hierarchical structure of semantic memory imposes severe constraints on the diffusion of activation. For example, it was assumed that, in order to check for the truth of a sentence such as 'canaries have skin', the activation goes from canary to bird, then to animal and finally reaches the property skin. In line with this logic, the fact that both canaries and penguins are birds implies that the response time to check the sentence 'canaries are birds' should be the same as the time necessary to check the sentence 'penguins are birds'. However, many experiments (e.g. Juola and Atkinson, 1971; Rips *et al.*, 1973) have shown that not all assumptions of Collins and Quillian's (1969) model are consistent with the empirical evidence, thus casting doubts on the model. These and other issues led Collins and Loftus (1975) to propose a new model, in which the hierarchical structure of the model was eliminated. Concepts are connected in a network with no constraint as to how related concepts should be organised. For example, the concept 'mammal' is in no way more or less important than the concept 'dog'. In addition, the activation of one concept does not require the activation of the other. This freedom in the dynamics of the model allows information to propagate in every possible direction and provides memory with a considerable amount of flexibility. An example of the portion of knowledge of an individual is provided in Figure 7.3.

A central notion in the 1975 version of the model is that of **spreading of activation**. Telling someone the word 'car' will activate the node for 'car'. The activation will then spread to all the connected nodes such as 'bus' or 'street'. The level of activation is then spread further from any active node to any associated node. (For an example of this, see Box 2.3 in Chapter 2.) The fact that the revised model did not include a hierarchy had the consequence that any node could activate any other node. The semantic network is now free from constraints, and activity can spread unreservedly.

There are no limits to the number of items that can be touched by the spreading of activation. For example, when writing a report, if you are looking for a synonym for the word 'big', the activation spreading from the node 'big' will touch upon all the words you know that are related to 'big'. Some of these words are synonyms of 'big' and may fit better in the specific sentence of your report. This example shows that spreading activation has a huge effect in terms of generating meaning.

Collins and Quillian's model of human memory was essentially a cognitive model. Bower (1981) extended this model by adding emotions. Just as in the previous model, memory nodes were linked to one another, but they were also linked to emotional responses, which were also coded as nodes in the network. For instance, the concept of a spider could be associated with fear. As a result of the spreading activation in the network, seeing a spider would generate fear (see also Chapter 14).

Stop and Think Identity
Considering that our memory stores our past experiences and that these shape our future behaviour, can our identity be reduced to our memories?

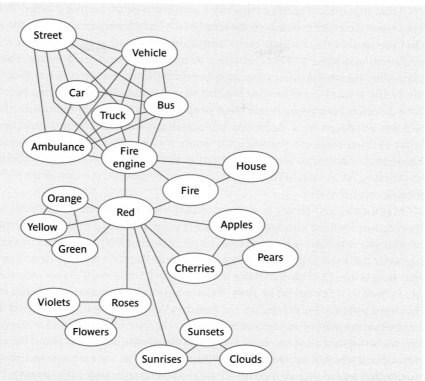

Figure 7.3 A subset of the nonhierarchical semantic network proposed by Collins and Loftus as a model of semantic memory
Source: Collins and Loftus, 1975.

Memory for events

So far, we have considered semantic knowledge: knowledge referring to general facts. However, many memories have such a strong personal colour that psychologists have believed for decades that they are encoded in specific memory structures. This intuition has turned out to be correct. Episodes of our life are encoded in another form of memory: episodic memory. As noted above, **episodic memory** refers to memory for the events that people have experienced on their own and that can be situated in time and space. A subclass of episodic memory, called **autobiographical memory**, concerns personal experiences that are important in one's life. Your first date, for example, is unique in the sense that you cannot repeat it or change it, nor can you improve its memory. Actually, if you close your eyes and re-experience the event, you may feel what you felt then. The experience cannot be replaced by another one. Other events in one's life, such as witnessing a car accident, are also personal memories that do not encode general knowledge.

Stop and Think Negative memories should fade away

Autographical memory allows us to re-experience past experiences. Yet, if these experiences are negative and thus likely to be detrimental to health, why is it that they do not fade away with time?

Autobiographical memory includes another type of memory called **flashbulb memories**. These memories are formed whenever an event has a strong emotional resonance for the person. On hearing about a dramatic event, a memory is formed as an image. The term was first coined by Brown and Kulik (1977) and refers to unexpected and vivid events. Examples of flashbulb memories are what Americans remember doing when they first heard about the 9/11 attack on the World Trade Center or what the British remember doing when first hearing about the 7 July 2005 London bombings. It has been proposed that flashbulb memories show little forgetting and are produced by a dedicated biological mechanism: modulation (Brewer, 1992). Many types of memories are formed in a brain region called the hippocampus (see Chapter 3). Emotional systems can modulate activity in the hippocampus and thus accelerate the formation of memory. As a result of this dynamic aspect of emotion, memories are built in one shot rather than in several trials.

Methodological issues have been raised about flashbulb memories, which question the mechanism we have just described. Since it is not ethical to traumatise participants for the sake of studying memory, it is impossible to generate flashbulb memories in the laboratory. To circumvent this ethical problem, Winningham *et al.* (2000) had the neat idea of testing participants in real life. O. J. Simpson is a famous American football player who was accused of killing his ex-wife and her friend in 1994. After a long and extensively mediated trial, the verdict was delivered publicly six years after the murder. Winningham and colleagues assessed the memories of two samples of students. One sample was tested five hours after the verdict and the other sample was tested after one week. Both samples were questioned about the characteristics of the situation in which they learned about the verdict (to assess memory accuracy) and how relevant this verdict was to them (to establish the emotional relevance of the event). The participants had to fill in a similar questionnaire eight weeks after the reading of the verdict. The results show major inconsistencies between the initial report and the report eight weeks after. These inconsistencies were more marked for the group that was tested immediately after the event. This finding constitutes strong evidence against the view that flashbulb memories are built in one shot. The conclusion might well be that flashbulb memories are normal memories associated with a high degree of confidence (Talarico and Rubin, 2003).

Another important topic in the field of personal memories is **eyewitness testimony** (Wells and Olson, 2003). This type of memory has an impact beyond the field of psychology. In many countries, eyewitness testimony is considered as acceptable evidence in trials; it is important, therefore, to ensure that the facts reported by witnesses are reliable, as they are sometimes key to establishing whether suspects are guilty or not. Eyewitness testimony is a very good illustration that visual memory does not work like a camera. As memories are consolidated over time, they might be distorted if they are not consolidated. The seminal studies on eyewitness testimony were carried out by Elisabeth Loftus and her co-workers in the 1970s. The experimental paradigm consisted of showing short video clips displaying simple events, such as a car accident at an intersection. Then, Loftus asked the participants about what they saw. Loftus and Palmer (1974) found that participants' perception of what occurred depended upon the way the question was put to them. Asking how fast the vehicles were running when they *smashed into* each other yielded higher speed estimates that asking how fast they were running when they *hit* each other. This experiment, as well as similar experiments carried out by Loftus and colleagues, shows that memories are fragile. Loftus went on to further investigate the vulnerability of memory. Together with Zanni (Loftus and Zanni, 1975), they showed participants a movie of a car accident that did not contain any broken headlight. Participants were asked whether they had seen *the* or *a* broken headlight. Participants asked about *the* broken headlight were more likely to report seeing one than participants asked about *a* broken headlight.

Loftus's research raised the crucial question as to whether memories can be altered or even invented. Surprisingly, it turns out that people can recall events that have never occurred. False memories can refer to events as inconsequential as being lost in a shopping mall (see Box 7.1), having a ride in a hot-air balloon (see Box 7.2) or remembering a road sign (see Box 7.3). They can also refer to impossible events such as abduction by space aliens (Clancy, 2005)! Such experimental results would be mere anecdotes if our memories did not impinge on our attitudes towards objects or people. Geraerts *et al.* (2008) tried to make a pool of 180 participants believe that, as children, they became ill after ingesting egg salad. While only a minority was sensitive to the manipulation, the effect was long lasting: four months after the experiment, this minority still avoided egg-salad sandwiches. The influence of memories on our actual behaviour is thus noticeable.

Such laboratory manipulations show the fragile nature of memory, but are laboratory manipulations as reliable as real-world experience? To answer this question, Yuille and Cutshall (1986) contacted witnesses of a real dramatic event where a shop owner killed a robber. Several months after the event occurred, the witnesses were still very accurate in the description of events from real life. Thus, it seems that emotionally laden events lead to vivid and robust memories. This natural experiment casts doubt on the idea that people are not accurate when remembering events. The results of Loftus's studies on the one hand and Yuille and Cutshall's study on the other teach us two interesting lessons. First, normal memories are fragile and may be distorted. Second, emotionally loaded memories are less sensitive to manipulations.

Box 7.1 RESEARCH CLOSE-UP: Shopping mall

The purpose of Loftus and Pickrell's (1995) study was to implement a false memory. Such a deception occurs rarely in psychology today and is to be used with caution to avoid the risk of harming anybody (see Box 7.2). The experiment had two phases. In the first phase, interviews with participants' relatives were conducted to identify three important events of the participants' childhood. During this interview, the experimenters checked that the participants have never been lost in a shopping mall. In the second phase, a booklet was sent to the participants. It included the three real events, as reported by the relatives, and a fictional one: being lost in a shopping mall. Upon receipt, the participants were called to schedule two interviews to talk about these events. In the first interview, the participants went through any possible detail that could be retrieved from memory. The interviewer pressured by asking for details and comparing the participants' recall of the event to the description given by the relatives. In the second interview, the participants underwent the same procedure and were eventually debriefed about the true purpose of the study. Out of the 24 participants, six 'remembered' the false event in both interviews. An astonishing demonstration that encouraging people think about a false event can sometimes create a new memory!

Box 7.2 RESEARCH CLOSE-UP: **Ethical issues in psychology**

How far can psychologists go to understand the workings of the mind? To discuss this difficult question, let us take a concrete example. Wade *et al.* (2002) doctored a photograph to make participants believe, contrary to reality, that they had had a hot-air balloon ride when they were children. The procedure was as follows. In a first phase, they asked a selected set of confederates to recruit a family member who would be the 'target' for the implant of the false memory. The confederates then provided a true photograph of each target, taken during their childhood. In a second phase, the experimenters used computer-assisted techniques to design a photograph where the targets appeared in a hot air balloon. Finally, the targets were called on for three interviews. Typically, the interviewer reassured the participants if they failed to retrieve the event at the first trial, but still pressed for details. The results revealed an astonishing trend: the more interviews were conducted, the more the targets tended to recall false events about the air balloon ride. A real brainwash!

This experiment, together with the ones carried out by Loftus and colleagues, shows that memories can be distorted: for example, by using doctored material. Beyond its interest for psychology, this experiment also poses the question of the kind of techniques that can be used by psychologists. The limit of how far scientists are allowed to manipulate people for the sake of scientific enquiry is a difficult one to set. On the one hand, if such studies are not conducted, we might not know the answer to crucial aspects of human cognition. On the other hand, it is difficult to set a clear line between ethically acceptable and misguided research. Many national psychological societies have taken measures to limit unethical research, and have provided guidelines for all students and academics undertaking psychological research. For example, the *American Psychological Association* emphasises the importance of confidentiality in using the participants' data. It is also good practice to inform the participant about the purpose of the study if this does not introduce noise in the data. Except in very rare cases, there is no need to intrude into participants' privacy, invade their social sphere or submit them to deception, as in Wade *et al.*'s (2002) study. Obviously, research projects should be compliant with law.

Box 7.3 CLASSIC EXPERIMENT: **Remembering what never occurred**

Chapter 4 has taught you that we can see things that do not exist. It turns out that we can also remember things that never occurred. Elisabeth Loftus, David Miller and Helen Burns (1978) published an article reporting six experiments that tested how much distortion can be introduced in the formation of one's memory. The typical procedure is simple. Participants are exposed to a series of items like in any other recognition task. Following this, they are asked to complete some task, such as filling a questionnaire. This intermediary task between stimulus presentation and recall aims to distort the participants' memories by introducing false elements. Finally, there is a recognition test.

In one classical experiment of Loftus *et al.*'s article, the participants were shown a series of slides (much like a movie) depicting an accident where a car hit a pedestrian. The critical slides were picturing a car at a crossroads. For half the participants, there was a STOP sign next to the car and, for the other half, there was a YIELD sign (see Figure 7.4).

Figure 7.4 Car at the crossroads
Critical slides used in the acquisition series.
Source: Slides used in Loftus *et al.*, 1978. Reprinted with permission.

In the second phase of the experiment, participants were given a questionnaire with several questions, one of which was phrased as follows: 'Did another car pass the red Datsun while it was stopped at the STOP sign?' The crucial point is that the sign was either consistent or inconsistent with what the participants had seen. In other words, some of the participants who actually saw a STOP sign were asked about the red Datsun while it was stopped at the YIELD sign. Then, after 20 minutes spent completing an irrelevant task, participants had to complete a recognition test. Slides were displayed by pairs and participants had to point out which one was displayed in the first phase of the experiment. Here lies the surprise: participants who were misled by the information in the questionnaire were more prone to recognise the wrong sign – that is, the participants who had seen a STOP sign and were then questioned about the YIELD sign recognised more often the YIELD sign as the correct answer than the participants who were not misled. They remembered what had never occurred!

It is important to make a distinction between visual illusions and false memories. Visual illusions are real experiences of a non-existing reality; false memories are real memories of a perceptual experience that did not occur.

Stop and Think Memory and adaptation
Memories of the past, such as those induced by Geraets *et al.* (2008), influence our attitudes towards objects. What is the practical interest of this link between memory and behaviour? And how could it lead to difficulties in adaptation?

Prospective memory

Another type of declarative memory is **prospective memory**, which can be defined as the ability to programme oneself to retrieve information from memory at a given point in the future. The target of the memory is typically an action (e.g. 'When I get to the office this afternoon, I must call John'). This type of memory differs radically from all others forms of memory considered in this book in that it is the only one to concern the future and not the past (retrospective memories).

We can distinguish between two types of prospective memory: *event-based* ('I will call John on my arrival') and *time-based* ('I will call John at 7 pm'). Logie *et al.* (2004) tested whether prospective memory imposes a high demand on working memory. To do so, they asked participants to simultaneously complete a typical working memory task (arithmetical operations) and a prospective memory task. If prospective memory uses part of the working memory resources, then a more complex task should impair prospective memory performance more. The authors tested their hypothesis with both time- and event-based tasks. In the time-based task, participants had to press a space bar on a computer every three minutes. The event-based task consisted in saying 'animal' each time an animal appeared in a 17-minute film. Two levels of difficulty were implemented in the arithmetical task. The results showed that high-demanding arithmetical operations impinge more on prospect memory performance, demonstrating that prospect memory and working memory use the same resources.

Research has demonstrated that, when we use prospective memory and wait for the relevant cue, we mobilise part of our attentional resources to monitor the prospective time or event. The advantage of the monitoring strategy is that we do not miss the cue (whether time or event based) so that the action is performed in due time. However, waiting for a cue that shows up a long time after the prospect memory has been formed incurs a high cost. McDaniel and Einstein (2000) have proposed that prospective memory is underpinned by similar mechanisms to retrospective memory. They suggest that an association is formed between the cue and the action to perform. Then, when the person perceives the cue, the activation spreads to the action, triggering its execution.

Forgetting

The usual and most widespread conception of **forgetting** is the one of a mere loss of information. However, research has shown that different types of forgetting occur simultaneously. A first central distinction can be made between pathological forgetting and normal forgetting. It may seem surprising to qualify a loss of information as normal, but it is reasonable to assume that one does not need to record all the information received from the environment. Most of what we see or hear is of no relevance to what we do. Given that memory has clear-cut limits in terms of speed of processing, it is easy to conclude that forgetting is necessary: a piece of information that is not going to be useful in the future should be dismissed. This line of reasoning also provides an explanation of what can be considered as pathological forgetting: a form of forgetting that deletes potentially useful information. We discuss pathological forgetting later in this chapter, when we deal with amnesia.

Normal forgetting refers both to the inability to access the information that is still stored, just like when your computer does not find an existing file on the hard drive, and the actual deletion of this information, just like when your favourite files were erased by a computer virus. Another useful analogy for the first case is that of an encyclopaedia. In order to access the huge amount of information in an encyclopaedia, we need an index. When part of the index is damaged (e.g. because the pages are not readable), we cannot access the relevant information. Applied to long-term memory, this analogy means that to access semantic and episodic information (the content of the encyclopaedia), we need an index. This index consists of *retrieval cues*: that is, cues that make it possible to reach a node in long-term memory. For example, the cues 'mouse', 'smart', 'cute' and 'Disney' are likely to elicit the concept of 'Mickey Mouse'. But if we delete part of the index, say 'mouse' and 'smart', and are left with the cues 'cute' and 'Disney', then we are unlikely to retrieve the node 'Mickey Mouse', given the many Disney characters that are cute. When part of the index is damaged, information stored in long-term memory cannot be accessed any more, although it is still there. Memory traces are typically indexed in different ways, and it is often possible to access a trace that was forgotten using a different set of cues. In our example, using the cues 'Minnie Mouse' and 'Goofy' might do the trick.

The second type of forgetting relates to deletion of memory traces. We do not need all the information we have come across in our life to make correct decisions in the future. The information that is no longer useful can be discarded. Of course, our brain does not know for sure whether some information will be useful or not in the future, and can only estimate a probability for this based on how useful this information was in the past. Unlike computer systems, there is no recycle bin where memories are put for immediate and definitive deletion. Rather, memories fade away gradually with time. Naturally, the more robust the memory, the more time will be required to delete it. This natural phenomenon is difficult to study, as most laboratory experiments last one hour or less. It is difficult to ask a participant to come on a regular basis (e.g. twice a month) over a long period of time (e.g. five years). Because of this methodological problem, only a few experiments have addressed the question of how memories stored in long-term memory fade away, with the noticeable exceptions of studies by Bahrick and Conway (Bahrick, 1984; Conway *et al.*, 1991). More recently, Bahrick *et al.* (2008) conducted a study about how forgetting occurs over the long term. They contacted 276 alumni who had graduated up to 54 years before. Participants were asked to provide their grades from memory and to rate how confident they were. These grades were then compared to the real grades, which were retrieved from the school's archives. Two types of error were distinguished. When a course was not recalled and thus a grade not retrieved, this was counted as an error of omission. When a grade was provided but was not accurate, this was counted as an error of commission.

Three aspects of Bahrick *et al.*'s (2008) study are of interest. First, a mathematical function could relate memory loss and time. Second, loss of information was distinguished from memory distortion. This distinction is important because it might help identify which factors distort our personal memories. Finally, the influence of academic performance was factored in. The sample was divided into three groups, each group being defined by their grade point average (GPA), so that accuracy of memory for academic life can be correlated with that of academic performance. Figure 7.5 shows the extent to which very old personal events are forgotten.

Figure 7.5 shows that, just like forgetting with STM, the decline in long-term memory accuracy follows a power function, in that there is a rapid decline after graduation followed by a slower decline with time. As we could have expected, the better the students the better the memory for grades. It is worth noting that, after nearly half a century, participants were able to recall 80 per cent of their grades accurately. It is likely that memory accuracy is even better for more important events in one's life.

Figure 7.6 shows that errors of omission increase with time, a result that is typical of normal forgetting. What is interesting is that errors of commission are fairly constant during life. Of these errors of commission, 81 per cent inflated the actual grade, making it better than it actually was. Distortions occur soon after graduation, remain constant during the retention interval, and are greater for better students and for courses students enjoyed most. This would suggest that memory of events that occurred long ago is distorted by how we felt about the event as much as by what actually occurred.

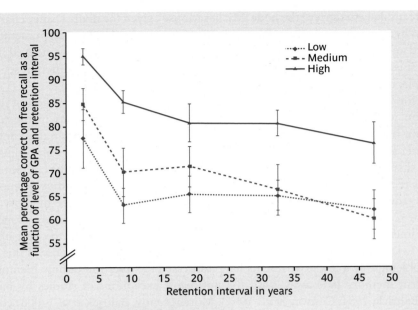

Figure 7.5 Bahrick *et al*. (2008) experiment: accuracy
Retention over a long period of time: percentage correct as a function of retention interval and GPA score.
Source: Data from Bahrick *et al.*, 2008.

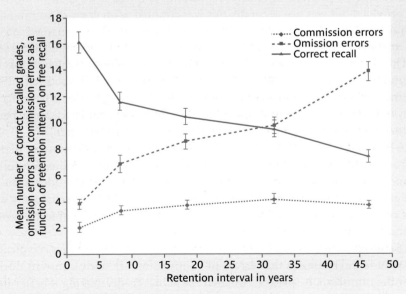

Figure 7.6 Bahrick *et al*. (2008) experiment: accuracy
Retention over a long period of time: types of errors as a function of retention interval.
Source: Data from Bahrick *et al.*, 2008.

Non-declarative memories

Non-declarative memories refer to a wide range of different memories. They may be as simple as **classical conditioning** or as complex as playing the piano. Still, they have in common the notion of action and thus are often related to performance. The retrieval of non-declarative knowledge (such as driving) does not require many resources from the cognitive system and in particular does not fill short-term memory. This feature makes non-declarative memories very useful in that they do leave free room for other processing to take place. However, the downside of this mode of functioning is not insignificant. As the retrieval of these memories is automatic, their execution cannot be controlled, as we have seen in Chapter 5. As a result, non-declarative memories lack flexibility.

Why do we have a memory for behavioural patterns? For their survival, all animals depend on their ability to behave quickly and accurately. The ability of a given individual creature to adapt to the environment where it lives becomes crucial in the competition for resources. The broad distribution of non-declarative memories across the animal kingdom explains why a substantial amount of research on this form of memory has been done with animals. This is in contrast with studies considering declarative memories, which typically rely on language. The areas in the brain in charge of processing language are obviously specific to humans and, for this reason, it is difficult to study declarative memory in animals. For simple and non-declarative forms of learning, humans and mammals use the same parts of the brain, and thus studies can be carried out with animals as well.

Skill acquisition

What is so fascinating in the Olympic Games that makes hundreds of millions people watch the event every four years? The answer is: performance. The issue is how much better one can become with training. Michael Phelps won eight gold medals in swimming at the Beijing Olympics in 2008, breaking many previous Olympic and world records. The relationship with memory does not seem obvious at first sight. But let us consider a different view of swimming. We were all born with a built-in motor system. Swimming results from the modification of motor programmes so that our coordinated movements make us float and advance in water. As we do not know how to swim before training, the motor system has to learn a motor programme, a *how to* memory that enables it to perform specific actions. Improving the quality of the programme by engaging in training leads to improvement in performance. Training to swim is thus improving the quality of the motor programme in charge of making one person swim. Phelps has a very good motor programme served by a gifted body and physiology! Improvements in built-in performance systems are not restricted to motor systems. Low-level perception can also be improved, as is shown by **perceptual priming**, where the perception of a stimulus is enhanced by the earlier presentation of another stimulus. This is a form of non-declarative memory, because the perceiver cannot control how the stimuli are processed. (The topic of skill acquisition overlaps with that of expertise, and we will take up some of the issues of this section in Chapter 12.)

We start our analysis of skill acquisition with motor skills. The purpose of skill acquisition is to refine the representation of actions so that the task becomes effortless. Learning is the acquisition of more appropriate representations of actions: that is, learning correct movements according to the task demands until a threshold of acceptable performance is achieved. When you learn to swim, you first need to use a float until you are able to float by yourself. Improving beyond this first threshold does not relate to your ability to carry out the basic task, but rather to the ease and efficiency with which you can perform it. The relationship between training and improvement is not linear: that is, for a similar duration of training, the trainee improves more in the early than in the latter stages. This is well illustrated by an experiment by Salthouse (1986). Participants were asked to type digits displayed on a screen on two separate keypads. They had to use the left keypad if the digits were displayed with a large font and the right keypad if the font was small. The numbers were arranged using a standard telephone display on each keypad. Participants were asked to use a specific key mapping of the fingers so that learning was the same for everyone. A training session consisted first of 39 blocks of 100 digits each, during which the number of digits displayed at a time was manipulated. The participants underwent 20 training sessions.

Figure 7.7 shows performance as a function of training session. We can see that response time (between key strokes) does not decrease by the same amount between two sessions. This is an illustration of the fact that skill acquisition does not follow a linear pattern. Also, performance tends to reach a limit after the eighteenth session. Obviously, improvement in a motor performance is limited by physiology. Since you need a minimum amount of time to perceive the stimulus and then to actually move the fingers, response time cannot be inferior to the sum of these two durations.

We now turn our attention to perceptual priming, which is a perceptual form of memory. In a study using priming, Hamann and Squire (1997) aimed to show that perceptual memory is

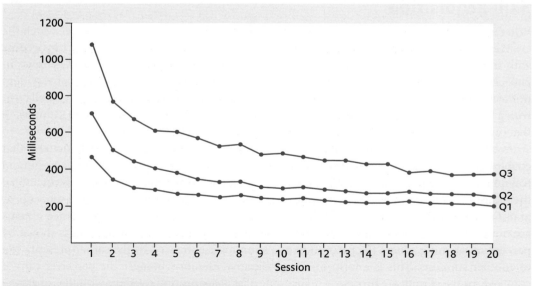

Figure 7.7 Salthouse's (1986) experiment

Mean performance (RT) as a function of training session. Means across the four subjects of the first (Q1), second (Q2 or median) and third (Q3) quartiles of the distribution of interkey intervals.

Source: Data from Salthouse, 1986.

independent of declarative memory. To do so, they wanted to establish that perceptual priming is an independent type of perceptual performance. The idea was to compare the performance of amnesic and healthy participants on declarative and priming tasks. The authors reasoned that, if declarative and priming memories were two facets of the same general memory system, then the loss in performance in one task should be mirrored in the other – that is, the loss of declarative memory should lead to a loss of priming performance. Thus, the amnesic patients should perform poorly in both tests, while the healthy should perform well in both tests. On the other hand, if priming and declarative memory are two separate memory systems, then the amnesics should perform well on the priming task but not on the declarative task, while the healthy participants should still perform well on both tasks.

Four amnesic patients and seven healthy participants took part in the experiment. Among the amnesic patients, Hamann and Squire paid particular attention to E.P., a patient who had a severe form of amnesia: E.P.'s amnesia was so severe that he did not recognise the experimenters after 40 sessions took place. There were four tasks: the two priming tasks tapped perceptual priming, and the two recognition tasks tapped declarative memory. In all four tasks, participants first read aloud a list of 24 words. In the *word-stem completion task*, participants had to complete a word based on its root. For example a trial may be 'P R I M _ _ _'. In the *perceptual identification task*, a word was briefly presented and immediately covered with a mask. Participants had to say which word was presented. In the first recognition-memory task, called *yes/no paradigm*, participants were presented with 24 novel and 24 studied items, one at a time; they had to indicate whether the item was (or was not) part of the list of words they had just read. In a second recognition task, a *forced-choice paradigm* was used. A pair of words made of one novel and one studied word was presented, and participants had to decide which word was in the first list. Note that with the recognition memory tasks, unlike the perceptual identification task, items remain on the screen until the participants reply.

The results (see Figure 7.8) showed that amnesic patients perform as well as healthy participants on priming tasks and, as expected, perform close to chance in declarative-memory tasks. In particular, E.P. performed at a level similar to healthy participants in word-stem completion, and was even superior to some of them in the perceptual identification task. In general, the pattern of results obtained by the group of amnesics was consistent with the notion that perceptual priming is a form of memory underpinned by different mechanisms from declarative memory.

If perception has its own form of memory, it is likely to improve with training. The idea that perceptual memory is highly specific and that it can be improved has been tested by Karni and Sagi (1991). As we have shown in Chapter 4, perception is carried out by integrating raw visual materials in a cascade of processing stages taking place unconsciously, until representations of objects are formed. Integration takes place in several stages, each stage accomplishing a specific function. The first stages of integration take place in early visual areas. The fact that these areas present **retinotopic maps** suggests that the perceptual skills acquired by training one specific region of the visual field will not be transferable to another sub-region.

Karni and Sagi's (1991) participants were asked to judge the orientation of rapidly presented stimuli (light bars presented for 10 ms). The central idea was to modify the orientation of some of the lines in every quadrant to assess how fast the eye detects the difference. To ensure that there was no eye movement, a decision task was superimposed. Prior to orientation judgement, the participants had to point out whether a letter in the centre of the screen was either a T or an L.

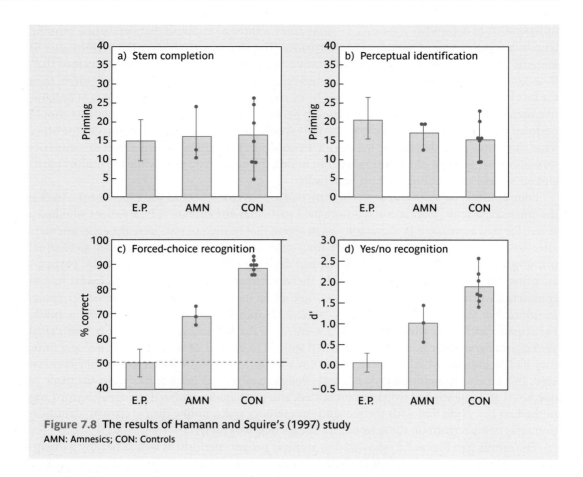

Figure 7.8 The results of Hamann and Squire's (1997) study
AMN: Amnesics; CON: Controls

The results showed that the rate at which performance improves is very high at first and then decreases. This result is similar to what has been observed with motor skills. After five to ten consecutive sessions, the participants reached a limit in improvement (the median improvement was 48 ms). The interesting result was that, whenever performance improved in one quadrant, the expertise acquired did not transfer to the other three quadrants. This result suggests that some form of learning takes place in early visual areas. This form of learning is automatic, and outside the control of attention – consciousness has no control or possible influence on the retrieval of the memory. In a sense, the perceptual system attunes itself to incoming stimuli and tasks.

Power law of learning

Many psychologists have been interested in quantifying the influence of training on performance. When performance is measured in response time and training in terms of number of trials, it is possible to plot performance as a function of trials (see Figure 7.9, left panel). The key result of this kind of research is that improvement in performance always follows a similar trend. There is a quick improvement at the beginning followed by adjustments of performance.

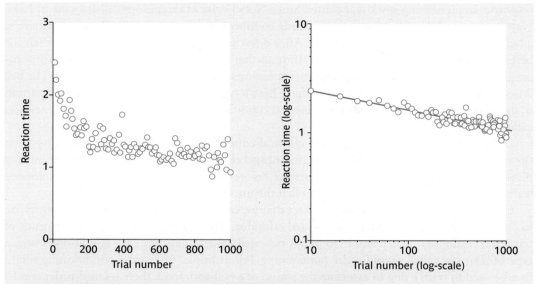

Figure 7.9 Illustration of the power law of learning (imagery data)
Left: data plotted in linear coordinates. Right: data plotted in logarithmic coordinates.

The change in performance becomes increasingly smaller until there is no noticeable change and the system has reached a limit in terms of performance. It is possible to fit such results with several mathematical functions. In a seminal paper, Newell and Rosenbloom (1981) showed that power functions fit this type of data very well. Power functions have the form: $y = ax^b$, and one interesting feature of these functions is that, when the two axes are expressed as logarithms, one obtains a straight line (see Figure 7.9, right panel). Thus, all sorts of learning and training experiments yield a straight line – the simplest function one can have. That is why psychologists often talk about the **power law of practice**.

Acquiring and changing habits

The scientific study of **habits** (acquired and unconscious dispositions to act in a given way) started at the end of the nineteenth century and has been dominated by behavioural experiments on animals. As a result of its history, we have inherited many terms that were introduced long ago. We consider in turn classical conditioning, instrumental conditioning, non-associative learning and consolidation.

Classical conditioning

If you present a piece of meat to a dog, it is going to salivate. The piece of meat is called the *unconditioned stimulus* because it does not require the presence of any other specific condition to be effective. For the same reason, the response is called the *unconditioned response*. Classical conditioning is the mechanism by which a new, neutral stimulus comes to elicit an automatic response. In pioneering work that earned him a Nobel Prize in Physiology or Medicine in 1904, Ivan Pavlov used the salivating reflex to study conditioning (Pavlov, 1927). He repeatedly rang a bell before presenting dogs with meat. After a few sessions, dogs started salivating when the bell rang, even in the absence of meat. A stimulus that elicits a response after a learning procedure is called a *conditioned stimulus*, and such a response is called a *conditioned response*. The bell is associated to the salivary reflex, so we have here a type of *associative learning*. In recognition of the importance of Pavlov's work on classical conditioning, this type of learning is sometimes called *Pavlovian conditioning*.

Let us summarise what characterises classical conditioning. First, the relationship between the unconditioned stimulus and the unconditioned response should be innate. In the learning phase, the conditioned stimulus is presented before the unconditioned stimulus. Following learning, the conditioned stimulus must elicit the unconditioned response.

Classical conditioning illustrates the fact that we can associate two elements in memory: an unconditioned stimulus and a conditioned stimulus. The pairing takes place as the result of temporal contiguity. It is possible to pair a new neutral stimulus with the conditioned one, a type of learning called *second-order conditioning*. For example, first-order conditioning might first be used to train a dog to associate the sound of a bell with food; then, second-order conditioning might be used to associate a light with the sound of the bell.

Instrumental conditioning

The second type of associative learning is **instrumental** (or **operant**) **conditioning**. It is concerned with how individuals select the most appropriate action from the repertoire of possible actions. The selection of appropriate actions in any given environment is the key to animal survival. At any moment in time, many actions can be performed in relation to the environment. Many of these actions do not have any effect. Some, under specific circumstances, might turn out to be fruitful. These actions thus have a utility regarding some goal, and this is what instrumental conditioning is helping to develop. For humans, this mechanism can be transposed to the exploration of new environments. Let us consider for example the first time you use a new piece of software. You try by clicking here or there until you get the effect you want. Each action is judged as to whether it is appropriate with respect to the outcome it yields, and this is learned by instrumental conditioning. Instrumental conditioning is thus the pairing between an action and its effect on the environment.

Let us consider a more controlled experiment. A rat is put in a box, which is equipped with three levers connected to mechanisms that are invisible to the rat. Pressing one lever delivers a small piece of food. Pressing any of the two other levers does not trigger any action. This kind of box was designed by Skinner, a leading behaviourist whom we have already met in Chapter 2, to test how the repertoire of the animal varies when we associate a positive or a negative outcome to a given behaviour. At the start of the experiment, the rat has never entered the box and has no experience of the levers. The probability of the rat pressing any one lever is 1/3. At some point, the animal will explore its environment and eventually will press the levers. When the lever yielding food is pressed, the rat associates the pressing of the lever to the effect of receiving food. Thus, the probability of the behaviour consisting of pressing the food-providing lever will increase. The food strengthens the probability of occurrence of the behaviour: it is a *reinforcer*. Whenever the outcome of an action is negative (e.g. an electric shock), the effect is to lower the probability of occurrence of the behaviour, and the stimulus is termed a *punisher*.

Many experiments using this paradigm have explored the notion of *discriminative stimulus*. For example, the effect of pressing the lever can only be effective if a red light is on. The animal thus learns that the action has an effect on the environment only when some specific conditions are met. The Skinner box also facilitates the provision of more or less food, thus enabling analysis of how the magnitude of the incentive changes the behaviour of the animal.

Non-associative learning

We end our exploration of human memory systems with the most basic forms of learning, habituation and sensitisation. They concern the modulation of the strength of an automatic response as a result of experience. **Habituation** is the progressive extinction of behaviour in response to a repetitive harmless stimulation. Habituation enables you to read this book without paying much attention to the background noise (e.g. the humming of your computer) that would otherwise disturb you. **Sensitisation** is the exact opposite: a magnification of behaviour in response to a meaningful stimulation. A practical joke of dubious value consists of frightening a friend. If you have been the target of such a joke, you may remember how sensitive you were to all stimuli just after having been frightened – you had been sensitised.

Most of our knowledge on the biological underpinnings of non-associative learning comes from studies that Nobel Prize winner Eric Kandel and his co-workers performed on a simple sea slug, the *Aplysia Californica* (Kandel, 1976). The interest in understanding the biology behind habituation and sensitisation is that it makes the understanding of other forms of memory much easier, because the same biological mechanisms (or variants of them) are in use.

All *Aplysias* have exactly the same neural circuits. A determined number of neurons, connected in the very same way, form a neural circuit that is strictly analogous from one individual to another. A simplified version of one of these circuits is presented in Figure 7.10. The *Aplysia* has a very simple and straightforward reflex: if you touch the siphon, the gill withdraws. As all *Aplysias* are similar, their circuits are inborn: all *Aplysias* withdraw the gill in response to a touch of the siphon. If you repeatedly but gently touch the siphon, the withdrawal will become slower and slower and will eventually not occur any more. This progressive extinction of a behavioural response is the typical end product of habituation. Whenever soft stimulations are applied often and repeatedly, the reflex vanishes for a long time. The habituation has thus led to changes in the *Aplysia's* long-term memory. For sake of *economy*, it is not worth learning a specific response to an innocuous stimulation.

Now, consider sensitisation with the *Aplysia*. If we touch the siphon and apply a shock to the tail, the animal withdraws the gill with vivacity. A later gentle shock on the siphon also elicits a vigorous withdrawal of the gill. As with habituation, if the first shock is followed by a period of calm and the next siphon touches are benign, the animal comes back to its baseline behaviour. However, repeated shocking of the tail will enhance responsivity, to the point where withdrawal is carried out whatever the intensity of the touch on the siphon. The neural circuits of *Aplysia* have also been used for studying the biological basis of classical conditioning (Kandel, 1976).

Stop and Think Brainstorming
Find ten different examples of memories that combine different memory systems.

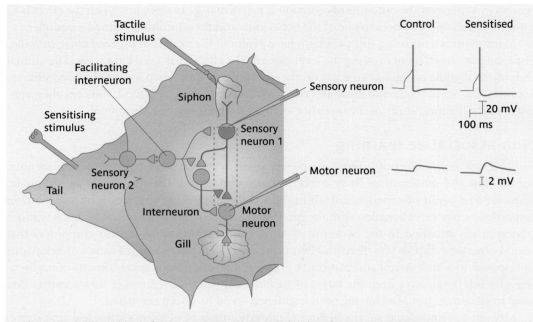

Figure 7.10 Illustration of the anatomy and neural circuits of the sea slug *Aplysia*
Sensitisation is produced by applying a noxious stimulus to the tail of the *Aplysia*, activating sensory neuron 2. This in turn activates a facilitating interneuron that enhances transmission in the pathway from the siphon to the motor neuron.
Source: Kandel *et al.*, 2000.

Consolidation

Those who play the guitar or the piano may want to read this section with particular attention. The fact that non-declarative memories depend upon rehearsal and are built gradually over time poses the question of what is the best training schedule: that is, do skills improve much if one trains two hours a day in one session or two sessions of one hour each? Baddeley and Longman (1978) carried out an experiment aimed at answering this question.

They went to a post office and recruited postal workers who were being trained on a new, mechanical letter-sorting system, where the correct postcode had to be typed in on a keyboard similar to a standard typewriter. Postal workers were randomly assigned to one of four possible training schedules. Baddeley and Longman manipulated both the number of sessions per day (one or two sessions) and the duration of the session (one or two hours). All groups were trained for 60 hours in total. All but one group underwent further training of 20 hours. After training, the participants were tested after one, three and nine months. Performance was assessed on the correct number of keystrokes per minute.

Figure 7.11 shows a series of counterintuitive results. First, after 60 hours of training, the group in which participants trained for one hour a day performed better than the group who received two hours of training a day. The second result of interest is that two sessions of one

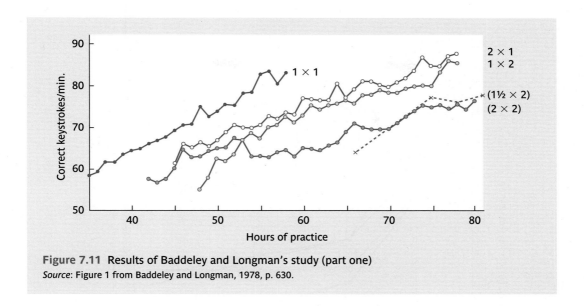

Figure 7.11 Results of Baddeley and Longman's study (part one)
Source: Figure 1 from Baddeley and Longman, 1978, p. 630.

hour each are more efficient than one session of two hours. This result is of key importance for applied psychology. It shows that distributed practice is better than massed practice. The third result of interest is that two sessions of two hours are worse than one session of two hours. This result shows the limit of improvement with distributed practice. It is not the multiplication of sessions that makes memory better.

Motor skills are thought to be robust – that is, they are supposed not to fade away with time. For example, once you have learned how to ride a bike, you know how to do it even after a long period of inactivity, without taking a refresher course. Let us now examine these ideas in the light of Baddeley and Longman's results. As shown in Figure 7.12, most of the participants had a drop of performance of about 30 per cent after nine months. This might seem like a huge drop in performance. However, one should remember that the participants were trained for only 80 hours and that they had no practice in nine months. Also, it is likely that the task was quite hard and that the postal workers did not have enough training to stabilise performance.

In sum, Baddeley and Longman's study has taught us that performance does not necessarily reflect the amount of time in training and that motor skills are robust. Do not spend ten hours in a row playing the guitar, but try to have shorter sessions more often!

Pathological forgetting

Most of cognitive psychology is concerned with normal functioning, typically trying to find out which cognitive processes carry out specific functions. However, the functions of memory are never more keenly felt than when the system is not working properly. The Ancient Greeks noticed this and were already interested in explaining the failures of memory. Hence, from the beginning, research on memory processing has placed strong emphasis on its failure. Cognitive

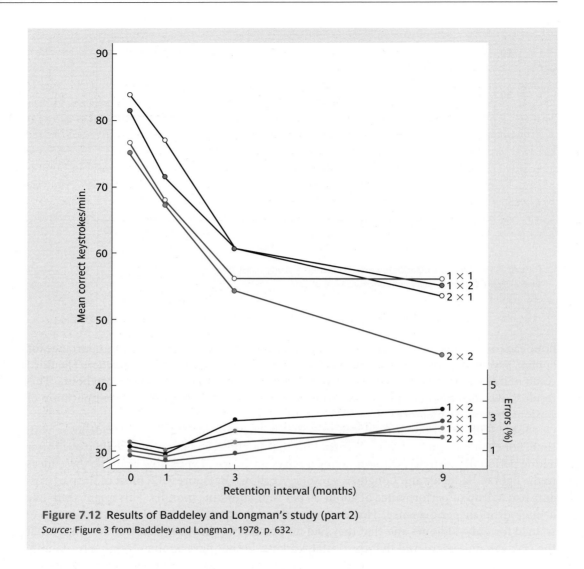

Figure 7.12 Results of Baddeley and Longman's study (part 2)
Source: Figure 3 from Baddeley and Longman, 1978, p. 632.

psychology and neuroscience have now much to say about memory failure. Memory pathologies are divided into two categories. **Retrograde amnesia** is the inability to recall part of your past. **Anterograde amnesia** is the inability to encode new memories. Note that the terms refer only to a set of symptoms and not to the causes of the pathology.

Retrograde amnesia typically occurs after illness or an accident. Contrary to common belief, the patient does not lose all memories at once. Rather, there is a gradual loss of memory. For example, consider a patient who had an accident in his mid-40s. He may still have memories of his childhood and teenage years intact. Then, he may suffer some memory loss from his young adulthood. Finally, the closer we get to the time of the accident or illness, the less reliable or indeed existent are the memories. Retrograde amnesia works backwards, and touches more recent events. The severity of retrograde amnesia depends on how deep into the past memories are erased. Unfortunately, owing to the fact that memories are often lost as a result of tissue damage, it is not possible to restore these memories.

Anterograde amnesia occurs whenever the anatomical brain structures in charge of storing new memories (e.g. the hippocampus) are damaged. The patient's memory will be forever limited to what they had experienced before the illness. This form of memory loss has a major negative impact on the patient's social and family life. Even though patients are as intellectually efficient as they were before the onset of the illness, they cannot perform tasks at appropriate moments. Obviously, this inability to know what to do means that patients are often unemployed, so seriously affecting their family life. As with retrograde amnesia, anterograde amnesia develops as a result of brain damage. As damage cannot be repaired, the disease is irreversible. Some pathologies show both retrograde and anterograde amnesia. An, unfortunately common, example is Alzheimer's disease (see Box 7.4).

Box 7.4 EVERYDAY APPLICATION: Alzheimer's disease

Alzheimer's disease (AD) is the most common form of dementia. Generally diagnosed after 65 years of age, it affects more than 25 million people worldwide. AD is characterised by a progressive loss of cognitive functions. Two of the first symptoms are difficulty in memorising new information (anterograde amnesia) and the loss of memories of the past (retrograde amnesia), starting with more recent events. Non-declarative memories tend to be spared; for example, patient suffering from AD can learn new procedural skills (Hirono *et al.*, 1997).

The causes of the disease are not yet known with certainty, but are thought to be related to changes at the cellular level (Toates, 2007). In particular, it is thought that the presence of abnormal tissue in the brain, known as 'neurofibrillary tangles' or 'senile plaques', leads to the destruction of neurons. This process appears to start with the medial temporal lobe, and in particular the hippocampus (see Chapter 3), which explains both the development of memory problems and the loss of spatial orientation shown by AD patients. As the disease progresses, the structural damage to the brain becomes considerable (e.g. atrophy of the structures in the medial temporal lobe, enlargement of sulci and shrinkage of gyri), and can easily be seen in images obtained with structural MRI (Frisoni *et al.*, 2010).

In a moving book that has been described as the 'greatest love story of our age', John Bayley, a former professor of English at Oxford, describes how AD affected the writing skills of his wife, Iris Murdoch (Bayley, 1998). Murdoch (1919–1999) was a noted writer and philosopher, selected by *The Times* as one of 'The 50 greatest British writers since 1945'. Her last novel, *Jackson's Dilemma* (1995), which was written after the onset of AD, was received politely but coldly by critics. Garrard *et al.* (2005) systematically compared Murdoch's last book with two of her previous novels (*Under the Net*, 1954, her first novel, and *The Sea, The Sea*, 1978, arguably her best book). They found a marked reduction in language complexity in *Jackson's Dilemma*. However, the effect was centred in vocabulary richness, while the use of **syntax** and the overall structure of the book were unaffected (see Chapter 9). Specifically, in her last book Murdoch used a smaller vocabulary more frequently. Garrard *et al.* concluded that this result is in line with previous research suggesting that the decline trajectories of syntax and vocabulary are different in AD.

Chapter summary

This chapter has surveyed the numerous types of memories that constitute long-term memory, and has reviewed the criteria used to describe how memory systems behave. First, there is the type of information they store. The main distinction here is between declarative and non-declarative memories. Second, there are the processes in charge of storing and retrieving memories. Some forms of memory are stored in one shot (e.g. flashbulb memories), while others necessitate many repetitions to reach an acceptable encoding level (e.g. skills). We can also distinguish the memories on the basis of whether they are accessible to conscious control. These criteria help establish a classification of our memory systems; however, you should keep in mind that another arrangement of these criteria would lead to an altogether different taxonomy.

Declarative memory is divided into semantic memory and episodic memory. Semantic memory relates to meanings and concepts. Semantic information can be put into words and can be used to make sense of the world. It can be combined to form more complex forms of memory such as scripts, which encode a typical sequence of events such as going to the doctor. Even though they are more complex, these memory records are used to interpret common situations. Episodic memory stores specific events of one's life. A subpart of episodic memory, called *autobiographical memory*, stores personal experiences that have special importance.

Non-declarative memories refer to many types of behavioural modulations. Perceptual and motor-skill acquisitions refer to gradual improvements in performance as a result of practice. While classical conditioning reflects the association of a stimulus with behaviour, operant conditioning is the modulation of the use of a particular behavioural pattern as a result of the feedback from the environment.

Records in real life might mix all kinds of memory. For example, a C major chord consists of the notes C, E and G. Such a piece of knowledge can be encoded in a verbal format or in a visual one (e.g. by visualising a keyboard). The two forms of coding coexist in musicians. Long-term memory is a huge database of records that vary in type and complexity and, further, that can be associated with each other. This high level of complexity makes it a rich body of information for us to use and underpins the performance of experts.

Further reading

The idea of retrieval cues acting as an index to long-term memory was proposed by Simon (1996) and plays an important role in CHREST (Gobet *et al.*, 2001), one of the cognitive architectures we discussed in Chapter 2. For memory disorders (and more), Oliver Sack's book (1986) *The man who mistook his wife for a hat* is an entertaining and useful read. It presents neurological diseases through a series of short stories. The book was published in the 1980s but is still a classic in the field for those who are willing to learn, without having to assimilate a daunting number of biological details. Practical implications of memory research can be found on several websites. That of Elisabeth Loftus (http://faculty.washington.edu/eloftus/) is of high relevance. The reader interested in understanding the biological underpinnings of all forms of memory can refer either to *Memory: From mind to molecules* (Squire and Kandel, 1999) or, for a more informal reading, to Kandel (2006).

PART 3

Complex cognition

Part contents

Chapter 8

Concept formation and categorisation

CHAPTER PREVIEW

☑ Concepts are important for interacting with the world, and thus for survival. They enable inferences and predictions to be made about the behaviour of objects and organisms, and are essential in the use of language.

☑ Classical theory, also known as defining attribute theory, proposes that we categorise objects and organisms using definitions. This is reasonable in the way we learn and use artificial categories, but less so with natural categories.

☑ According to the prototype approach, items to categorise are matched, feature by feature, to the best representative of each category, known as *prototypes*. The approach successfully accounts for a number of experimental data with natural categories, such as the presence of typicality gradients and the role of context. However, it fails to account for how we learn artificial categories and how we relate concepts to our general knowledge of the world.

☑ Researchers in the prototype tradition have noted that people tend to use hierarchies with three levels: superordinate, intermediary and subordinate. With many categories, one level has a special status, called the *basic* level, and this tends to be the intermediary level.

☑ Exemplar theories propose that we categorise items by comparing them, feature by feature, with all the memory traces of what we have perceived in our life. Just like prototype theories, these theories do a good job in explaining typicality gradients and the role of context. They are weaker at explaining how concepts are organised hierarchically and how they relate to other types of knowledge.

☑ Explanation-based theories propose that concepts are interwoven with other types of knowledge and that people use common-sense explanations to categorise objects.

☑ People use different strategies for categorising objects. The strategies they use are partly determined by cognitive limits in attention and short-term memory.

Introduction

Imagine that you lived in a world without concepts. You would not be able to classify any of the objects that fill your life – humans, cats and other animals, cars, books. You would look at your hand every time as if for the first time, and you would not be able to recognise your face. Spoken language would be a meaningless stream of sounds, and written language would be as bewildering as other types of visual information. You would not have a notion of self, and would not be able to recognise other humans as such. Clearly, conceptual knowledge is essential for living our lives: by categorising organisms and objects, we can be aware of their properties even though they may not be clearly visible at that instant, we can make inferences about them, and we can predict their behaviour. In short, conceptual knowledge enables us to interact with the environment (see Box 8.1).

In Chapter 7 we discussed several ways in which knowledge is represented in the mind. In this chapter we focus on conceptual knowledge, an essential aspect of semantic knowledge. As stated by Murphy (2002), concepts act as the 'glue' of our mental world. They enable our knowledge of the world – not only the physical, but also our personal and social worlds (see Box 8.2).

Tentatively, we can propose a few definitions – some of them will be qualified by what follows in the chapter. A **concept** may be defined as the building block of semantic knowledge (e.g. 'dog'). A **category** is a class of concepts that share some common properties (e.g. the members of the category 'animal' are living organisms capable of voluntary movement). A **natural category** (or **natural kind**) is a group of entities that exist in the natural world (e.g. 'fish' or 'flower'). An **artefact category** is a group of man-made objects that are designed with a specific goal or function in mind (e.g. 'boat' or 'computer'). A **nominal category** (or **nominal kind**) is a group of objects or ideas that are put together based on an arbitrary characteristic (e.g. the concept of a positive number, or the concept of the things that can be found in the office of the Prime Minister of Thailand).

Box 8.1 IN FOCUS: **Funes the Memorious**

If you want to uncover the mysteries of human concepts, the best way is not to read an introductory textbook on cognitive psychology (not even this one...) or even a monograph on concepts and categories. Instead, you should read the works of the Argentine writer Jorge Luis Borges, who, more than anybody else, has explored the conceptual world of humans. In his short story *The Aleph*, he tells how he saw the Aleph, 'the only place on earth where all places of the universe are seen from every angle, each standing clear, without any confusion or blending'. In another short story, *The Library of Babel*, he describes a library containing all books of 410 pages, including a book that is the perfect summary of all the books contained in this library. Borges speculates that this library contains all the information contained in all the books in any language, past, present and future. In *Funes the Memorious*, he tells the story of Ireneo Funes, a young Uruguayan, who, after suffering a horseback riding accident, had a perfect memory.

> He knew the forms of the clouds in the southern sky on the morning of April 30, 1882, and he could compare them in his memory with the veins in the marbled binding of a book he had only seen once, or with the feathers of spray lifted by an oar on the River Negro on the eve of the Battle of Quebracho. Nor were these memories simple – every visual image was linked to muscular sensations, thermal sensations, and so on. He was able to reconstruct every dream, every daydream he had had. Two or three times he has reconstructed an entire day; he had never once erred or faltered, but each reconstruction had itself taken an entire day. '*I, myself, alone, have more memories than all mankind since the world began,*' he said to me.
>
> (Borges, 1962)

In spite of all these memories, or rather because of them, Funes was not able to form concepts: 'It bothered him that the dog at three fourteen (seen from the side) should have the same name as the dog at three fifteen (seen from the front)'. Interestingly, Luria (1968) reports the real case of a mnemonist suffering from the same type of hypermnesia as Funes (although of course to a lesser extent), and notes that this individual also had serious difficulties using concepts.

Box 8.2 RESEARCH CLOSE-UP: **A small introductory experiment**

Psychologists have devised a large number of experiments to study the way concepts are represented and used by our cognitive system. Two main classes of experiment stand up. In the first class, a series of examples, which may belong to two or more categories, are presented, and the task is to correctly predict membership. Feedback is usually given after each attempt. In the second class of experiments, examples of well-known concepts are presented (e.g. 'apple', 'bird'), and participants have to respond in one of several ways: for example, by categorising them ('is an apple a fruit?') or stating the extent to which they are a good example of a given category.

Let us illustrate these two types of experiment by a simple example. First, consider the stimuli in Figure 8.1, hiding the labels with a sheet of paper. These items belong to one of two categories: 'glap' and 'bomp'. For each row, try to predict their category, and then look at the answer. Once you have done this, go through the items that belong to the 'glap' category, and rate, on a scale of 1 (not at all) to 7 (perfectly), how well they correspond to this category.

These two types of experiment have uncovered a large number of phenomena, and this chapter will discuss some of the most important of them. As you can imagine, several theories have been developed to explain these phenomena. These theories are traditionally grouped into four approaches – classical, prototype, exemplar and explanation-based – and the chapter will follow this convenient organisation.

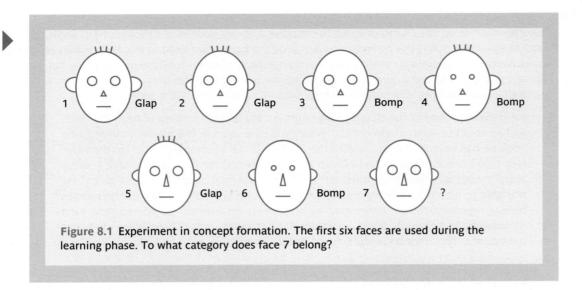

Figure 8.1 Experiment in concept formation. The first six faces are used during the learning phase. To what category does face 7 belong?

Classical theory of concepts

A natural way to consider concepts, which goes back to the Ancient Greeks (e.g. in the works of the great philosopher Aristotle), is to consider them as definitions. In this context, a **definition** is a rule containing features that are together *individually necessary and jointly sufficient* for category membership. 'Individually necessary' means that all members of the category have each of these features, and 'jointly sufficient' means that, when all these features are present in a given instance, this instance must be a member of the category. Features that are part of such a definition are called **defining features** (or **defining attributes**). To classify an object, one simply considers the features in the concept in turn and tests whether they are matched by the properties of the object being classified.

For example, a bachelor is defined as an adult male who is not married. If any of these features is missing, it means that a necessary feature is not present, and therefore the example is not a member of the category 'bachelor'. Obviously, an adult male who is married would violate the rule, and thus would not be a member of the category. If all three features are present, then we know enough to conclude that the person in question is a bachelor.

It is no accident that this approach has a mathematical beauty and logical elegance to it. Mathematics and logic use this kind of approach to categorise the objects they deal with. For example, a non-zero integer is either even or odd, but cannot be both, and the rule is that an integer is even if it can be divided by two and otherwise will be odd. Historically, this view has been favoured by philosophers (Frege, 1984; Pitt, 1999), linguists (Katz and Fodor, 1963) and psychologists influenced by philosophy (Bruner *et al.*, 1956).

Definitions are crystal-clear, and this has several important consequences. First, category membership is binary: that is, an object is either a member or not a member of a category. There is no intermediary solution. As former US President George W. Bush said to the governments of other countries after the 2001 bombing of the World Trade Center: 'Either you are with us, or you are against us.' Second, through its definition a concept will select *all the members* of the category, and *only its members*. Third, classification is not affected by context: that somebody is a bachelor is not influenced by the time of the day, the weather or the geographical location. Finally, concepts can be organised using a **hierarchy of inclusion relations**. A classic example is that of biological taxonomy: a mouse is a mammal; a mammal is a vertebrate; and a vertebrate is an animal. Another example is offered in Figure 8.2.

Empirical data supporting classical theory

In their book *The Study of Thinking*, Bruner *et al.* (1956) used geometrical shapes of various colours, size and number to study how people attain concepts. They used different types of concepts, but focused on the following three types. **Simple concepts** are defined by a simple attribute: for example, 'objects have to be triangles to belong to category X'. With **conjunctive concepts**, several attributes have to be met together: for example, 'objects have to be square *and* black to belong to category X'. Finally, **disjunctive concepts** require that at least one attribute is present: for example, 'objects have to be square *or* black to belong to category X'. Disjunctive concepts, which are rarely used in real life, were by far the hardest to learn.

In line with what we have said in Chapter 6, Bruner and colleagues also found that people found it difficult to identify the categories when information about previous trials had to be kept in short-term memory. By contrast, using external memory aids such as paper and pencil

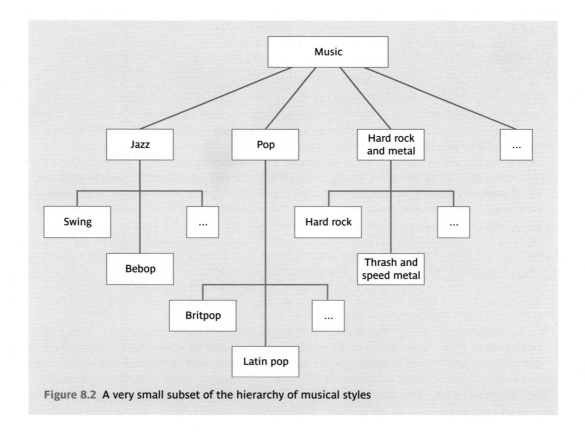

Figure 8.2 A very small subset of the hierarchy of musical styles

made the task much easier. Thus, limitations in attention and short-term memory led participants to develop a number of strategies, among which three were particularly prominent. With *successive scanning*, participants keep a single hypothesis in mind (e.g. 'square and blue'), and limit their attention to cases that offer a direct test of the hypothesis. With *conservative focusing*, participants start with a positive instance of the concept, and then alter this concept by changing only one feature at a time, testing its validity with each new positive instance, and ignoring the negative instances. For example, if 'square and blue' was the first positive item, participants could try 'square and red' as their next hypothesis (see Box 8.3 for a detailed example). *Focus gambling* is a similar strategy, except that more features can be changed. Crucially, the choice of strategy in this type of task is affected by constraints imposed by time pressure and limits in memory capacity (Simon, 1996). In fact, even if the optimal strategy were taught to participants, they would not be able to use it because it requires memory storage much larger that humans' short-term memory capacity.

Problems with classical theory

Problems have been identified with classical theory, both from theoretical considerations and experimental research. A first theoretical objection is that it is not clear how the sometimes

---

Box 8.3 RESEARCH CLOSE-UP: **Example of strategy use: conservative focusing**

The conservative focusing strategy is a strategy commonly used by participants. The first positive example is taken as the hypothesis, and then only one feature is changed when positive instances do not match the hypothesis. Negative instances are ignored. Let us illustrate this strategy using the stimuli displayed in Figure 8.1 and assuming that the task is to learn to identify faces that belong to the 'glap' category. The first face belongs to this category – it is *a positive instance* – so we choose its description as positive hypothesis: **large eyes, large ears, with hair and short nose**. The next face, which is also a positive instance, does not fully match the current hypothesis. Thus, we change our hypothesis by changing one feature so that it corresponds to the new face. We thus change the second feature from **large ears** to **small ears**, and keep the other features unchanged. So, our hypothesis is now: **large eyes, small ears, with hair and short nose**. The third and fourth faces do not belong to the category 'glap' – they are *negative instances* – so we do not change our hypothesis. The fifth face is a positive instance, but does not fully match the current hypothesis. So we change one feature that does not match: amend **short nose** to **long nose**, and the hypothesis is now: **large eyes, small ears, with hair, long nose**. The sixth face is a negative instance, so we ignore it. We can now deal with the last face, and test whether it matches our current hypothesis; three of the features are correct, but **without hair** should be **with hair**. So we decide that this face is not a member of the 'glap' category.

You might have noticed two interesting characteristics of this strategy. First, it throws away a lot of information: the negative instances are not used to revise the hypothesis, and the old trials are simply forgotten. Second, and this actually justifies the first characteristic, this strategy does not impose much load on short-term memory, as the only thing that has to be memorised is the last hypothesis.

incorrect information we receive from the environment could lead to the type of clear-cut concepts, not to mention beautiful and perfect hierarchies of concepts, proposed by this approach. A second, more fundamental objection was proposed by the Austrian philosopher Ludwig Wittgenstein (1953). In a classic piece, he argued that it had been impossible to identify the necessary and sufficient conditions for many, if not most concepts. Wittgenstein took the example of the concept of a 'game', and argued that there is no group of clear-cut features that will distinguish things that are games from things that are not games. For example the property *being played*, which seems necessary, is not sufficient, as many things (such as musical instruments) are played but are not games. Conversely, properties that seem sufficient for defining a game – for example, the rules of *Monopoly* – are not all necessary as there are many games that have rules different from *Monopoly*. Rather, Wittgenstein argued that the different members of a concept share **family resemblances**: members of a category resemble each other in different ways, and the features that mostly determine resemblance for a pair of members may not be the same as the features that characterise resemblance for another pair.

Wittgenstein (1953) proposed a purely theoretical argument, but the importance of family resemblance for concepts has also been established empirically. Rosch and Mervis (1975) asked participants to list the attributes of members of categories, such as fruit, vegetables and vehicles. They found that participants often produced non-necessary attributes and that, in general, participants' responses had the structure of family resemblance. In a follow-up experiment, Barsalou (1983) went one step further and actually explained to the participants what the phrase 'necessary and sufficient properties' meant. He then asked them to provide necessary and sufficient properties for deciding whether objects were members of a given category. Again, and in spite of these very specific instructions, participants' answers corresponded to family-resemblance structures.

Rosch's results established empirically that objects are not classified in a binary, yes-or-no fashion. Later research has also shown that people disagree when categorising objects and that classification is not stable over time. McCloskey and Glucksberg (1978) asked participants whether certain objects were members of specified categories, and then re-tested the same participants a week later. They were first of all interested in peripheral cases, such as *tomato* (as a member or not of the category *fruit*) or *amoeba* (as a member or not of the category *animal*). With these cases, they found not only that there was a fair amount of disagreement between people at a given time (between-subject disagreement at one time), but also that some people changed their view between the two test times (within-subject disagreement between times). These results make it hard to argue, following classical theory, that concepts capture *all and only the members* of a category.

The final main prediction of classical theory follows from the assumption that concepts are organised in a strict hierarchy. If this is the case, a clear prediction is that membership judgements should be transitive: if Xs are Ys, and Ys are Zs, then Xs are Zs. For example, if cats are mammals, and mammals are animals, then cats are animals. Hampton (1982) showed that this is not always the case. For example, although his participants agreed that car seats were chairs and that chairs were furniture, they disagreed that car seats were furniture. According to classical theory, they should have agreed with this last statement.

In sum, the classical view explains some data from concept attainment experiments, where artificial material is used, but has difficulties with more naturalistic categories. Clearly, people can learn some concepts in the way proposed by classical theory, and output clear-cut definitions for them. However, as soon as one moves to naturalistic concepts, the theory has difficulties. Thus, experiments show that the categories used by people do not always satisfy the rather idealistic requirements proposed by classical theory. The importance of the idea of family resemblance in many of the concepts we used led researchers away from experiments with artificial categories and towards experiments using natural categories, and spurred the development of prototype theories.

Prototype theories

The important role of typicality has already been mentioned a few times. It is therefore not surprising that some psychologists have developed theories based on this notion. The key idea is that the concepts are organised around prototypes (Rosch, 1973). Different theories have been proposed around this idea, but we need not be concerned by the subtle differences between them. For our purpose, we define a **prototype** as the *most typical* member of category (e.g. for the category of dogs, German shepherd), or a *set* of such members (e.g. golden retriever, German shepherd and collie). Prototypes are represented as a set of **characteristic features**: that is, features that best describe the prototypes, although it is important to stress that these features are not necessary in the sense of classical theory. According to Rosch, characteristic features are found by averaging the description of all the members of a given category we have met in our life, and taking the features that recur most often. (See Box 8.4 for an example.) For example, a characteristic feature for the concept of 'bird' is the ability to fly. While this applies to most birds, there are birds that do not fly (ostriches, penguins). This is why these features are characteristic and not defining: they work most of the time, but not necessarily all the time.

During classification, the features of the concept are matched against the properties of the object being classified, and an overall measure of similarity is measured. Every matching feature increases similarity, and every mismatching feature decreases similarity. If the object and the concept are similar enough – that is, if similarity is larger than a pre-defined threshold level – then the object is classified as a member.

More often than not, these features are sufficient, but there may be cases where this is not true. Also, note that these features are not necessary in the sense of classical theory; rather, they tend to correlate with category membership. Because there are differences in how attributes are perceptually salient or useful for categorising an object, it is reasonable to assign different *weights* to these features, ordering them according to how well they identify members. For example, the feature 'barks' is more informative than the feature 'drinks water' in deciding whether an animal is a dog, and thus should have a larger weight.

Evidence supporting prototype theory

We have already described some of the evidence supporting prototype theory when we discussed the data problematic for classical theory. For example, we noted that people tend to list characteristic features, and not defining features (Barsalou, 1983). In addition to this, there is considerable empirical evidence that concepts have a **typicality gradient**: that is, some members of the category are seen as closer to the prototype than others. Rosch (1975) was the first to show this empirically. Asking participants to rate the typicality of items, she showed that typicality

Box 8.4 RESEARCH CLOSE-UP: **Prototypes in action: an example**

Let us illustrate the use of prototypes with the stimuli presented in Figure 8.1. We first create a prototype for each category by assuming that each feature is set to the value that occurs most frequently within this category. For example, with the 'glap' category, the feature **eye size** is always set to **large**, so we give this value to the prototype. The feature **ear size** is set once to **large** and twice to **small**, so we give the value **small** to the prototype. By processing the four features of each category in a similar fashion, we obtain **large eyes, small ears, with hair and short nose** as the prototype for the 'glap' category, and **small eyes, large ears, without hair, and short nose** as the prototype for the 'bomp' category. Figure 8.3 shows these two faces. Note that the prototype may not correspond to an existing instance, as it is just an average. For example, the prototype for the bomp category is none of the stimuli of Figure 8.1.

In order to categorise the final face, we match its features with each prototype. There are two matches with the 'glap' prototype, and only one match for the 'bomp' prototype, so we decide that the last face belongs to the 'glap' category.

There actually exist different ways of computing similarity. For example, different weights can be used for the features, and some features can be totally ignored. Moreover, different measures can be used to measure the similarity between a new object and prototypes. (See Murphy, 2002, for details.)

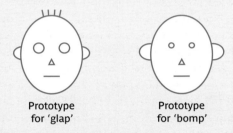

Prototype for 'glap'   Prototype for 'bomp'

Figure 8.3 Prototypical faces
The prototype for the 'glap' category is the same as the second face in Figure 8.1. However, the prototype for the 'bomp' category is not the same as any of the faces in Figure 8.1.

ratings range from highly typical members (e.g. *robin*) through atypical members (e.g. *penguins*) to non-members (e.g. *bats*) (see Table 8.1). This result has been replicated for colour categories, natural kinds, artefacts, social categories, etc. Using a verification task, where participants have to answer 'yes' or 'no' to statements such as *tomato is a fruit*, Smith *et al.* (1974) showed that high- and low-typicality items produced rapid verification times, and that borderline cases were slower. Mervis *et al.* (1976) showed that, when people have to enumerate as many members from a category as they can, prototypes tend to be mentioned first. Finally, it is interesting that typicality gradients exist even with artificial categories. When discussing clear-cut categories earlier, we gave the example of odd and even numbers. Armstrong *et al.* (1983) found that, even in this case, there is a typicality gradient: numbers such as 22 and 4 are seen as better examples of even numbers than 18 or 26, and take less time to answer.

Experiments supporting the hypothesis of typicality gradient also support the notion that the boundaries between categories are fuzzy or ill-defined. If some items receive no high rating for any category and low rating for several categories, then there is uncertainty about category boundaries. It is interesting to note that fuzziness in classification is not due to a lack of information, since participants receive full information in these experiments.

Table 8.1 Results of Rosch's (1975) experiment

The ten most typical and least typical items for the categories Fruit, Sport and Bird. Items were rated from 1 (very typical) to 7 (very atypical). Rosch (1975) collected data from ten categories, which had between 50 and 60 members each.

Category					
Fruit		Sport		Bird	
Most typical					
orange	1.07	football	1.03	robin	1.02
apple	1.08	baseball	1.05	sparrow	1.18
banana	1.15	basketball	1.12	bluejay	1.29
peach	1.17	tennis	1.15	bluebird	1.31
pear	1.18	softball	1.29	canary	1.42
apricot	1.36	canoeing	1.41	blackbird	1.43
tangerine	1.36	handball	1.42	dove	1.46
plum	1.37	rugby	1.43	lark	1.47
grapes	1.38	hockey	1.44	swallow	1.52
nectarine	1.52	ice hockey	1.45	parakeet	1.53
Least typical					
pawpaw	4.30	pool	3.82	duck	3.24
coconut	4.50	billiards	3.95	peacock	3.31
avocado	5.37	hunting	4.05	egret	3.39
pumpkin	5.39	jump rope	5.00	chicken	4.02
tomato	5.58	camping	5.07	turkey	4.09
nut	6.01	chess	5.07	ostrich	4.12
gourd	6.02	dancing	5.49	titmouse	4.35
olive	6.21	checkers	5.64	emu	4.38
pickle	6.34	cards	5.79	penguin	4.53
squash	6.55	sunbathing	6.75	bat	6.15

Source: Data from Rosch, 1975.

Other experiments have shown that some concepts can be unstable. For example, Roth and Shoben (1983) have shown that typicality ratings are affected by the context. Participants rated cows and goats as better examples of animals than horses and mules after reading a text about milking, while the opposite was true when the passage, and thus the context, was about riding. Prototype theory can account for this dependence on context: for example, by assuming that context leads to a change of the similarity threshold or by increasing the weights of one or more attributes.

Evidence against prototype theory

An important limitation of prototype theory is that it assumes that people use only fairly superficial features for categorising objects. Authors such as Murphy and Medin (1985) have argued that, rather than surface features, people use more central attributes. A later section, devoted to explanation-based theories, will describe what kind of more essential features and beliefs people might be using. For the time being, let us simply note that prototype theories use only surface features and cannot include such central attributes.

Another issue is that, while well established, typicality effects may not necessarily tell us much about the causal mechanisms engaged. For example, it could be the case that typicality is only an end product of other classification processes that do not use typicality. (We will consider such a possibility when dealing with the exemplar approach.) In other words, the fact that participants can judge the typicality of items does not necessarily imply that it is important in the way they represent these items. A final weakness of the theory is that, while some abstract concepts (such as *work of art*, *science* and *crime*) do show a prototypical structure, others do not (e.g. *belief* or *instinct*) (Hampton, 1982).

Hierarchical structure and basic level

Research based on prototypes has also uncovered an intriguing effect. For many concepts – but by no means all of them – it seems that the intermediate level of abstraction plays a critical role, to the point that it has been called the *basic level*. Rosch and colleagues (Rosch *et al.*, 1976) presented concepts organised in three levels: superordinate level (e.g. furniture), intermediate level (e.g. chair) and subordinate level (e.g. desk-chair). They found that the basic level played a special role in several tasks. When asked to list features common to superordinate level, intermediate (basic) level and subordinate level categories, participants listed 3, 9 and 10.3 features, respectively. What is interesting here is that there is a large gain when one goes from the superordinate level to the intermediate level, but only a small gain when one goes from the intermediate level to the subordinate level. When asked to say whether the picture of an object was a member of a category, people were faster with basic-level categories than with superordinate categories. Finally, when asked to name pictures of objects, Rosch *et al.* found that participants were more likely to choose names at the basic level.

Using the results of these experiments, Rosch and colleagues proposed that the intermediate level is cognitively critical, because what this level does is not only to maximise the dissimilarity between categories, which makes it possible to discriminate between different categories, but also to maximise the similarity within a given category, which means that this category can be used efficiently. This means that, at the basic level, members of a category have similar shapes and can be interacted with in the same way. This is also the level where objects tend to be named, both by adults and children.

Are the basic levels used to categorise objects innate, perhaps because they offer an optimal level from a perceptual point of view? Two types of evidence suggest that this is not the case. First, what counts as a basic level varies as a function of expertise (Tanaka and Taylor, 1991). For example, while American (non-expert) students use 'bird' to name pictures of birds, bird experts name them using terms such as 'sparrow' and 'robin'. Thus, the subordinate level of non-experts has become the basic level of experts, who could provide more specific terms at the subordinate level, or even at a level below, if required to do so. Second, different basic levels are used in different cultures (Berlin, 1992; Malt, 1995). Typically, while individuals in non-industrialised societies use the biological genus to name plants (e.g. 'maple'), individuals in Western countries use the level above (e.g. 'tree'). Thus, it is as if there were an expertise effect at the level of entire societies.

Exemplar-based theories

Just as with the prototype approach, similarity plays a central role in exemplar-based theories. However, while the former approach assumes that we keep only a few prototypical representations, exemplar-based theories assume that we hold a large number of memory representations, called **exemplars**. It is proposed that we store a representation of an external object in memory every time we see it or somehow deal with it. Thus, for each category, we have millions of instances stored in our long-term memory. When an object is presented, all instances are matched in parallel against it using some measure of similarity, and the instance most closely matching it is retrieved (see Box 8.5 for an example). Note that the match need not be perfect – just that the selected instance has a higher match than the other instances. It may seem counter-intuitive and wasteful in resources that we store so many instances, but a number of computational models have implemented this idea (Smith and Minda, 2000), showing that it is theoretically possible.

Box 8.5 RESEARCH CLOSE-UP: **Exemplars in action: an example**

As with the other theories, we can illustrate how exemplars are used with the stimuli of Figure 8.1. When categorising the last stimulus, what we do is to compare it with each of the instances stored in long-term memory. We will assume that each instance is fully stored in long-term memory when seen – a central assumption of this theory, but also a debatable one given what we know from research into long-term memory (see Chapter 7). Every time a feature of an instance matches the stimulus, the similarity scores for the category to which the instance belongs increase by one. So, for example, matching the first instance (**large eyes, large ears, with hair and short nose**) with the last stimulus (**large eyes, small ears, without hair and long nose**) gets only one match (**large eyes**), so we increase the similarity score of category 'glap' by one. When we do this for all the instances of each category (which we encourage you to do), we find that the 'glap' category gets six matches, whilst the 'bomp' category gets four matches. Thus, we decide that the last stimulus is more similar to the 'glap' category, and thus that it belongs to this category. As with prototypes, researchers have proposed different ways of computing similarity.

Evidence for the exemplar view

The exemplar view can readily explain typicality gradients and other typicality effects. The two key assumptions are that each exemplar is linked to a specific category, and that matching is faster when there are many similar instances, because more exemplars are going to 'vote' for a given category than if there are just a few exemplars. Faster naming of typical instances is explained by this faster matching. Typicality gradients are also explained by the fact that typical instances have more exemplars 'voting' for them.

Exemplar theories can deal with atypical cases more readily that prototype theories can. For example, penguins are atypical birds in the sense that they cannot fly. However, according to exemplar theories, exemplars have been stored for penguins every time we have seen a picture of them. Thus, some fairly high similarity resemblance can be computed for them. This is hard to explain for prototype theory, as penguins would have to match the prototypical representation of birds, which they do not. The exemplar view can also account for the instability of concepts. The context is part of the information that is encoded in the description of the object. As a consequence, matching objects in different contexts will retrieve different instances, and thus different concepts.

An advantage of the exemplar approach over the prototype approach is that it keeps information about variability, as all the instances are stored in long-term memory. By contrast, prototypes are averages of instances, and thus lose any information about variability. The notion that variability is used by people has been documented in an experiment by Rips and Collins (1993), who used the fact that rulers and pizzas have the same size on average (12 inches, i.e. 30 cm), but different variability: while pizzas vary wildly in size, rulers pretty much always have the same length. They presented participants with an unknown object 18 inches long (about 45.7 cm), and asked them whether it was more likely to be a pizza or ruler. Rips and Collins reasoned that if people use average properties only, as proposed by prototype theories, they should choose the pizza and the ruler with equal probability. By contrast, if people take variability into account when categorising objects, as proposed by exemplar theories, they should choose the pizza, because they know that pizzas vary in size while rulers do not. The results showed that people chose the pizza more often, which thus supported exemplar theories.

Weaknesses

A key assumption of the exemplar-based approach, and indeed of the prototype approach, is that category membership judgement and typicality should co-vary. However, dissociations have been demonstrated. We have seen earlier that people use a binary way of classifying odd and even numbers, but also make typicality judgements that are (presumably) based on similarity with prototypes or instances. In that case, category membership judgement and typicality *do not* co-vary.

Another important weakness of this approach is that, beyond their similarity, it has nothing to say about how concepts are related to each other, and in particular does not make any prediction as to how concepts are (possibly) organised in hierarchies. A final weakness is that, as noted above when we discussed the classical view, some concepts can be described using arbitrary definitions (for example the concepts used in Bruner *et al.*'s (1956) experiments). Some of the members of such categories will share little similarity with each other, and any theory solely based on similarity will fail to explain how humans can use such concepts.

Stop and Think Best way of studying
When you study material for a class, is it better to learn many exemplars or to acquire just a few prototypes summarising what happens with many exemplars? If you think that the answer depends on the topics being studied, give examples.

Explanation-based theories

When dealing with prototype theory, we noted that one of its weaknesses was that people sometimes use central features rather than superficial ones; when dealing with the exemplar approach, we noted that it failed to explain how concepts are organised and how they are possibly linked to each other. Explanation-based theories were developed to remedy these (and other) weaknesses. The central theme of these theories is that people use common-sense explanations to categorise objects (Murphy and Medin, 1985); these explanations are motivated by the kind of intuitive theories that people have about the world. These common-sense explanations, which might differ from one domain to another, specify what attributes should be used for categorising objects. So, for example, when classifying abstract drawings of faces that actually follow an arbitrary classification rule (like the faces we used in Figure 8.1), participants might remember that eyes are very important in identifying people and thus that the size of the eyes in the stimuli is likely to be a very predictive feature (see Box 8.6). The importance of the attributes in the explanations provided by the theory varies: some attributes may play a central role, while others are less important. Thus, a distinction is made between diagnostic and surface attributes. With this approach, concepts are considered as parts of knowledge in general, and thus links are made with general theories of long-term memory.

Evidence for explanation-based theories

Compared to the three previous theories, where concepts seem to exist independently of the way our knowledge of the world is stored in long-term memory, the idea of linking concepts to other types of knowledge is intuitively plausible and seems a clear advantage. The theory also explains why classification times sometimes vary depending on the task. In tasks where a rapid

---

Box 8.6 RESEARCH CLOSE-UP: **Explanation-based theory in action: an example**

Returning to our Figure 8.1, we can illustrate the explanation-based approach. Our experience in recognising faces tells us that eyes are the most predictive feature. We also know that hair length is a poor cue, because hair appearance can easily be changed. Similarly, ear size is a poor diagnostic cue, because the ears are often hidden behind the hair. Finally, we have learned from our experience that nose length is not reliable for categorising people. In sum, we are left only with eye size. Glaps always have large eyes, while bomps tend to have small eyes, except for the third face, which has large eyes. Our knowledge of the world tells us that perception is sometimes unreliable, so we decide not to take this instance into consideration. As our rule is that glaps have large eyes and bomps small eyes, we conclude that the seventh face is a glap.

identification is required, people will use a measure of similarity based on superficial features. In tasks where time is not essential but the quality of categorisation is, people will rely on more central features and on the type of explanations they provide. This approach also has a means to explain why some concepts seem more natural and coherent than others: if an explanatory theory can be found, coherence will increase. This kind of theory also explains why classification can vary between contexts: different attributes – either superficial or central – are used.

Weaknesses

The main weakness of explanation-based theories is that they lack specificity. It is not clear what exactly a 'theory' is, and even less how it relates to other parts of semantic memory. There is also a serious danger of circularity of definition: concepts are based on explanations, but explanations themselves depend on concepts. This circularity is not necessarily fatal to this approach, but the only way to avoid this potential issue is to specify exactly the relations between concepts and explanations, which is not done in current theories. Another potential problem relates to the amount of cognitive processing that is required. It is proposed that processing a concept involves processing the common-sense knowledge that is associated with this concept. However, how does the mind know when to stop? For example, if you see a picture of a dog, this will activate the knowledge that dogs are hungry because they need food for survival, which might lead to the knowledge that dog food can be bought in supermarkets, presumably because the owner of the supermarket wants to make profit, which in turn leads to the knowledge that profit is linked to the price of the goods, and so on *ad nauseam*. Clearly, such processing is intractable from a cognitive point of view, and the explanation-based theories should provide the means to explain how the use of knowledge stops at some point.

Role of strategies, attention and short-term memory

Using four main approaches, we have reviewed a considerable amount of empirical evidence on categorisation. Although none of the four theories has provided a perfect account of the available evidence, it is currently thought that the exemplar theories do the best job (Murphy, 2002). It has also been proposed that it might be ill-advised to look for a single mechanism, and that the different approaches we have reviewed might account for diverse aspects of the data. People might use alternatively definitions, prototypes, exemplars and explanations in different situations or in different domains. For example, the early work by Bruner *et al.* (1956) strongly suggests that, with artificial domains, people use the type of definitions and rules proposed by the classical approach. There is also evidence that people tend to use prototypes at the beginning of learning a domain and exemplars later on (Smith and Minda, 2000). In addition, exemplar models provide a good account of the data when the number of instances in a category is small, as it is possible to memorise individual stimuli, but prototype models seem more suitable to explain how people deal with categories that contain a large number of instances, where learning all stimuli is not possible.

Finally, human cognition is very flexible and participants often follow the type of classification strategy implicitly or explicitly suggested by the experimenter. This has been clearly established by Medin and Smith (1981), who gave different instructions to different groups of subjects as to which strategies should be used to learn the categories (one of the strategies required the use of prototypes, and another used a combination of rules and exemplars). The results clearly showed that participants could use whatever strategies they were instructed to use, which strongly suggests that people use not only one mechanism in real life, but a combination of mechanisms. In a similar vein, Markman and Ross (2003) have emphasised that the way instances are processed determines how they are going to be learned. Learning by classifying instances (e.g. 'Is a mushroom a vegetable?') will lead to a different type of categorisation than making inferences about these instances (e.g. 'Will this mushroom poison me?').

An obvious conclusion of these observations is that theories of categorisation should pay more attention to the strategies used. More specifically, computer models of categorisation should incorporate the possibility of using different strategies rather than being limited to just one mechanism. This is just what Gobet *et al.* (1997) did. They describe a model that simulated the data of Medin and Smith's (1981) experiment, where, as we have just seen, participants were instructed to use different strategies. The model, based on the chunking mechanism discussed in various places in this book, could follow different strategies depending on the instructions of the experimenter. Gobet *et al.* also emphasised the importance of goals and attention when learning categories. Focusing one's attention on different aspects of the stimuli will lead to the learning of different categories.

When discussing Bruner *et al.*'s (1956) research, we have also seen that the limited capacity of short-term memory affected the strategies used by the participants. Thus, while this chapter started by emphasising the unique role of concepts, it is now clear that concepts do not stand in isolation, but are linked to several of the cognitive functions we have discussed so far in this book, most notably attention, short-term memory and semantic memory. Crucially, some of the critical features we had identified in previous chapters – e.g. role of attention and limited capacity of short-term memory – again play a considerable role in predicting how people deal with concepts. This reuse of theoretical terms across different cognitive domains is a good example of theoretical parsimony.

Stop and Think Strategies

The role of strategies in categorisation has been illustrated by the work of Bruner *et al.* (1956) and Medin and Smith (1981). But if participants can change the strategies they use at a whim, what does the study of categorisation tell us about human cognition?

Stop and Think Babies and animals

Do babies have concepts? Do animals have concepts?

Chapter summary

Concepts are (relatively) stable cognitive structures that are fundamental to cognition and action. They make it possible to classify objects and represent them when reasoning, and they support the semantic processing of language. Most of the empirical evidence derives from experimental studies on classification. Four classes of theories have dominated the field. In order of historical appearance, they are the classical theories, prototype theories, exemplar theories and explanation-based theories. While there has been clear progress in our understanding of concepts, all the theories discussed in this chapter have shortcomings. A point that is often neglected by these theories is that people have to abide by the cognitive limits we have identified in previous chapters, and always strive to encode information economically. To do so, people use different strategies depending on the type of information they are dealing with (e.g. natural concepts vs artificial concepts), and the goal they have in mind.

Further reading

The standard work by Bruner *et al.* (1956), which uses a classical approach, is still well worth reading. It covers a broader ground than many of the current studies on categories. In *The big book of concepts*, Murphy (2002) provides an extensive discussion of current research. Useful reviews of literature are also offered by Markman and Ross (2003) and Ashby and Maddox (2005). Giannakopoulou (2003) critically discusses prototype theory with respect to word meaning.

Chapter 9

Language

CHAPTER PREVIEW

☑ Linguistics is the study of language, and psycholinguistics is the study of the psychological aspects of language.

☑ Human language is unique in the animal world because of the following features: use of arbitrary symbols, rules organised in a hierarchical structure, generativity and continuous evolution over time.

☑ According to Chomsky, the input that children receive does not contain enough information for them to learn language. Therefore, the knowledge of the central principles of language must be innate. This view has recently been criticised, as computer models have shown that the input in fact contains much useful information.

☑ It is remarkable that we can understand speech that easily, as it is an almost continuous stream of sounds that are often articulated together, not to mention differences in accent and pitch of voice.

☑ There is considerable disagreement in the theories explaining how syntax is processed. Some theories assume that processing is serial with strong constraints on the capacity of working memory, while others assume that it is highly parallel with few memory constraints.

☑ Text comprehension involves a complex interplay between the external text and long-term memory knowledge. The most successful explanation of how this is done is provided by Kintsch's construction-integration model.

Introduction

Of all the cognitive functions discussed in this book, language is clearly the one that is uniquely human. While animals are known to communicate in various ways, they are not even close to using anything like human language. In particular, the modes of communication they use lack the following features of human language (Brown, 1973; Clark and Clark, 1977): (a) use of *arbitrary symbols* – for example, 'tree' in English, 'Baum' in German and 'arbre' in French all refer to the same object; (b) *hierarchical structure*, where each level (e.g. the level of sounds or the level of words) follows specific rules; (c) *generativity*, in the sense that an infinite number of utterances can be produced by a combination of symbols; and finally (d) *dynamic evolution* in the sense that human languages keep changing.

These features make language both a fascinating and complex topic of research. Unlike perception, learning, memory, and even problem solving and creativity, we cannot use experiments or observations with animals to understand human language. While some research has been carried out with chimpanzees, dolphins and parrots, among others, the results very clearly indicate that whatever is acquired by these animals is very far from human language. In addition, there is a fundamental difference: in these experiments, animals are taught and with extreme difficulty learn very basic elements of language, while human infants acquire language seemingly effortlessly, even when no attempt is made by parents to teach them anything. In fact, in some cultures, adults rarely speak directly to their young children (Pinker, 1994). In spite of this, children learn language as rapidly as in cultures where parents spend a great deal of time looking after the linguistic development of their children.

Some definitions

Linguistics is the science of studying language; it is concerned with the properties shared by all languages or how languages have evolved over centuries and millennia. *Psycholinguistics* studies the psychological aspects of language: for instance, how children acquire language or how the capacity of working memory affects language processing. The study of language is usually divided into phonology, syntax, semantics and pragmatics. **Phonology** is concerned with identifying the rules followed by the basic speech sounds of specific languages, called **phonemes**. A phoneme is the smallest class of speech sounds that leads to meaningful differences in a given language. For example, /l/ and /r/ are two phonemes in English, so that 'royal' and 'loyal' have different meanings. (Note that two slashes are used to indicate phonemes.) This is not the case in languages such as Japanese and Thai, where /l/ and /r/ do not lead to differences in meaning and are thus considered as a single phoneme. Similarly, consider the sound [p] when you say 'pit' and 'spit'. If you put your hand in front of your mouth, you will notice that there is a puff of air in the first case ([p] is 'aspirated'), but not in the second. These two sounds are different, but correspond to only one phoneme in English. By contrast, they correspond to two different phonemes in Hindi or Thai. (The phoneme with the aspirated sound is denoted as /pʰ/ and the phoneme with the plain sound is denoted as /p/). Incidentally, the phonemes of your native language will determine what phonemes are easy to learn in a new language. Thus, native speakers of Japanese will have difficulties in learning the distinction between /l/ and /r/ in English, and native speakers of English will struggle to discriminate between /p/ and /pʰ/. Different languages use different sets of phonemes, and most languages have only between 20 and 37 phonemes (Maddieson, 1984)

Syntax studies the system of rules specifying how words are combined in sentences. The focus is on the order of words and on the use of **grammatical morphemes**, which consist of function words (e.g. 'the', 'on') and inflectional endings (e.g. the use of the suffix –ed indicates the past tense in English). Consider the following three sentences (the star indicates an ungrammatical sentence):

1   The boy throws a stone.
*2   The a boy stone throws.
*3   The boy throw a stone.

The first sentence is grammatically correct. The second is grammatically incorrect because it uses a word order that is not admissible in English, and the third is grammatically incorrect because the verb 'throw' lacks the required –s suffix.

Semantics studies how meaning is expressed in languages. The relation between syntax and semantics is not straightforward. For example, Chomsky's (1957) sentence 'Colorless ideas sleep furiously' is grammatically correct English but does not make much sense. By contrast, *'The boy throw a stone' is grammatically incorrect but makes perfect sense.

Finally, **pragmatics** is concerned with the communicative functions of language: that is, how language affects others' behaviour. For example, if you ask your friend 'Can you please open the window?' the intended message is that you want your friend to open the window, and just answering 'Yes, I can' to your question, without doing anything, would be considered rude.

Box 9.1 EVERYDAY APPLICATION: **From Grice to Australia**

We have defined pragmatics as the study of intended meaning. If we ask somebody 'Do you have the time?', we expect that she will tell us the hour of the day rather than just say 'yes'. How do people know when to use a meaning different than the literal meaning, and how do they know which intended meaning among the multiple possible ones?

In an influential paper called 'Logic and conversation', the British philosopher Paul Grice explored these issues (Grice, 1975). He first introduced the *cooperative principle*: people cooperate when participating in a conversation – that is, they tend to be helpful, informative and relevant. Grice then expanded this principle into four maxims (now known as *Grice's maxims*). The *maxim of quality* states that speakers are not expected to say something false or something for which they do not have sufficient evidence. The *maxim of quantity* states that speakers are expected to provide the right amount of information, given the purposes of the conversation. In particular, they are expected not to be more informative than is necessary. The *maxim of relation* states that speakers are expected to say things that are relevant. Finally, the *maxim of manner* states that speakers are expected to be concise and orderly, and to avoid being obscure or ambiguous.

These maxims are fairly straightforward, and an example of violating the maxim of quantity will suffice. When you ask somebody 'How are you today?', you do not expect an answer such as 'This morning at 9 am, I had a slight headache. So I took an aspirin. At 10 am I felt fine. At 11 am I felt fine too. At 12 noon I wasn't sure I felt that great, but I didn't take any medicine ... [and so on until the state of health at 10 pm].'

These maxims, and the cooperative principle in general, assume that much of what seems important for a clear understanding is left unsaid and that listeners have to make many inferences. Grice gives the following example:

Speaker A: *I am out of petrol.*
Speaker B: *There is a garage round the corner.*

The obvious inference is that a garage is a place that sells petrol, and that A should go there to fill up. Other inferences are less obvious: the garage is open, it sells petrol at a reasonable price, it is not burning, and so on. Indeed, making only the relevant inferences while avoiding making an indefinite number of trivial inferences is a problem that has marred artificial programmes written to carry out conversations (Pinker, 1994).

It is sometimes possible to 'flout' these maxims, that is to violate them intentionally. This is what happens with humour, sarcasm, irony, and so on. For example, after seeing a mediocre film a disappointed movie-goer could say that 'the movie was *terrific*'.

Although no systematic study has been carried out across cultures, it is fairly well established that the extent to which Grice's maxims are followed varies from culture to culture. A nice example is offered by Australian aborigines (Walsh, 1994). First, some of the original maxims are not followed. For example, given the significance of kin in Aboriginal social interactions, the maxim of manner is not respected: from a pragmatic point of view, it is better for an Aborigine to be (to non-Aboriginal ears) obscure, ambiguous and wordy than to be brief. Second, some new maxims must be introduced to explain the way Australian aborigines carry out a conversation. Walsh suggests to create the *maxim of epistemic discretion*: you are expected to speak about what you know, except if your age or gender is inappropriate, or if there are other people who are expected to speak in your place.

You might think that all this is not uninteresting, but without any practical applications. You would be wrong. The style of conversation described by Walsh has led, together with other factors, to numerous difficulties of communication in Australian courts. Noting that a disproportionately high percentage of Indigenous Australians are likely to be arrested and imprisoned, Stroud (2006, p. 3/11) comments that 'even though an Indigenous offender "appears" competent in the language, cultural differences may lead to the offender not being able to tell their story, and misunderstandings on the part of the interviewer or prosecutor'. To remedy this situation, a new type of court has been created in Australia: the 'koori' (Aboriginal) courts. In these courts, where justice is carried out in a culturally sensitive fashion, the judge sits at a table with the defendant, who is accompanied by members of the family, elders and other respected individuals in the community. Legal jargon is not allowed, and plain language is used. There is provision for enough time for sharing information, in particular with respect to cultural matters. According to Stroud, a preliminary evaluation of the programme reports important benefits. In particular, reoffending rates have decreased, with some regions having a rate as low as 12.5 per cent compared to a general level of recidivism of 29.4 per cent.

The importance of development

Given that one of the characteristics of language is the ease with which it is learned by children, it is impossible to understand language without considering, even briefly, how it is acquired. We have seen in Chapter 2 that one of the main attempts to understand the mechanisms underpinning language using principles from animal research led to an impasse. Skinner's book *Verbal Behavior* (1957) had argued that language is learned by reinforcement, just as pigeons learn to peck on a key for food. Thus, children would be reinforced positively when they produce correct utterances and not when they make mistakes. However, anecdotal evidence suggests that children pay little attention to feedback given on the syntax, as they seem to focus on the semantics and pragmatics of what is being said. McNeill (1966, p. 69) gives the following example:

> **Child:* Nobody don't like me.
> **Mother:** No, say, 'Nobody likes me.'
> **Child:* Nobody don't like me.
> **Mother:** No, say, 'Nobody likes me.'
> [This dialogue is repeated eight times]
> **Mother:** Now listen carefully, say, '*Nobody likes me.*'
> **Child:* Oh! Nobody don't *likes* me.

The thrust of Chomsky's (1959) scathing review of Skinner's book was that language, in particular syntax, is made of rules, and the type of reinforcement learning proposed by Skinner, and indeed any kind of learning mechanism, cannot lead to the acquisition of these rules. One key argument in Chomsky's reasoning is that the input that children receive – typically the speech of their parents and siblings – contains numerous mistakes, false starts, unfinished sentences, and thus is simply not sufficient for conveying the rules of language. This is known as **the poverty of the stimulus argument.** According to Chomsky, the only solution to the problem that language is too difficult to learn is to assume that, in fact, there is no learning at all: knowledge of the syntax (also called *grammar* in this context) must be innate. More specifically, he proposed that children are born with what he calls knowledge of **Universal Grammar** (UG): knowledge of the key principles that subtend all possible languages. These principles are instantiated differently in different languages, and what has to be learned is the value of specific parameters. Let us consider two such parameters. The first is whether the subject has to be present, or whether it can be omitted. In English, subjects must be present. So, while the following utterance is correct

4　**We** are going to the beach

the following utterance is incorrect

*5　Are going to the beach.

By contrast, Spanish allows subject-less sentences. Thus the following two sentences are correct:

6　**Nosotros** vamos a la playa.

7　Vamos a la playa

The second example is the parameter stipulating word order. In English, this parameter is set to Subject – Verb – Object (SVO). Thus, the following utterance:

8 Ali ate the apple

is correct, while the following utterance is not:

*9 Ali the apple ate.

Other languages have this parameter set to a different value. For example, Turkish has this parameter set to Subject – Object – Verb (SOV), as shown in the following example:

10 Ali elma yedi (literally: Ali the apple ate).

Chomsky also made a distinction between competence and performance. **Competence** refers to the idealised knowledge that individuals have of their language; **performance** refers to the kind of utterances individuals actually produce. Because of limitations in working memory or attention, among other reasons, we make errors when we speak although, according to Chomsky, we have a perfect competence of the language – we were born with UG.

Chomsky had a considerable impact not only on linguistics, but also on psycholinguistics, and we will review below some of the research influenced by his ideas. However, some of the key assumptions he made about language acquisition have been criticised recently, in particular the argument of the poverty of the stimulus. There is increasing evidence that the environment provides much more information than had been assumed by Chomsky, and a number of simulation models have shown that much grammatical knowledge can be learned from child-directed speech (Redington *et al.*, 1998). At several places in this book, we have mentioned that **chunking** is a central mechanism for human learning and cognition generally. This applies to language as well. With respect to syntax acquisition, Freudenthal and colleagues (Freudenthal *et al.*, 2007) have shown that a simulation model based on the idea of chunking could reproduce several phenomena in the way children acquire language: for example, errors in the use of verbs. With respect to vocabulary, Jones *et al.* (2007) have shown that chunking provides a plausible mechanism as to how phonemes are grouped together to form new words. Together, simulation models show that the input received by children contains a substantial amount of information, and that fairly simple learning mechanisms can extract the statistical properties of the input that are useful for acquiring language.

In the remainder of this chapter we will proceed following the hierarchical structure of language: we start with the building blocks of words (sounds in speech and letters in written language); then we consider how words form sentences; and, finally, we discuss text and discourse comprehension, which deals with the understanding of a group of sentences.

> ### Box 9.2 IN FOCUS: **Key questions in the study of language**
>
> In addition to trying to identify the mechanisms enabling children to learn language seemingly effortlessly, research on the psychology of language has also addressed a number of central questions that echo those addressed in previous chapters. Are processes underpinning language serial or parallel? That is to say, is language processed through a sequence of processing stages, each dealing with one aspect of language (e.g. phonology, syntax, semantics) in full, or are all these processes carried out in parallel, with feedback loops continuously occurring between them? A related question asks whether language processing is modular or non-modular. That is to say, are some processes exclusively devoted to specific aspects of language, perhaps in a dedicated brain region, or are these processes more general? A recurring theme relates to the flow of processing – a theme we have discussed at length in Chapter 4. Is processing mostly top-down (i.e. concept-driven), or is it bottom-up (i.e. data-driven)? Or, perhaps, is it some combination of the two? Finally, what is the relationship between syntax and semantics? Which one, if either, comes first? This chapter will try to provide answers to these questions, although many of them do not have (yet) a clear-cut answer and are still the object of intense research and debate.

Speech production

To produce sounds, we use a combination of organs (among others: vocal cords, nasal cavity and mouth (see Figure 9.1) to create sound waves. These sound waves can be displayed as spectrograms (see Figure 9.2). Linguists have classified phonemes as a function of two aspects of articulation. The *place of articulation* indicates where in the mouth the air flow is obstructed (e.g. by the action of the tip of the tongue on the upper teeth to produce the phoneme /t/). The *manner of articulation* describes how the air flow is obstructed. For example, with stop consonants (/p/ and /d/), there is first total blockage of the oral and nasal cavities, which allows air pressure to build up and then to be released suddenly. With voiced consonants (/d/, /b/), the vocal cords vibrate, which is not the case with voiceless consonants (/t/, /p/). You can feel the difference by putting your fingers on your larynx when saying /b/ and /p/: your vocal cords will vibrate in the first case, but not in the second. (You can find a systematic discussion of the place and manner of articulation in the textbooks on linguistics and psycholinguistics mentioned at the end of this chapter.)

As noted in Chapter 6, many errors in recall experiments are due to the similarity shared by phonemes. Most confusable consonants differ by only one distinctive phonemic feature. For example, /b/ and /p/ are both produced in the anterior part of the mouth by the lips, and are distinguished only by the fact that /b/ is voiced while /p/ is voiceless. As you have probably experienced on a poor-quality phone line, distinguishing these two phonemes can be problematic.

Speech perception

On the listener's side, sound waves are collected by the ear and translated into neural signals. The brain then translates these neural signals into phonemes. Phonemes are then combined to form words. Whether this happens sequentially, as suggested here, or in parallel, has been the subject of considerable debate, as we shall see.

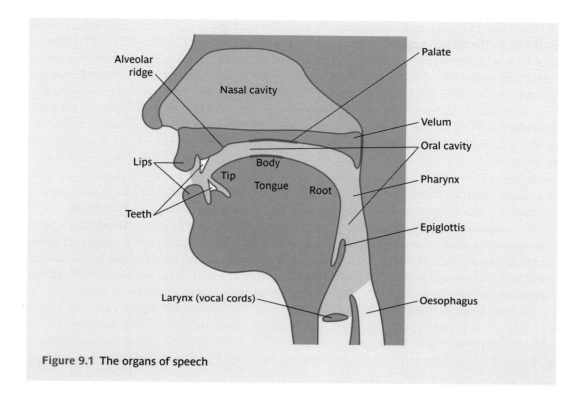

Figure 9.1 The organs of speech

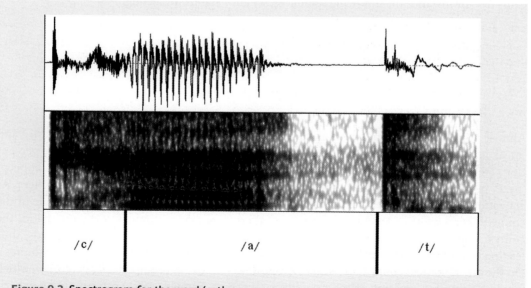

Figure 9.2 Spectrogram for the word 'cat'
Source: Courtesy of Dr Maria Uther, Brunel University.

Speech perception comes so naturally that we take it for granted. However, it is a challenging problem, as the following facts will make clear. People speak with a variety of accents, different speeds, and different pitches of voice. Even a word as simple as 'the' can be pronounced in at least 50 different ways (Waldrop, 1988)! Fluent speakers can perceive up to 50 phonemes per second (Foulke and Sticht, 1969). This is in spite of the fact that phonemes do not come as a neat sequence of independent sounds, but overlap and interact – a phenomenon called **co-articulation**. For example, as we have seen earlier, the phoneme /p/ is pronounced differently in 'spit' and in 'pit'. Moreover, and this is actually implied by co-articulation, the sound pattern of phonemes is not invariable. A phoneme is actually a class of related but different sounds, sometimes called *phones*, which are perceived as belonging to the same category. In addition, the speech signal is continuous, and one important task of the listener is to find the boundaries of words – a task known as **word segmentation**. Pauses in speech are not a reliable indicator of word boundaries, as they often occur within words. If you are still unconvinced that speech perception is difficult, consider the following result. Pollack and Pickett (1964) extracted single words and sequences of words from conversational speech. Participants could barely understand half of the single words. It is not that the quality of the recordings was poor, as the recognition rate jumped up to about 90 per cent when sequences of seven words were presented.

We have noted in Chapter 4 that we can sometimes 'see' objects that do not exist (e.g. Figure 4.8). The same happens with language. A particularly good example of this is offered by the *phonemic restoration effect* (Warren and Warren, 1970). In this type of experiment, a sentence is spoken with the manipulation that one phoneme has been deleted and replaced by an extraneous sound such as a cough. Surprisingly, participants do not notice this alteration and, even when they are told beforehand of the manipulation, they cannot identify the phoneme that has been deleted. Typically, the semantic context will determine how the cough will be perceived. Consider for instance the following sentences, where * stands for a cough:

1 It was found that the *eel was on the axle

2 It was found that the *eel was on the shoe

3 It was found that the *eel was on the orange

4 It was found that the *eel was on the table.

   * = meaningless sound

Almost all participants hear 'wheel' in the first sentence, 'heel' in the second, 'peel' in third and 'meal' in the fourth. The classic explanation of this effect is that context helps phoneme perception. So, for example, knowing that we are talking about oranges might activate the concept 'peel', perhaps with the kind of spreading of activation proposed by memory researchers. As activation is higher, one is more likely to perceive that word. But what is the exact role of the context? A moment of thought leads to two alternative explanations. On the one hand, the context could have a bottom-up effect, in that it affects how listeners perceive sounds, thus leading to an increase of sensitivity (i.e. the ability to discriminate between different sounds). On the other, context could affect decisions about words that were imperfectly perceived, which would be a post-perception effect. To address this issue, Samuel (1981) carried out an experiment in which words were presented either with the target phoneme replaced with meaningless noise such as a cough – this is similar to Warren and Warren's (1970) experiment – or with the target phoneme still present but with noise added. The participants' task was to discriminate between the two kinds of stimuli; in other words, they had to tell when the target phoneme was present, and when it was absent. The results showed that the participants could not do so reliably. This suggests that the phonemic restoration effect is due not to a bottom-up effect – participants cannot discriminate between the two conditions, indicating that sensitivity is not increased by the presence of the phoneme – but rather to a top-down effect, the context being used to bias the response (see Box 9.3).

Theories of speech recognition

Given the challenges that speech recognition poses, it is not surprising that several theories have been developed to explain it, and we briefly discuss three of them. Motor theory (Liberman *et al.*, 1967; Liberman and Mattingly, 1985) is not only the oldest of these theories, but it is also the most counter-intuitive. It proposes that listeners perceive words by reproducing the movements of the speaker's vocal tract. Thus, the motor system devoted to speech is used both for producing speech through articulation and for analysing speech. We have seen earlier that speech is often 'noisy', and the idea of motor theory is that simulating the motor movements engaged in speech improves the reliability of the speech input and reduces its variability. At first glance, the theory has serious weaknesses. Its thrust is the hypothesis that motor articulation leads to less variable and therefore more reliable information than input speech. But this is not the case: there is in fact much variability in articulation (Dromey and Sanders, 2009). In addition, infants excel at speech perception although they are not particularly good at articulation

---

Box 9.3 CLASSIC EXPERIMENT: **The McGurk effect**

Other cues in addition to context help speech recognition. We use prosodic cues such as stress and intonation, as well as non-verbal cues, such as hand gestures. We also often watch the lips of the speaker, even though we are not aware of it. A classic demonstration of our use of lip-reading is the McGurk effect (McGurk and MacDonald, 1976) (see Figure 9.3). In this experiment, a video is modified so that while the voice repeats 'BA', the lips repeat 'GA' in synchrony with the voice (see Figure 9.3). The surprising result is that participants report hearing neither 'BA' nor 'GA', but 'DA', which is a combination of auditory and visual features. The effect is very robust, and is, for example, still obtained with a female face and a male voice. Perhaps surprisingly, seeing affects hearing.

Figure 9.3 The McGurk effect
Source: McGurk and MacDonald, 1976.

(Tsao *et al.*, 2004), which seems to directly contradict the prediction of the theory. However, the theory gains support from data in neuroscience. In particular, it has recently been proposed that some neurons in the premotor cortex – the so-called 'mirror neurones' – are implicated both in the perception and the generation of motor movements. For example, Rizzolatti and Craighero (2004) have shown that these neurons fire both when a monkey grabs food and when it sees another monkey grabbing food. Thus, it would seem at least plausible that similar neurons are implicated in the perception and production of speech, although the validity of this hypothesis is debated (for a discussion, see Lotto *et al.*, 2009).

The second theory – cohort theory (Marslen-Wilson and Tyler, 1980) – is interested in the time course of the processes leading to word recognition. It is an interactive theory, in the sense that bottom-up and top-down processes are intermingled. As soon as the first sounds of an utterance are perceived, all the words that are consistent with these sounds are activated. These words are called the 'word-initial cohort'. When additional sounds are perceived, the words that are not consistent with the new information (either the sounds themselves or the context that is being inferred from these sounds) are deleted from the cohort. The process continues until only one word remains in the cohort. This final stage is called the 'recognition point'. The central characteristic of the theory – the strong interaction between different types of information, including lexical, syntactic and semantic – turned out to be overemphasised. A variety of experiments using priming (e.g. Zwitserlood, 1989) have shown that the context has relatively little influence early in speech recognition. To account for these results, a revision of the theory (Marslen-Wilson and Warren, 1994) assumes that context starts to influence word recognition only late in the process. Another change in the revision of the theory is that words, rather than being or not being members of the cohort, have a graded membership: the likelihood of being part of the cohort is a probabilistic function of the number of features in the utterance corresponding to a given word.

The final model we consider is McClelland and Elman's (1986) TRACE model. Just like the cohort theory, this is an interactive model, which simultaneously makes use of different types of information. The major difference is that it is implemented as a computer model (a connectionist model, to be precise), which makes it possible to predict with precision the behaviour of the model. (See Chapter 15 for a discussion of the use of computer models in cognitive psychology.) As shown in Figure 9.4, the model consists of three layers of units. At the bottom, we have the input layer, where the distinctive auditory features are represented, such as place and manner of articulation. The middle layer consists of phonemes, and the output layer consists of words. To differentiate between, for example, the first and second phoneme of a word, the units encoding phonemes are duplicated for each possible position of a phoneme. So, for example, the /t/ in TICK is encoded by a different unit from the /t/ in CAT. The same applies to the phonetic features of the phonemes.

The connections between the layers are excitatory. So, if /c/ and /a/ are activated for the first and second phoneme respectively, they will further activate all the words starting with these phonemes. Significantly, this is also valid in the opposite direction: from words to phonemes. To continue our example, if the word CAT is activated, it will activate back to the phonemes /c/ and /a/. By contrast, the connections within layers are inhibitory. This means that units within a layer compete against each other by lowering the activation of the units they are connected to until one unit receives all the activation (this is the principle of 'winner takes all'). For example,

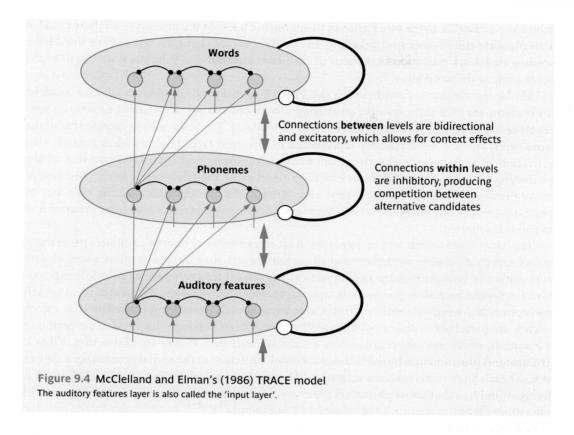

Figure 9.4 McClelland and Elman's (1986) TRACE model
The auditory features layer is also called the 'input layer'.

Text within the figure:

Words

Phonemes

Auditory features

Connections **between** levels are bidirectional and excitatory, which allows for context effects

Connections **within** levels are inhibitory, producing competition between alternative candidates

if the words CAT and CAN are activated because the first two phonemes recognised are /c/ and /a/, these two words will compete to win the activation from their direct competitor (as well as from other words partially activated, such as COP).

Connectionist models are difficult to understand, as much is going on at the same time (that is the point of parallel processing!) and processes are carried out over a large number of iterations, called *cycles*. It might therefore be useful to look in some detail at how activation spreads in our example. At the beginning of the simulation, the links between the units have preset values, which reflect knowledge of a specific language (English in our case). The model knows, for instance, that the phoneme /b/ is voiced and is pronounced by opening the lips. By contrast, the activation of the nodes is random. In the first cycle, the input is presented to the input layer, which activates the relevant features. In our case, the presentation of the input CAT coded as phonemic features activates the feature units. The units in the middle and output layers do propagate activation as well but, because their activation is random, we need not be concerned with this at the moment. In the second cycle, the input keeps activating units in the input layer as in the first cycle. In addition, the units in the input layer send inhibitory activation to the other units in the input layer, and also send activation to the units in the phoneme layer. In the third cycle, we have the same state of affairs for the input layer as in the previous cycle, but now the newly activated units in the phoneme layer propagate activation in three ways: backward excitatory activation to the input layer, forward excitatory activation to the output layer, and inhibitory activation to the other units in the phoneme layer. In the next cycle, all these kinds of activation are still present and spreading. In addition, we also have the units of the word layer sending excitatory activation backwards to the phoneme layer and inhibitory activation to the other units in the word layer.

This is the elegant way with which the TRACE model (and other connectionist models) implements the idea that cognitive processing is both bottom-up (from input data up to concepts) and top-down (from concepts down to input data). The concepts are represented in the word layer, and the input data are represented in the input layer. The key ideas here are that activation spreads in both directions, can be both inhibitory and excitatory, and that all the processing is done in parallel. How exactly connectionist models work is fairly complex, as many processes occur at the same time and many cycles are repeated, and the only way to predict the behaviour of the model is often to implement the model as a computer program and to run this program.

The TRACE model has several strengths. As it is realised as a running computer program, it is well specified – a clear advantage over the cohort model, for example. It offers a very elegant explanation of how bottom-up and top-down processes interact. It offers a plausible explanation for several empirical phenomena, and we consider two of them here: categorical speech perception and word superiority effect. **Categorical speech perception** is the fact that speech sounds are perceived as phonemes with a sharp distinction, although the physical properties of the sounds, which are often continuous, do not warrant such a clear-cut distinction. TRACE explains this phenomenon by the 'winner-takes-all' principle: at the end of processing, only one node at each layer receives all the activation. The **word superiority effect** (Cutler *et al*, 1987) is the phenomenon that target phonemes are recognised faster when they belong to a sequence of phonemes that form a word, as compared to a non-word. TRACE explains this by the fact that the word level feeds activation back to the phoneme level, which makes it easier for the target phoneme to reach sufficient activation and thus be recognised. (We will see later that there is a visual word superiority effect as well, which can be explained by the same mechanism.) However, TRACE is not without weaknesses. Its vocabulary is limited to one-syllable words, and it is not clear that the simulations would scale up to larger vocabularies and longer words. Moreover, it does not learn. Finally, it tends to make top-down effects stronger than they are in reality. For example, Frauenfelder *et al.* (1990) carried out an experiment in which French-speaking participants had to detect the presence of target phonemes. The critical condition used non-words very similar to words (for example, *vocabulaite* instead of the real word *vocabulaire*, where the phoneme /t/ has replaced /r/). According to TRACE, *vocabulaite* should be assimilated to *vocabulaire* because of top-down influence, and then participants should not detect the presence of /t/. However, this was not the case.

Visual word recognition

So far, we have dealt with auditory input. In industrialised societies, visual input also provides an important source of linguistic information through reading. Most children in these societies receive substantial training in reading from about the age of six, with the result that reading is a highly efficient and automatic process with adults. For example, adults routinely read about 200 words per minute. A classic demonstration of the automaticity of reading is provided by the

Stroop effect (Stroop, 1935), which we have already met in Chapter 5. Although the task is to name the colour in which words are written, and not to read the words, people cannot help reading them. In general, similar phenomena as the ones we have described with auditory input have been identified with visual input. For example, Neely (1977) has shown that context affects reading and word recognition in particular. There is also a **word superiority effect** with visual input (Reicher, 1969) (see Figure 9.5). In the word condition, a word is briefly presented with a letter underlined, followed by a mask. Then, two letters are presented, and the task is to indicate which letter was underlined. The sequence of events is the

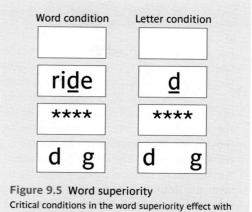

Figure 9.5 Word superiority
Critical conditions in the word superiority effect with visual presentation.

same with the letter condition, with the difference that that a single letter (also underlined) is presented instead of a word. The results show that participants are more accurate when the letter is presented as part of a word. Participants are also more accurate when the letter is part of a word (BLINK) as opposed to a non-word (e.g. LKFIN). A final interesting result is the **pseudo-word superiority effect**: performance is better when the letter belongs to a non-word that is pronounceable (e.g. FLINK) as compared to a non-pronounceable non-word (e.g. LKFIN). A connectionist model called the Interactive Activation Model (McClelland and Rumelhart, 1981), similar to the TRACE model that we have considered with auditory input, can reproduce these phenomena.

Stop and Think Speed reading – It's about some Russians
Woody Allen once joked that he took a speed-reading course and then read Tolstoy's hefty *War and Peace* (1475 pages) in one hour. And it worked! His summary of Tolstoy's great book was: 'It's about some Russians.' At the same time, speed-reading companies argue that the speed of reading can be considerably increased: up to 25000 words a minute, one company claims. Based on what you know about attention, memory and language, decide who is right – Woody Allen or the speed-reading companies?

We know much about how the eyes move during reading, in great part due to the use of eye trackers (see Box 9.4). The eyes do not move smoothly, but by saccades. **Saccades** last about 10–20 milliseconds and are ballistic – that is, they cannot be stopped or changed once started. Note that saccades can be forwards or backwards; in the latter case, we speak about **regressions**. Between two saccades, the eyes stay still in what is called a **fixation**. Fixations last 200–250 milliseconds with good readers, and can be much slower with poor readers or with children learning to read. Fixation duration is also affected by the difficulty of the text. Most of the information is extracted during fixations, and little if any information is gathered during the saccades. While foveal (central) vision is used for analysing the letters in detail, parafoveal vision is also used to roughly perceive words a few letters away and estimate where the next fixation should land.

Box 9.4 RESEARCH CLOSE-UP: **Eye-movement studies of reading**

For both practical and theoretical reasons, a considerable amount of research has been devoted to the study of reading. In particular, much research has been carried out with an eye tracker, an apparatus that records the position of the eyes (see Rayner, 1998, for an extensive review). Beyond just recording eye movements, research has also used eye trackers to modify the display in real time as a function of the position of the eyes. Figure 9.6 illustrates two of these techniques: the moving-window technique and the boundary technique. With the **moving-window technique**, the display is greyed except the letters preceding and following the fixation point. The visible part of the display changes with each new eye fixation. Varying the size of the window makes it possible to make inferences about the size of the visual span. With the **boundary technique**, the text a few letters after the fixation point is changed. As with the previous technique, the content of the display changes with each new fixation. Varying the distance of the changed letters and measuring reading speed provides information about the number of letters that are used in peripheral vision.

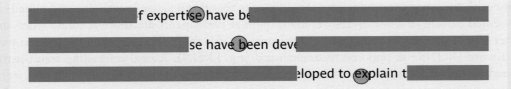

Figure 9.6 Examples of techniques used in eye-movement research on reading
Top. The *moving-window technique*. Each line shows how the display changes a function of an eye movement. The grey circle indicates the fixation point. *Bottom.* The *boundary technique*. Each line shows how the display changes a function of an eye movement. The grey circle indicates the fixation point. Note how some of the words in the display are changed (e.g. structure → expertise).

An important concept is that of the **perceptual span**, also called the **effective field of view**, which is the span from which information can be used for reading purposes. The perceptual span consists not only of foveal vision, but also of parafoveal and peripheral vision. A number of factors affect perceptual span, including the expertise of the reader, the difficulty of the passage, word frequency and the size of the font used. In languages such as Dutch, English and French, the perceptual span is at most four letters to the left of fixation, and about 14–15 letters to the right of fixation. This asymmetry is explained by the fact that there is more information on the right of the word currently being fixated. That this asymmetry is not the product of low-level aspects of the visual system itself has been established, because we get the opposite distribution (about 15 letters to the left and 4 letters to the right) in languages such as Hebrew that are read from right to left.

Not all words receive the same attention during reading. Functions words (e.g. 'the', 'a', 'for', 'on') tend to be skipped and are fixated only 20 per cent of the time. Contents words tend to be fixated about 80 per cent of the time. As you might expect, common words are not fixated for as long as rare words, and words that are predictable – typically short words – are fixated only for a short amount of time, if at all. Finally, rare and difficult words often increase the time the following word is fixated, a phenomenon called the **spillover effect**.

Syntactic processing

So far, our discussion has focused on the processing of letters and words. We can now move one level up in the hierarchy and consider how sentences are processed from a syntactic point of view. We have seen earlier that modern theories of syntactic processing tend to be influenced by the work of Noam Chomsky, and we need to briefly introduce some of the key ideas he put forward. The central question he wanted to answer is: how can humans produce an infinite number of new acceptable sentences and no unacceptable sentences? One of the many solutions he proposed – Chomsky has been extraordinarily productive, writing a book with a new theory every few years – is the idea of a phrase-structure grammar (see Box 9.5).

To explain how parsing is carried out, Frazier and Rayner (1982) developed an influential model, called the **garden-path model** because it explains phenomena where people are misled or 'led up the garden path' by ambiguous sentences. When people listen to or read a sentence, it is assumed that a parse tree is constructed incrementally. For example, looking at Figure 9.7, after hearing 'The boy', one would construct a partial tree containing S and NP. A key assumption of the model is that only one (partial) tree is constructed at time, even when several trees are possible. This assumption, which minimises the load of working memory, makes sense given the research we have reviewed in Chapter 6. Frazier and Rayner assume that meaning is involved only after a syntactic parse tree has been constructed. Thus, we have here a serial, bottom-up model, which assumes that the simplest syntactic structure is always chosen. More specifically, the model makes two important assumptions in order to explain which tree is constructed when several options are present. The first one is *minimal attachment*, which says that preference is given to the tree with the smallest number of nodes. Consider the following sentence:

11   The horse raced past the barn fell.

Most people have difficulty understanding this sentence – even after reading it several times. The minimal attachment principle can explain this difficulty as follows: in English, all sentences require a main verb, so it is natural to consider that 'raced' is the main verb. The alternative and, as it turns out, correct interpretation, is to consider 'raced' as part of a relative clause modifying 'horse': The horse, which raced past the barn, fell. However, this involves a more complicated structure, and people consider this interpretation only after the more natural and simple one has failed (see Figure 9.9).

Box 9.5 RESEARCH CLOSE-UP: **Phrase-structure grammar**

A **phrase-structure grammar** is a set of generative rules that show how syntactically correct (and no incorrect) sentences can be constructed from basic components (Chomsky, 1957). The sentence, which is represented as an inverted tree, is first constructed using grammatical categories; then, these categories are instantiated with real words. The idea is illustrated in Figure 9.7, which depicts a simple grammar for a small subset of English. We have three rules: S = NP + VP means that a sentence (S) is made by putting together a noun phrase (NP) and a verb phrase (VP). We do not yet know what NP and VP are, but this is explained by the following two rules. A noun phrase (NP) is defined as an article (art) plus a noun (N). A verb phrase (VP) is defined as a verb (V) plus a noun phrase. We also need to know the words (called *terminals*) that can be used for each of the grammatical categories, and this is indicated at the bottom left of the figure. For example, the article (art) can be either 'the' or 'a'.

Generating a sentence starts with the symbol S, which is unpacked into NP and VP, as shown in the tree on the right of the figure. We keep unpacking information, adding more branches to the tree, until all the bottom nodes are terminals. For example, as indicated in Figure 9.7, we can produce the sentence 'The boy read a book.' Other possibilities include 'A boy was a boy' or 'The book read a boy.' The last example illustrates an important aspect of phrase-structure grammar: it is only about syntax, and semantics does not play any role. Our example used a very simple grammar, but it is not hard to show that such grammars are very powerful (for details, see the Further reading section at the end of the chapter). In fact, just adding a few rules allows the generation of an infinite number of utterances, such as 'You think that the boy read a book', 'I think that you think that the boy read a book', and so on.

Psychologists have carried out considerable research to test the validity of phrase structure grammar and other types of grammar. They have in particular devoted much time to the following question, known as **parsing**: how do people construct a syntactic tree when they hear or read a sentence? To do so, they must analyse the syntactical structure of a sentence and come up with a tree stipulating the way the words are combined. It turns out that this is a difficult problem, because many sentences are ambiguous in the sense that they can lead to different trees. Figure 9.8 illustrates such a case. With sentence A, 'boring' has been parsed as an adjective, indicating a feature of the students. With sentence B, 'boring' is now part of the verb phrase, and indicates an action that is performed on the students.

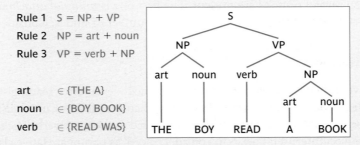

Rule 1   S = NP + VP
Rule 2   NP = art + noun
Rule 3   VP = verb + NP

art   ∈ {THE A}
noun   ∈ {BOY BOOK}
verb   ∈ {READ WAS}

Figure 9.7 A simple example of phrase-structure grammar

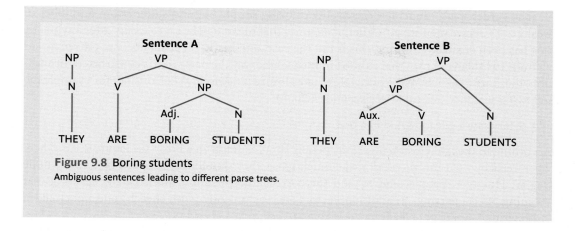

Figure 9.8 Boring students
Ambiguous sentences leading to different parse trees.

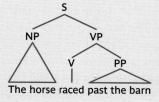

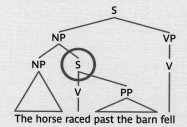

Figure 9.9 Example of minimal attachment

The second assumption is *late closure*, according to which the parser tries to attach new words to the current phrase (see Figure 9.10), which minimises the number of phrases in the parse tree. Consider the following sentence, taken from Frazier (1987):

12 Because he always jogs a mile seems like a short distance to him.

Most people have difficulty parsing this sentence, because they follow the principle of late closure and attach 'a mile' to 'jogs', which leaves 'seems' hanging in the air. When it is realised that 'a mile' is in fact the subject of 'seems', parsing can be carried out without difficulty.

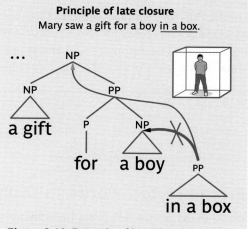

Figure 9.10 Example of late closure

The garden-path model has the quality of being simple but also suffers from a number of weaknesses. As we mentioned earlier, it assumes that meaning plays a role only after a syntactic tree has been created. However, this is not the case, and many experiments (e.g. Carreiras and Clifton, 1993) have shown that context influences the way the parse tree is constructed. In addition, there are cases where the principle of late closure is not followed. Consider for example the following sentence (example by Fernández, 2002):

13 Mary saw a gift for a boy in a box.

According to the late-closure principle, people should attach 'in a box' (see Figure 9.10). Then, when realising that this does not make much sense, they should reattach 'in a box' to the node 'a gift'. However, people tend to find the correct interpretation immediately, showing that meaning affects parsing. In addition, factors such as prosody (with speech) and punctuation (with written language) play important roles as well.

To some extent, the weaknesses of the garden-path model exemplify the weaknesses of Chomsky's theories in general: the role of meaning and context is underplayed, while empirical research suggests that these two variables are essential. More recent theories have tried to re-adjust the balance. An excellent example of this trend is offered by MacDonald *et al.*'s (1994) constraint-based theory. In this theory, and in direct opposition to the garden-path model, all the useful information is brought to bear as soon as possible and in parallel: the parser uses grammatical knowledge, lexical knowledge and information about frequency of interpretations. The key idea is that of constraint satisfaction: while a single constraint might not be sufficient to make a decision, taken together multiple constraints have the effect that only one interpretation of the sentence is possible. Interestingly, the theory assumes that all possible parse trees are constructed in parallel, again a clear difference in comparison to the garden-path model.

The theory has the advantage of explaining how context affects syntactic processing, something that the garden-path model could not do. However, it can also be criticised on several grounds. First, several essential aspects of the theory are left unspecified. It is one thing to propose that all knowledge is brought to bear in parallel when processing sentences, but it is another to fully implement this idea in a running connectionist model, something that MacDonald and colleagues do not do. Second, the idea that multiple parse trees are formed is not supported by empirical data and seems uneconomical, given the known capacity limits in working memory. In fact, there is little empirical evidence to support this hypothesis.

Stop and Think Language and artificial intelligence
Children can use their native language nearly perfectly after four or five years, but computers struggle to understand natural language after more than 50 years of research. In particular, parsing is still an unsolved problem for machines. Why do you think this is the case?

From printed words to sounds

While many researchers were busy trying to understand how the eyes move during reading, another group of psychologists were interested in how speech sounds are accessed during reading. This domain of research is interesting because it affords the possibility of discussing the role that neuropsychological data have played in some parts of cognitive psychology, and in particular how such data can help test theories. It will also allow us to present one of the great theoretical debates in cognitive psychology: the debate between rule-based accounts and connectionist accounts.

In this field of research, the typical task consists of presenting a string a letters on a computer display and asking the participants to read it aloud. The stimuli can be either words (e.g. CAT) or non-words (e.g. FASS). Two variables are of interest. First, stimuli can be *regular* or *irregular* (Coltheart, 1978). With regular stimuli, the pronunciation can be predicted by applying **spelling-to-sound rules**, also known as *grapheme–phoneme conversion* rules. (**Graphemes** are the basic units of a written language.) Some examples of such rules are given below:

'a'   → /a/
'ph' → /f/
'ave' → /eiv/
'int' → /int/

So, 'cat', 'gave' and 'mint' are regular words, as their pronunciation can be derived from the application of rules. By contrast, 'have' and 'pint' are irregular words, as the application of the rules would lead to an incorrect pronunciation. It is interesting that non-words tend to be read using these rules; for example, 'mave' would rhyme with 'gave', and 'rint' would rhyme with 'mint'.

The second important dimension of stimuli is consistency. *Consistent* stimuli have a pronunciation similar to the majority of words with a similar spelling (known as 'neighbours'), while *inconsistent* stimuli have a different pronunciation (Glushko, 1979). The top of Figure 9.11 shows an example of a consistent word, and the bottom an example of an inconsistent word. In Figure 9.11, *friends* denote words that have a similar pronunciation as the target word, while *enemies* denote words that have a different pronunciation. So while 'posh' agrees with the pronunciation of all neighbours, 'mint' is less consistent as there are three friends but one enemy.

Much is known about reading words and non-words. Inconsistent words take longer to name than consistent words, and rare words take longer to name. There is also an interaction between word frequency and consistency, in that the effect of consistency is weaker with highly frequent words and stronger with less frequent words. Finally, adults read over 90 per cent of non-words with a regular pronunciation.

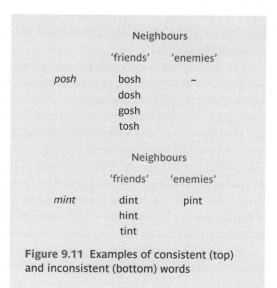

Figure 9.11 Examples of consistent (top) and inconsistent (bottom) words

Neuropsychological syndromes of reading

Understanding reading has obvious applied implications, as one would be in a position to develop better instructional methods for teaching children how to read. About 10 per cent of children and adults in the UK suffer from **developmental dyslexia**, which makes it hard for them to read and write. In this section, we will be concerned with another type of dyslexia, **acquired dyslexia**, which affects patients who were able to read normally in the past but now suffer from a number of impediments as a result of brain damage following, for example, a stroke or dementia. There are different types of acquired dyslexia, and patients suffering from each type show diverse types of difficulties in reading. *Surface dyslexia* patients have difficulties reading irregular words, although they can read most of regular words and non-words correctly. *Phonological dyslexia* patients have problems reading non-words and unfamiliar words, but can read familiar words. Finally, *deep dyslexia* patients show more severe symptoms: in addition to difficulties in reading unfamiliar words, they also commit semantic errors when reading. For example, 'swine' could be read as 'pig'. It should be pointed out that the symptoms shown by these types of dyslexia are often not as clear-cut as described here, a state of affairs typical in neuropsychology.

Theoretical explanations of acquired dyslexia

Dual-route model

Several theories have been proposed to explain both normal reading and the types of acquired dyslexia we have just presented, and we consider two of them here: the **dual-route model** (Ellis and Young, 1988) and the family of connectionist models developed by Seidenberg and McClelland (Seidenberg and McClelland, 1989) and Plaut *et al.* (Plaut, McClelland, Seidenberg and Patterson, 1996). The central disagreement between these theories is whether they assume that humans use rules (the position of the dual-route model) or not (the position of the connectionist model).

The dual-route model consists of a number of processes, as shown in Figure 9.12. A visual analysis system extracts perceptual features, and, at the other end, a phoneme-level system produces phonemes. These two systems are assumed to exist but are not described in any detail in the model. The focus of the model is on the internal 'boxes'. It is assumed that reading is carried out through two main modes of processing: a lexical and semantic mode on the one hand, and a grapheme–phoneme conversion mode on the other. The first mode of processing consists of two routes. In the lexical route (route 3 in Figure 9.12), information about pronunciation is extracted from the *lexicon*, which can be seen as a large database containing the words known by a person. In the lexical-semantic route (route 2), the model uses information from the semantic system in addition to information from the lexicon. Finally, route 1 uses the type of grapheme-conversion rules we have discussed above (e.g. 'p h' → /f/).

The model assumes that normal readers use both routes with familiar words, but that the lexical routes are faster, as the pronunciation of a word is already known and does not have to be generated by the letter-by-letter application of rules. Both routes are independent of each other. The model does a good job at explaining data from normal reading. For example, people can read irregular words (because they use the lexicon) and they tend to use a regular pronun-

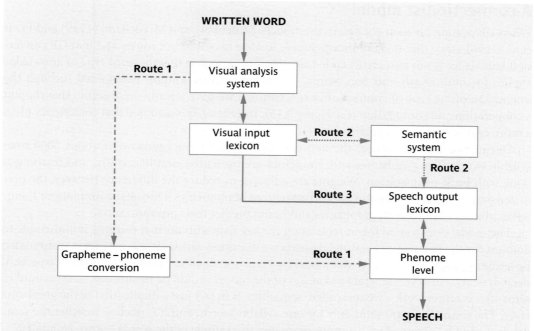

Figure 9.12 The 'dual-route' model (after Ellis and Young, 1988)
The model is called 'dual-route' rather than 'triple-route' because the key distinction is between route 1, on the one hand, which uses grapheme–phoneme conversion rules, and routes 2 and 3, which use the lexicon.

ciation when they read non-words (because they use graphemes-to-phonemes rules). It is also consistent with most neuropsychological data. Surface dyslexia is explained by damage to routes 2 and 3 but with route 1 intact. Thus, the only possibility in this case is to use route 1 and grapheme-to-phonemes rules – hence the difficulty with irregular words. Phonological dyslexia is explained by damage to route 1 only. In this case, grapheme-to-phonemes rules cannot be used, and unfamiliar words and non-words cannot be read. Finally, deep dyslexia is explained by damage to routes 1 and 3, so that only the semantic system (route 2) can be used. Unfortunately, this system is also partly damaged, which leads to the severe symptoms displayed by patients suffering from deep dyslexia.

However, the assumption of independence of routes, which is at the core of the model, is disputable. For example, Glushko (1979) showed that the consistency of neighbouring lexical items affects the reading of non-words, which should not be case if the two routes are independent. Similarly, Kay and Marcel (1981) showed that the brief presentation of words affects pronunciation of non-words. The non-word 'RASTE' is normally pronounced as /reist/; however, if CASTE is presented first, then RASTE tends to be pronounced as /ra:st/. To address some of these criticisms, the dual-route mode has been implemented as a computational model combining a rule-based and a connectionist approach (Coltheart *et al.*, 2001).

A connectionist model

When advocating for their connectionist models, Seidenberg and McClelland (1989) and Plaut *et al.* (1996) argue that it is not indispensable to have two different routes and that GP conversion knowledge is not necessarily coded as rules. They propose that the same type of knowledge applies for both words and non-words. The correct pronunciation is obtained through the interaction of the type of connectionist mechanisms we have already discussed in this chapter – cooperation and competition (see Figure 9.13). In general, it is assumed that consistency plays a more critical role than regularity.

During the learning phase, the network receives extensive exposure to about 3000 one-syllable words. The graphemes and phonemes are presented simultaneously, and learning is done with **back-propagation**. Weights are adjusted to reduce the difference between the predicted pattern of phonemes and the correct pattern of phonemes. During the simulations themselves, the network receives graphemes and has to predict their pronunciation.

The model does a good job at replicating the key data with normal reading. It is also able to account for the patterns of acquired dyslexia we discussed earlier. Surface dyslexia is simulated by lesioning the network. A related model by Plaut and Shallice (1994) accounts for aspects of deep dyslexia. However, several weaknesses of the model should be mentioned. The account of semantics is rather weak – what is called 'semantics' is in fact just a duplication of the grapheme layer. The simulations are valid only for one-syllable words, and it is unclear whether the same results would be obtained with a more representative sample of the words known by adults.

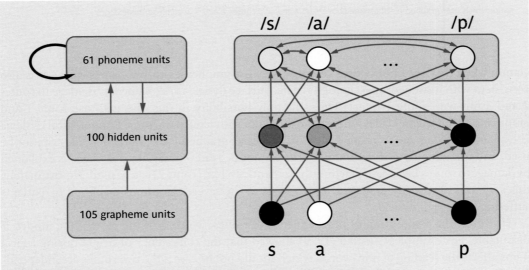

Figure 9.13 Plaut *et al.*'s (1996) model of how written words are read
Source: After Plaut *et al.*, 1996.

Text comprehension

The final level of analysis of this chapter is comprehension of an entire text, which has typically been studied with visual input. This level builds on the material we have considered so far – perceptual analysis of letters, word identification, syntactic analysis – but the focus of interest is at the semantic level: the way people understand the text. In addition to putting together material from this chapter on language, we will also use material from Chapters 6 and 7. In fact, specific topics of interest will be the roles of working memory and the role of long-term memory knowledge on text comprehension.

Capacity theory

The aim of capacity theory (Just and Carpenter, 1992) is to understand some of the variables that affect comprehension while reading. The emphasis is on the role of *working memory*, which is defined here as the part of memory that enables both processing and storage of information. The capacity of working memory is limited, and varies across individuals. Just and Carpenter argued that the *reading-span task*, originally developed by Daneman and Carpenter (1980), is the proper way to measure working memory capacity. In this task one presents a list of sentences that must be read for comprehension; at the same time, the last word of each sentence must be memorised. Thus, the task engages working memory both for processing (understanding the sentence) and storage (memorising the last word). For example, if the following sentences are presented

> When at last his eyes opened, there was no gleam of triumph, no shade of
> *anger*
> The taxi turned up Michigan Avenue where they had a clear view of the
> *lake.*

you should remember the words 'anger' and 'lake'.

Reading span has been shown to correlate with comprehension of a text (.80), which clearly supports the idea that the capacity of working memory is important in reading. (Incidentally, the correlation between reading span and verbal intelligence is .60.) There is also good evidence that participants with a high reading span can make more use of semantic cues and can maintain two different syntactic interpretations in parallel (Just and Carpenter, 1992).

Just and Carpenter partly implemented their theory in a computer model called CC-READER (for Capacity-Constrained READER). CC-READER is a parallel production system in which a capacity parameter limits the number of productions that can be held simultaneously in working memory (see Figure 9.14). This parameter can be varied in order to simulate individual differences. The two key assumptions of the model are that there is a trade-off between storage and processing, and that working memory limitations lead to errors in reading. Although capacity theory deals with all aspects of language, the specific computer implementation mainly deals with syntactic processing.

In general, Just and Carpenter (1992) provided convincing evidence that working memory plays an important role in reading, and that there are large individual differences. However, the theory has received some criticism. It is unclear to what extent the reading span measures something specific to reading or just reflects general attentional resources. For example, Turner and

> ## If you see a determiner (a, the)
> →
> Start a new noun phrase
> Expect the phrase to end with a noun
> Expect the noun to be preceded by modifiers

Figure 9.14 Example of a production in CC-READER

Engle (1989) have developed what they called an 'operation span', which also correlates highly with language comprehension. In this task, participants have to verify whether the result of a series of arithmetic operations is correct, whilst at the same time memorising the last word of each line. For example, with the following line

'IS $(3 \times 3) - 4 = 2$? TRAIN'

they should say 'no' and memorise the word 'TRAIN'.

A second issue relates to the origin of the working-memory differences. Just and Carpenter argue strongly that these differences are innate in nature. However, it could be countered that, rather than innate working memory differences causing differences in the efficiency of language processing and comprehension, it is rather knowledge-based differences in language processing and comprehension that cause differences in working memory. For example, Ericsson and Kintsch (1995) have proposed that extensive practice with reading leads to differences in knowledge, and that good readers can use knowledge structures held in long-term memory to supplement the capacity of working memory. Finally, the theory is somewhat circular: reading comprehension is explained by correlations with a reading task.

Importance of knowledge

While recognising words and processing the syntax of sentences clearly requires access to knowledge stored in long-term memory, the role of previous knowledge is even more important during text comprehension. When we read, we continuously make inferences, and it is actually known that skilled readers make better inferences (Oakhill *et al.*, 1986). We also use the type of **schemas** and **scripts** that we have discussed in Chapter 7. These well-integrated knowledge structures, which possess both a core and slots, are important for understanding a text, because they not only provide a framework that allows filling in gaps in the text and making inferences, but they also make it possible to store new information rapidly in long-term memory, through the presence of slots. However, a limit of most schema theories is that they are unspecified (Lane *et al.*, 2000).

Walter Kintsch is probably the scholar who has most contributed to our understanding of comprehension processes. In the influential model developed with Van Dijk (Kintsch and Van Dijk, 1978), he argued that text comprehension has two basic levels of analysis: the **argument**, which refers to the meaning of a word, and the **proposition**, which refers to a phrase or clause, or, more precisely, the minimal combination of words of which one can say whether it is true or false. So, for example, the sentence 'Romulus, the legendary founder of Rome, took the Sabine women by force' contains four propositions:

1 Romulus: took women by force
2 Romulus: founded Rome
3 Romulus: was legendary
4 Women: Sabine.

The first proposition occupies a more important role, as the other three propositions just qualify it.

According to Kintsch and Van Dijk, processing a text produces two types of structure. The **micro-structure** connects propositions together, and the **macro-structure** consists of a reduced version of the micro-structure, to which schematic knowledge has been added. The macro-structure only keeps a subset of the original micro-structure, because the theory assumes that it is stored in a memory buffer that has a limited capacity. The theory correctly predicts that reading time is a function of the number of propositions, and not of the number of words, and that the way the text is structured as propositions predicts priming better than distance expressed in words. For example, in our Romulus example, 'took' is primed better by 'Romulus' than by 'Rome', although 'Rome' is adjacent to 'took' while 'Romulus' is five words away. Data also show that memory for the micro-structure is good in the short term, but then decays rapidly, while memory for the macro-structure is less sensitive to time. However, many aspects of the theory are unspecified: it is unclear how propositions are formed, and how schemas interact with propositions.

In later work, Kintsch (1988) developed the construction-integration model (see Figure 9.15), which provides more details on the mechanisms involved during text processing than did Kintsch and Van Dijk's (1978) model. The model proposes that processing text leads to three levels of representation: surface, proposition (also known as the 'textbase') and situational. When a text is read, words from the external representation are coded into an internal linguistic representation consisting of propositions, which Kintsch calls *surface representation*. Then, these propositions are placed into a short-term buffer, called the *propositional net*. Information from long-term memory (semantic knowledge, inferences) is retrieved and added to the propositional net, forming the elaborated propositional net, where each proposition has a level of activation. These steps constitute the construction phase of the model. Not all information in this net is useful or even relevant, and propositions below a certain level of activation are culled by a process called *integration*. The outcome of this selection process is the text representation, which can be used both in producing language and storing new knowledge in long-term memory, with what Kintsch calls *episodic text memory*.

The model postulates a number of fairly complex mechanisms, and only aspects of it have been studied empirically. Kintsch *et al.* (1990) tested the assumption of three levels of text representation. They showed participants descriptions of standard situations (e.g. going to the movies) and gave them a recognition test either immediately after, after 40 minutes, after two days or after four days. They found that surface information, while fairly good with immediate recall, declined rapidly. The decline was slower for propositional information, and there was virtually no loss of information as a function of time for situation information. These results are consistent with the predictions of the construction-integration model.

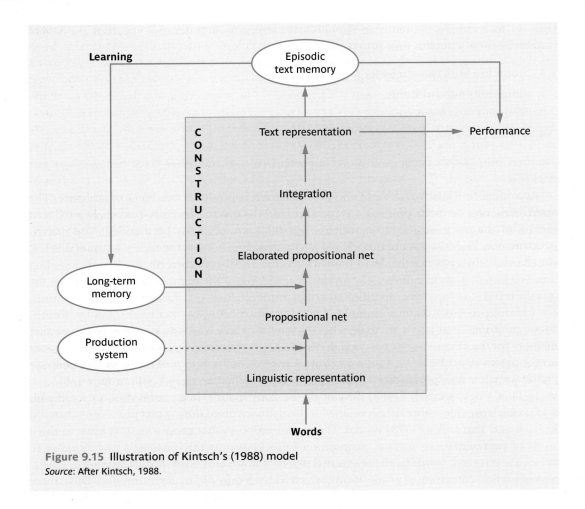

Figure 9.15 Illustration of Kintsch's (1988) model
Source: After Kintsch, 1988.

Stop and Think Clear writing (a)
Using what you have learnt in this chapter and in Chapter 6, propose a few guidelines that would enhance the quality and clarity of your writing.

Stop and Think Clear writing (b)
Advice often given to people willing to improve their writing is that 'writing is revising'. Why do even good writers have to revise and rewrite their text? Why can't they just put on paper what is in their head?

Chapter summary

Two key aspects of human language are its hierarchical structure and its use of arbitrary symbols. Research into the cognitive psychology of language has been heavily influenced by Chomsky, although some of his hypotheses, in particular that grammar cannot be learned and is therefore innate, have been challenged. Language engages both bottom-up and top-down mechanisms, and a recurring question has been the extent to which these two types of mechanism interact.

Data from speech perception (e.g. the phonemic restoration effect) and syntactic processing (e.g. the influence of semantics on syntactic processing) suggest that they do. At the same time, the data also suggest that this interaction is not massive, and that processing goes through a series of well-differentiated but also overlapping steps, starting with phonological processing and ending with semantic and pragmatic processing. The importance but also the limits of the interactions of bottom-up and top-down processing are well illustrated by the fact that theoretical models are located at different places on the continuum bottom-up and top-down processing. For example, the garden-path model of syntactic processing is essentially bottom-up, and the constraint-based model assumes full interactivity. The research on acquired dyslexia has shown how data from patients suffering from brain damage can help discriminate between cognitive theories. Finally, the work on reading and text comprehension has highlighted mechanisms that are also essential in other cognitive domains: role of attention in what gets stored in short-term memory and possibly learned, the impact of limitations of working memory on performance, and the importance of information stored in long-term memory, including chunks and schemata, in how the (linguistic) world is perceived and understood.

Further reading

Pinker (1994) has written an entertaining book on language, broadly inspired by Chomsky's theories. A classic introduction to psycholinguistics is Clark and Clark (1977). More recent introductions are provided by Taylor and Taylor (1990) and Harley (2008). Ellis and Humphreys (1999) present a detailed overview of connectionist models of language; interestingly, this book also includes reprints of several of the key papers discussed. Kintsch (1998) deals in detail with text comprehension.

Chapter 10

Reasoning and decision making

CHAPTER PREVIEW

After studying this chapter you should be able to do the following:

☑ Research into reasoning focuses on tasks where all the information necessary for a correct solution is known. By contrast, research into decision making uses tasks characterised by uncertainty.

☑ When we reason about something, we usually form a belief and then look for positive evidence that confirms the belief. This tendency to look for positive evidence, called 'confirmation bias', is in stark contrast to *scientific thinking* where much emphasis is also placed on negative evidence – an approach known as *falsifying*.

☑ Most of our thinking is based on our previous experience. We solve problems by forming an internal representation in our mind and using our knowledge. This is one of the reasons why we often do not perform well on artificial problems.

☑ When making decisions, we do not take into account every relevant factor, a task that would be beyond the boundaries of our limited cognitive apparatus. Instead, we use cognitive shortcuts (heuristics), which enable us to look at a few important factors and make a reasonable, but not necessarily the best, decision.

☑ The disadvantage of using mental shortcuts is that our knowledge on which they are based is sometimes incorrect. The consequences are cognitive biases, which are the main focus of researchers in decision making.

☑ Cognitive biases do not mean, however, that we are irrational. Once problems have been phrased in a more realistic way so that we can use our experience, we often turn out to be rather good decision makers.

Introduction

Animals are remarkable creatures capable of incredible feats, some of which we will consider in the next chapter, on problem solving. However, none of us would think of them as having capabilities that are thought to be exclusively human: animals do not talk nor are they able, among other things, to do complicated arithmetic. Or are they? Around a hundred years ago, there was a horse in Berlin whose intellectual prowess challenged the very notion that there are exclusively human abilities. When asked by his owner Wilhem von Osten, a respected mathematician, to multiply 4 by 4, the remarkable horse would tap his front hoof 16 times and stop. The Clever Hans, as the German public called him because of his intellectual powers ('*der kluge Hans*' in German), could not only do simple arithmetic tasks such as adding, subtracting, dividing and multiplying, but could also read and spell using a previously established system of tapping that translated letters into numbers.

The exhibitions with Clever Hans attracted increasing public curiosity. Sceptics asked whether the animal had been misunderstood because of its inability to use language. Von Osten demanded a scientific inquiry. Finally, the Berlin scientific establishment sent a young psychologist, Oskar Pfungst, to examine more closely the possibility that the animal possessed human-like intelligence. It was quickly established that there was no scam involved. Von Osten certainly was not a cheat; Clever Hans would tap the right number of times when any other person would show him a board with an arithmetical assignment. Instead of gathering additional evidence on the mathematical genius of Clever Hans, Pfungst tried to identify occasions

Figure 10.1 Clever Hans and von Osten in Berlin at the turn of the twentieth century overshadowed even the recently opened underground subway (not shown in the picture!)
Source: © Alamy/Mary Evans Picture Library.

when Clever Hans failed to calculate correctly. One such instance was when von Osten, or any other person who acted as the examiner, did not know the answer to the problem: Clever Hans was lost. He could only tap the correct answer in around 8 per cent of instances, which was in stark contrast with his almost perfect performance when the examiners knew the problem (and therefore the answer). It turned out that Clever Hans indeed had remarkable powers, but they did not have much to do with mathematical ability (Pfungst, 1965). He was very good at picking up visual cues, no matter how slight, from the examiners. After presenting the question, the examiners would bend forward, look at the hoof which was the sign for Clever Hans to start tapping. When Clever Hans tapped the right number of times, the examiner would slightly straighten and glance up, which was the sign for Hans to stop tapping.

Stop and Think Learning by Clever Hans

The signs and cues picked up by Clever Hans were almost unnoticeable, and completely unintentional. They were nevertheless enough to shape the behaviour of the animal. Can you provide a plausible learning mechanism using Chapter 7 to explain how Clever Hans behaved so perfectly?

The multiple forms of thinking

Thinking is obviously a key characteristic of human – and perhaps animal! – nature, and psychologists have studied this question from different angles, which can be grouped into three categories. Historically, the first people to investigate the 'laws of thought' were the philosophers Aristotle and Leibniz, as well as the mathematician Boole, who all proposed that human thought functions like the laws of logic. This hypothesis has inspired a considerable amount of research in cognitive psychology in the field of **reasoning**, which we will consider in the first part of this chapter. We talk about **inductive reasoning** when probable conclusions are derived from the available statements (also called **premises** in logic), and **deductive reasoning** when the conclusions necessarily follow from the premises. The second main hypothesis, discussed in the second part of this chapter, is that humans think using the laws of probability, and that we attempt to optimise our choice when trying to make decisions, combining the value of the possible outcomes with their probability of occurring. The considerable research that has been carried out on this question in psychology and economics is known as **decision making**. An interesting characteristic of these first two approaches is that the experimenter typically provides a set of options, and the participant has simply to select the correct solution from this set. The issue of how participants come up with the solutions themselves is studied by a third group of research on thinking, based on the idea of search in a problem space, which we will discuss in Chapters 11 and 13. The emphasis is on how people find their way in the maze of possible solutions, the size of which can often be considerable (think of choosing the perfect present for an acquaintance or selecting articles to include in an essay). A related research field, known as **analogy making**, is interested in the extent to which knowledge acquired in a domain can be transferred into a different domain, thus facilitating thinking.

Although these approaches differ in the types of task studied and the theoretical assumptions made, it is important to realise that they all study the same question: thinking. In addition, they all reach, through different routes, the same conclusions that echo those made in previous chapters: knowledge stored in long-term memory is essential to thinking, limits in attention and short-term memory make seemingly simple problems very hard indeed to solve, and the extent to which attention is directed to the key aspects of the problems is an excellent predictor of whether people will find a good solution.

Scientific reasoning

Oskar Pfungst's approach to the problem raised by Clever Hans is often used as a primer for scientific thinking. Confronted with numerous instances supporting the hypothesis that Hans had mathematical ability, Pfungst tried to falsify this hypothesis instead of gathering more confirming evidence. According to Karl Popper (1968), the famous philosopher of science, **falsification** is the only valid way to test the validity of theories (see Box 10.1). Gathering more positive evidence for a certain claim can only bring us so far, because no claim can ever be completely confirmed. No matter how many instances of positive evidence we have collected, it is always possible to come across a piece of evidence that will turn out to be negative (this is known as 'Hume's problem of induction', after the eighteenth-century Scottish philosopher). Consider the following real-life example. For many centuries, it had been believed that all swans were white. Then, in the eighteenth century, black swans were found in Australia (Sutherland, 2007). In general, instead of possibly wasting years and years gathering more positive evidence, one

Box 10.1 RESEARCH CLOSE-UP: **The basis of scientific thinking**

The notion of falsification is the crux of the scientific method. In order to establish a causal link between two occurrences, finding a relation between them is necessary, but it is not sufficient. For any conclusion about causality, it is necessary to conduct a falsification experiment. On a more philosophical level, the scientific method and the falsification strategy correspond to John Stuart Mill's (1843) rules of inductive logic. If we are to conclude that X causes Y, we need the rules of **agreement** and **difference**. The rule of agreement states that if X is followed by Y, then X is sufficient for Y, and could also be the cause of Y. However, the mere co-occurrence of X and Y does *not* mean that X causes Y. For the causal relation we need the rule of difference – if Y does not occur when X does not occur, then X is necessary for Y to occur.

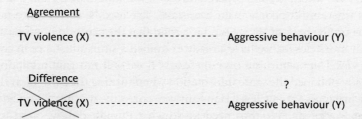

Agreement

TV violence (X) --------------------- Aggressive behaviour (Y)

Difference   ?

TV violence (X) --------------------- Aggressive behaviour (Y)

Figure 10.2 Mill's rules of agreement and difference with the example of the influence of TV violence on children's aggressive behaviour. The real question is whether aggressive behaviour will be shown even if there has not been exposure to TV violence.

ought to look for negative evidence immediately. If there is none, we can be more certain than before that a particular claim is valid. This strategy of falsification in the scientific method may at the moment sound abstract and alien to you, and there is a good reason for this, as you will soon see. It is, however, as important in everyday life as it is in science and may save you from many irrational beliefs.

Stop and Think Induction rules and experimental design

In psychology, experiments often involve two groups of participants: an experimental group, which receives a treatment of interest, and a control group, which does not receive the treatment. Why do you think it is necessary to use a control group? Would it be possible to conclude a causal relationship between the treatment and the factor measured solely on the results of the experimental group? What does this have to do with Mill's induction rules?

Let us consider one of the most famous experiments in cognitive psychology, the **selection task**, developed by British psychologist Peter Wason (1966, 1968). Cards have a number on one side, and a letter on the other side. You are presented with four cards with the following numbers and letters:

Using these four cards, your task is to find out whether the rule – *if a card has a vowel on one side, it has an even number on the other side* – is correct. You should turn over only the necessary cards. Before reading further, try to figure out which card(s) should be turned over, keeping in mind Popper and Pfungst's strategy of falsification.

Most people opt for the cards 'E' and '4', or even 'E' alone. The card with 'E' seems to be a good choice and is chosen by most people – if the other side does not show an even number, we can be certain that the rule does not apply for this set of cards. But what if there is indeed an even number on the other side? We would need to proceed further if we want to be certain that the cards follow the rule. This is where most people make a mistake. The card '4' seems like a natural choice. If there is no vowel on the back of '4', we can be certain that the cards do not follow the rule. But if we think about it more closely, we have already examined a similar instance in choosing the card 'E'. If we get a vowel upon turning over the card '4' we will not gain additional information, because we already obtained the same information when turning the card 'E'. If this reminds you of finding more instances when Clever Hans answers correctly, it is not a coincidence – the same mechanism is at work here. We thus need to do what Pfungst did; we need to try to find an instance where the rule is not valid, we need to try to falsify it if we are to be certain that it is indeed valid. We already know that 'E' has an even number on the back. The real question is whether the vowel will appear when we turn over the card that does *not* contain an even number. The presence of the vowel on the back of '7' would immediately falsify the rule. In conjunction with 'E', turning the card '7' offers the fastest way of finding out whether the rule is correct.

Box 10.2 RESEARCH CLOSE-UP: **Wason's 2 4 6 problem**

To further illustrate the notions of confirmation and refutation, let us take a look at an ingenious experiment by Peter Wason (1960). The participants are given the sequence 2 4 6 and told that the sequence follows a particular rule. The task of the participants is to find out the rule by producing sequences of three numbers. They could produce as many sequences of three numbers as they wished and would receive a simple YES or NO as feedback after each sequence. On the basis of the first 2 4 6 sequence, most participants formed a rule involving a sequence of even numbers increasing by two. Their test sequences were similar to 6 8 10 or 12 14 16. In both instances they received YES as feedback. After they received enough positive evidence, they would stop and state the rule – increasing by two. To their amazement, the rule that they generated and saw confirmed was wrong! The rule was simply any sequence of increasing numbers. The co-occurrence between positive feedback and the sequences involving increasing numbers by two was enough for most unsuspecting participants. They never thought of trying to disprove their rule by a sequence such as 8 6 10 or 1 7 32. Wason's deceptively simple *2 4 6 problem* uncovers a deeply rooted human tendency to look for evidence confirming one's beliefs. It also shows why scientific thinking is inherently difficult and why humankind needed centuries to come up with a method – the scientific method based on experiments – powerful enough to produce significant breakthroughs, which only happened really in the past two centuries.

Theories of reasoning

Why do people choose the cards 'E' and '4' in the selection task when they contain the same information? Before turning to the theoretical explanations of people's failure to reason properly (scientifically), let us introduce a practical observation. In all instances mentioned so far, the claims did not matter much to the participants. Nevertheless, they regularly looked for instances that were confirming the claim and did not search further. They fell prey to the **confirmation bias** – a human tendency to confirm views held rather than falsify them (see Box 10.1 and Box 10.2). The situation is even more complicated when people hold strong beliefs, as is often the case in everyday life. Consider the following example: Tom is a gullible person believing in extrasensory perception. He has just thought of his best friend John and at that exact moment the phone rings. Surprise, surprise, John is on the other end of the line! This just happens to be one of the many instances when Tom thought of John and John called him within seconds. This must be telepathy, Tom is certain. It just cannot be a coincidence that, over and over again, when he thinks of someone, that person calls him within seconds. While Tom is preoccupied in confirming his belief in telepathy by recalling instances when John called him when he had thought of him, he readily forgets the instances when he thought of John but John did not call him. It could be that telepathy sometimes works and sometimes does not, but a safer guess is that the confirmation bias, and perhaps other cognitive biases which we will consider later in the chapter, are at work here. It is not surprising then that lay people are susceptible to the confirmation bias when their strongly held views are in question (see Box 10.3 and also Box 10.4).

Box 10.3 CLASSIC EXPERIMENT: **Lord, Ross and Lepper's (1979) experiment on the death penalty**

Lord *et al.* (1979) devised a cunning experiment to show what happens when confirmation bias and strongly held beliefs combine forces. They asked participants what they thought about the death penalty. Then, they divided participants into two extreme groups which formed the two levels of the first independent variable of their experiment: for the death penalty and against the death penalty. The people who were indifferent towards the death penalty were excluded from the experiment. The participants then read two out of four studies that examined the effects of capital punishment on the murder rate. Two of the studies were of a longitudinal character and showed the number of murders before and after the introduction of the death penalty within various states in the USA. Although the methodology in both studies was the same, each of these two studies had a different conclusion – one suggested that the death penalty was successful, the other that it was not. The other two studies were of a cross-sectional character, comparing the number of murders between different states that did or did not introduce the death penalty. Again, one of the two studies presented positive evidence for the death penalty, while the other presented negative evidence. The study type (longitudinal/cross-sectional) presented the second independent variable, while the outcome (positive and negative conclusion) was the third independent variable (see Figure 10.3).

All the participants had their attention drawn to the drawbacks in the two types of study. The longitudinal studies contained a flaw in that many factors other than capital punishment can play a role in the decrease of murder rates in one state over time (e.g. decreased

Participant	Group (1st IV)	Study type (2nd IV)	Outcome (3rd IV)	Study
1	**Pro** death penalty	Longitudinal	+	1
		Cross-sectional	–	4
2		Longitudinal	–	2
		Cross-sectional	+	3
...		...	...	...
15	**Anti** death penalty	Longitudinal	+	1
		Cross-sectional	–	4
16		Longitudinal	–	2
		Cross-sectional	+	3
...		...	...	...

Figure 10.3 The design of Lord *et al.*'s (1979) experiment

consumption of narcotics). The cross-sectional studies, by contrast, compared different states, where the murder rate can be equally dependent on other factors than the introduction of the death penalty (e.g. in one state the murder rate could already be very low before the introduction of capital punishment). In short, all participants were told that both types of studies had serious shortcomings. Each participant was asked to read two stories, one longitudinal and one cross-sectional. One of the studies provided positive evidence for the death penalty, the other negative. The order of presentation of the outcome variable (positive vs negative) and the type of design (longitudinal vs cross-sectional study) was counterbalanced. Using the same attitude scale employed to initially allocate participants into two groups, Lord and his colleagues measured the strength of participants' belief after they read the first study, and after they read both studies. The dependent variables were thus the strength of the attitude before, after reading one study, and after reading both studies.

All participants believed that the study that favoured their own views was more convincing and better conducted than the study that ran counter to their belief. In accordance with confirmation bias, they easily noticed the flaws in the study that ran counter to their views, but failed to notice similar flaws in the study that favoured their views. Another sign of confirmation bias was the intensity of attitude after reading the first study. The attitude towards capital punishment was intensified after reading the first study where the study confirmed their view; there was no change when the evidence went against it. After reading both studies, this time exposing themselves to both positive and negative evidence, all the participants even strengthened their initial view: opponents of the death penalty were more against it and proponents more for it!

You have certainly come across examples of people not taking into account the seemingly obvious weaknesses in their position, while easily disregarding the strengths of the opposing arguments. The study by Lord and colleagues shows impressively how far these double standards can go. In the next two chapters you will see the mechanism behind this remarkable mental blindness.

Stop and Think Political life and first impressions

Why do you think that supporters of a particular political party attend only meetings of that party? Why do people tend to read newspapers that publish commentaries close to their hearts? Why do you buy the magazine/newspaper that you read? Why do you think first impressions are important when meeting new people?

Pragmatic reasoning schemas

Wason's selection task is admittedly abstract and probably not very relevant in everyday life. However, a variation of this problem – with exactly the same logical structure as the original selection task – is closely related to our everyday experience. You are a policeman enforcing the rule that only persons over 18 can drink beer. In other words the rule is: *if someone in the bar is drinking beer then that person must be over 18.* You enter a pub and the owner claims that the four persons in the bar at the moment follow the rule. The first is drinking beer, the second is drinking coke; the third is obviously over 18, while the last seems under 18:

Beer	Coke	22	16

Whom will you check to find out whether the owner is telling the truth? In this case, it seems obvious that the person drinking beer is relevant, as is the person who seems under 18. If the first happens to be under 18 and the second is drinking alcohol, the owner's licence will be taken away. The person drinking coke is not important nor is the person clearly over 18. This seemed childishly simple in the comparison with the mind-boggling classical selection task. Around three out of four participants get the answer correct in the pub problem (Griggs and Cox, 1982) while rarely more than one person in ten gets it right in the original selection task with abstract material. Yet, the two problems are essentially the same.

The classical selection task and its real-life version belong to a broader category of problems that involve '*if* something *then* something' statements. These *if–then problems* are also called **conditional problems**. Both problems are solved using the same formal rules of logic. The first rule, *modus ponens*, is quite intuitive – if *p* then *q*. In the classical selection task, *p* would be a vowel (card E) and *q* would be an even number (card 4), while in its real-life version *p* would be the Beer card and *q* would be the 22 card. The other rule, called *modus tollens*, is much less intuitive – if *not q* then *not p*. To successfully solve the classical selection task, people need to realise that they need to check the 'if *not q* (card 7) then *not p* (card K) rule' in combination with the obvious if *p* then *q* rule. As we have seen, the application of *modus tollens* represents the main stumbling block in solving the classical selection task. This rule is easier applied in the real-life version of the selection task (*not q* would be the 16 card and *not p* would be the Coke card).

Nevertheless, some theorists (Rips, 1994) argue that people actually use universal logical rules when solving such problems, with both abstract problems and examples from real life. However, there seem to be clear differences between the two problems. In the pub example we can use our previous experience, while in Wason's selection task we do not have any experience to fall back on. According to Cheng and Holyoak (1985), people use **pragmatic reasoning schemas** based on experience to accommodate abstract knowledge structures. In the pub case, the schema invoked could be called the 'permission schema', because it is about being allowed to drink alcohol. Since there is, usually, no experience to fall back on in the case of the cards in Wason's selection task, no pragmatic schema can be invoked. Consequently, we fail miserably (for more examples on reasoning in familiar and unfamiliar domains, see Bruner *et al.*, 1956; Tschirgi, 1980; Wilhelm and Beishuizen, 2003).

The pragmatic reasoning schema model emphasises the role of experience and context in contrast to universal logical rules (of which most of us have little or no experience). The role of context is also evident in the following example (Manktelow and Over, 1991). A mother wants her child to tidy up his room, while the child wants to play. The mother enforces a rule by telling the child: *if you tidy up your room, then you can go out and play*. Now, which of the following four instances do you need to check out to find out whether the mother applied the rule?

Tidy	Untidy	Play	No-play

If the mother applied the rule, the instance where the room is *tidy* should lead to play, while the instance where there is *no play* should *not* result in a tidy room, as then the mother would have broken the rule. So far, the example is similar to the classical selection task and the pub problem. Now, imagine that it is the child who sets the same rule, and that the mother wants to find out whether the child has broken the rule. How would the mother proceed? Suddenly, the right answer is to check what happens when the room is *untidy* and when the child *plays*. Depending on the perspective and context, the answers can be completely different.

Mental models

Conditional problems are notoriously difficult, as we have already seen with the example of the selection task. According to Philip Johnson-Laird (Johnson-Laird, 1981, 2001; Johnson-Laird and Byrne, 1992), who was Wason's student, this is because we try to decode the meaning of every statement. On the basis of the meaning, we form internal representations of the statements. These internal representations are the **mental models** we use to deduce whether the statements and conclusions are correct. Imagine you are told that:

- John is taller than Paul
- Paul is taller than Dave.

You will easily represent these two premises and realise that John is also taller than Dave. Imagine, however, that there is another statement saying that Mitch is shorter than Paul. You will update your mental model and will be able to identify John as the tallest, followed by Paul. On the basis of your mental model you are certain that Dave and Mitch are shorter than Paul, and in particular John, but you will not be able to tell who is taller between Dave and Mitch. If this looks too easy, consider the following statements:

- All the artists are beekeepers
- Some of the beekeepers are chemists.

The question is whether all of the artists are also chemists. According to the mental model theory, you will solve this problem by making mental models based on the premises. You can imagine a row of artists, a row of beekeepers and finally a row of chemists (see Figure 10.4). While all of the artists are also beekeepers, only some of the chemists are beekeepers (in other words, some of the chemists are *not* beekeepers). Now you can verify whether all artists are also chemists by checking the mental model (all artists would need to be beekeepers and chemists). Given that there are some beekeepers who are not chemists, you will reject the conclusion.

• artist	=	beekeeper	=	chemist	
• artist	=	beekeeper	=	chemist	
• artist	=	beekeeper	=	chemist	
•		(beekeeper)	=	(chemist)	
•		(beekeeper)	=	(chemist)	
•				(chemist)	
•				(chemist)	

Figure 10.4 Artists, beekeepers and chemists mental model

Both pragmatic reasoning schemas and mental models draw on our experience and our knowledge. Unlike pragmatic reasoning schemas, mental models do not rely on pragmatics but rather on the pure meaning of the statements. Both models are, however, in stark contrast to the theories that propose that we behave strictly according to logical rules (Rips, 1994).

Decision making

In the previous examples we had all the information necessary to come to a conclusion. As we all know, this is rarely the case. In everyday life we are forced to make decisions, some of them of great importance for our future, without knowing all the information. This uncertainty forms the main characteristics of **decision making**. Last year you were at an important crossroads in your life. You had to choose whether to study, what to study and where to study. These are all important decisions that depended on many factors, including your wishes and your estimated potential. Do you remember how you arrived at the decision to study, how you selected psychology or a related field, and how you chose the university? One school of thought argues that people take all the available pieces of information and weigh their importance using numbers. More specifically, they attribute a value to each option, and estimate the probability that this option will occur. By multiplying the value of an option by its probability, one gets its **expected utility**. The best solution is the option with the largest expected utility. If this sounds like economics and mathematics to you, it is not by chance – this is the way people are thought to make decisions in classical economics. All factors would be taken into careful consideration in order to obtain the optimal choice – in our case, in which university to enrol. According to this approach, people are **maximisers**: they always select the optimum option.

Now, we all know this is *not* exactly the way you came to your choice of what and where to study, nor is it the way to make less important decisions (e.g. to read this chapter to the end rather than going out with friends). This is what Herbert Simon (1957) observed when he went back to his hometown Milwaukee to examine how people make decisions in a naturalistic context. Simon observed the managers in the recreation department of the city administration when they were allocating budgets. He found that they did not consider all options, did not weigh the available information, and did not try to explore the whole problem, searching for the optimal solution. Instead, they would take an option, figure out whether it is worth going for, and decide to pursue the option if it led to good enough results. Thus, people were **satisficers** rather than maximisers. One obvious reason for this strategy was the limitation of the cognitive system we have been talking about in the previous chapters. People are simply incapable of holding and processing a lot of information in their minds, and often they cannot even access this information because of the time that this would take. They certainly are not irrational, but they display a **bounded rationality** owing to their cognitive limitations. Simon, who obtained the Nobel Prize in Economics in 1978 for this and related findings, found that people would use various strategies, shortcuts and rules of thumb when exploring potential solutions. These strategies, called **heuristics**, will be featured in the next chapter, on problem solving, another area shaped by Simon's research. Heuristics are of crucial importance in this chapter too, but in another light. Daniel Kahneman and Amos Tversky continued Simon's research on heuristics and showed when this can lead us astray. This research into human decision making, which we will describe in the next section, earned Kahneman the Nobel Prize in Economics in 2002.

The availability heuristic

You have heard it many times – flying is safer, much safer, than travelling by car (you are about 10 000 times more likely to die in a car accident than in a plane accident). And yet, millions of people, maybe including you, experience much more fear travelling by aeroplane than by car. Why, when faced with a decision to take a plane or a car, do people prefer a more dangerous mode of transport? One of the reasons is our previous experience. It is not only our personal experience of travelling with cars and planes, although this is clearly important, but also the experiences of others we have heard of and read about. An accident in a car usually ends up in a small number of casualties and rarely features in the news. A plane crash, on the other hand, makes headlines. This is not only because, unfortunately, many people lose their lives, but also because it is a rare event. When trying to decide on which is safer, people base their decision on their experience. Unsurprisingly, when they try to remember bad things that happened with cars and planes, the plane accidents will be more available from their memory – thanks to the powerful encoding caused by the gruesome coverage in newspapers and its emotional impact (see Chapter 7). A recent sad example of the dangers and power of the **availability heuristic** is offered by the aftermath of the tragic events of 9/11. Scared by these events, which featured aeroplanes, many people who usually took planes decided to travel by car. The roads, not nearly as safe as the air in normal times, became even more crowded and this resulted in unnecessary deaths – in the three months following 9/11, about 350 more people in America lost their lives in car accidents than usual (Gigerenzer, 2004).

As mentioned above, Kahneman and Tversky (1973a; Tversky and Kahneman, 1974) described in detail the dangers of the human tendency to use previous experience to make decisions. One of their famous examples is the following:

> If a word of three letters or more is sampled at random from an English text, is it more likely that the word starts with 'r' or has 'r' as its third letter?

Please try to answer this question before reading on. Probably you will try to recall the words that start with an 'r' and others who have an 'r' in the third position. It turns out that it is fairly easy to generate words when an 'r' is in the first position, but it is hard to come up with the second type of word. In fact, there are more words with an 'r' in the third position than words with an 'r' at the beginning. If you do not believe us, just go back and count the number of the two types of words in this paragraph. (However, be wary of generalising from a small sample!)

Stop and Think Self-contribution in a group
When asked to estimate their contribution to a joint project such as in discussion groups, sports or even marriage, what do people do? Do they underestimate or overestimate their involvement? Why do you think this is the case?

Stop and Think Everyday examples of the availability heuristics
Why do lotteries proudly present their past winners and give them considerable publicity? Why do people believe that they are more likely to win the lottery than be struck by lightning, when the reverse is true? Why do fruit machines make such a noise when somebody wins?

Representativeness heuristic

All gamblers experienced it – their favourite number or combination of numbers has not come up for a while. If you play the lottery and your favourite combination of numbers has not come up for years, the chances are that you have experienced it too. It is a belief that your favourite combination or number *must* come next. After all, it has been a while since it appeared last time and, if there is nothing fraudulent going on, your feeling tells you that it should come soon. But somehow it rarely comes. Take the example of coin tossing. Your friend tosses a perfectly balanced coin five times and each time it is heads. Surely, the next one should be tails? You put your money on it but, surprisingly, it is heads again! You are furious with your friend, accusing him of cheating. You should not be certain, however. The problem is that the coin has no memory – the sixth tossing is the same as any other. The chances are 50 per cent that it will be heads, the same as for tails. Hence, it is perfectly possible to get six heads in a row. If your friend, however, obtains 600 heads out of 600 tosses, then you should immediately cancel your friendship!

The problem is that we take a short sequence of six tosses as representative of a much longer sequence such as of 500 or 1000 tosses. According to the **law of large numbers**, we should expect around 50 per cent of heads only in a large number of tries, such as in 600 tosses. Only large samples are sufficient to predict an outcome. However, it is conceivable that there will be six heads in six tosses (the exact probability is $(.5)^6 = .016$). This tendency to expect that possible outcomes will even out in small samples is called the **gambler's fallacy**. The gambler's fallacy is an example of a wider heuristic called the **representativeness heuristic**. Decisions are inevitably based on personal experience and available examples. The problem is that we often consider just a few instances to build an opinion about something or to arrive at a decision. Sometimes it even takes a single instance – a vivid example of a relative who lived a long and healthy life despite being a heavy smoker will often suffice to persuade a person that smoking cannot be that deadly. In order to obtain a fair idea about somebody or something, we need to base our decision on a large number of instances and not just a few or a single one.

Stop and Think Why do skilled gamblers (and psychologists!) prefer large samples?
Players of Texas hold'em, or any other kind of poker, claim that, despite the fact that the cards are randomly drawn, it is a game of skill. What makes poker a game of skill? When does it become a game of skill? Similarly, why do psychologists insist on large samples?

Stop and Think Representativeness example in squash
The rules of squash were changed so that a set now lasts until 9 points rather than 15 points, as was the case earlier. Who benefited from this change: better or worse players?

Neglect of base rates

People also have a tendency to disregard **base-rate information** – that is, the frequency with which certain events or attributes occur in the underlying population – when estimating the likelihood that somebody belongs to a specific group. For example, if you hear that your new neighbour in London is a professor who likes poetry, is rather shy and is small in stature, would you think that he is a professor of Chinese studies or of Psychology? As it turns out, most people would think that the description fits better a professor of Chinese studies (Kahneman and Tversky, 1972, 1973b). The problem is that there are so many more professors of Psychology than Chinese studies in England that it is highly likely that there are more professors of Psychology who are shy, small in stature and write poetry than all Chinese studies professors taken together. People often look at what is presented to them and forget about the background information concerning the population.

If this all looks somewhat artificial to you, you may be interested to hear that it has serious consequences in real life. For example, important decisions in medicine suffer from the neglect of base rate. Imagine that one of your friends, John, decides to have a routine HIV test. He does not consume drugs, is heterosexual, has no partner who uses drugs and is not a haemophiliac. In this population, the prevalence of people infected by the virus is 0.01 per cent (i.e. one person

---

Box 10.4 EVERYDAY APPLICATION: **Paranormal beliefs**

In his show *Trick of the Mind*, the magician Derren Brown gives a group of five young people a personalised horoscope upon receiving their birth dates. The same procedure was repeated with people from the USA, the UK and Portugal with identical results – youngsters thought that the horoscope fitted them at least 80 per cent, and most said that it was almost entirely correct.

In fact, this experiment had been done more than 60 years ago with the same result (Forer, 1949). The idea is rather simple and consists of including a number of the so-called **Barnum statements** that fit anyone. For example, does this claim fit you: *'At times you are extroverted, affable and sociable, while at other times you are introverted, wary and reserved'*? You will be hard-pressed to find instances where the most extrovert person did not have her introvert moments. You certainly know that it applies to you! But that is not the whole story. As it turns out, we do not only seek to confirm our beliefs, but we also remember positive evidence much better, even if we may have encountered more negative evidence (Nisbett and Ross, 1980; Pitz *et al.*, 1967). It is thus not surprising that people recognise themselves in tailor-made horoscopes or astrological readings. Helped by the Barnum statements, they tend to remember the hits that they look for in the first place rather than the misses to which they pay little attention. Next time your friend asks you to read their horoscope, you may want to pull a Derren Brown on them by reading another horoscope.

Astrology and horoscopes are just two instances of how prone people are to succumb to the confirmation bias with non-scientific 'phenomena'. This tendency has been stable through the years, as can be seen by the continuing popularity of extrasensory perception, alien abduction and telepathy – three out of four Americans believe in some kind of paranormal occurrences (Shermer, 2002). The situation is probably not very different elsewhere in the world. We will not go into detail about how people come to believe in such things (see Shermer, 2002) but will rather try to sketch out how they persist in their beliefs. We have already seen that focusing on positive evidence, the confirmation bias, is at least partly responsible for beliefs in telepathy. Two other candidate explanations are selective memory and neglect of the underlying population rate. Representativeness probably plays a role in situations where a single occurrence becomes a basis for a belief (e.g. encounters with aliens, UFOs). Finally, the classical study by Lord *et al.* (1979) demonstrated to what lengths people are willing to go to defend their views on such matters. The power of beliefs, when combined with cognitive biases, is not to be underestimated!

in 10 000 will be infected). The test for detecting HIV is fairly sensitive and specific, almost 100 per cent sure – it detects 99.9 per cent of infected cases (sensitivity) and gives a negative result in 99.99 per cent of the cases where the person is not infected (specificity). The outcome of the test is that John tests positive for HIV. What is the probability that John is indeed infected by the HIV virus? Most of the people, basing their answer on the positive HIV test and the high detection rate of the test, estimate that the chances that John is actually infected are very high – 99.9 per cent or even 100 per cent. You may be shocked to find out that the likelihood of John really being infected with HIV is only 50 per cent. (This probability can be computed using something called *Bayes' theorem*, although we will see a simpler way to obtain the correct probability shortly.) People, even experts such as medical doctors or social workers working in the area, are often so impressed by the high detection rate (i.e. sensitivity) of the HIV test that they forget that a person from a non-risk group is highly unlikely to be infected with HIV. In a later section we will take up the reasons why people, including many medical experts diagnosing patients (Gigerenzer, 2003), fail to solve this and similar problems. But first, we need to clear up what it means to be rational, and whether humans are indeed rational.

(Ir)Rationality?

The research programme on heuristics and biases in human thinking and decision making, which Tversky and Kahneman started almost 40 years ago, paints a rather bleak picture of human **rationality**. However, this does not really dovetail with our experience: although we probably do not always make optimal decisions, at the same time we do not feel that our decisions are particularly bad. Certainly, we would not think of ourselves as irrational! Gigerenzer strongly opposed the idea that humans are as prone to errors as is suggested by Kahneman and Tversky. For example, take the errors caused by the availability heuristic. Gigerenzer *et al.* (1999) claim that there is nothing wrong, and mostly there is much good, in using our previous experiences and recognition shortcuts to come to a decision. Sometimes simple rules can produce equal, if not better, decisions than complex sophisticated rules that take numerous factors into account.

For example, a simple heuristic based on recognition can be highly efficient. If you are asked to estimate the size of a city, say the German cities Herne and Cologne, you may fall back on the things you know about them. You happen to have heard of Cologne – it has a famous cathedral and a football club – while Herne does not ring a bell. Consequently, you decide that Cologne has a larger population. American students used the **recognition heuristic** over 90 per cent of the time even when they were provided with information on the presence or absence of a premiership football club in the city (a sure sign that the city is large). The recognition heuristic is extremely simple, intuitive and quite efficient (Goldstein and Gigerenzer, 2002).

Similarly, the problem with the HIV test above is one of representation and not human irrationality. In order to decode the problem, it is necessary to have a good knowledge of probabilities (or percentages, which are similar to probabilities – a .01 probability corresponds to 1 per cent), something most people, including experts who should know better, are not very skilled at. The calculations using probabilities are relatively new, having been extensively in use only for the past 50–60 years. In contrast, people have been using frequencies for a long time. Gigerenzer had an idea that makes the HIV and similar problems easy to solve, just by changing their representation in our minds. Instead of dealing with probabilities, we should use frequencies, as they occur often in everyday life. Out of 10 000 people (level I in Figure 10.5) from the non-risk group, one will have HIV while 9999 will not (level II). The one that has HIV is highly likely to test positive, because there is a 99.9 per cent chance that the test will be positive (level III). We also know that the test gives negative results in 99.99 per cent of cases when the person is not infected. Hence, out of the 9999 uninfected people, 9998 will get a negative test (99.99 per cent out of 9999 is 9998, as .9999 × 9999 = 9998). Thus, out of those 9999 uninfected persons, one will nevertheless be diagnosed with HIV (level III). This leaves us with two persons who test positively for HIV. Since only one of them is really infected, the probability of the person from the non-risk group being infected positively is only 50 per cent (one out of two). Empirical studies (Gigerenzer, 2003) show that people are indeed fairly good at solving such problems when they use frequencies.

Thus, people can be good at making decisions with the same problem that was so difficult with probabilities. They just need to change their representation, something we will encounter again in Chapter 11. But why is there such an insistence on errors in the literature on decision making? We encountered a similar trend in Chapter 4, where optical illusions are one of the favourite topics of researchers. One of the reasons is that the mistakes of our cognitive system tell us something about how it functions. This may sound paradoxical at first, but consider the now (hopefully!) well-known examples of Clever Hans, Wason's 2 4 6 problem and falsification in general. Obtaining additional evidence of the supposed ability of Clever Hans would bring us only so far. Maybe we would eventually stumble on the real cause of Hans' remarkable performance. A fair guess is that it would take a while. Instead, we focused on trying to establish rela-

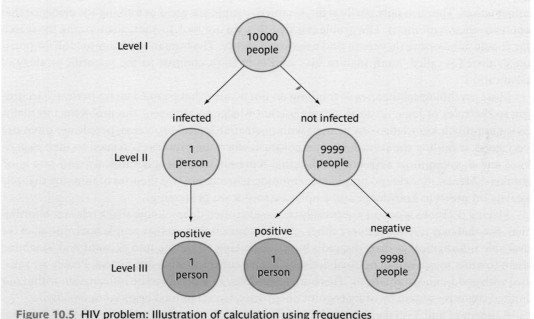

Figure 10.5 HIV problem: Illustration of calculation using frequencies

tions between factors when the performance is disabled, when it does not appear any more. Obtaining evidence when our cognitive system processes information without difficulty is the same as gathering evidence about Hans' mathematical exceptionality. It is without doubt useful and insightful, but after a while we gain little more information. Examining the processes and analysing the situations when the system does not function perfectly, on the other hand, gives us the opportunity to obtain new, important information.

Are we rational, then? Are there biases and illusions in our thinking and decision making? You saw that it is also a matter of representation and context. A slight change and we behave very rationally. It should be noted, however, that not all biases disappear when the context is changed (Sides *et al.*, 2002). Even if they did, it would not change the fact that in certain situations humans do not behave rationally. As Piattelli-Palmarini (1996) cunningly noted, erasing the arrows in the Müller-Lyer illusion (see Chapter 4) and perceiving the lines as equal does not change the fact the lines are not perceived as being equal when the arrows are present. Similarly, it is beyond doubt that humans are not that bad at making decisions, since our species is well adapted to its environment. Considering our limited cognitive resources, we are probably doing pretty well in an environment as complex as our world. Rather than aiming for perfect solutions, we have developed useful cognitive shortcuts that spare us the need for lengthy calculations that would probably be beyond our capabilities anyway. Everything has a price, and the price of our 'bounded rationality' and adaptability is mercilessly uncovered by the seemingly trivial problems invented by the researchers on the cognitive biases.

Chapter summary

Most people think that they are not bad at drawing conclusions when given the necessary information. They are only partly right. Granted, people are good at looking for evidence that confirms their hypothesis. The problem is that they do not look further, abandoning the search for conclusions before they try to find negative evidence. The human tendency to look for positive evidence is called 'confirmation bias' and is in stark contrast to the scientific strategy of falsification.

Most psychological theories of thinking do not assume that people behave perfectly according to the rules of logic. Instead, people use knowledge to represent the problems internally. Since not much knowledge can be used with normative logical problems, people are often not very good at finding the conclusions. In contrast, when the problem is related to their experience and they can form a meaningful internal representation, people suddenly turn into good thinkers. Mental models and pragmatic reasoning schemas are two theories of thinking that rely heavily on previous knowledge and emphasise top-down processing.

Making decisions is not easy, especially because we often do not know all the relevant information. But that may not be necessary either – Herbert Simon showed that people rarely use all of the available information at their disposal. Instead of taking all factors into account and weighting them in order to achieve an optimal decision, people consider only a few factors. People are satisfied with good-enough solutions. This human tendency to accommodate information within our limited cognitive system by using cognitive heuristics, Simon termed *bounded rationality*.

Kahneman and Tversky extended Simon's research on heuristics, showing how dangerous relying on them can be. The most famous heuristics they identified, sometimes called 'cognitive biases', are the availability and representativeness heuristics. The availability heuristic is the tendency to make a decision based on the instances that come first to our mind. The problem occurs when these instances are heavily biased in comparison with the actual frequency of events. The representativeness heuristic corresponds to the tendency to make a single instance or only a few instances characteristic of a whole group of events.

While Kahneman and Tversky paint a rather bleak picture of human rationality, Gigerenzer and others take a more positive stance. Heuristics are usually useful and efficient, as demonstrated by the example of the recognition heuristic. Moreover, most of the biases can be 'debiased' by using appropriate internal representations of problems. The emphasis on errors and biases in thinking and decision making as well as in science in general is not a chance occurrence. Errors and biases give us additional insight into the mechanisms of our mind that the instances without errors do not offer.

Further reading

Markman and Gentner (2001) provide a useful review on thinking and its relation to other higher-level cognition. The classical papers by Kahneman and Tversky (Kahneman and Tversky, 1973a; Tversky and Kahneman, 1974) should not be missing from the library of any psychologist. Gigerenzer's entertaining book *Reckoning with risk* (2003) is a good start to becoming familiar with his counterattack on the Kahneman and Tversky's heuristics programme. Finally, the two popular books by Sutherland (2007) and Piattelli-Palmarini (1996) not only contain relevant everyday examples of the theories presented in this chapter, but are also such a joy to read that it is impossible not to recommend them in conjunction with this chapter.

Chapter **11**

Problem solving

CHAPTER PREVIEW

- ☑ Problems can be solved by trial and error, an approach that does not require much understanding. Problems can also be solved by a sudden flash of insight that produces an 'a-ha' experience.

- ☑ Most of the problems we face in everyday life do not require particularly insightful solutions, but rather need to be worked out in a deliberate fashion.

- ☑ Given that our cognitive system is limited and cannot completely deal with the full complexity of most problems, we are required to use cognitive shortcuts: strategies that lead to acceptable solutions most of the time. These problem-solving strategies are also called heuristics.

- ☑ Problem-solving strategies are usually investigated with puzzle-like problems where the influence of previous experience is minimised.

- ☑ One of the main ingredients of intelligent thinking and problem solving is the ability to use previously acquired knowledge in similar situations. Analogical problem solving seems to be particularly difficult when there are no obvious similarities between situations.

Introduction

Clever Hans, whom you read about in the previous chapter, turned out to be more sensitive to remarkably subtle cues than intelligent in a traditional way. The ravens inhabiting the Japanese capital Tokyo, on the other hand, seem to be genuinely clever creatures, at least when it comes to cracking nuts. Faced with the problem of getting to the fruit hidden in the shell, many birds drop nuts from great heights. Since some nuts are inevitably harder to crack than others, it is not unusual to see birds, in particular ravens and crows, dropping nuts on a street and waiting for cars to do the job for them. However, collecting the cracked nuts can be problematic if you are in Tokyo with cars zooming around. The ravens in Tokyo found an ingenious solution to this problem: a raven would alight on a lamp post, drop a nut on the part of the street where there was a pedestrian crossing, wait for a car to drive over and crush it, drop to the ground and then, setting an example to all nearby children, wait for the green pedestrian light! Once the traffic lights changed and all the cars stopped, the raven would make its way to the opened nut and collect it.

We face all kinds of problems in everyday life. Some are so easy that one would never consider them real problems. Let us say that you are hungry, something you experience every now and then during every single day. It is likely that you will open the fridge and find something to eat, or, if you are outside, stop at a place that sells food. This is not exactly what we understand as problem solving – even animals are required to perform more demanding feats to be called problem solvers. Imagine, however, that you are hungry on a deserted island where there is nobody and nothing in sight. The difference between the two problems is that in the former case you can call on your previous experience. You are likely to solve the problem by recalling previous instances from your memory. In the deserted island scenario, you will need to be imaginative to find food as you will probably never have experienced any similar situation. Coming up with solutions in new situations is the kind of problem solving we will examine in this chapter.

In research into **problem solving**, the problems are general in the sense that everybody understands what the desired end goal is and that it is possible to achieve it, although it may not be immediately clear how to do this. The main idea behind this approach, which is typical of the whole experimental approach in cognitive psychology, is to study the processes involved in problem solving without contamination from other processes such as learning, memory and familiarity. Just as in the research on attention, perception, memory and learning, the goal is to uncover pure, basic processes, only this time the processes are those behind problem solving. As you will realise reading this chapter, this is even more difficult with problem solving than with other cognitive phenomena. Trying to solve the desert island problem, we may fall on our previous experience or theoretical knowledge about seas, islands and creatures inhabiting them. We may not have exactly the same experience with the problem, but we may have enough knowledge about the relevant parts or tools that we can make use of in the current situation. This application of acquired knowledge in new situations is called **transfer** or **analogy making**. Thus, memory, learning and transfer are all inevitably connected with the problem-solving process. That is also one of the reasons why problem-solving research was left at the outskirts of mainstream experimental psychology. It is difficult to investigate something you can hardly define and distinguish from other related phenomena.

The striking example of ingenious problem solving by no less than 'bird brains' in Tokyo unavoidably draws the question of how it is achieved. Did it take ravens years until they came up with the solution, or was it a sudden flash of brilliance by a single raven? Did the solution then spread through imitation, or was it left up to every raven to reinvent it? These are just a couple of questions the research on problem solving is trying to answer. While it mostly deals with human problem solving, the very first experiments were conducted with animals.

The Gestalt approach

In a circus it is not unusual to find cats playing the piano, pigeons following instructions printed on cards or pigs putting a coin in a money-box (which is, needless to say, in a pig's shape). While these feats are remarkable at first sight, there is nothing particularly amazing about them. The animals are painstakingly trained to execute a pattern or a sequence of actions leading to the desired goal. Their learning is not based on an insightful reflection but rather on a **trial and error** approach. In a classical study carried out by the American behaviourist Thorndike (1898), hungry cats had to pull a lever to get out of a cage and get to food. They tried and tried unsuccessfully to reach the food while moving around the cage. Eventually, by chance, they would press the lever, which would open the door and lead them to food. One would think that this success would be enough to learn to obtain the food next time. However, the cats still spent a considerable time fooling around until they pressed the lever again. In the next trials, they spent less and less time, until they could finally find the solution immediately. Although the cats could then solve the lever problem without trial and error, they needed dozens of trials to form a close association between a behaviour sequence and its consequences (see Chapter 7). While the end product of a cat deliberately pulling a lever to get to food might look impressive, the whole process of forming associations is unspectacular. For intelligent behaviour to be established we would expect the cat to pull the lever immediately after the first successful trial.

You may by now be disappointed with those American cats that look rather dull in comparison with the Japanese ravens. It is possible, however, that the behaviour of the ravens is also the consequence of trial and error, and we are only admiring the highly sophisticated end product. A German scientist, Wolfgang Köhler (1921), provided evidence that animal behaviour can also be insightful. Working in exile on the Canary Islands during the First World War, Köhler conducted a number of ingenious experiments with chimpanzees showing that they are capable of **insightful problem solving**. Chimpanzees would be placed in a cage with two sticks and food, usually bananas, placed outside. Food could not be reached with either of the two sticks, but the sticks could be extended by combining them into a single stick. At first, a particularly clever chimpanzee called Sultan was, as most of his peers, frustrated by not being able to reach the food with the sticks. He would then withdraw into a corner of the cage and sit still. At some point he would suddenly jump up, rush to the sticks and put one on the other, and reach the food! Sultan was also able to solve other similarly difficult problems such as putting two containers one on top of the other to reach bananas hanging from the ceiling. In all instances Sultan would spend some time, usually after unsuccessful attempts and just before finding the solution, seemingly doing nothing.

The study by Köhler was also the first piece of research on problem solving by Gestalt psychologists, already prominently featured in Chapter 4. As with perception, the Gestalt school emphasised that a problem is a whole that is more than the sum of its individual elements. When the current perception of the elements of the problem is insufficient to solve the problem (for example, two sticks of insufficient length), a new representation of the relations between the problem elements is necessary – combining the two sticks into one of sufficient length. The moment this **restructuring** happens is usually connected with the 'a-ha' experience of a sudden realisation (see also Chapter 13 for the processes involved in insight problem solving).

While it is unclear whether the animals are able to experience such insights, as initially shown by Köhler (see Box 11.1), it certainly occurs often among humans. Consider the two-string

Figure 11.1 Sultan with sticks and boxes

Sultan solving a problem by putting together two sticks (left) and stacking boxes (right).

Box 11.1 RESEARCH CLOSE-UP: **The feathered ape in your garden**

Just like humans, animals can use analogies. It is reported that Sultan, the chimpanzee we met at the beginning of the chapter, once felt hungry but, since no experiment was running at the time, could not stack containers together to reach the bananas hanging from the ceiling. With his empty belly rumbling, Sultan used what was at hand – he led Köhler under the bananas and when the unsuspecting man was well positioned, he simply jumped on his shoulders to reach the food! Unfortunately, like most of Köhler's sensational findings, this amazing display of analogy has not been replicated in other studies with apes (e.g. Povinelli *et al.*, 2000). The main difference between Köhler's studies and later experiments was that Köhler used apes that were captured in the wild, while the other studies carried out experiments with apes raised in captivity. A possible explanation, then, is that Köhler's chimpanzees had the opportunity to learn some of their behaviours from their peers.

However, similar behaviours have been replicated in other animals. The most famous of all was Betty, a female crow captured in Oxford. Weir *et al.* (2002) reported an experiment in which Betty had to retrieve food placed at the bottom of a tiny vertical tube. Since the tube was too narrow, the bird could not use her beak. The experimenter also put two aluminium wires nearby – a straight one that could not be used for

Figure 11.2 Betty at work, hoping Abel is not around

Source: Weir *et al.* (2002).
Courtesy of Alex Kacelnik.

food retrieval, and a bent one that was suitable as a tool. The initial idea was to see whether Betty could pick the right tool to retrieve the food. As in life, serendipity plays a role in science. Betty was always accompanied by Abel, an older male crow (not captured in the wild like Betty but bought from a zoo). Unfortunately, Abel would repeatedly snatch the bent wire and fly away with it. Poor Betty was left with the unusable straight wire. After several attempts to retrieve the food with it, Betty arrived at the ingenious solution of bending the wire using the edges of a nearby brick and using the bent wire to retrieve the food! In the next trials Betty did not even attempt to use the straight wire but would immediately start bending it. At the same time, Abel would simply observe Betty at work. During the whole period of the experiment, Abel never once tried to bend the straight wire. He did, however, display another kind of intelligence. Once Betty was about to pull the container with the food out of the tube, Abel would fly down to the tube and take the container! Abel might not have been bright enough to bend the wire and retrieve the food, but he would not have gone hungry, that is for sure!

problem (Maier, 1931). Two strings are hanging from the ceiling and your task is to tie them together. The strings are long enough to be tied together, but they are so far away from each other that it is impossible to connect them in the most obvious way – you would have to let one string go in order to reach the other. Some other material is at hand, including a pair of pliers. You may wonder what pliers are doing there when there is nothing to cut, but therein lies the trick! One needs to use the pliers as a pendulum, tying them to one string and setting the string in motion. That way one can reach the swinging string once it comes towards the other string. The problem turned out to be difficult even with subtle cues such as the experimenter brushing one string and setting it in motion. The main difficulty of the problem lies in what another Gestalt psychologist, Karl Duncker (1945), called **functional fixedness** – our tendency to consider only the usual function of objects. It is our everyday experience with pliers and their cutting function that makes the two-string problem so difficult. This was shown empirically by Birch and Rabinowitz (1951), who

Figure 11.3 Illustration of the two-string problem
Source: Maier, 1931.

first let two groups complete an electrical circuit by using either a switch or a relay. After this introductory task, the participants were given the two-string problem with a number of objects at their disposal, including the switch and relay that either group had received in the first task. Both groups had difficulties in solving the insight problem but eventually, after some hints (e.g. accidental brushing of the strings), they managed to swing one of the strings using one of the devices at hand. The two groups, however, chose markedly different devices – the group who had repaired the electrical circuit with a switch set the string in motion using the relay, while the group who had used a relay chose the switch to solve the two-string problem. Again, the immediate previous experience in using an object in a particular way makes it less likely to use it in other ways. Another dramatic example of the influence of our previous experience on problem-solving performance is offered by Luchins' (1942) classic water-jug task (see Box 11.2).

Box 11.2 CLASSIC EXPERIMENT: Luchins' (1942) *Einstellung* (mental set) effect

Most experiments in cognitive psychology have not been exactly close to real life. Some, however, such as the insight problems developed by Gestalt psychologists, are so much fun that they have been used in motion pictures. In the third instalment of *Die Hard*, the bad guy, Simon Gruber (played by Jeremy Irons), is looking to rob a bank and at the same time avenge his brother, Hans Gruber, killed in the previous instalment by John McLane (Bruce Willis). One of the tasks Jeremy Irons gives to Bruce Willis, accompanied by a sidekick Zeus (Samuel L. Jackson), is a brain teaser in the best Gestalt tradition. It is necessary to put exactly the weight of four gallons on the bomb in order to deactivate it. One pound more or less and the bomb will destroy the whole park. Besides water from the (elephant) fountain, there are only two jugs, one of three and the other of five gallons. Is it possible to obtain the required four gallons to save the people in the park?

One of the solutions, the one found by the good guys in the film, is to fill up the five-gallon jug and, using the water in this jug, fill up the three-gallon jug. Discard the water in the three-gallon jug and refill it with the remaining two gallons from the five-gallon jug. Then one would only need to fill up the five-gallon jug and use it to fill the smaller three-gallon jug, already containing two gallons, to the top. That would leave us with four gallons in the bigger jug. *Voilà*, the world saved once again!

If you think that this was a mean brain teaser by Simon, consider what Abraham Luchins (1942) did to his participants in the classical experiment on the *Einstellung* (mental set) effect. The participants had to solve similar water-jug problems, this time with three jugs of different capacities (127, 21 and 3 in arbitrary units – say, pints). There was no fountain as in the film, no real jugs either, only a paper-and-pencil brain teaser with the following rules – the amount of water was unlimited and the jugs could only be filled or emptied completely in order to keep track of the exact amount of water in the jug. The real cunning of the design is that Luchins gave his participants a few warm-up introductory problems. As shown in Table 11.1, we can get the amount required in the first problem (100 pints) by first filling up Jug B (127 pints), then pouring 21 pints from Jug B into Jug A, and finally pouring 3 pints from Jug B into Jug C twice (of course emptying Jug C once before the second filling). If you look at the five introductory problems, you will notice that they can all be solved using this method – filling up Jug B, emptying it once to Jug A and twice to Jug B.

Problems six and seven can also be solved using the same method (B – A – 2C), but also involve a trick that most participants do not notice – both problems can be solved using a much shorter solution: simply pouring Jug A into Jug C in the sixth problem, and pouring Jugs A and C into the empty Jug B in the seventh problem. These two problems are called *critical problems* because they involve two possible solutions: an old but long solution, and a new and shorter one. Surprisingly, 80 per cent of participants failed to spot the shorter solution and went with the familiar longer one. But the biggest surprise is yet to come. Luchins went a step further and presented another problem where only one solution was possible. The solution was not the familiar long one but rather the same simpler A – C solution. Since the familiar solution is inapplicable now, this kind of one-solution problem is appropriately called an *extinction problem*. Almost two-thirds of participants completely failed to solve the problem! By contrast, in a control group that was given the critical and extinction problems only, only 5 per cent of people failed to solve the extinction problem. These results are stunning given that this problem does not seem particularly difficult.

Luchins' ingenious experiment nicely illustrates the dangers of the mechanisation of thought. Once we have a good way of dealing with a situation, we tend to apply it to other similar situations too. In other words, to somebody with a hammer, everything looks like a nail! The problem is not only that we can fail to spot a better, more optimal solution, but that we can become completely blind to alternative solutions as illustrated by the surprising number of people who failed to solve the final extinction (1-solution) problem in the Luchins experiment.

Table 11.1 Luchins

Problem	Capacity of Jug A	Capacity of Jug B	Capacity of Jug C	Desired quantity
1	21	127	3	100
2	14	163	25	99
3	18	43	10	5
4	9	42	6	21
5	20	59	4	31
6	23	49	3	20
7	15	39	3	18
8	28	76	3	25

The first five problems are the introductory problems, which can be solved by B – A – 2C. Problems 6 and 7 can be solved by the same solution, but also by a shorter solution (A – C for Problem 6, and (empty) B + A + C for Problem 7). Problem 8 can be solved only by the short solution (A – C).

In the spirit of the previous problems, consider the following problem by Duncker (1945) originally used to illustrate the term 'functional fixedness'. You are given a candle, nails and a box of matches. Your task is to attach the candle to a wall next to the table so it does not fall down on the table. How would you proceed?

Figure 11.4 Duncker's (1945) candle and matchstick problem

The solution is given at the end of the chapter (Figure 11.11).

What is restructuring? The theory behind the insight phenomenon

The Gestalt psychologists showed that problem solving does not need to be a routine, laborious process and that it depends on the representation of the elements of the problem. They produced a number of ingenious experiments eliciting insight. However, they did not clearly specify the phenomena of restructuring and insight, let alone provide mechanisms to explain these phenomena. As we have seen in Chapter 1, cognitive psychology aims to explain, not just describe, phenomena.

Stellan Ohlsson's **representational change theory** (1992) uses Gestalt terminology and at the same time provides an elaborate mechanism which explains the processes involved in insight problems. Representational change theory focuses on the representation of the problems. When confronted with a problem, we try to make a mental picture of what the problem involves. In other words, we form an internal representation of the problem. For example, consider the mutilated checkerboard problem studied by Kaplan and Simon (1990): two diagonally opposite squares have been removed from a checkerboard and participants receive 31 dominos, each covering two squares (see Figure 11.5). The question is whether it is possible to cover the remaining 62 squares with the dominos. The description of the problem automatically activates knowledge related to previous experiences with boards and dominos. Thus, the first representation of the problem involves a board of 62 squares and 31 dominos, which will be used to cover the board. However, this is a rather inefficient representation given that there are almost 1 million possible permutations of the dominos – in Kaplan and Simon's study, a conscientious but unfortunate student spent 18 hours trying to obtain the solution mathematically, filling in numerous notebook pages in the process.

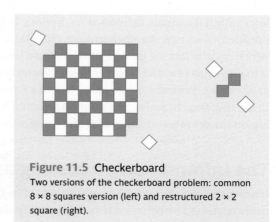

Figure 11.5 Checkerboard

Two versions of the checkerboard problem: common 8 × 8 squares version (left) and restructured 2 × 2 square (right).

What makes insight problems difficult is that generally the initial representation does not allow access to the necessary information. After trying for a while to cover all the squares, people realise that they need a new approach. Often, they feel that they are stuck, and that they have come to an impasse (block). In order to retrieve the necessary information, a new representation is required. This is done by elaborating and re-encoding the problem description. First, we may notice that one domino can cover only one black and one white square (re-encoding). Then, we may spot that the two missing squares, nowhere in sight in the original problem, were both white ones. Finally, by representing the problem in this way, it may suddenly strike us that there are 30 white squares and 32 black ones! After using 30 dominos on 30 white and 30 black squares, we are left with two black squares. You can also solve the mutilated checkerboard problem with a more ingenious and, of course, incredibly difficult, restructuring as shown in Figure 11.5. Alternatively, you can try the less abstract version of the same problem in the Matchmaker thought question.

Stop and Think Matchmaker problem and analogies

The mutilated checkerboard problem may look abstract and therefore difficult to solve. In contrast, a 'real life' version of the same problem called the 'matchmaker problem' (see below) looks almost trivial (Hayes, 1978). Would you say that people who previously solved the matchmaker problem would have fewer difficulties in solving the mutilated checkerboard problem since they are essentially the same?

In a small but very proper Russian village, there were 32 bachelors and 32 unmarried women. Through tireless efforts, the village matchmaker succeeded in arranging 32 highly satisfactory marriages. The village was proud and happy. Then, one drunken Saturday night, two bachelors, in a test of strength, stuffed each other with pierogies (dumplings) and died. Can the matchmaker, through some quick arrangements, come up with 32 satisfactory marriages among the 62 survivors?

Besides re-encoding and elaboration, the other process that leads to representational change – according to Ohlsson's theory – is constraints relaxation. A good example of this is the nine-dot problem, where one needs to connect nine dots with four straight lines without lifting the pencil (see Figure 11.6). When trying to solve this problem, you will probably first perceive the nine dots as a Gestalt, a unit (see Chapter 4). Consequently, the chances are that you will try to draw the four lines within the square delineated by the dots. In fact, the solution requires that you draw the lines outside this square. Another striking example is offered by the matchstick algebra problems, in which matchsticks are used to write down an (incorrect) equation with roman numerals. The task is to move just one stick in order to get a correct equation to work (Knoblich et al., 1999; Knoblich et al., 2001). Typically, when people try to solve this type of problem, they focus on the numbers in the equation. In reality, the solution sometimes requires relaxing this initial constraint by focusing on the operators (minus, plus and equal signs) rather on the numbers.

The information-processing approach

During the cognitive revolution mentioned in Chapter 1, the topic of problem solving, previously neglected by behaviourists, became popular again. The starting point was the observation that most of the problems in everyday life are solved in a fashion that does not involve the type

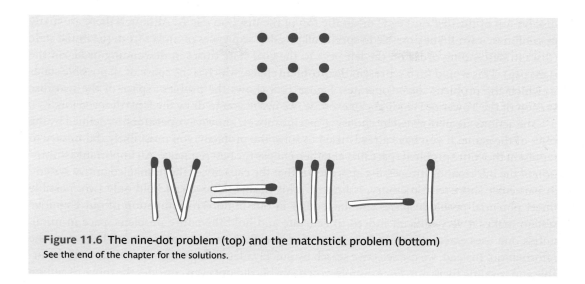

Figure 11.6 The nine-dot problem (top) and the matchstick problem (bottom)
See the end of the chapter for the solutions.

of insight characteristic of the Gestalt approach. For example, if you are about to go on a romantic date and your car does not start, you will probably try to fix it if the time allows. If that fails, you will probably resort to asking a friend to give you a lift or to relying on public transport. There is no place for insight here. A goal of the information-processing approach was to discover the problem-solving strategies that people use. Once identified, the strategies are then implemented in computer programs. If the programs capture the key processes used in problem solving, then they can solve problems just as humans can, which is of course of great interest in the field of artificial intelligence (AI). But it is not only AI that benefits from this approach. As mentioned in Chapter 1, computer simulations also inform psychological theories about the processes and mechanisms involved in human problem solving. In the case of problem-solving strategies, if the program does not produce results comparable to those of humans, which might include the presence of errors, then the theory is incorrect and needs modification. On the other hand, if the output of the simulations matches human behaviour, then one can have confidence that the program embodies a reasonable theory of human problem solving.

To illustrate the information-processing approach to problem solving, let us consider the four-disc version of the Tower of Hanoi problem (Newell and Simon, 1972). In the **initial state** of the problem, four discs of different sizes are stacked on the first peg, and the other two pegs are empty. The desired outcome, or **goal state**, is to have the same pyramid of four discs on the third peg. The rules of the problem, or **problem constraints**, are that (a) only one disc can be moved at a time, (b) a disc can be moved only if there is no disc on it and (c) a larger disc can never be put on top of a smaller one.

As you will realise when trying to solve this puzzle, the number of possibilities is quite large. Once we have moved the smallest disc to Peg B, and put the second disc on Peg C, we are left with a number of choices. We can, for example, move the disc on Peg C back to Peg A, a move that does not appear very smart, but that is nevertheless possible. We can also move the smallest disc on top of the disc on Peg C or on the top of the discs on Peg A. Although there are many possibilities, it would be possible to specify all possible sequences of moves from the initial state (discs in descending order on the left peg) to the goal state (discs in descending order on the right peg). This would then represent the **problem space**, which is the space of all possible states in which the problem solver operates. Figure 11.8 shows the problem space of the two-disc version of the Tower of Hanoi. As an exercise, we invite you to draw the four-disc version.

The actions are performed by choosing specific moves, known as **operators**, as defined by the rules of the game. If you have already tried to solve the problem, you most likely did not try to represent the entire problem space first and then choose the best sequence. An important assumption of the information-processing approach is that the capacity of the human cognitive system, in particular short-term memory, is limited. This means that we can hold only two, possibly three, potential problem spaces simultaneously in our mind. This limitation of our cognitive system makes it very difficult indeed to generate and hold the entire problem space in mind, unless one uses external aids such as paper and pencil, or even a computer, to help store the information. Instead, we use selective search by quickly identifying which moves are not reasonable and weeding them out. For example, you probably did not even consider the move of getting the smallest disc back on Peg A as your second move, because this would not bring you nearer to the desired goal state. This kind of strategy is exactly what we use in situations that put a burden on our cognitive system – we use shortcuts and rules of thumb, which are also called **heuristics**. As we have seen in Chapter 10, heuristics can lead us astray because they are not guaranteed to lead to the solution. In most instances of problem solving, however, heuristics are useful.

The particular heuristic of choosing a move that brings us nearer to the desired goal (and not choosing the one that takes us farther away!) is called **hill climbing** (Newell and Simon, 1972).

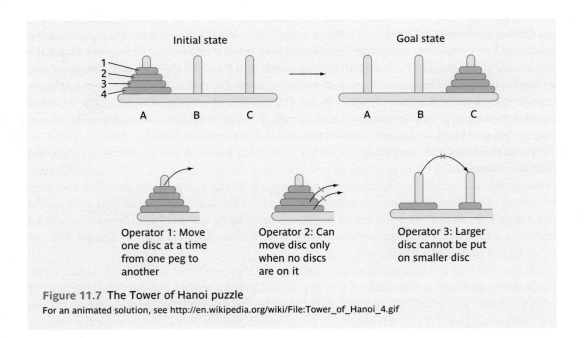

Figure 11.7 The Tower of Hanoi puzzle
For an animated solution, see http://en.wikipedia.org/wiki/File:Tower_of_Hanoi_4.gif

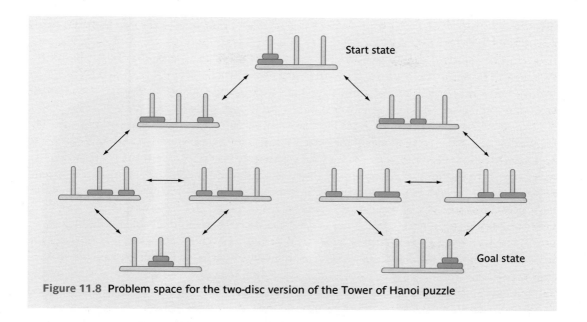

Figure 11.8 Problem space for the two-disc version of the Tower of Hanoi puzzle

This is a useful strategy, but it is also limited, because it does not involve a real understanding of the problem. Sometimes, we have to choose a move that leads us further away from the final goal in order to solve the problem. In such situations, hill climbing would not lead us to a correct solution.

A more efficient heuristic, based on a real understanding of the problem, is **means–ends analysis**. Once we understand that a problem may be complex as a direct consequence of its large problem space, we will probably try to break it down into more easily achieved subgoals ('ends'). Operations ('means') that would lead us to fulfil these subgoals would bring us nearer to the final solution. To go back to our example of the four-disc version of the Tower of Hanoi, one subgoal could be to put the largest disc on Peg C. Once we have achieved this, we are nearer to the final solution than previously, and the next plausible subgoal would be to put the second largest disc on Peg C, and so on until the smallest is put on Peg C. The sequence to achieve the first subgoal (moving the largest disc to its final location), is the following (discs are represented by Arabic numbers, and pegs by capital letters):

$$1 \rightarrow B; 2 \rightarrow C; 1 \rightarrow C; 3 \rightarrow B; 1 \rightarrow A; 2 \rightarrow B; 1 \rightarrow B; \text{ and } 4 \rightarrow C$$

Having put the largest disc on the third peg, a similar procedure can be used for the other discs.

Stop and Think **Understanding and learning**

Try to understand the things you learn! Using the knowledge you have just acquired about problem-solving heuristics, try to explain what would be a likely scenario for a person who tries to solve a problem for the first time. Hint – problem space, subgoals and heuristics are all important!

Figure 11.9 Herbert Simon (left) and Allen Newell (right) exploring the problem space of chess
Source: Courtesy of Carnegie Mellon University

The Tower of Hanoi and similar puzzles employed in the research on problem solving are **well-defined problems**, where all aspects of a problem are clearly specified. Most of everyday problems are **ill-defined problems**, where the goal and ways of reaching it are not easily identified. For example, there are quite a few solutions, some better and some worse, to avoid being late for a date. What we often forget is that even these small everyday tasks are problems and that their solutions feature heuristics. This hypothesis received strong empirical support from Newell and Simon (1972), who asked people to verbalise their thoughts while solving problems such as the Tower of Hanoi. Using the technique of **protocol analysis**, they were able to identify the strategies explicitly used in problem solving. In order to test their understanding of the problem-solving strategies, they developed a model called *General Problem Solver (GPS)*. GPS was implemented as a computer program and was able to simulate human problem solving pretty accurately in several different tasks such as proving theorems in logic and solving crypt-arithmetic problems.

Stop and Think Well-defined vs ill-defined problems
Why do psychologists prefer well-defined problems to ill-defined problems for their investigation? What do they gain and possibly lose by using artificial puzzles?

Making analogies

In the ideal case, we should learn something by solving a problem. Not only should we be able to solve the same problem when it appears again, but we should also be able to transfer what we had learned to situations similar to the original problem. The transfer of problem-solving strategies and solutions from one situation to a similar one is called **analogical problem solving**. Making analogies between seemingly unrelated situations is for many researchers the key factor in learning and creativity (Dunbar, 1997; Holyoak and Thagard, 1995). You may think that making analogies might not be that difficult, given how easily you have spotted the similarity between the matchmaker problem and mutilated checkerboard problem. It is one thing, however, to be told that there are similarities between two problems, but quite another to find the analogy yourself. It turns out that people can hardly make spontaneous analogies, no matter how obvious they may appear.

Consider the following insight problem by Duncker (1945). A surgeon needs to operate on a patient with a malignant tumour in the stomach. The tumour can be removed by directing a kind of ray towards it. However, a ray strong enough to destroy the tumour would also destroy the healthy tissue around it. A ray that will not harm the tissue, on the other hand, would be too weak to destroy the tumour. How would it be possible to destroy the tumour without damaging the healthy tissue? This is a rather difficult problem and only about 10 per cent of people can solve it without any help. Things are even worse: people find it hard to use whatever hints are provided. Even solving a related problem does not help much. Gick and Holyoak (1980, 1983) presented participants with a story of a general who has to capture a fortress. Numerous roads lead to the fortress but each of them contains mines. This prevents the whole army from using one single road. Yet, in order to overpower the enemy, the entire army must attack the fortress at the same time.

If this problem somehow reminds you of the previous tumour problem, it is because the two problems are analogical to each other – the ray is the army, the tumour is the fortress, the risk of damaging healthy tissue corresponds to the risk of detonating the mines, and finally, the surgeon is replaced by the general (see Figure 11.10). The general came to a clever solution that can be used in the tumour setting too – by spreading the army out on all the roads leading to the fortress, he would avoid losing soldiers to mines and would be able to attack with full power. In the tumour problem, as you can imagine, the surgeon needs to spread the ray by using several weak rays so that he does not harm healthy tissues while still converging on the tumour with full power. If you think that this seems obvious enough and participants given the fortress story first should be able to make the analogy to the tumour problem, you are in for a surprise! Only about 20 per cent of people made spontaneous use of the fortress story. Although the two stories are practically the same, it is only at a deep semantic level. They do not share surface similarities, which makes it difficult for participants to realise that they share the same deep structure. But when participants are directly told that the fortress story is relevant to the tumour problem, almost all of them find the correct solution.

Stop and Think Analogy between information-processing approach and cognition
When we try to explain something, we often use analogies. It is not different with scientific explanations – for example, blood circulation is explained using the analogy of a hydraulic system. The information-processing approach uses the computer as an analogy for human cognition. In a computer, which part corresponds to short-term and which to long-term memory?

The research on analogy makes the point that two problems must be perceived as similar if we are to make a successful mapping between them. The following experiment carried out by Perfetto and colleagues (Perfetto *et al.*, 1983) shows how similar the two instances need to be. The main story is to explain how a certain Reverend duly delivered on his promise to walk for 20 minutes on the surface of the Hudson River without sinking. The first group of participants were given the problem only. The other two groups were given a number of sentences to evaluate for truthfulness before facing the problem. One of the sentences contained the answer to the problem: 'A person can walk on frozen water.' The first group was informed about the relation between the sentences and the problem. Exactly as in Gick and Holyoak's (1983) experiment, this group was able to solve the problem. The other group evaluated the sentences but was not told about their relevance to the problem. Their ability to solve the problem was not better than that of a third group, which was given the problem only. There was no spontaneous transfer in the uninformed group.

In a follow-up experiment, the form of the sentences used for evaluation was changed (Adams *et al.*, 1988). Instead of the previous fact-orientation format, sentences that pose and answer the problem at the same time were used. For example, 'A person can walk on water [problem] if it is frozen [solution].' Evaluating these problems, participants were able to make spontaneous use of analogy. A plausible explanation for this result is that these sentences, unlike

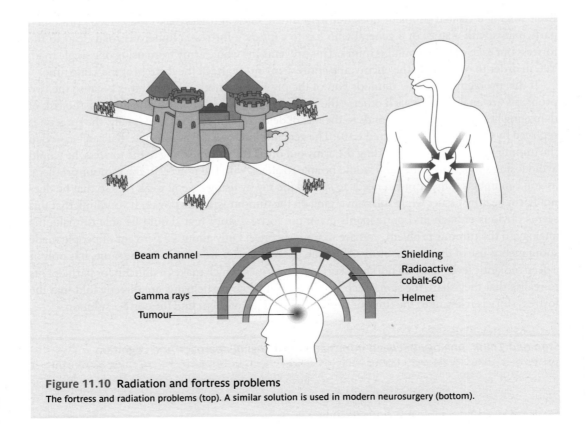

Figure 11.10 Radiation and fortress problems
The fortress and radiation problems (top). A similar solution is used in modern neurosurgery (bottom).

the sentences used in the mere evaluation condition, engaged the same mental processes as the actual problem. Once the problem has been represented mentally, it is not difficult to recall the idea linked to the key sentence.

Needham and Begg (1991) went one step further and showed that even trying unsuccessfully to solve a problem produces greater spontaneous transfer than rote learning of the problem and its solution. This result, which echoes findings in the literature on levels of processing (see Chapter 6), is of immense importance for you, as a student, and for us, as instructors. It shows that it is necessary to make the context of knowledge acquisition similar to the context in which the knowledge will be applied. Solving related problems and explicitly or implicitly understanding the principles behind the solutions will not only lead to the acquisition of rote knowledge, but will also produce better performance on seemingly unrelated tasks.

Chapter summary

Problem solving has been relegated to the margins of psychology for a long time. The main reason for this state of affairs was the negative view that behaviourism, the dominant school of thought in the first half of the last century, had of problem solving. From the perspective of behaviourism, problem solving was no more (and no less) than simple learning by associations, as exemplified by Thorndike's experiment. At the beginning of the last century, the Gestalt school showed that problem solving does not need to be a laborious process of association building, even among animals. Köhler's famous study with chimpanzees paved the way to ingenious explorations of insight with humans. Just as with perception, the Gestalt school emphasised that a problem is perceived as a Gestalt, which is a unit made of its components. The insight, accompanied with the 'a-ha' experience of sudden realisation, occurs when the elements of the problem are restructured in an appropriate way.

Despite their influence and some remarkably clever experiments, the Gestalt psychologists did not offer much more than a description of the processes involved during insight. Some 50 years later, Stellan Ohlsson presented a fully fledged cognitive theory of insightful problem solving that specifies the mechanisms and conditions through which insights occur.

Another important period for problem solving research was the cognitive revolution in the middle of the last century. Problem solving was seen as one of the central pieces of both artificial intelligence and cognitive psychology. The main goal of the research led by such eminent scholars as Nobel Prize winner Herbert Simon and Allen Newell was to discover the characteristic heuristics that people use when confronted with problems that are too much for the processing power of their limited cognitive system. These heuristics could then be implemented in computer programs. This would lead not only to the eventual automation of important problem-solving activities, but also to the development of explicit psychological theories whose assumptions can be tested empirically.

Solving problems should lead to better performance in other similar problems. While this seems true, as we will see in the next chapter, when the problems come from the same context or domain, people do not excel at problems that involve analogy at a deeper semantic level. The main difficulty seems to be finding the connection between problems that seemingly, at the surface level, do not have much in common.

Further reading

Emery (2006) provides a highly readable and entertaining overview of the research on bird intelligence. The seminal volume by Newell and Simon (1972) is still the reference for the application of the information-processing approach to problem solving. The topics of analogy and transfer have recently been reviewed by Barnett and Ceci (2002), while most original articles by Gestalt psychologists mentioned in the chapter can be found on Green's *Classics in the History of Psychology* Web page. The video showing the behaviour of Tokyo's ravens from the beginning of the chapter can be found, albeit in German, at www.spiegel.de/video/video-27770.html.

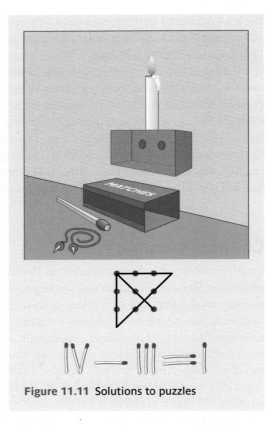

Figure 11.11 Solutions to puzzles

Chapter **12**

Expertise

CHAPTER PREVIEW

☑ We face many situations where we can use our knowledge. Situations similar to well-practised problems allow us to use specialist knowledge. The knowledge can be cognitive in nature, such as in chess, or perceptual-motor, such as in tennis or cricket. In all cases, we talk about expertise.

☑ Contrary to widespread public opinion, experts are not endowed with superhuman abilities. They use their knowledge of the domain, acquired through extensive experience and practice, to circumvent the limitations of their cognitive system.

☑ Knowledge enables experts to recognise situations that are similar to those previously experienced and stored in their memory. Once a problem has been recognised as a similar situation, suitable plans of action from previous situations become available.

☑ Sports and music may have an additional motor component in comparison to purely cognitive domains, but both kinds of skill rely on similar acquisition principles and thus theoretical explanations.

☑ Practice is undeniably important and may possibly make perfect, but mere exposure to an activity is not enough. To improve, it is necessary to carry out highly structured activities aimed at correcting weaknesses.

Introduction

Chess players face a daunting task. In an environment that has arguably more possibilities than atoms in the universe, they have to choose the right path. Similarly, tennis players returning a fast serve seem to be in the impossible position of reacting faster than seems humanly possible. The task is no easier for batsmen in cricket – not only do they have to react extremely rapidly if they are to have a chance to defend a fast ball, but they also have to deal with an uneven playing

Figure 12.1 Experts at work
Source: © Alamy

surface that can make the ball bounce unpredictably. Despite these problems, the best chess, tennis and cricket players regularly produce these seemingly impossible feats. The best chess players can not only play extremely well, but they can also take on several opponents at the same time, even without the sight of the chess board, and beat them easily. Returning tennis serves is a big part of the game just as is batting in cricket. The best tennis and cricket players not only manage to get the fastest balls back in the field but also to counter-attack with their return. How is this possible? Do they have superhuman abilities that make them faster and better than other mortals? What are the differences between experts and novices, and what lies behind these differences?

These are just a sample of the questions that research into **expertise** is trying to answer. Like the problem-solving research from the previous chapter, expertise deals with problems. Finding the best move in chess, returning a serve in tennis or batting a fast ball in cricket are all problems. In comparison to the problems commonly employed in the problem-solving research, the difference is that people studied in expertise research typically have experience with these problems. They have previously been confronted with the same or similar problems and they can also be certain that they will encounter similar problems in the future. This experience, or more precisely the difference in performance that it produces, is one of the main aspects of expertise. While problem-solving research focuses on heuristics that are flexible enough to be applied in most tasks, expertise deals mainly with knowledge that is specific to a particular domain. Capturing expert knowledge is complex, as has been painfully learned by researchers in artificial intelligence over the past decades. It turns out that it is much more difficult to simulate human performance using heuristics in **knowledge-rich domains**, such as chess, where people have large amounts of experience, than in **knowledge-lean domains**, such as the Tower of Hanoi, where everybody's experience is limited. In complex domains, such as chess and tennis, general heuristics are of limited use and completely overshadowed by domain-specific knowledge. The research on expertise thus deals with knowledge, its acquisition and its influence on cognitive processes.

There are vast individual differences between people in most endeavours, especially in complex ones. We may be able to swim but some of us are better than others; and there are only a handful of us who can compete at the highest level or be good enough to win eight gold medals at the Olympic Games, as Michael Phelps did in Beijing in 2008. A common assumption is that extraordinary performers must be extraordinarily endowed too. It is known, for example, that Michael Phelps has a very long arm length (wingspan) as well as joints that can bend further than most people's, turning his feet into virtual flippers. But sometimes, experts' amazing performances can lead to the creation of myths. It is reported that Ted Williams, arguably the greatest hitter in the history of baseball, could see the stitching on the incoming ball rotate, such was the power of his perception. Another often held assumption is that chess masters can foresee what their opponent will play many moves ahead. These exaggerated views fascinate and puzzle us when it comes to outstanding performance. In less extreme versions they form the basis of the **talent view**. According to this view, outstanding performances are inextricably related to inborn physiological and/or cognitive factors. In this chapter we will briefly review the opposing (deliberate) **practice view**, which postulates that practice overshadows inter-individual differences. In the next chapter we will continue the debate between talent and practice. However, cognitive psychologists are mostly interested in going one step further and uncovering the cognitive mechanisms that enable experts' outstanding performance. In this chapter we will uncover the basis of expertise in cognitive skills such as chess and how the cognitive mechanisms in such skills generalise to other seemingly different perceptual-motor skills such as tennis or cricket.

Cognitive expertise

The groundbreaking work on expertise was done by a Dutch psychologist, Adriaan de Groot (1946/1978). De Groot was interested in how chess experts think – that is, how they solve problems and find good moves when playing chess games. Among other things, one question he wanted to answer was whether chess experts are really able to look ahead further than their less skilled colleagues, as it is commonly assumed. De Groot investigated some of the very best players of his day using the **think-aloud technique** we have encountered in Chapter 11. Players were given a problem, an unknown position, and were asked to speak out loud when looking for the best solution. The **verbal protocols** that were obtained in this way were later analysed for a number of parameters, such as the number of different alternatives considered, the number of moves seen in advance and the strategies used. Amazingly, de Groot's research had all the ingredients that later became the hallmarks of modern expertise research (Ericsson and Smith, 1991): putting experts in the controllable environment of the laboratory, using experimental techniques, applying methods such as protocol analysis to extract strategies and other types of knowledge, and devising tasks that are relevant for the experts and so have a high level of **ecological validity**.

The most surprising finding of de Groot's study was that Grand Masters, who can be considered as super-experts, did not differ greatly in the structure of their search behaviour compared to ordinary experts. All players would first inspect the position and classify it as a certain type. On the basis of this classification, they would then retrieve common plans, likely courses of action and possible moves. Grand Masters hardly anticipated more moves than ordinary experts, but nevertheless clearly found better solutions. The difference was therefore not so much in the number of anticipated moves as in the ability to concentrate on the promising solutions and follow them up with a close investigation. The investigation itself did not seem to differ greatly across skill levels.

De Groot noticed that, during the first stage when players familiarised themselves with the problem, Grand Masters could grasp the essence of the position within seconds. In fact, Grand Masters had a better understanding of the problem after five seconds than weaker players after 15 minutes! This enabled them to direct their effort and cognitive resources – which were as limited as those of weaker players – to relevant solutions. Weaker players could not seize the fundamentals of the problem as quickly as that, which led them to investigate irrelevant solutions. Metaphorically, one could say that Grand Masters had the advantage of having a flashlight to orientate themselves in the jungle of possibilities, while weaker players were trying to do the same in the dark. The 'flashlight' was not, however, their superior ability to look ahead, but rather their experience and acquired knowledge. To test this hypothesis, de Groot used a task that later became a favourite among expertise researchers – the so-called **recall task**. Players are briefly exposed to an unfamiliar stimulus, in this case a chess position with around 20 to 25 pieces. Typically after five seconds, the stimulus disappears and players are asked to reconstruct it. De Groot found that Grand Masters could reproduce a complex chess position almost perfectly. In contrast, average players could recall only about half of the pieces. To see how much novices could recall, and for further evidence of the influence of knowledge about the limits of the cognitive system, see the classical experiment by Michelene Chi (1978) in Box 12.1.

How can chess masters remember so many pieces? Could it be that the capacity of their memory does not suffer from the limits of the cognitive system identified by Miller (1956) and others (see Chapter 6)? It was obvious to de Groot that experts do not have a superior memory in general, but he never published the necessary control experiment to rule out this possibility (Vicente and de Groot, 1990). Chase and Simon (1973a), however, did exactly that. They replicated de Groot's results of experts' superior memory for chess positions, but added a control condition where the pieces from a game position were randomly scattered on the board. The stimuli consisted of the same elements – identical chessboard, identical number and type of pieces – thus any difference between the recall of game and random positions should be due to the difference in structure. The recall performance of Chase and Simon's Grand Master suddenly fell to the level of novices – around four pieces (for the complete picture, see Chapter 15). What was the reason for such a stark decrease in performance?

To explain this finding, Chase and Simon (1973b) put forward the **chunking theory**. Chunking theory introduced an elegant way of reconciling results showing memory limitations with the results from the field of expertise, which at first seem contradictory. In short, experts' and novices' memories share similar properties, but experts can use their large knowledge base from long-term memory, acquired through extensive experience with the domain, to organise new stimuli in a more efficient way. Instead of remembering a chessboard piece by piece – as it is typical of novices – experts group pieces into **chunks** of up to three to five pieces. This enables them to remember all the pieces in a position, even with a board containing all the 32 pieces, which is below what can be coded with seven chunks of five pieces each. Also, they can do this while still respecting the well-known limits of short-term memory, which were at the time estimated at seven chunks (Miller, 1956). Remembering briefly presented positions with high accuracy is thus just the consequence of the well-developed knowledge structures that expert chess players have acquired. More generally, experts' superiority with the recall of meaningful stimuli has been replicated in numerous domains, such as sport, engineering, dance and music

Box 12.1 CLASSIC EXPERIMENT: Chi's (1978) experiment on the recall of chess positions and digits in adults and children

As we have seen in Chapter 6, short-term memory capacity is severely limited. We also know that people reach their maximum capacity in adult age. In other words, children have a less developed memory capacity than adults (Dempster, 1981), and a standard explanation is that memory capacity increases as a function of maturational processes in the brain (e.g. Casey *et al.*, 2005). In a study with child and adult chess players, Michelene Chi (1978) produced a striking demonstration that maturity is not the only factor affecting the capacity of short-term memory. Chi measured the digit span of adults and children by asking them to repeat a string of digits they had heard previously. The digit span is arguably the most popular measure of working and short-term memory. In addition, Chi gave de Groot's recall task to her participants; the children played chess at a good, albeit not expert, level, and the adults were chess beginners. Replicating previous results, she found that adults had a larger digit span than children (incidentally, this shows that there was no transfer from chess playing to digit memory). However, with the recall of chess positions, children easily outperformed adults, in spite of the fact that the adults had a more fully developed memory than the children. Chi's conclusion was that knowledge plays a key role in the development of memory.

As independent variables, Chi used level of maturity (adults vs children) and level of chess expertise (novices vs amateurs). The dependent variables were the number of digits and the number of chess pieces recalled. In the digit-span task, adults were the experts and children the novices, while the roles were inverted in the recall of chess positions. This way Chi's study convincingly showed that maturity is not the only factor affecting the capacity of working memory. This was also the first evidence that knowledge probably outweighs other relevant factors (e.g. capacity, strategies or metamemory) in the development of memory.

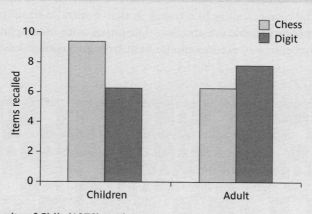

Figure 12.2 Results of Chi's (1978) study

Stop and Think Chi's (1978) design

Chi's experimental design was not complete. The experiment featured child chess experts and adult chess novices. What are the missing groups of participants?

(e.g. Ericsson and Lehmann, 1996; Vicente and Wang, 1998), and is thought to be one of the characterising features of expertise.

But what do these chunks have to do with chess experts' ability to find the best path in the jungle of possibilities? Chase and Simon's insight was that, when experts are faced with a chess problem, they automatically retrieve from their vast knowledge base not only chunks, but also, attached to the chunks, information about possible ways of dealing with the problem. If this seems unrealistic to you, imagine yourself in a dark room. The problem you face is to turn the light on, and you can bring a modicum of expertise to bear because you have faced similar situations previously. Through your experience with similar rooms, you have acquired a schema for rooms, which helps you to reach for the light switch automatically, because it is usually positioned sideways next to the door, and light up the room. You may think that chess is much more complex and unpredictable than the location of things in rooms. The principle, however, remains the same. Expert chess players have invested thousands of hours in playing and studying different positions. Through their experience, they have acquired highly specific patterns or schemas. Just like chess experts with meaningless positions, you would have great difficulty remembering where things were in a room if they had been randomly scattered around, with a chair, say, hanging from the ceiling.

It later became evident that the chunks proposed by Chase and Simon (1973a, 1973b) were too small and too simple to account for all the phenomena found in expertise research (Charness, 1976; Frey and Adesman, 1976). Most important, it is difficult to imagine how a chunk of just a few pieces could trigger complex solutions related to the whole situation. Gobet and Simon (1996b) proposed the **template theory**, which builds directly on chunking theory. Template theory retains the notion of chunks, but allows them to be grouped in higher structures, **templates**, which encode particularly well-learned chunks or situations (see Figure 12.3). Templates, which are a variant of the schemas we have considered in Chapter 7, are made up of two components. The core is similar to a chunk in that it encodes fixed information; by contrast, the slots can encode variable information. The importance of templates is that they show how higher-level, conceptual structures can be built from perceptual structures (chunks) and

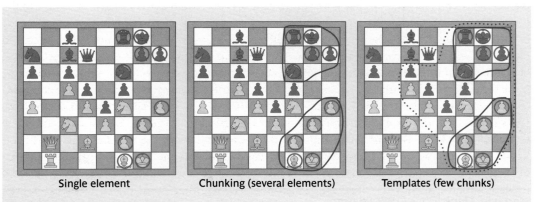

Single element   Chunking (several elements)   Templates (few chunks)

Figure 12.3 Chunks and templates
Illustration of similarities and differences between chunks and templates.

provide mechanisms for the rapid long-term memory encoding shown by experts. Loosely speaking, templates are created in situations in which the context presents both constant and variable information. Thus, variability during learning is predicted to facilitate the acquisition of templates and then foster better long-term performance. Substantial empirical evidence from education and training supports this hypothesis (Fazey and Marton, 2002; Shea and Morgan, 1979).

Stop and Think Templates in football

You have seen that the core of a template in chess consists of stable pieces that are found on the same squares in many situations. In contrast, the slots are less stable pieces, which can be found on different locations. Using your knowledge about templates, try to identify core and slots in some team sports: say, football.

Acquisition of (cognitive) skills

You may have noticed that experts' performance is often explained using IF–THEN rules: IF the situation is such and such, THEN do this and that. We have already seen an example of an IF–THEN coupling in Chapter 5. We step on the street only if we have looked to our left side and realised that there are no cars. This coupling between current situation and consequent action, first noticed by de Groot (1946/1978) in the protocols of chess masters, is at the core of theories about cognitive skill acquisition. One of the most popular theories is John Anderson's **Adaptive Control of Thought (ACT)**, which we briefly encountered in Chapter 2. As the name of Anderson's theory suggests, the general idea behind ACT is that organisms adapt to their environments through cognitive mechanisms (Anderson, 2005, 2007; Anderson *et al.*, 2004).

To illustrate the mechanisms and the main components of ACT, think of an everyday skill you are probably highly familiar with, such as typing or driving. You may be able to type words and whole sentences without looking at the keyboard, selecting the right letters without much effort. Similarly, if you are an experienced driver, you probably do not even think when changing gear. However, when you first started typing or driving, you had to pay close attention to the basic elements of the task. You needed to remember explicitly where letters are located on the keyboard. Changing gear also required your full attention, as you needed to press the clutch and figure out where to move the lever for the desired gear. According to ACT, basic facts about tasks are stored in **declarative memory** as a network of closely connected concepts. With time, these facts increase in number and sophistication. Through the process of **knowledge compilation**, we start using the knowledge from declarative memory to build specific **production rules**. IF a situation requires it, *then* an action or a series of actions is executed. Say, if we need to type the word 'DOG', we will automatically start the movements with the middle finger of the left hand (D), move swiftly to the ring finger of the right hand (O) and finish with the index finger of the left (G). Similarly, to switch from first to second gear we will first press the clutch and move the lever downwards. This way, we do not need to think about the clutch or where the letters are on the keyboard every time we need to change gear or type a word. Production rules are stored in **procedural memory** and enable fast performance without the kind of thinking and effort that would be required if we were to search for the right elements in declarative memory.

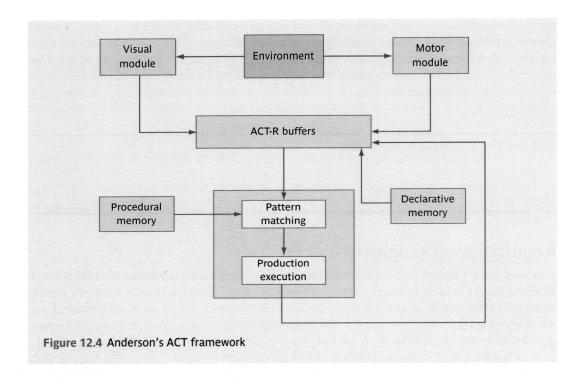

Figure 12.4 Anderson's ACT framework

Productions become increasingly complex as a consequence of the process of **composition** where a sequence of productions will be collapsed into a single large production. A given situation will typically fire several responses that are more or less adequate, and productions are further fine-tuned by strengthening the productions that led to successful outcomes and weakening those that did not. In contrast to the theories in Chapter 5, the ACT framework does not directly feature the notion of automaticity. Instead, the degree of automaticity is determined indirectly by the strength of productions (Anderson, 1982).

Our intuitions about the process of skill acquisition are well captured by the ACT framework: there is a progression from a declarative phase where we have to pay full attention to the task at hand, to the almost automatic procedural phase where we can execute the skill without much effort. One advantage of automatisation is that we may be able to use our cognitive resources for other aspects of the task and thus further improve our performance. On the other hand, automatisation is also accompanied by a curious phenomenon related to our conscious access to the information we use. For example, if you cannot verbalise what exactly you do when tying your shoelaces, your skill is probably at the procedural stage. In contrast, your young nephew who is going through a painful phase of learning to tie his shoes may explain to you in great detail what he is supposed to do and what he is actually doing. Experts often cannot explain their performance, as it relies on highly compiled actions from procedural memory, which seem to be beyond conscious access. It is certainly true that new driving instructors who are experienced drivers need to refresh their (declarative) memory on how to change gear when they embark on their new employment.

Stop and Think Experts as instructors
It is the usual practice to give teaching jobs to previously successful individuals in the domain. Instructors need to make their knowledge explicit in order to communicate it to students. What kind of problems might instructors experience when teaching beginners? Would this explicit verbalisation help them in their performance in the domain? Would some other, less skilled individuals, be more adequate teachers?

Box 12.2 RESEARCH CLOSE-UP: Why do good thoughts block better ones?

As you may have noticed by now, the main ingredient of expertise is recognition of previously encountered situations. Once the situation is recognised, a suitable plan of action is retrieved automatically. This is a highly efficient mechanism that we all use in everyday situations. But it also comes with certain costs. Once we find a good way of doing something, or form an opinion about somebody, it becomes difficult to see things differently. We have seen in the previous chapter that the behaviour of the participants in Luchins' classical water-jug study not only became inflexible, but also almost rigid. Similarly, the participants in Lord and colleagues' study on the death sentence (see Chapter 10) believed that they were evaluating studies objectively when in fact they showed blatant bias in favour of their preferred view. What is the mechanism behind these surprising phenomena?

Bilalić *et al.* (2008a, 2008b, 2010) investigated this issue by asking expert chess players to solve chess problems that resembled the *Einstellung* problems from Luchins' experiment. Each problem had two possible solutions: one familiar, but longer, and one less familiar, but shorter. It turned out that a number of experts could not find the optimal shorter solution. Why did experts fail to find the simple optimal solution? To answer this question, Bilalić and colleagues recorded the eye movements of chess experts (see Figure 12.5). Although all the players insisted that they had looked for a better solution after spotting the familiar longer one, the eye movements told a different story. Experts still lingered and examined the elements of the previously retrieved solution while not paying much attention to the elements of the optimal solution. When the *Einstellung* effect was removed by disabling the familiar longer solution, experts managed to find the optimal solution without much difficulty. Their attention, as measured by their eye movements, focused more and more on the relevant aspects of the optimal solution. Why did the expert players fail to find the optimal solution in the presence of a highly familiar solution, but found it easily when the familiar solution was removed? The first thought experts had was related to the familiar solution: it was the first production fired from their memory upon recognising the situation. Experts then tried to look for a better solution, but their attention had already been influenced by the previously retrieved thought, which still guided their perception. They assumed that they were examining new solutions, and undeniably did so, but those new solutions were related to the first retrieved solution. This study shows us how dangerous *Einstellung*-like situations can be even for highly motivated experts. As the great economist John Maynard Keynes once aptly put it, 'The difficulty lies, not in the new ideas, but in escaping from the old ones, which ramify ... into every corner of our minds.'

▶

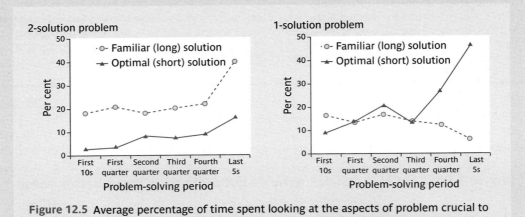

Figure 12.5 Average percentage of time spent looking at the aspects of problem crucial to the familiar solution and optimal solution as a function of time, for players looking at the 2-solution problem (left-hand side) and players looking at the 1-solution problem (right-hand side)

Perceptual-motor expertise

So far, we have examined the nature of expertise in cognitive skills such as chess. We have seen that chess experts do not have superior general cognitive abilities, and, in particular, superior memory. Does this finding also apply to domains such as sports and music where not only perceptual ability but also rapid motor behaviour is needed? It is one thing to perceive a ball rapidly; it is another to react successfully to it. Could it be that top-level tennis and cricket players are more talented physically than other mortals? This is certainly a common assumption among the public. While this notion is sometimes distorted to ludicrous heights, as we saw earlier when mentioning the legend about the baseball's great Ted Williams, it is difficult to deny that generally a faster reaction time, no matter how small the difference, would give experts a significant edge over other people in most competitive perceptual-motor activities.

It seems, however, that the best athletes are not faster in reacting to simple stimuli such as pressing a key on a visual signal than their weaker colleagues. They are also not faster than young people who do not actively pursue sport activities (Whiting, 1969). The laboratory studies of reaction times (Beggs and Howarth, 1970; Keele and Posner, 1968) find that a simple reaction time of a motivated participant is almost never faster than 200 milliseconds. How then can tennis players return a ball served at a speed of over 150 miles per hour (240 kilometres per hour)? It takes less than 500 ms for the ball to reach the player, and the player not only needs to determine the side, the distance and possibly the spot on which the ball will land, but also needs to execute a complex movement. On first consideration, it seems impossible to play such balls, let alone play them well, and yet world-class players manage this routinely. Could it be that laboratory measures of reaction time are simply invalid for world-class athletes? Or do expert tennis players use some other strategies to circumvent the limits of their motor system, just as chess players did with the limits of their cognitive system?

Psychologists have tackled this question using the **occlusion paradigm** (Abernethy and Russell, 1987; Jones and Miles, 1978). For example, with expert and novice tennis players as participants, they would present a tennis video with the full service motion until the ball was hit by the racquet, and ask them to predict on which side and at what distance the ball would land. Unsurprisingly, skilled tennis players were better than novices at predicting the landing position. The crucial condition was whether they would be able to do it when parts of the body or even the racquet were occluded when the ball was hit. The performance of both experts and novices suffered most when they could not see the motion of the racquet before the impact. This means that the position and movement of the racquet are particularly important for successful returns (Abernethy *et al.*, 2001). Furthermore, experts seemed to use additional cues to make their prediction. When the motion patterns of the whole body were occluded, or when the arm holding the racquet was not visible, experts' performance suffered while the prediction of novices did not (Abernethy and Russell, 1987). Tennis players thus use advanced perceptual cues to predict where the serve will fall. Through extensive practice and experience, players have

Box 12.3 RESEARCH CLOSE-UP: Ecological validity and expertise – are laboratory findings applicable to the real world?

The real-world applicability of research in cognitive psychology is sometimes questioned. This is because most of the experimental approach, which is at the heart of cognitive psychology, uses stimuli completely devoid of the everyday flavour that things normally have (e.g. the nonsensical trigrams used by Ebbinghaus, 1913). Is it possible that some of the laboratory findings, such as the time needed to react to stimuli, are simply invalid in the case of highly skilful individuals? The best cricketers, especially batsmen, seem to be a good example. Although we find irregular playing surfaces in other sports, say tennis on clay, bad wickets are regular occurrences at cricket matches. The slightly raised sewn seam on the ball does not make it easier for the batsman either – it produces unexpected bounces on a regular basis. This unexpectedness means that previous anticipatory cues may not be of much use to batsmen. Is it any wonder then that some fans believe that the very best batsmen are almost superhuman? Peter McLeod (1987) of Oxford University found an ingenious way to test whether the batsman's reaction time was really superior to what is usually obtained in the laboratory. Instead of depending on good luck, and fishing for unexpected bounces, McLeod prepared a wicket covered in matting under which, unknown to the batsmen, there were a number of long, half-round dowels. When the ball bounced between the dowels, it changed direction unpredictably. The main interest of the study was in how batsmen would cope with such bounces. By disabling the use of advanced cues, it was expected that batting would depend primarily on fast reflexes. McLeod measured whether expert cricketers were able to initiate the movements necessary to adjust the bat in less than 200 ms, universally thought to be the fastest reaction possible. Analysing the films frame by frame, he found that none of the expert cricketers initiated the bat adjustment in less than 200 ms after the ball bounced. Thus, the laboratory findings also apply to the real world and with world-class experts. However, a delay of only 5 to 10 ms in the initial adjustment often results in the inability to defend against a fast and precisely pitched ball. World-class cricketers may not have superhuman reflexes, but their skill at batting is nevertheless astonishing!

fine-tuned their perceptual and attentional system to pick up such advanced cues. Just like expert chess players' considerable knowledge enables them to concentrate on promising paths, expert tennis players' perception of advanced cues gives them an immense advantage over less skilled opponents. Similar findings were obtained when the occlusion paradigm was employed in cricket. The position of the bowler's front foot, hand and arm at the moment of the release of the ball seems particularly important for a successful prediction of the type and length of ball (Müller *et al.*, 2006).

Stop and Think Keep your eye on the ball!

Standard advice given by coaches to young players for successful batting in cricket and serve returning in tennis is to keep one's eyes on the ball at all times. Given that balls reach a speed of over 100 mph in cricket and even 150 mph in tennis, is this advice feasible? What other strategy could be useful?

Deliberate practice

How do tennis and cricket players acquire knowledge structures that enable them to anticipate the future so successfully? It certainly helps to be exposed to the domain or, in other words, practice does not hurt. Yet, we all know of people who have spent years and years playing tennis or cricket but do not seem to improve at all. Practice may make perfect, but what kind of practice? Anders Ericsson and colleagues (Ericsson, 2006; Ericsson *et al.*, 1993) propose that only certain types of practice result in performance improvement. In order to improve, it is necessary to engage in highly structured activities that aim to eliminate weaknesses and consequently improve performance. These activities, called **deliberate practice**, not only need to be at the appropriate level of difficulty, but must be monitored, usually by a coach or trainer, so that constant feedback is provided. One can easily imagine Venus Williams making the same backhand shot over and over again with feedback from a specialised coach in order to improve this aspect of her game. If it sounds like a really hard job, and maybe a little boring too, this is no surprise – deliberate practice is not meant to be inherently enjoyable. Playing with friends just for fun, or even serious competition, does not count as deliberate practice. During a playful interaction with friends the last thing on our minds is to try to improve an aspect of our game. Similarly, serious competition does not provide enough possibilities for focused practice. People who play for enjoyment do not seem to improve much despite logging in hours and hours of seemingly relevant exercise.

There is overwhelming evidence that deliberate practice indeed predicts part of the differences between experts and novices. International-level violinists and pianists may have not spent more time altogether with their instrument than their weaker colleagues at the national level. They did, however, practise considerably more deliberately (Ericsson *et al.*, 1993). Similarly, there is evidence that deliberate practice in chess (e.g. predicting the next move in games played by masters, in particular when done alone) explains a good proportion (about 40 per cent) of the difference between players of various skills (Charness *et al.*, 2005). This result has also been found in a number of different sports such as hockey and wrestling (Ward *et al.*, 2004). At the same time, there are domains for which it is difficult to pinpoint activities that would satisfy all the requirements of deliberate practice (e.g. Abernethy *et al.*, 2003). Scientific activities, for example, do not provide immediate feedback, which makes it difficult if not impossible to practise deliberately. In addition, other kinds of practice, such as competition, may also be relevant and even better predictors of expertise than actual deliberate practice (e.g. Campitelli and Gobet, 2007). Still, this aspect of deliberate practice theory is hardly controversial. Most people will probably agree that there should be a distinction between different activities in any domain. Ericsson's distinction between different types of activities based on effort certainly reminds us of the idea of levels of processing (Craik and Lockhart, 1972), which we encountered in Chapter 6. It is common sense that more effort and more focused effort should produce a better performance.

However, other aspects of deliberate practice theory are highly controversial. Ericsson takes the extreme position that deliberate practice is not only necessary, as even hardcore proponents of the talent account acknowledge, but also sufficient to achieve the highest possible levels of performance (Ericsson and Charness, 1994). In that regard, the earlier individuals start with systematic practice, the better performers they will become, because they will have more opportunities to log in the necessary amounts of practice. Early signs that made parents seek specialists to coach their child are explained away with the argument that children were only exceptional in their parents' eyes and in comparison with immediate neighbourhood children (Bloom and Sosniak, 1985). Consequently, it is not innate talent but rather the *perception* of talent that drives parents to invest time and money in supporting their children's careers. According to Ericsson, deliberate practice is the sole determinant of exceptional performance, its pace of acquisition and final level.

These extreme environmentalist views are bound to produce excitement from researchers in the domains of giftedness, intelligence and other related fields who are usually proponents of the talent view (see Bock and Ackrill, 1993; Howe *et al.*, 1998, and in particular the accompanying replies). According to the talent view, practice, deliberate or any other, is necessary for the attainment of exceptional levels of proficiency, but is not sufficient. Other innate characteristics such as intelligence and reaction speed, or a combination of these abilities, are more important. Innate abilities are stable, difficult-to-modify traits that constitute natural talent. Although practice is an essential part of the development of excellence, only people who are talented will achieve the highest skill levels (Chassy and Gobet, 2010).

The talent versus practice debate is just another version of the old bitter **nature versus nurture controversy**. A person's behaviour and traits can be seen as the product of biologically inherent factors (nature) and particular experiences (nurture). It is difficult to study the real causes of the differences between people, because both nature and nurture factors are inextricably connected to each other. The complexity of the issue inevitably leads to ambiguous and inconclusive findings. However, the consequences of the nature versus nurture debate for real life are immense. If we decide to value the nature factors more, we may employ selection strategies based on these factors. In contrast, the policies related to the nurture factors would focus more on motivation and willingness to put effort into a particular activity. Who gets the opportunity to go to school, to study, to get a certain job or to pursue a particular hobby, largely depends on our social policies, which are in turn influenced by our beliefs about the respective role of nature and nurture. Although it is difficult to make firm conclusions regarding the nature versus nurture controversy, the sheer importance of the issue makes its resurgence a common occurrence. In the next chapter, we will encounter another version of the same debate.

Stop and Think Michael Phelps' physical advantages
As previously mentioned, Michael Phelps' physical advantages (e.g. big armspan and flexible joints) could have played an important role in his swimming performances. How exactly could these advantages enhance his performance? And if physical advantages are that important, how is it possible to explain the curious case of another famous swimmer, Mark Spitz? Spitz won seven gold medals at the Munich Olympic Games in 1972, at the same time setting seven world records. Many believed that these world records would hold good for years to come. However, if Spitz swam at the Beijing Olympic Games in 2008 with the same times that seemed so incredible in 1972, he would not have been able to qualify even for the semi-finals. How can you explain this?

Cognitive and perceptual-motor skill – two worlds apart?

Cognitive skills such as chess and perceptual-motor skills such as tennis, cricket and music share much more ground than may be apparent at first sight. Some of the most popular theoretical explanations of perceptual-motor skills (Adams, 1971; Newell, 1991; Schmidt, 1975) involve mechanisms that are similar to those used in the classical theories of cognitive skills (Anderson, 1982; Chase and Simon, 1973a; Gobet *et al.*, 2001; Gobet and Simon, 1996b; Newell, 1990). In both domains, chunking is typically used to explain how people acquire increasingly sophisticated knowledge about the environment. Most theories also assume that people need to focus their attention on the most relevant cues if they are to have a chance of finding a satisfying solution in the forest of possible paths. Selective attention may be the consequence of the limited resources that plague even the most skilful practitioners, but it does the job when it is guided by previously acquired knowledge. We have seen that both expert chess players and tennis players use their knowledge of the game to anticipate future developments. Unlike novices who are overwhelmed by the complexity of the environment, experts are able to retrieve appropriate productions from their vast knowledge base. Thus, the underlying mechanism behind experts' performance in both domains is the recognition of patterns in the environment that are automatically connected to the retrieval and execution of sequences of actions.

It is not a surprise that the findings from cognitive domains have often been replicated in perceptual-motor domains. Experts in perceptual-motor domains also encode and retrieve meaningful, that is game-related, information more effectively than novices (for a review, see Williams *et al.*, 1999). Experts also seem to possess more extensive declarative and procedural knowledge, although it is rather difficult to assess the amount of procedural knowledge (Williams and Davids, 1995). Most important, there seems to be a consensus that experts in both cognitive and perceptual-motor domains do not have to be endowed with exceptional hard-wired properties of their physical system to produce amazing feats. Where they really excel is in finding ingenious ways around their limited cognitive system. While this may take away some magic from the very best performances, it also raises interesting questions as to how these skills are acquired.

Chapter summary

Research on expertise deals with problems that actually appear in real life and for which people can acquire a great deal of expertise. While problem-solving research focuses on general heuristics, expertise mainly deals with domain-specific knowledge.

A common assumption is that exceptional performers are also exceptionally talented. The main finding in expertise research is that there are actually no great differences in basic cognitive abilities between differently skilled performers. In other words, their inherited physical properties, often called *hardware* by researchers, are not necessarily different.

De Groot's (1946/1978) seminal studies of chess players' thinking demonstrated in a convincing manner that domain-specific knowledge is the main ingredient of expertise. Using the recall paradigm with stimuli within the domain of expertise but without meaning, Chase and Simon (1973a; 1973b) corroborated de Groot's conclusions and also showed that experts do not have a better general memory. This finding led to the chunking theory (Chase and Simon, 1973a; 1973b), later modified in template theory (Gobet and Simon, 1996b), which proposed an elegant way of explaining experts' extraordinary feats while at the same time respecting the cognitive limitations that have been uncovered by experimental research. Using the computer analogy, one can say that de Groot and others showed that the *software* of experts is much more sophisticated than that used by lesser experts and novices.

The ACT theory of skill acquisition, developed by Anderson, is one of the most elaborated theories in cognitive psychology. To explain experts' performance, it uses the transition from a slow effortful *knowing what* knowledge, stored in declarative memory, to a fast, precise and almost effortless *knowing how* knowledge, stored in procedural memory. Experts possess fine-tuned sequences of actions, organised as productions, which fire automatically when a condition is satisfied. As with other production systems, the condition part of the productions in ACT tests for information in working memory, which often includes a description of the problem situation in the environment.

It is universally agreed that practice is necessary for acquiring the extensive declarative and procedural knowledge that experts use to circumvent the limits of their cognitive system. Ericsson's deliberate practice framework identifies necessary ingredients (e.g. identification of weaknesses, appropriate level of practice, constant feedback and focused effort) for successful training. Given that research into expertise focuses on the difference in experience and practice between differently skilled performers, the next logical step would be to try to explain expertise differences solely through differences in practice. The hard-line proponents of deliberate practice theory have done exactly that.

A recurring theme of this chapter has been that it is possible to generalise the findings from one domain of expertise to other domains. It may look easy to use the mechanisms uncovered in chess research to explain performance in board games such as Go or draughts; however, it is not obvious how the same mechanisms are applicable to traditional sports such as tennis and cricket. At first sight, these perceptual-motor domains appear totally different from cognitive domains. Interestingly, research has shown that the acquisition mechanisms (e.g. chunking, creation of production rules) behind superior performance are similar in cognitive and perceptual-motor skills.

Further reading

Gobet *et al.* (2004) provide a comprehensive overview of the research on board games and on cognitive expertise in general. The books by Williams (Williams and Hodges, 2004; Williams *et al.*, 1999) deal with sport expertise. The most comprehensive selection of overview articles on expertise is the handbook edited by Ericsson *et al.* (2006). The talent vs practice debate, one of the recent reincarnations of the old nature vs nurture controversy, is elaborated in the target article by Howe *et al.* (1998) and numerous comments by other researchers. An accessible summary of the research on music expertise is provided by Sloboda (2005). If you want to find out more about returns in tennis, the following site provides information: http://tennis.about.com/od/serve/a/javagameintro.htm.

Chapter 13

Creativity

CHAPTER PREVIEW

☑ Most of us think that creativity should produce something *novel* or *original*. Besides novelty, researchers often claim that creativity should also produce something *valuable* or *useful*.

☑ Although researchers need a *product* to be certain that real creativity is at work, what they are really after are the *processes* that led to the product as well as the *person* who started it all.

☑ As it is often inconvenient to wait for a creative product (and the processes accompanying it) to occur, most research techniques involve interviews with creative persons, analyses of their self-reports, case studies and similar approaches that do not involve direct experimental manipulation.

☑ A common assumption among laypeople and some creativity researchers is that creativity, which leads to products that are so new that they are different from anything else, cannot be explained by the type of ordinary cognitive processes we have met in the chapters on expertise and problem solving.

☑ In contrast, most cognitive psychologists believe that creativity is an extension of ordinary processes we all employ in problem solving. To support their claims, they try to reproduce major scientific breakthroughs under controlled laboratory conditions.

Introduction

Albert Einstein once said that 'I'm enough of an artist to draw freely on my imagination, which I think is more important than knowledge. Knowledge is limited. Imagination encircles the world' (in an interview published in the *Philadelphia Saturday Evening Post*, 26 October 1929). One would guess that if somebody knows what **creativity** is, then it certainly would be Einstein, the person most people would think of when asked about creative genius. Einstein's statement also captures perfectly the opinion that most laypeople have about creativity. There must be something extraordinary, almost mysterious, involved in the creative process; otherwise it would be easy to explain it with plain thinking and drawing upon the world's knowledge. But consider for a moment another highly creative person, Thomas Edison, a prolific inventor – he had more than a thousand patents to his name – who invented the first commercially viable electric light bulb. Edison thought that he simply had to find the right solution to the electric light bulb problem because he had already run out of unsuccessful solutions! There was nothing extraordinary in the creative process for Edison. Producing breakthrough inventions simply required the type of ordinary thinking skills we are all equipped with and the type of ordinary knowledge we can all acquire. What then is the origin of creativity? Do we need to rely on mysterious forces such as imagination to produce highly creative products, or will common knowledge do? Can anyone be creative?

It is difficult to find a more important topic of research than creativity. It is because of human creativity that we are able to use cars, trains and airplanes as means of transport, and enjoy other pleasant aspects of life such as music and art. If we uncover what lies behind creativity, it seems obvious that we may reap great benefits by incorporating the findings into the education and training of future generations, and even writing computer programs that lead to creative outputs.

Figure 13.1 Creative persons and their products
Einstein sailing a boat and Edison surrounded by light bulbs.
Source: Albert Einstein © The Print Collector/Alamy. Thomas Edison © Pictorial Press Ltd/Alamy

Creativity research, however, faces many obstacles. To begin with, defining creativity is problematic. Most researchers argue that a **creative product** should be original and valuable or useful (Boden, 1990; Csikszentmihalyi, 1988; Sternberg, 1999). We also have to take into account the **creative process** that brought the product to life, and in particular establish whether the creative process recruits mechanisms that are found in other fields of cognitive psychology. Finally, in addition to the product and process, we should not forget the **creative person**, who is the originator of the product and the process. Add to this multilayered nature of creativity the fact that life-changing creative inventions occur very rarely and certainly not in the laboratory of experimental psychologists, and it becomes obvious that research on creativity faces many problems. In the following pages we will see how creativity researchers have tried to solve the problems posed by this difficult subject of investigation.

The creative product

Einstein's theory of relativity and Edison's invention of the electric light bulb are without doubt creative products. They are certainly original – the world had previously not seen them in that form. They are also valuable because we can now produce huge amounts of energy from tiny amounts of mass and enjoy the advantages of fully lit houses. Creativity can be seen on a much smaller scale too. Using a pram as a shopping cart once the children have grown up is certainly original and valuable, if not life changing. However, to be creative, is it enough for the product to be original to the person who produced it, or should it be new to the whole world? Consider the following scenario: you are reading this book and suddenly you think of a clever experiment that would answer an important theoretical question. You are very excited and want to inform your professor about your discovery when, upon turning the next page of the book, you find out that this experiment has already been carried out. It is an unfortunate situation, but does it really mean that you were not creative? After all, you could not have known about the existence of this experiment. The idea was novel, at least to you.

The other part of the definition – about the value of a creative product – is arguably even more problematic. It might be easy to define value in science by seeing how useful the discovery is in real life, as was the case with Einstein's and Edison's creative products. But how to define value in the arts? Some currently well-known artists, say the Impressionists from the nineteenth century, produced beautiful and highly valued paintings. However, their masterpieces were at the time greeted sceptically by art critics and the public in general. In contrast, the most valued artists of that period are now only a footnote in the history of art. How can it be that some products, and inevitably the people who produced them, are seen as creative in one period of time, only to lose their creativity and become ordinary in another?

It may be difficult to give a definitive answer to the above problems (Weisberg, 2006). It does seem, however, that by reducing the creative product to originality, especially to the person, it becomes easier to define the object of study and carry out experiments on their creation in the laboratory. Finally, although creative products are fascinating, what we are really after in the study of creativity are the mechanisms and processes that brought them to us.

The creative process

The most obvious way of investigating the creative process is to see what the creative people have to say about the way they accomplished their amazing feats. In such self-reports, which are different from the verbal protocols we have encountered in Chapter 11 because self-reports are not obtained during or immediately after the creative feat, we often find references to extraordinary, almost mysterious, forces and processes. Wolfgang Amadeus Mozart, for example, is said to have produced whole compositions almost effortlessly, without any need for revision (Ghiselin, 1952). August Kekulé, the founder of modern chemistry, said that the idea for the structure of benzene, an important organic compound, came to him while he was 'dreaming' of a snake. The snake association brought Kekulé to the right path of assuming that the benzene structure forms a closed ring of carbon atoms (Roberts, 1989). The poet Samuel Taylor Coleridge, one of the founders of the Romantic movement, described the writing process of his famous poem *Kubla Khan* in a similarly mysterious vein. While reading about Kubla Khan's adventures, Coleridge dozed off and continued to sleep for several hours, dreaming about Kubla Khan's palace. After waking up, he felt the immediate urge to take a pen and start writing. According to Coleridge, he wrote effortlessly and 'without any sensation or conscious effort' a long poem of over 200 lines (Ghiselin, 1952).

These personal reports by eminent, and without doubt creative individuals, fit in nicely with speculations about creativity by another eminent person, French mathematician Henri Poincaré (1913). According to Poincaré's self-observations, the processes of **incubation** and **illumination** are of crucial importance to creativity. During the process of incubation, the creative idea is being developed. This does not necessarily mean that the person has to deliberately think about the problem. Poincaré argued it is often the case that the person is doing an unrelated activity while the mind is doing the work unconsciously. It is then often the case that the solution will be triggered by seemingly unrelated external events such as dreaming about a snake in Kekulé's case. This process of sudden realisation is called *illumination*. If this reminds you of the 'a-ha' experience in insight problems (cf. Chapter 11), it is not a coincidence. Many researchers believe that similar processes are at play in the creativity process (Csikszentmihalyi, 1996; Simonton, 1999).

Wallas (1926) developed Poincaré's observations into a full-blown theory of the creative process that is considered useful right to the present day. In addition to the processes of incubation and illumination, there are also the stages of **preparation** and **verification**. In the stage of preparation, which precedes incubation and illumination, the person gets to know the problem, deliberately gathers information and consciously tries to solve the problem. The process of verification involves, as the name implies, checking out the solution produced in the illumination phase.

What are the processes in the incubation period that enable creative people to find the right solutions? There are different explanations, which tend to be based on the idea that some kind of unconscious processing of the information gathered is happening – while the preparation stage is taking place. Unconscious thinking is often assumed to be superior and more effective than conscious deliberation. One idea is that unconscious thinking is not very different from conscious thinking but is much faster (Koestler, 1964; Poincaré, 1913). Consequently, incubation provides more effective thinking although the person is not actively thinking about the problem. A related idea is that unconscious processing is more efficient because it loosens the everyday associations between concepts and enables access to new ones, which are much more uncommon and normally beyond conscious access (Csikszentmihalyi and Sawyer, 1995; Mednick, 1962; Simonton, 1999) (see Box 13.1).

The explanation of the creativity process through the notion of unconscious looks plausible. Some of the creative products are so novel and groundbreaking that it is natural to imagine that extraordinary processes have been involved in their creation. This also provides a plausible

---

Box 13.1 RESEARCH CLOSE-UP: In search of the creative potential

Psychologists like to test people. Thus, it is not surprising that there have been numerous attempts to measure creativity or, more precisely, the potential for creativity. Most tests for measuring creativity have been developed based on Guilford's (1950) idea of **convergent** and **divergent thinking**. Convergent thinking is typical for situations where only one answer is correct. An example is offered by the kind of questions found in intelligence tests. By contrast, divergent thinking produces ideas that move away from the ordinary. For example, the usual function of pliers is to cut and not to hang as a pendulum as in Maier's two-string problem (Maier, 1931; see Chapter 11). Divergent thinking is also at the core of some of the most popular tests of creativity (Guilford, 1967; Torrance, 1974), where one needs to find as many unusual functions of an object as possible.

A slightly different approach was taken by Mednick (1962), who proposed that creative people produce original and unusual ideas because of the underlying structure of their associations in long-term memory. In Mednick's remote associates tests (RATs), one needs to produce a word that fits well with three target words (see Figure 13.2).

As you may have noticed, these creativity tests do not have much in common with specific domains of creativity. They are general tests thought to identify people who could be creative in any domain. Looking for general and basic capabilities is one of the main characteristics of the psychometrics approach in psychology. Just as we can test for general intelligence and memory capacity, we should also be able to test for creative potential. The big idea behind the psychometrics approach is that measures of general capacities provide information about how successful people will be in specific domains. Creativity tests do predict future creativity to some degree (Brown, 1989). However, they seem to be highly confounded with intelligence tests (Barron and Harrington, 1981), which makes it difficult to say what exactly predicts creativity.

Divergent thinking test

- What can we use a BRICK for?
- What can we use a PAPER CLIP for?

Remote associates test

Find the word that relates to the following three words: Cherry Time Smell
(Answer: BLOSSOM)

Figure 13.2 A sample of items found in creativity tests

explanation for a number of curious and otherwise inexplicable reports by famous creative people. However, there are several problems with this explanation. One of them is that the evidence is almost exclusively based on a selection of self-reports. There are also self-reports of other kinds contradicting this account. Most notably, we have seen that Edison believed he managed to invent a commercially viable light bulb through a combination of knowledge and ordinary thinking. As discussed in Box 13.2, the view that simple mechanisms are at play is also shared by Nobel Prize winner Herbert Simon, whom we have encountered several times in this book, most notably in Chapters 10 and 11. A critical weakness of the unconscious-processing hypothesis is that it is difficult to judge how reliable these self-reports are. As a rule, they are produced long after the actual events. No matter how remarkable these scientists and inventors were, it is likely that their memories suffer from the same fallibility as the memories of ordinary people (see Chapter 7). For example, Kekulé told the story about the snake at the celebration of his great discovery, some 35 years later. (He also spoke of 'daydreaming', and not of 'dreaming' as it is commonly translated.) Similarly, Coleridge seems to have worked deliberately on his *Kubla Khan* poem earlier: a different version of the same poem in Coleridge's handwriting has been found (Schneider, 1966). Obviously, a more reliable approach is needed to investigate creativity.

One such approach consists of using all available information and resources about a significant achievement and trying to reconstruct its development. Applying this **case study approach** to creativity, researchers have shown that there may be nothing mysterious in a number of groundbreaking scientific breakthroughs such as the discovery of the structure of the DNA

Box 13.2 RESEARCH CLOSE-UP: **Problem-space explanation of incubation**

Among the cognitive psychologists who have argued that creativity can be explained by the mechanisms used to explain 'normal' problem solving, Herbert Simon has been the most vocal. For him, scientific discovery, the type of creativity he was most interested in, is simply the outcome of the kind of search mechanisms that he had proposed together with Allen Newell to explain how people solve simple problems such as the Tower of Hanoi puzzle (see Chapter 11). More specifically, Simon (1966) argued that incubation could be accounted for by the problem space theory as well. Problem solving involves two types of information. First, there is control information – information about goals and sub-goals – which is stored in short-term memory. Second, there is factual information – information about the properties of the problem itself – which is stored in long-term memory. Simon argued that, during what Wallas (1926) called the 'preparation phase', factual information found when searching a specific subgoal may sometimes not be available to other subgoals. This might hinder the discovery of the solution. For example, Poincaré did not realise that a type of mathematical technique he used to solve one aspect of his problem (i.e. one subgoal) could also be used to solve a different aspect of the problem (i.e. another subgoal). During incubation, control information disappears much quicker than factual information, as the former is stored in short-term memory and the latter is stored in long-term memory. Thus factual information becomes much less context-sensitive, and can now be used in other parts of the problem space. This increases the likelihood of finding a solution, and the fact that it was 'already there' can produce the appearance of a sudden insight and illumination.

molecule by Watson and Crick, and the invention of the steam machine by James Watt (Weisberg, 2006). Although there were various twists and turns, hardly any of the aforementioned breakthroughs involved anything resembling the processes characteristic of incubation and illumination.

What, then, is the support for incubation and unconscious thinking? The evidence for them is ambiguous. On the one hand, there are numerous self-reports of incubation, illumination and similar phenomena, but these are difficult to verify. On the other, the laboratory studies with simple and complex everyday problems produced little evidence for the existence of incubation (Dodds *et al.*, 2003). In those few studies that found some evidence (Dijksterhuis *et al.*, 2006), it is far from clear that the underlying mechanism is unconscious processing. You may think that this is strange given the large amount of evidence for the 'a-ha' experience in insight problems. However, there is evidence that the insight problems can be solved using normal problem-solving strategies and do not necessarily have to produce an 'a-ha' experience (Fleck and Weisberg, 2004; MacGregor *et al.*, 2001; Perkins, 1981; Weisberg and Alba, 1981). This all fits well with the views of some researchers, who do not think that we need the unconscious and other similarly mysterious and vaguely defined terms to explain creativity (Ericsson, 1998; Newell *et al.*, 1962; Weisberg, 2006). Simple, ordinary thinking processes and strategies that manipulate necessary knowledge should be more than enough.

The advocates of this line of reasoning usually point out the studies which investigated creative processes under controlled laboratory conditions. Qin and Simon (1990), for example, let undergraduate students solve the same problem that German astronomer Johannes Kepler was facing when he worked out the equation which describes how long it takes for a planet to go around the sun depending on its distance from the sun (Third Law of Planetary Motion). The students got the same data that we know Kepler had at his disposal describing the behaviour of a few planets. However, the context was changed – the variables of distance and period were changed into x and y. Almost a third of students found Kepler's Third Law of Planetary Motion in an hour or less. Similarly, when Langley *et al.* (1987) showed to professional mathematicians and physicists the data that Max Planck needed to develop his theory of blackbody radiation, almost all of them found the correct equations successfully within a mere three minutes. Dunbar (1993) created a laboratory simulation of Monod and Jacob's discovery of genetic control. In all of these studies, undergraduate students and in some cases even schoolchildren were able to replicate the famous breakthrough discoveries. There were no mysterious processes involved, just the common problem-solving strategies (heuristics) we have encountered in Chapter 11, in combination with relevant knowledge (see Box 13.3).

Despite these scientific findings, the notion of **creative problem solving** and thinking (de Bono, 1973; Osborn, 1953) is highly popular today. Indeed, you have probably encountered popular commercial programmes that aim to enhance creativity in any kind of context. This is in particular the case among business enterprises that are interested in the newest techniques for enhancing productivity in their employees. Without going into too much detail, most creative problem-solving techniques rely on the concepts of divergent thinking and unconscious processing we discussed earlier in the chapter (see Box 13.1). While these techniques are certainly not harmful per se and may even prove useful to a certain degree, it is difficult to see how they can provide a major improvement in thinking and problem-solving performance given the evidence we have considered in this chapter and in Chapters 11 and 12.

Box 13.3 RESEARCH CLOSE-UP: **Natural and artificial creativity**

How would you rate a picture created by a computer? We have put this question to hundreds of undergraduate students, and most of them found the painting creative (between 4 and 5 on a scale ranging from 0 – not creative, to 5 – highly creative). AARON, a computer program developed by artist-turned-computer-scientist Harold Cohen has created many paintings which you can see here: www.kurzweilcyberart.com. Many people are repulsed by the idea that computer programs can be creative, but this is actually a rather direct prediction of the problem space theory we have discussed in Chapter 11 (see also Box 13.2 in this chapter). Newell and Simon (1972) argued that problem solving, of which creativity is just a special case, can be described as a search through a problem space. Using a number of heuristics, which can be general or domain specific, people mentally generate possible actions; the value of these actions is then evaluated, and the best one is chosen. In many artistic and scientific fields, it is actually possible to list the type of heuristics that people use, consciously or unconsciously. For example, in science, successful researchers love finding problems and exploring variations of a solution, and they show a readiness to change direction and to redefine problems. If you are interested in becoming a researcher in psychology, you can consult the interesting article by McGuire (1997), which lists 49 heuristics for making discoveries in psychology.

If creativity is about carrying out searches and using heuristics, then computers should be able to be creative as well: they are exceedingly good at searching, and humans can provide them with the necessary heuristics. There are actually many examples of programs in artificial intelligence that show, to various degrees, creativity, both in the arts and in science (see Boden, 1990, and Langley *et al.*, 1987, for extensive discussions). We have already mentioned AARON in the field of visual arts. AARON (Cohen, 1981) is a production system that draws pictures and paintings following a number of rules and constraints (e.g. 'don't put too many people in the scene'). While limited in its style, it can be seen as creative within it, and critics who are unaware of the origin of the drawings and paintings agree that they have a high aesthetic value. As you can imagine, many of these critics suddenly changed their minds when it was pointed out to them that a computer program was the origin of these creations!

Simon himself has actually applied his theory of problem solving to artificial scientific discovery and developed several programs that can be seen as creative. We consider two examples here. The Logic Theorist (Newell *et al.*, 1958) specialised in proving theorems in logic; it actually found some proofs that were more elegant than those proposed by some of the leading mathematicians in the field. KEKADA (Kulkarni and Simon, 1988) provided a detailed simulation of the discovery of the urea cycle by Krebs in 1932 – not a mean feat as this later earned Krebs the Nobel Prize in Physiology or Medicine. KEDADA used heuristics implemented as productions. It could make theoretical inferences, assess the acceptability of its theoretical knowledge and propose experiments that would test its theories.

Currently, artificial intelligence systems, sometimes coupled with robots, play a non-negligible role in scientific research, either as tools used by humans or as true discoverers. For example, a 'robot scientist' developed at Aberystwyth University autonomously generates hypotheses in genomics and physically carries out experiments aimed at testing these hypotheses – all this without human help!

(See http://www.aber.ac.uk/compsci/Research/bio/robotsci/press/)

www.kurzweilcyberart.com

Stop and Think Is it possible to think out of the box?
It is often said that stepping back enables us to break away from the chains of knowledge and look at the problem with a fresh mind. This is the main assumption behind many popular creative programmes that can be summarised under the creative problem-solving movement and their mantra of 'thinking out of the box'. Are we, however, able to think out of the box if the box is the very knowledge that defines us?

The creative person

If the creative process is not so mysterious, what about the creative person? Are creative individuals really that different from other mortals? Do they have superior innate characteristics that constitute their special creative talent or do they have to go through the same laborious processes of creation as other people? One of the common assumptions among creativity researchers is that the ability to build unusual associations between concepts somehow underlies creativity. A surprising result is that people who are particularly good at generating unusual associations tend to be diagnosed as manic depressive or schizophrenic. The manic phase of bipolar disorder is characterised by restlessness, immense self-belief and greatly enhanced productivity. Similarly, schizophrenic patients are well known for the strange and bizarre ideas they produce. In fact, it has been found that manic depression and schizophrenia occur more often among creative people than among ordinary people (Jamison, 1993). The so-called **mad genius hypothesis** has attracted much attention among researchers and laypeople. It is certainly an interesting idea, which is aligned with most modern theories of creativity, taking into account not only the creative process, but also the creative person and the environment (Amabile, 1996; Csikszentmihalyi, 1996; Simonton, 1999; Sternberg and Lubart, 1995). However, a more pressing question, with more important repercussions, is the relationship between creativity and knowledge.

Stop and Think Causal relationship between mental illness and creativity
We learned in Chapter 10 that an association between two phenomena does not mean that one is the cause of the other. Bearing this in mind, consider the relationship between mental illness and creativity. Which is the cause and which the consequence?

You have probably heard the stories of young Einstein being described as a 'lazy dog' by his professor, or of Mozart being able as a child to compose music of which some more experienced composers could only dream. Apparently, Einstein and Mozart did not need the kind of extensive practice that is necessary for other experts (see Chapter 12). These observations seem to directly support an extreme version of the talent hypothesis and to pose a serious challenge to the practice view. They also uncover the dual and difficult position of knowledge in creativity research. If we start by defining creativity as something original and novel, we should not then be surprised that creative products have only that much to do with what is known. After all, creativity should go beyond previous knowledge and expertise, break links with the past, and move away from stereotypical thinking. According to this view, knowledge is necessary for creativity, but too much of it can be harmful (Amabile, 1996; Csikszentmihalyi, 1996; Frensch and Sternberg, 1989; Sternberg and Lubart, 1995).

Upon closer examination, at least some of these common assumptions do not seem to stand up to scientific inquiry. For example, it is known that Mozart's father, Leopold, was a professional musician who took the greatest interest in the development of his son's talent. He would give Mozart pieces written by other composers from which the young Mozart had to create new arrangements. More to the point, there were actually no original pieces of music in the early compositions of Mozart (Hayes, 1989(a)). Mozart's first masterwork, his Piano Concerto no. 9, came some 15 years into his musical career. Similarly, the Beatles – arguably the greatest pop band ever – broke on to the world scene in 1963 with hits such as 'She Loves You' and 'I Want to Hold Your Hand'. They came seemingly out of nowhere and became an immediate hit, topping the music charts all over the world. However, the Beatles too had spent a considerable time honing their skills before the breakthrough. Originally, the Beatles played very few songs written by Lennon and McCartney. As they became more experienced, their repertoire increasingly included their own songs. By the time they had issued the albums *Revolver* and *Sgt. Pepper's Lonely Hearts Club Band* – revolutionary albums that most consider their unique contribution to pop music – they had been in the music business for almost ten years (Weisberg, 1999).

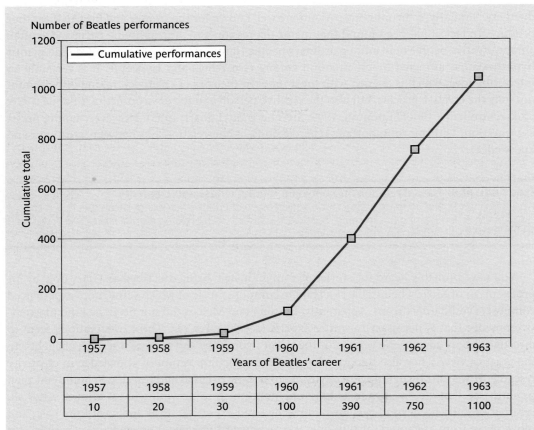

1957	1958	1959	1960	1961	1962	1963
10	20	30	100	390	750	1100

Figure 13.3 The Beatles – learning to make hits
Source: Weisberg, 1999.

You may have noticed that there was hardly complete agreement between researchers in the previous chapters of this book. Disagreement has never been clearer than with creativity, which seems to be extraordinary, if only because it is extraordinarily difficult to study. One may think that it is the typical question as to whether a bird in the hand is worth two in the bush, but if you were given the choice, what would you choose – Einstein's imagination or his knowledge?

Chapter summary

We have seen that creativity is a difficult topic to study. Researchers first need to agree about the definition of a creative product. Once this is done, they also need to look at the creative process behind creativity. Finally, they need to investigate the creative person behind both processes and product. The low frequency of creativity occurrences that are both valuable and novel for everybody means that researchers need to focus mostly on secondary data, such as self-reports of famous creators.

Poincaré (1913) and Wallas (1926) identified different stages in the creative process, among which incubation and illumination are the most important. One of their assumptions was that it is not necessary to think deliberately, and thus consciously, about a problem in order to be creative. Anecdotal evidence suggests that some of the greatest discoveries might have been made without any conscious thinking. The notion that unconscious thinking can help creativity by relaxing the connections between concepts and enabling the establishment of remote associations is an influential view of creativity. This can be seen in numerous questionable programmes that use thinking strategies to help people free themselves from common ways of looking at problems. Similarly, the potential for creativity has been measured by numerous tests that typically measure the production of remote associations between concepts.

Some researchers have pointed out that anecdotal evidence is not reliable and that it is not wise to base whole theories of creativity on it. Thorough analyses of case studies mostly suggest that incubation is not necessary for creativity. The experimental evidence for unconscious thinking and incubation in general is also at best flimsy. Similarly, there are contradictory findings about the relationship between knowledge and creativity. On the one hand, it seems obvious that creativity goes beyond the known, and breaks links with the past. On the other hand, even the most talented among us, such as Mozart, seemed to have had to acquire considerable amounts of knowledge before making their mark in the world.

Further reading

Runco's review (2004) briefly presents the current directions and trends in the research on creativity. A more detailed account of research and theory can be found in the book on creativity by the same author (Runco, 2006). Klahr and Simon (1999) provide an overview of different approaches to the study of scientific discovery. Weisberg's book on creativity (2006) is interesting not only because it provides a highly readable summary of previous research, but also because it tries to explain creativity in terms of ordinary thinking processes, using as evidence detailed case studies of famous discoveries.

PART 4

Advanced topics

Part contents

Chapter **14**

Emotion and cognition

CHAPTER PREVIEW

☑ Affective sciences are concerned with emotions, mood, motives and feelings.

☑ Emotional responses are object-triggered episodes. They frame the mind and prepare the body to undertake specific actions. Emotions constitute a primitive cognitive system.

☑ Emotions are discrete entities with specific influence on cognition. They can be classified along many dimensions, the crucial ones being *valence* and *arousal*.

☑ We can distinguish between basic emotions (all shared by the members of a species) and ontogenetic emotions (depending on the experience of a given individual). Basic emotions are shared with animals. Ontogenetic emotions display more individual variability.

☑ Emotions emerge as the result of the appraisal of a situation and include a cognitive component. They can influence several aspects of the cognitive system: perception, memory, decision making and judgement.

Introduction

To many scientists, emotions look like an esoteric topic. They are difficult to define, not easy to generate without raising ethical issues, and the effects obtained in one experiment sometimes do not show up in the next. For these reasons, and also due to the fact that emotions are not a central topic for cognitive psychology, relatively little research has been carried out into cognitive psychology on emotions. However, there has been a clear increase of interest in this topic with the emergence of brain-imaging techniques, with the consequence that we know much more now than two decades ago about how emotions are linked to cognition and how they are implemented in the brain.

In the first section, we provide a working definition of emotions. You will discover that emotions are a complex and archaic cognitive system. This makes their definition a hard task. Then, we explain why emotions exist. This will help not only in understanding why we have emotions but also in appreciating why emotions impose such a grip on cognition. Having set the stage, we describe the structures and mechanisms underpinning emotions. We will also spell out the process by which emotions develop within the cognitive system. Finally, we will show how they impinge on cognitive processing by boosting some components and nearly shutting down some others.

What emotions are and what they are not

Affective sciences are concerned with emotions, mood, motivation and feelings. **Emotions** are primarily responses to stimuli in the environment. There are several features that make emotions unique. First, emotions are mind–body responses triggered by a chunk of information (usually a recognised object, see Chapter 4). Second, they have a short duration – they generally last just for a few seconds, although they can sometimes last for a few hours. Third, they generate a subjective experience: feeling. Fourth, they generate action tendencies (Frijda, 1993), in the sense that each emotion increases the likelihood of people acting in a specific way. For instance, fear tends to cause flight behaviour. Finally, emotions are accompanied by a recognisable facial expression, which makes them a quick and efficient way to communicate our feelings to others (Ekman, 1999).

The fact that emotions are generated in response to an object and that they last for a short period of time distinguishes them from **mood**. Mood is the baseline of the emotional system; it is what we feel when nothing is stimulating the emotional system. There are interactions between emotions and mood. For example, a strong emotion such as the one arising after winning the National Lottery will change the baseline level for much longer than a few hours. By contrast, a very bad mood will moderate the impact of positive emotions. **Motivation** characterises the response to a goal rather than to an object. For example, if your blood is lacking sugar, your brain is going to inform you that you need sugar, and you become hungry. The motivation to go for food is the result of the goal to be achieved. Motivation is thus a force driving you to achieve a goal. The more attractive the objective is, the more you are willing to go for it.

What are emotions for?

Emotions can be understood as an archaic cognitive system. The emotional system is a basic form of information processing over which humans have little or no control. For example, you are strolling in a forest and, unfortunately, you meet a bear. This encounter is likely to trigger fear, and fear in turn is going to generate body changes that prepare for flight. In such a context, fear has helped you to save your life by preparing you to undertake the most appropriate action when confronted by danger. (The example of a bear encounter in a forest is a standard, often cited in emotion literature. Running away is likely to be the emotional response that most of us would have. However, it might not be the safest one – what to do if you find yourself in that unpleasant situation is discussed at http://en.wikipedia.org/wiki/Bear_danger.) You did not have to think about the fact that you have to run away (i.e. about preparing muscles by increasing tonus and raising heartbeat), it was just done. Emotion saved time, which is invaluable considering the danger you faced. This is what emotions are for: to provide the body and mind with a rapid adaptation to a relevant stimulus. If some food is not suitable for ingestion, then you are disgusted even before it touches your lips. If some rewarding event is bound to happen, then you will be happy. Emotions are fast, but short-lasting, adaptive responses to a stimulus. Since emotions made their appearance prior to high-level cognition during the course of evolution, high-level cognition (e.g. thinking, planning and use of language) can be considered not only as an advance but also as an add-on to the emotional system. High-level cognition was built upon emotion but in no way replaced it. Once the conscious form of cognition made its appearance, it developed so narrow a link with the emotional system that the two systems are now entangled: emotion and cognition work in concert. This conclusion is in stark contrast to the trivial view that emotions and cognition are two different entities. Actually, we notice that both systems are at work only when they are conflicting and returning opposite conclusions to our consciousness.

Using this evolutionary viewpoint, we could explain the difference between positive and negative emotions. **Positive emotions** are expected to occur whenever a reward is under consideration, while **negative emotions** mark the consideration of a dark perspective.

Hence, a crucial factor characterising a given emotion is **valence**, that is whether it is positive or negative. The second factor is the intensity of the emotion: often referred to as **arousal**. Arousal is in some sense the degree of the response. You can experience a weak, average or strong feeling of fear. This gradation will be reflected in the intensity of arousal. Arousal can be defined as the degree to which the autonomous nervous system (ANS) is activated; that is, how active are physiological parameters such as heart rate. It has been shown that the pattern of ANS responses is emotion specific: each emotion triggers a unique emotional state (Collet *et al.*, 1997; Ekman *et al.*, 1983).

Stop and Think Apparent paradox
Considering that negative emotions are generated by potentially negative events and that positive emotions are indicators of a lack of danger, how can you explain the experience of being happy and sad at the same time?

The structure of emotions

The term 'emotion' encapsulates two different facets: the emotional response and the emotional experience. The **emotional response** concerns the actual changes that take place in your body and mind. The **emotional experience** occurs whenever you become conscious of such changes. These two facets led scientists to consider the time course of the generation of an emotional response. Such a model of emotion is presented in Figure 14.1 (after Phillips *et al.*, 2003).

An appraisal module is in charge of evaluating the emotional relevance of the incoming stimulus. A bear triggers fear, and a chair does not trigger any emotional response. Whenever

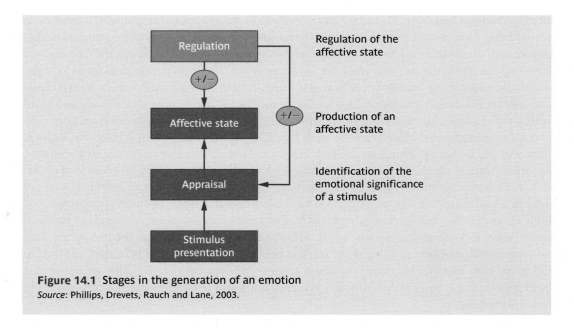

Figure 14.1 Stages in the generation of an emotion
Source: Phillips, Drevets, Rauch and Lane, 2003.

appropriate, the appraisal module outputs an emotional response which is forwarded to the affective state module. The affective state module holds the current emotional state. When no emotional responses influence its content, this component returns the baseline value, which is mood. When an emotional response is triggered, the emotional system tunes the values of valence and arousal so as to match the query and thus trigger the pattern of responses that characterises the emotion. Finally, when the emotional response has been effectively carried out, the feedback from our senses (both external and internal, see Chapter 4) informs our consciousness about our emotional state; this is when the emotional experience starts. The flow of information between the emotion-related modules is supplemented by regulatory mechanisms which ensure that emotional responses (or expressions) are not too strong or too weak for the situation at hand. One can distinguish between two types of regulation: the first is automatic and the second is activated through conscious thought (e.g. 'I should calm down'). The former type of regulation starts when the emotion is triggered and thus before the process reaches the stage of emotional experience. The second form of regulation is conscious and thus arrives after we become aware of the changes in mind and body. This view of how the emotional responses are triggered assumes that we know that a given stimulus (i.e. the bear) has some emotional value. How do we know this?

Stop and Think Sad music

Among the many possible media that convey emotions, music is one of the most efficient. Using what you know about emotions, how would you explain the fact that people like to listen to sad songs while this triggers negative emotional experiences, which, by definition, we are programmed to avoid. Do you think that all listeners are self-destructive?

Basic emotions and ontogenetic emotions

The fact that we know what is and what is not dangerous is not always due to learning. Ekman (1999) has shown that the facial expression of some emotions does not change from one culture to another, while other emotions elicit differential expressions across cultures. Making the assumption that some emotions are innate, Ekman investigated the notion of basic emotions: in-built emotional systems. The invariability of the expression of some emotions across cultures shows that these emotions are included in the genetic plan that builds our nervous system. This makes sense from an evolutionary perspective. Each species faces different predators, and accordingly has to be familiar with the typical cues signalling their presence. It is thus to the advantage of a species to be equipped with an alert system.

Fear is a good example of an automatically programmed response. Humans are now not really in danger in most environments (except from other humans), but we had been for about two hundred thousand years. Basic emotions are hardwired into our genes. It follows that these emotions are implemented by a specific neural circuit that does not differ from one member of a specific species to another. All basic emotions are shared by all members of the species. While the debate as to which emotions are basic and which are not is still raging, there is some agreement among scientists about at least some basic emotions: fear (to flee, mainly), anger (to fight) and disgust (not to touch).

Stop and Think How much of an animal are we?
If we share most of our emotional system with animals, we can say that animals suffer, are scared or are angry. Distinguishing between emotions and empathy, provide arguments about whether animals can have empathy.

The dichotomy between basic and non-basic emotions implies that part of our emotional system emerges during the course of development. Emotional differentiation is the process by which new emotional responses are available to the emotional system. As these emotions are the result of learning, their expression differs much more between individuals.

The interaction between emotion and cognition

We have already pointed out that emotion and cognition work together. This section is concerned with ways of differentiating the influence of the two systems. Let us carry out a brief experiment. Please close your eyes and think about your first date. Try to envision the details of the face of your partner, the whispers, the first touch, the first kiss. It is likely that, in a sense, you re-experience the emotion you felt at the time. It is obvious that the experience was not hardwired in your genes, because specific events had to occur for the emotion to be associated with them. Indeed, emotional learning consists mostly of pairing an emotion with a perceptual chunk (see Chapter 7). How does this happen? LeDoux's (1998) studies on fear answer this question. LeDoux has shown that one specific neural circuit is in charge of triggering the fear response. More specifically, he has shown that the neural circuit coding for a neutral stimulus (a sound) becomes associated with the fear response by Hebbian learning (see Chapter 3). Emotional learning shows how an emotional response and a representation are associated to form a cognitive-emotional chunk of information.

Emotions are able to influence various aspects of human cognition. The influence of emotion on perception can be demonstrated through simple experimental procedures. Öhman *et al.* (2001) used a detection task to test the hypothesis that emotions draw attention to fear-relevant stimuli. The displays were arrays containing nine images that were either fear-relevant (e.g. spiders and snakes) or emotion-free (e.g. flowers and mushrooms). In half the stimuli, one dissonant image of another category was inserted in the array of a given category (for example, one image of a spider with eight images of flowers). The results show that participants were faster to detect the fearful stimuli hidden in the non-emotional display.

Stop and Think Emotions in social communication

If emotions are a form of simple cognition, what is missing to the individuals who cannot recognise the features of emotions in others' faces? How does this impair their social life and why?

It will come as no surprise that emotions have a huge influence on memory. Among the countless studies conducted to examine how different emotions influence various forms of memory (see Chapters 6 and 7), we will follow the study of LaBar *et al.* (1998), who examined how neutral stimuli come to be associated with fear responses. The goal was to show that the **amygdala** (i.e. the brain structure in charge of triggering fear) has the ability to pair a neutral stimulus to the fear response. In a conditioning paradigm, participants were shown visual cues that were either predictive of a shock or neutral. In a second phase, there was no mapping between the stimulus and the shock so that the pairing would become extinct: that is, participants would learn that the stimulus was no longer predictive of a shock. The results showed that the amygdala was highly active during both the acquisition and the extinction phase. The study was among the first to examine the role of the amygdala in humans and to show that it is involved in both the creation of the conditioned response and its extinction. This finding is to be added to the numerous neuroscientific experiments showing that the brain regions in charge of emotional generation and regulation cooperate tightly with the brain regions in charge of cognitive operations. For example, the anatomical structure in charge of consolidating semantic memories is under the direct influence of the very same amygdala (see LeDoux, 1999, for a review). Emotions modulate not only basic cognitive processing but also high-level thinking, as can be seen in Box 14.1. The link between emotion and high-level cognition is also clearly visible in several mental disorders. Box 14.2 discusses the case of depression, and shows how therapies based on cognitive processing can be used to alleviate the emotional cost of depression.

Positive emotions

It is easy to get the idea that negative emotions are the responses provided by an alert system. But what about the role played by positive emotions? Are they the responses of another alert system, which would direct our attention to 'positive threats'? Here is where the symmetry between negative and positive emotions breaks down. Positive emotions have been shown to facilitate problem solving and decision making (Isen *et al.*, 1987; Isen and Means, 1983). More important, they have also been shown to facilitate the recovery from negative emotional episodes. Fredrickson and Levenson (1998) ran an insightful study on how positive emotions build our sense of self. They put a group of participants in an anxiety-provoking situation. Then the

Box 14.1 CLASSIC EXPERIMENT: Bechara – emotions and decision making

To demonstrate that emotions influence decision making, Bechara and colleagues (Bechara *et al.*, 1994; Bechara *et al.*, 1996) have run experiments comparing the performance of normal participants with those suffering from lesions in the prefrontal cortex, which is known to be a region of the brain which processes emotions. In Bechara's (1996) experiment, participants were presented with four decks of cards and provided with a fictional bank account of $2000. Each card could credit or debit the fictional account. In addition, each pack was designed either to win or lose money on average. The participants were instructed to pick one card at a time in any pack and try to win as much money as they could. The operation was repeated many times while the experimenters recorded skin conductance as a measure of arousal. The results revealed that, after some trials, normal subjects tried to avoid the two packs that were programmed to lose money. Furthermore, while the normal participants showed differences in skin conductance when they were about to take a card in a positive compared to a negative pack, the participants with prefrontal lesions did not manifest any change. The results suggest that participants with lesions had lost the ability to compute the emotional value of an item, thus impairing their ability to feel the difference between a positive and a negative feedback on one's action.

Bechara's experiment should not make you believe that all negative emotions are the same. As we have mentioned previously, each emotion has a specific pattern of responses. This is as true for the modulation of cognitive processes as it is for the pattern of ANS responses. Lerner and Keltner (2001) have shown that fear and anger, while being two negative emotions, trigger different attitudes towards the evaluation of risk. In doing so, they demonstrated that valence is an important but not sufficient dimension for predicting people's reactions.

Box 14.2 EVERYDAY APPLICATION: Therapy – memory structures, emotions and cognitive therapy

Research on cognition and emotion has led to important applications to psychopathology and clinical psychology. A classic illustration is the development of cognitive therapies: an arsenal of techniques aimed at repairing the emotion–cognition link. As an example, let us look at Beck's theory of depression (Beck, 1975, 1978; Beck *et al.*, 1979). According to Beck, information processing in depressive patients is determined by their cognitive structures – that is, the set of mechanisms that interpret perceptual input (see Chapters 4 and 7). While these structures apply some distortion to social reality even with healthy individuals (see Chapter 18), the distortions are so severe with depressed patients that incoming information is systematically interpreted in a negative way: such patients do not consider positive information. Thinking processes might also be contaminated: there is a tendency to generalise only bad experiences, inevitably leading patients to conclude that they are weak and useless. Another typical trait is that failures are considered much more important than successes. All these beliefs 'push' patients to believe that life is worthless. What is interesting is that everyone holds such automatic interpretative mechanisms. For reasons belonging to patients' pasts, their cognitive structures appraising reality have been damaged. Cognitive therapies are designed to put these structures back into order.

▶ In a typical cognitive therapy, patients first identify the situations or cognitions that make them react inappropriately. Then, they are encouraged to stop whenever negative feelings are emerging and engage in a backward analysis of the chain of thoughts until the false or distorted beliefs are identified. Once these are isolated, patients challenge them and start using correct beliefs. Challenging false beliefs means that patients falsify the wrong cognitions that are at the centre of the depression by testing whether they hold true in all circumstances. For example, if John isolates the belief that he is unable to work properly, he can ask himself whether he has *never* done anything positive by working. Focusing on his successes will help him change the belief by specifying the precise circumstances in which he fails. To change a distorted mechanism is time consuming and difficult: patients have to monitor their own thoughts all the time. This constant conscious supervision aims to prevent the triggering of incorrect beliefs or to stop them as soon as possible. Here too, we have an example of how knowledge stored in long-term memory (see Chapter 7) is used to interpret reality, and how this knowledge influences our emotional life.

participants watched a film, in which emotional content was manipulated. A subgroup of participants watched a happy film, a second subgroup watched a neutral film, and a third subgroup watched a sad film. Measures of heart rate and blood pressure were taken before the anxiety-provoking event, before watching the film and after watching the film. These measures reflect the arousal elicited by the negative emotional experience. The data revealed that participants' emotions went back to baseline faster after having watched a positively loaded film. This experiment shows that positive emotions interact with negative ones and can 'undo' the effect of negative emotions. (Box 14.3 explores the links between emotions and music, and Box 14.4 discusses the mother of all positive emotions: love.)

Box 14.3 IN FOCUS: Music – perceptual structures, emotions and music

One of the world leaders in the psychology of music, John Sloboda, has provided a valuable demonstration of the link between music structure and emotions (Sloboda, 1991). Sloboda asked his participants to identify the passage in their favourite pieces of music that induced emotional responses. Then, he analysed the musical structure of the portion of the score that was emotionally laden and found that some musical structures are associated with specific emotional responses. For example, the results revealed that delaying final cadence leads to negative emotions that are close to pain ('tears' in Sloboda's taxonomy). On the other hand, new or unprepared harmony tends to trigger shivers. This link between perceptual patterns and emotional responses is more subtle than might first appear. With suitable training, perception can catch very subtle differences (see Chapter 4). The same piece of music can be played with microvariations that change the local patterns of sound. When intended to embody different emotional expressions, these microvariations lead to perceptions of different expressions, each expression being recognised beyond doubt (Gabrielsson and Juslin, 1996). What does this tell us about what we feel when we listen to music? Beyond the personal memories that can be attached to a specific piece of music, the link between perception and emotion is not limited to fear conditioning: there is probably something intrinsic to music that generates emotions.

Box 14.4 IN FOCUS: **Love**

Surprisingly, love has not been the focus of much emotional research. If fact, it has largely been neglected: for the thousands of studies dealing with each and every aspect of fear, we find only a handful about love. This is astonishing, considering the influence of love on human behaviour. Even the law acknowledges the very existence of love, as judges take it into consideration when setting the tariff in murder cases. Perhaps, some theorists think that love is not enough of an emotion or that it is too complex to be studied with the classical experimental paradigm.

According to Sternberg (1986), love can take a number of different forms. For example, it can be romantic or companionate. To account for the variability of forms of love, Sternberg proposed that love is the result of the interaction between three dimensions. The first dimension is intimacy, the second passion (referring mostly to physical attraction) and the last decision making. 'Intimacy' describes all the behaviours that aim to be close to the loved person and to generate the warm security that emerges from this. This component of love does not include physical attraction, which is dealt with in the passion component. The passion component encapsulates all the strong feelings and may trigger romantic love. Finally, the decision-making component reflects the willingness to engage in the future with the loved one.

Theories of emotions, or better said: attempts to theorise emotions!

There are countless theories about emotions. Some address their social aspects, their influence over the cognitive system, or their interaction with basic physiological processes. Some theories are supposed to account for all possible emotions while others address only some specific ones. In the brief tour that follows we contrast different views of what emotions are. All theoretical ideas except the last one deal with the nature and classification of emotions, and use the cognitive approach. The last theory is that of Paul MacLean, who put forward not only a theory of emotions but also a paradigmatic view of the brain. His theory accounts not so much for emotions as for the relationship between emotions and cognition.

Figure 14.2 presents two influential theories of emotion: that of Roseman (1991) and that of Watson and Tellegen (1985). A comparison between these two theories yields interesting results. First, it is striking that the two theories do not address the same set of emotions. How can we agree on a theory of emotions if we cannot agree on the entities under study? In addition to this, as the figure shows, the two theories are built on different classification criteria. While Roseman considers the nature of the agent and the power that one has on the situation, Watson and Tellegen consider affect and engagement. The result is that we have two dramatically different theories of emotion. Hence, instead of presenting a necessarily restricted and arbitrary set of theories, we must discuss some of the central ideas explored by theories of emotion.

Several theorists have developed different, yet consistent, ideas about what emotions are. A prominent idea is that emotions arise as a result of an appraisal (i.e. an evaluation of reality). The classification of emotions depends then upon the criteria that one uses to explain how one

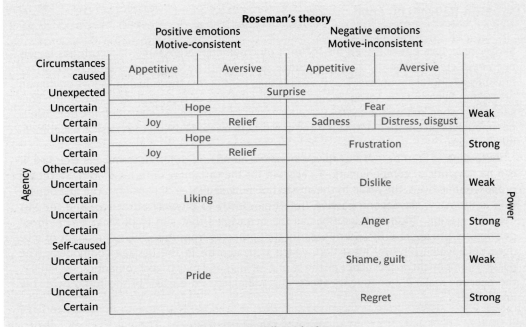

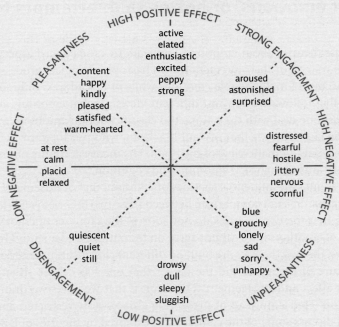

Figure 14.2 Comparing theories: the emotion theories of Roseman (1991) and Watson and Tellegen (1985)

evaluates reality. This appraisal process is at the core of many theories. Lazarus (1982), for example, divides the process into three stages. In the first stage, the situation is evaluated as positive, irrelevant or negative. This stage provides the agent with basic information about what to do. In the second stage, the emotional system assesses the resources needed to cope with the situation. Finally, the first and second evaluations are integrated to determine the course of action. Frijda (1993) insisted on the fact that emotions are associated with a stimulus and that they prepare the body for action. Emotions are thus transient states of action readiness. We might be tempted to believe that the action to undertake mainly depends on the valence of the emotion – positive emotions attract and negative emotions repel – but the story is not that simple. Lerner and Keltner (2000) have demonstrated that emotions of the same valence (i.e. anger and fear) have opposite effects on risk perception. Fear makes us very sensitive to risks, while anger wipes out any sensitivity and pushes us to undertake immediate action.

It is now clear that a central factor in the generation of emotions is the nature of the stimulus. Two dimensions are of great relevance: certainty and control. Certainty refers to the degree to which future events seem predictable. Control refers to our ability to have control over the situation. You will notice that the second dimension relates directly to the second stage posited by Lazarus (1982). Anger and fear are supposed to be different regarding both dimensions. An angry man undertakes an action because he thinks that he controls the situation and the outcome is predictable. A fearful man is not certain of what is going to happen and he would rather flee than try to control this uncertain and unpredictable environment. These fictive cases illustrate, if still need be, that emotions and cognitions are rooted in one another. In spite of this close relationship, some theorists have developed interesting ideas as to how we can distinguish the two processes on the basis of anatomical data.

MacLean (1990) had a simple idea: the brain is actually made of three layers (see Figure 14.3). Each layer reflects one evolutionary stage in the course of evolution from the basic brain of the reptile to ours. The innermost layer is responsible for automatic behaviour such as the regulation of vital parameters. The second layer is responsible for a simple form of cognition, which is supposed to point to environmental cues of what is potentially beneficial or harmful. You have probably guessed that this second layer, the limbic system, refers to the emotional system (see Chapter 3). The last layer is the neocortex. It is because this layer is more extensively developed in humans that they are different from other species in using symbols and abstract concepts.

For MacLean, the inherited past from faraway ancestors is thus still present in our brain. Of course, the theory posits some control mechanisms to regulate the flow of information between the layers. In this context, the cognition–emotion relationship

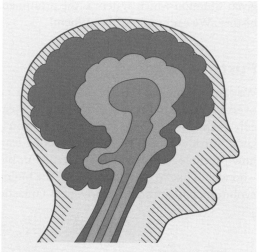

Figure 14.3 MacLean's triune brain theory
Source: eruptingmind.com.

refers to the links established by evolution between the second and third layers. The interesting question is: which layer takes control of the behaviour: the emotional one or the intelligent one? The human brain is not exempt from oddities in that we sometimes react inappropriately or, even worse, quite strangely. This non-rational behaviour can easily be explained by MacLean's theory: old programmes have taken control of us and run without our being able to control them. MacLean's view makes sense from an evolutionary point of view.

Stop and Think The reasons of the heart

The French philosopher Pascal said: 'Le coeur a ses raisons, que la raison ne connaît point', which might be translated as 'The heart has its reasons, which reason knows nothing of.' How would you explain scientifically what he meant? Take MacLean's theory as a theoretical framework.

Chapter summary

Emotions are short-lasting, mind–body responses elicited by representations (whether brought about by perception or retrieved from long-term memory). The emotional response is a specific pattern of changes taking place in brain and body. Emotions influence many aspects of cognitive processing, but each emotion influences the whole spectrum of processes differently. Negative emotions are discrete entities modulating our cognitive 'life' so as to attune it to the needs required in specific circumstances. Positive emotions have a role in building what we are and increasing our resistance to negative life episodes.

Many aspects of our lives are concerned with the state of our emotional system. Usually, we note the presence of emotions when the emotional system fails or overrules cognitive, rational processing. It is then that we realise that this system, usually silent, can take control of the cognitive system and betray our deep feelings about a situation. Emotions and cognitions are so tightly connected that it is very difficult to disentangle one from the other and determine in a given situation which system is the prominent one. Emotions are a gift from our evolutionary history. We cannot do without them!

Further reading

We can recommend three books, each with a different purpose. Frijda (2006) gives an excellent overview of emotions, and everything is explained by a master of the domain. This is undoubtedly one of the best books to start with if you intend to study emotions. LeDoux (1999) is a very good introduction to the biology linking fear to cognition: a must if you want to understand how psychological concepts are rooted in biology. Panksepp (2004) is for advanced students who would like to delve deeply into the biology of emotions and understand the links between evolution, biology and psychology. A fantastic yet complex book.

Chapter 15

Computational modelling

CHAPTER PREVIEW

☑ Theories in psychology can be divided into informal and formal. Formal theories can in turn be divided in computational and non-computational theories.

☑ The main computational approaches consist of symbolic modelling and connectionist modelling.

☑ Computational modelling offers several advantages: development of well-specified theories, the capability of predicting complex behaviours and the possibility of systematically exploring the effect of specific variables on behaviour. These advantages are much more difficult to obtain with informal theorising.

☑ Computational modelling has disadvantages as well: it is not easy to learn, there is a danger of overfitting models to data, and it is difficult to compare different models.

Introduction

Human cognition is obviously very complex – as shown in many chapters of this book – and it is therefore difficult to formulate theories of cognition. The issue is that many mechanisms occur simultaneously, at different levels of analysis. At a low level, think of the way neurons transmit information through neurotransmitters (see Chapter 3). At an intermediate level, think of the way features are combined together in visual perception (see Chapter 4). Finally, at a high level, consider how percepts lead to the retrieval of information about the people you love or information that you have acquired during your entire life (see Chapters 4 and 7). Although most theories in psychology (including cognitive psychology) are formulated verbally, it should be made clear that this type of representation is insufficient to explain the complex mechanisms related to cognition.

As we have seen in Chapter 2, researchers in cognitive psychology and allied sciences have developed new media for representing theories, often using techniques imported from other fields. Globally, these techniques are called **formalisms**, and the theories developed with them are called **formal theories**. For example, when Peterson and Peterson (1959) proposed that forgetting in short-term memory follows a power function (see Chapter 6), they used the formalism of mathematics (or algebra, to be more precise). We have seen many examples of such formal theories in this book, with a particular emphasis on computer models. When dealing with perception, we studied the mechanisms postulated by Marr (1982). When dealing with language, we spent a fair amount of time discussing how two different formal theories (Coltheart *et al.*, 2001; Plaut *et al.*, 1996) could explain the data on acquired dyslexia. However, what we have not yet discussed in detail are the properties, advantages and disadvantages of formal theories. The aim of this chapter is to address these issues, and in particular to explain how computational models are used to develop theories of cognition. (This chapter will use computer modelling, cognitive modelling, and computational modelling as synonyms. Note also that, in practice, little distinction is made between computational *theories* and computational *models*. See Chapter 2 for a discussion of these terms.)

A taxonomy of formal modelling

As we have just seen, **formal theories** are models that are expressed using some kind of formalism – that is, a system of rules that are rigorously defined. **Informal theories** are simply theories that are expressed using natural language (e.g. English). Baddeley's theory, which we have discussed in Chapter 6, is a good example of an informal theory.

There are two main classes of formal theories in cognitive psychology: computational theories and non-computational theories. **Computational theories** are theories that are expressed as computer programs. **Non-computational theories** are theories that use a different type of formalism (e.g. some type of mathematics). To confuse matters somewhat, a theory can start as a non-computational theory (e.g., a theory using differential equations – equations describing behaviour as a function of time) but can be later implemented as a computer program and thus become a computational theory.

With the exception of mathematics and formalisms coming from linguistics, largely influenced by Chomsky's theories, cognitive psychology has mostly used computational modelling. Computational modelling can in turn be divided into different approaches. **Symbolic modelling** assumes that cognition requires the manipulation of symbols: that is, patterns that represent other things. As discussed at length in Newell and Simon (1972; Simon and Newell, 1976), the 'physical symbol hypothesis' clearly states that these symbols are not just abstract entities, but are instantiated physically. With humans, these patterns are implemented as neural activity; with computers, they are realised as electrical activity. It is important to stress that neural activity and electrical activity are not the levels of analysis that symbolic modelling deals with. While it assumes that these levels exist, it focuses on the level at which symbols are manipulated. A large number of symbolic models use rules, including production rules, but there are other possible formalisms as well, such as decision trees and semantic networks (see Chapter 2). Symbolic models have also tended to simulate high-level cognition, such as playing chess, carrying out arithmetic operations or driving. Classic examples of symbolic models are Soar (Newell, 1990) and the models of scientific creativity developed by Langley *et al.* (1987). (For the difference between cognitive modelling and artificial intelligence, see Box 15.1.)

Neural modelling, or **connectionism**, argues that human cognition is best modelled using mechanisms that are known to happen at the neuronal level (e.g. McLeod *et al.*, 1998). However, when modelling phenomena in cognitive psychology, researchers are not interested in the biological details of how real neurons function. Instead, they are actually using neuronal mechanisms as an analogy. For example, as we have seen in Chapter 9, 'neurons' (or more neutrally 'units') can represent words. The interest is in how behaviour, including learning, can be simulated by the pattern of activity of the neurons and the links connecting them. Most of the connectionist models in psychology have used mechanisms (such as back-propagation, discussed in Chapter 2) that have little biological plausibility. In recent years, however, there has been a trend towards using models that better respect the constraints imposed by biology (e.g. O'Reilly, 1998).

It is possible to have theories that are **hybrid**, in the sense that some of the components can be classified as symbolic and others as non-symbolic. A good example of a hybrid architecture is ACT-R (Anderson *et al.*, 2004). At the symbolic level, ACT-R uses a production system for procedural memory as well as a semantic network for declarative memory. At the non-symbolic level, ACT-R explains how activation is spread across the nodes, and stores procedural and declarative knowledge using mechanisms borrowed from connectionism.

The field known as **embodied cognition**, which brings together researchers from a large variety of fields including cognitive psychology, computer science, robotics and philosophy, has recently criticised traditional research in cognitive psychology in that it neglects the body (e.g. Pfeifer and Scheier, 1999). For example, while eye movements are sometimes recorded, very little is said about the contribution of the body in general to cognition. Yet all forms of

Box 15.1 IN FOCUS: Cognitive modelling vs artificial intelligence – the case of Deeper Blue

Computational modelling and artificial intelligence pursue different goals. Computational modelling is about simulating human behaviour (including the errors humans commit in a specific task) while artificial intelligence is about producing computers that show intelligent behaviour, regardless of whether or not they use the same mechanisms as humans.

In other words, computational models need to 'be' smart, whereas artificial intelligence merely needs to 'look' smart. With artificial intelligence, there is no interest in producing errors and, in fact, errors should be avoided. A striking example that artificial intelligence programs can display remarkable behaviour without teaching us anything about cognition was offered by Deeper Blue, a computer developed by IBM. In May 1997 Deeper Blue beat chess world champion Garry Kasparov in a six-game match by 3½ – 2½. It accomplished this feat mainly by brute force, being able to evaluate 200 million moves per second. By comparison, humans rarely evaluate more than 15 moves per minute (Campitelli and Gobet, 2004; De Groot, 1978).

biological cognition, from insects to humans, rely on a body. The idea that one needs to consider the body to understand the mind is not new. It was actually one of the cornerstones of Piaget's theory of cognitive development (Flavell, 1963; see also Chapter 2). With respect to formal modelling – both symbolic and non-symbolic – the criticism again is that the models totally ignore the body, and thus lack a component that is essential to understand cognition. Embodied cognition researchers argue that, in order to incorporate the body in simulations, one has to carry out simulations with robots (Pfeifer and Scheier, 1999). Thus, for example, to understand how people form concepts, one would observe how a robot navigates in its environment and categorises the objects it encounters: for instance, as either useful or useless objects. Researchers in traditional cognitive psychology reply that current robots are so different from the human body that such simulations negate the very goal of embodied cognition (e.g. Lane and Gobet, 2001). It is therefore preferable to follow standard scientific method, by simplifying the scientific questions in order to obtain tractable solutions. In this case, the simplification is achieved by studying specific aspects of cognition – e.g. perception, memory or language – while ignoring the entire cognitive and bodily system with all its complexity.

Stop and Think Theories as computer programs

In 1957 Herbert Simon predicted (among other things) that within ten years (a) a computer program would be world chess champion and (b) 'most theories in psychology would take the form of computer programs or of qualitative statements about computer programs' (McCorduck, 1979, p. 167). Computer programs now routinely beat world chess champions – although this took longer than predicted by Simon – but not all, and not even most, theories in psychology are implemented as computer programs. Looking at recent issues of journals publishing research in cognitive psychology, such as *Psychological Review*, *Cognitive Psychology* and *Cognitive Science*, try to estimate the proportion of theories that take the form of computer programs. Why has Simon's prediction been incorrect in this respect?

Stop and Think Divide and conquer

Most computational models, including connectionist models, have little to say about the biological substrate of cognition. This is an example of the 'divide and conquer' approach in science, where large and difficult questions are split into smaller, more manageable questions. Is this a reasonable approach to studying cognition?

Strengths of computational modelling

Whatever the specific methods they utilise, cognitive modellers argue that their approach offers several important advantages over informal theorising or other types of formal modelling. First, developing a computer model requires a clear and rigorous specification of the mechanisms and parameters underpinning a theory; if this is not done properly, the computer programs just will not run. As we have seen in Chapter 2, and as has been argued for centuries by philosophers of science, this request for being clear and avoiding vagueness is one of the key requirements for developing valid theories. In particular, well-specified theories – including, of course, computer models – make it possible to derive testable predictions.

Second, computer programs afford the possibility of simulating complex behaviours, both qualitatively and quantitatively, irrespective of the number of variables involved. The claim here is that informal theories simply cannot do that, because the limits of human cognition make it impossible for a theorist to keep track of all the constraints involved. The claim is also that other formal methods, in particular mathematical modelling, are not flexible enough to provide veridical models of cognition. For example, to use a case in point provided by Newell and Simon (1972), a mathematical model of language would have to translate everything into numbers, while a symbolic model could simply treat words as symbols.

Third, formal models make it possible systematically to manipulate some variables in order to explore their effects on behaviour. This enables a better understanding of the dynamics of a system, dynamics that can be quite complicated because of the large number of variables involved and also because many of these variables show a complex, non-linear behaviour. This possibility of manipulating some variables while keeping others constant can also help to study the environment systematically, as this often plays an important role in determining human behaviour. For example, by manipulating the input received by models of language acquisition, one learns not only about the models themselves, but also about properties of the environment. A nice illustration of this method is provided by Freudenthal *et al.* (2009), who showed how small differences in the frequency of infinitives (e.g. 'to like', in English) in speech heard by children speaking Dutch, German and English led to subtle differences in the way children later use these infinitives.

Fourth, models provide explanations that are 'sufficient', in the sense that they can reproduce the behaviour under study. For example, a good model of how people solve the Tower of Hanoi puzzle should be able to find a solution, a good model of driving should be able to drive a car (preferably under human supervision, for safety reasons), and a good model of reading should be able not only to reproduce the eye movements of poor and good readers, but also to understand what is being read. While not all models are able to carry out the tasks under study fully, many of them can reproduce at least some important aspects of behaviour.

Finally, computer models can have important implications beyond basic research, and lead to applications. For example, precisely specified theories of acquired dyslexia can inform the design of therapies, or at least suggest compensating strategies (Plaut and Shallice, 1994), and models of learning and expertise have led to the design of training methods. A good example of this is the work carried out at Carnegie Mellon University in Pittsburgh on developing computer tutoring systems teaching geometry and algebra based on the ACT-R computational theory of cognition (Anderson *et al.*, 1995; Koedinger and Corbett, 2006); these systems are now used successfully in thousands of schools in the USA. Box 15.2 offers another nice illustration of the benefits that modelling can have for everyday life.

Box 15.2 EVERYDAY APPLICATION: Mobile phones and driving

Driving is a complex task where perceptual, motor and cognitive processes are continuously integrated. In recent years the use of mobile phones while driving and the potential distraction they cause have received much attention. Many countries have actually banned the use of mobile phones while driving, as there is good empirical evidence that operating them increases the risk of an accident. A fair amount of research has been carried out in cognitive psychology to pinpoint what are the exact effects on attention of using a mobile phone and thus on the driver's ability to react to traffic hazards (for example, see Crundall *et al.*, 2005; Strayer *et al.*, 2003).

▶ Salvucci and Macuga (2002) tackled this problem using computational modelling. They were interested in building models that could predict the impact of dialling on driving performance. Using the ACT-R architecture (Anderson *et al.*, 2004), they developed models of four methods of dialling used by commercially available mobile phones, and combined these models with a model of driving (mostly steering and speed control). Simulations with the models made it possible to generate a priori predictions about driving performance. The simulations made the interesting prediction that driver performance would be more affected by dialling methods that made high visual demands rather than by methods that had long dialling times. An empirical study with a driving simulator and with a typical driving task (driving down a winding lane in a construction zone at varying speeds) validated the models' predictions. This research has real-life applications, as it provides a means for mobile phone developers to design interfaces that minimise attentional load.

Box 15.3 RESEARCH CLOSE-UP: **Can models predict new phenomena?**

In principle, one of the strengths of having theories stated precisely – for example, in the form of computer models – is that they make it possible to derive clear-cut predictions. Ironically, this has often been seen as one serious weakness of cognitive modelling. The contention is that modellers tend to focus their interest on simulating data that have already been collected, and therefore their models are not in a position to make new predictions. This criticism often comes together with the complaint that modellers often adjust the parameters of their models to improve the fit between theory and data (see Box 15.4), which in fact makes it impossible to make new predictions.

This might well be the case, but there are also some nice examples where computer models have led to new predictions. As we have seen in Chapter 12, De Groot (1978/1946) showed that chess masters are much better than weaker players at recalling a briefly presented chess position taken from a tournament game (see Figure 15.1). Players at master level demonstrate almost perfect memory for the entire position, but weaker players hardly remember 50 per cent of the pieces. But what happens when the pieces on the board are shuffled so that one obtains a random position? In a follow-up experiment, Simon and Chase (1973) found that there were no differences in the recall of random positions between their three subjects: a master, an amateur and a novice. This result, which provided a dramatic illustration of the role of knowledge in expertise, became a classic in cognitive psychology, widely cited in articles and in textbooks.

However, the CHREST model (Gobet *et al.*, 2001; Gobet and Simon, 1996a) made predictions about the recall of random positions that were contrary to this received wisdom. CHREST simulates the acquisition of chess expertise by scanning a large number of games played by masters and extracting patterns of pieces ('chunks') that recur often in these positions. With positions taken from games, a version of CHREST, having learned a large number of chunks, can recognise more chunks on the board than a version having learned a small number of chunks, replicating the expertise effect. However, contrary to expectation, the model also predicted a small, but robust skill effect with the recall of random positions: simply by chance, a model with more chunks in long-term memory would sometimes recognise patterns in

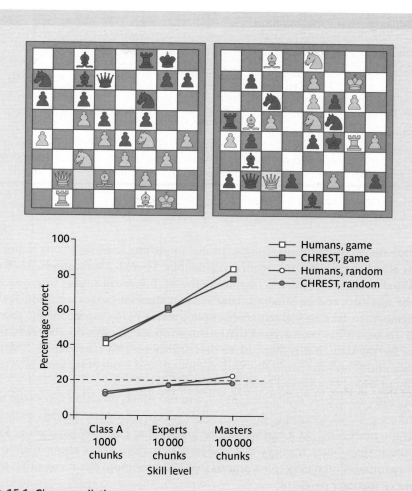

Figure 15.1 Chess prediction

Top: examples of game (left) and random (right) positions. Bottom: recall performance of human players with game and random positions.

random positions. Collection of new data, as well as re-examination of previous experiments having used random positions, showed that masters were consistently better than weaker players at recalling such material, although the skill differences were typically small. Only one study – that of Simon and Chase (1973) – observed a different result! Interestingly, CHREST not only predicted that there should be a difference between skill levels, but also predicted absolute recall percentages that were very close to the values observed with humans.

Stop and Think Mechanisms and data
Consider the TRACE model (McClelland and Elman, 1986), which we have discussed in Chapter 9. How do specific mechanisms explain specific aspects of the empirical data?

Stop and Think Experimental approach and computer modelling
Choose one computational model that was described in some detail in a previous chapter of this book. Using this model and the data it was supposed to explain, compare and contrast the computational approach with the experimental approach. To what extent are they complementary? In opposition?

Stop and Think Simulating free will
Computer models can simulate simple phenomena such as the pattern of eye movements of somebody reading a text and the number of items that can be recalled after brief presentation. But can they simulate more complex 'phenomena' such as free will and consciousness?

Issues

With its emphasis on mechanisms, computational modelling imposes strong requirements for what counts as an 'explanation' in cognitive psychology. There is a stark contrast between explanations realised as computer models (say, using the ACT-R architecture) where each cognitive step has to be specified, and explanations couched in natural language (say, Baddeley's theory of working memory, to take an influential example), where many aspects of the theory remain unspecified. In fact, it has been argued that many informal theories do not really provide any explanation for the data, but rather just re-describe them with fancy labels. Owing to these requirements, and somewhat ironically, with computational modelling, some interesting issues are raised about what constitutes a good theory in science.

To begin with, computer models might require too much precision too early: that is, currently cognitive psychology simply does not allow precise computer models to be developed. This view is too pessimistic, as it can actually be argued that cognitive psychology knows more about cognition than other sciences that are seen as mature know about their own subject matter. For example, Simon (1992) has argued that we know more about cognition than physics knows about elementary particles.

A second difficult issue concerns the way different models can be compared, in particular when they differ in their complexity and in the number of parameters they use (Richman and Simon, 1989; Ritter *et al.*, 2003). One theory might account for a small number of phenomena almost perfectly, but also contains a large number of free parameters that can be adjusted to the data. Another might have few parameters and account for many phenomena reasonably well, but far from perfectly. Which theory should be preferred? This issue relates to the danger of developing models that **overfit** the data (Roberts and Pashler, 2000); Box 15.4 discusses the question.

A third issue relates to the difficulty in separating, in a given model, what constitutes the theoretical claims and what should count as just implementational convenience (Cooper *et al.*, 1996; Lane and Gobet, 2003). For example, a computer model might have a statement for printing the results of the simulations on the screen. Is this part of the theory? The answer is obviously negative, but other cases are more borderline. For example, connectionist models – such as the ones we have discussed in Chapter 9 – come with a specified number of units. Is this part of the theory, or is it just an artefact of the way the theory was implemented? A fourth issue is

Box 15.4 RESEARCH CLOSE-UP: **Fitting and overfitting data**

Mathematical models and computer programs typically contain two types of parameters: **fixed parameters** and **free parameters**. Fixed parameters cannot be changed to account for a set of data. For example, if your theory assumes that the capacity of short-term memory is limited to seven items for everybody, then this value cannot be changed. Free parameters can be adjusted to a new set of data. For example, if you assume that the capacity of short-term memory varies as a function of individual differences, then you can use different values for different individuals. One way to do this is simply to search the value that gives the best fit for the performance of each individual. Let us say that you are modelling performance in an arithmetic task, and that one parameter of your model is the capacity of short-term memory. Then, you could run a few simulations with different values for this parameter (say, 5, 7 and 9) and select the value that provides the closest simulation for each individual. Thus, Peggy could be assigned a short-term memory capacity of 5, and Mary a capacity of 9. This way of estimating parameters uses the data one wishes to simulate, and although it is common practice in modelling – for example, in neural-net modelling – it has serious drawbacks, as we will see in the following paragraphs. A better approach would be to estimate the capacity of short-term memory independently – for example, by giving a memory test to each participant – and then to use these empirical values when carrying out the modelling.

What is then the problem with using the data one wishes to simulate to estimate parameters? Intuitively, this sounds like cheating or at least like circular reasoning: one uses the data one wants to simulate to set the parameters of the model, and then one claims that the model can simulate the data! This practice is actually common in science, in particular when estimating statistical models. The real problem is when too many parameters are estimated in this way. Consider a simple case, where one wishes to fit data points with a mathematical function (see Figure 15.2(a)) – a common task in mathematical modelling. One could opt for simplicity and choose a linear function. In fact, a linear function ($y = a + bx$) gives a pretty good fit: 95 per cent of the variance is explained (see Figure 15.2(b)). Note that two parameters (a and b) are estimated from the data.

But one could also try to get a better fit. Why not estimate more parameters from the data? In fact, as is shown in Figure 15.3, one can fit the data perfectly using a polynomial function ($y = a + bx + cx^2 + dx^3 + ex^4 + fx^5$) with six parameters. Of course, using six parameters for fitting six data points is not particularly economical, and is actually bad scientific practice – it even has a name: **overfitting**. Interestingly, this conclusion dovetails with our intuitions: the linear function seems to summarise the data better than the polynomial function. Indeed, it could be argued that the polynomial function really fits statistical noise in the data. A different set of data from the same phenomenon will show the same linear trend, but the errors will be different and another polynomial will have to be found to fit the new data. Although the function in Figure 15.3 fits the data perfectly, it gives only the *illusion* of a good description, because it is not able to generalise beyond the specific data used to estimate it.

The issue is then to find mathematical models (and the same applies to computational models) that account for the data reasonably well while at the same time remaining simple and not overfitting the data. There is no general solution to this question, but two proposals might be mentioned here. Simon (1992) has argued that one way to assess the success of a model is by considering the ratio of the number of data points explained by the number of free parameters in the model. Similarly, Newell (1990) has proposed that, if one develops a 'Unified Theory of Cognition' that is applied to many phenomena, then this problem disappears because the data will force the theory to settle on fixed rather than free parameters.

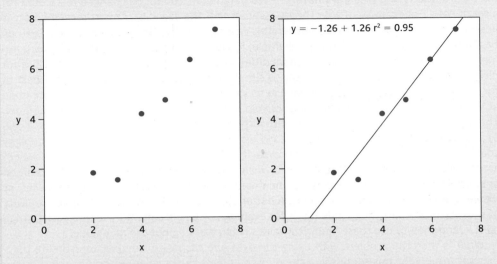

Figure 15.2(a) What mathematical function fits these data best?

Figure 15.2(b) Using a linear function to fit the data
Although the fit is not perfect, a linear function captures the trend in the data fairly well.

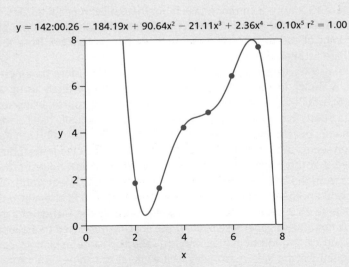

$$y = 142{:}00.26 - 184.19x + 90.64x^2 - 21.11x^3 + 2.36x^4 - 0.10x^5 \; r^2 = 1.00$$

Figure 15.3 Using a polynomial function with six parameters to fit the data
Although the fit is perfect, the function will not generalise to new data describing the same phenomenon.

that there are no standard rules for developing a model, and that researchers use a variety of different techniques for comparing the models and for comparing models against empirical data (Pew and Mavor, 1998; Ritter *et al.*, 2003; Roberts and Pashler, 2000). A final issue is that computer modelling requires distinct skills in computer science and in cognitive psychology, skills that might be time-consuming to acquire.

Given these matters of contention, one might wonder why researchers should bother with cognitive modelling at all – but of course, most of these issues are present because everything must be specified in detail in a computer model. While discussions with verbal theories often centre on clarifying the meaning of different concepts, such discussions are vastly more sophisticated with formal models, and would focus on how changing the value of a specific parameter affects the predictions of the model.

Scope of models

Reflecting on what should be in a model has led researchers to ponder what should be the scope of models: is it enough just to explain a few phenomena, as is the case with most models in cognitive psychology, or is better to develop large-scale theories that can simulate many phenomena in many different domains? As we have seen in Chapter 1, Newell (1990) has passionately argued that the limited scope of many models in cognitive psychology is a hindrance to progress, and that large-scale models should be developed. Such models, which are known as *cognitive architectures*, provide simulations for a large number of phenomena. Several architectures are currently developed, among which three can be said to be prominent. ACT-R (Anderson *et al.*, 2004; Anderson and Lebière, 1998) is the most comprehensive architecture, and has simulated a wide variety of phenomena ranging from simple memory experiments to driving to learning geometry. CHREST (Gobet *et al.*, 2001) has been used to simulate phenomena in domains such as concept formation, verbal learning, expert behaviour and language acquisition. Finally, Soar (Newell, 1990) has simulated data in domains such as memory, problem solving and concept formation.

Chapter summary

There is no doubt that computer models have provided a very useful contribution to cognitive psychology. They are tangible proof that our understanding of cognition has advanced to the point where one can develop detailed models that can simulate the data, sometimes with surprising precision. We have seen that a number of technical issues are still pending, which mostly centre on what constitutes a theory and on how theories should be compared with human data. It is important to note that many non-formal theories cannot even take part in this type of debate, because they are simply unable to make clear-cut predictions. Finally, computer models are not only important for the development of theories in cognitive psychology, but can also have repercussions for applied science.

Further reading

There are surprisingly few good introductions to computer modelling in psychology. The problem is that most focus on a specific approach rather than on computer modelling in general. General overviews are provided by Pew and Mavor (1998) and Ritter *et al.* (2003). Bechtel and Abrahamsen (1991), as well as McLeod *et al.* (1998) provide good introductions to connectionist modelling. ACT-R is described in Anderson and Lebière (1998), Soar is discussed in Newell (1990), and Gobet and Lane (forthcoming) provide an introduction to the CHREST architecture.

Chapter

16

The cognitive neuroscience of visual perception

CHAPTER PREVIEW

☑ After activating cells on the retina, the visual input is sent to the occipital lobe via the optic nerve.

☑ There are two main visual pathways, one dealing with colour and shape, and the other dealing with spatial processing, including motion.

☑ In the occipital lobe, different areas specialise in shape, colour and motion processing.

☑ The lower part of the temporal cortex deals with object recognition. The failure to recognise objects, people or sounds is called *agnosia*.

☑ One of the great mysteries of psychology and neuroscience is how the diverse aspects of the visual input, which are processed in different parts of the brain, are put together so that we have the impression of perceiving a single object. One hypothesis is that this is made possible by neural synchrony, where neurons coding for components of the objects fire at the same rhythm.

Introduction

Light is the fastest element in the universe. It is therefore to be expected that creatures whose perceptual system is based on light have increased chances of survival. Through natural selection, species have developed various ways of seeing the world. Some animals see infrared radiations and others see ultraviolet radiations. Humans have developed a visual system mainly based on colour and brightness.

We know a great deal about the human visual system. This is in part due to the fact that our visual system is similar to that of other primates, which makes vision easier to study than functions that are uniquely human, such as language. In addition, most of our cortex is also devoted to visual processing in one way or another.

The goal of this chapter is to weave together some of the threads that we have introduced in Chapters 3, 4, 6 and 7. More specifically, this chapter will discuss the visual system in some depth and present all the main steps from the point in time where light hits the retina to the point where visual memories are accessed. This will enable us to illustrate, with more detail than has been possible in previous chapters, some key points about how the brain brings about cognition.

Point of contact

The point of contact of our organism with light is the **retina**, which is a layer of cells lying at the back of the eye. The retina, which is very thin (about 0.5 mm), is made of a wide variety of neurons. It is an active system integrating visual information before it is sent to other visual areas for in-depth analyses. There are three major classes of functional neurons in the retina: photoreceptors, bipolar cells and ganglion cells, which are connected laterally by horizontal cells and amacrine cells (see Figure 16.1). Starting from the back of the eye, we first find the **photoreceptors**, which are in charge of capturing light. We then find an intermediate layer, which consists of **bipolar cells**. Finally, we find ganglion cells. **Ganglions cells** are output units, which forward information to other cortical and subcortical anatomical structures. Their axons form the **optic nerve**. The organisation of these three layers is rather counterintuitive, as the photoreceptors are in the back and the ganglion cells are in the front. This means that light must go through the ganglion and bipolar cells before it can be processed by photoreceptors.

The process by which photoreceptors transform light energy into neural signals is called **transduction**. Two types of photoreceptors are in charge of carrying out transduction: *rods* and *cones*. The retina contains about 120 million rods and 8 million cones. Their density differs depending on their distance from the **fovea** (see Figure 16.2). The fovea, which is roughly the central part of the retina, is about 1 mm in diameter – about the size of a pinhead. It is the portion of the retina where acuity is the highest. **Rods**, which are shaped like cylinders, as their name suggests, are concerned with light intensity. They are particularly responsive in dimly lit conditions and provide information about shades of grey. The density of rods is high near the fovea – but not on the fovea itself – and decreases towards the periphery of the retina: there are about 175 000 rods per mm² near the fovea and 50 000 rods per mm² at 80° from it. When compared with other retinal regions, the fovea itself includes few rods. **Cones**, which are shorter and thicker than rods, are concerned with colour detection. They

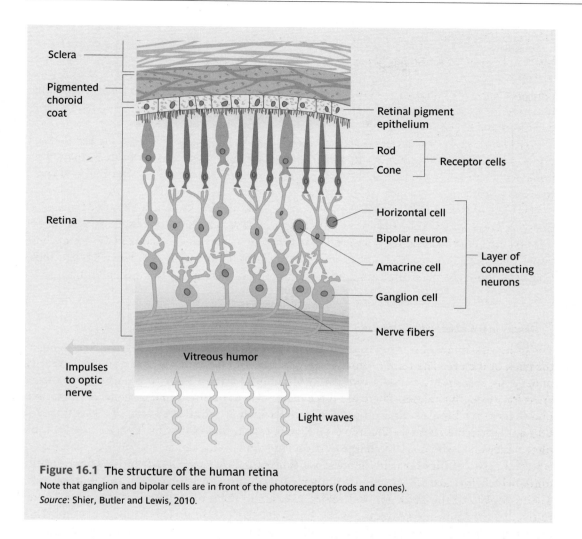

Figure 16.1 The structure of the human retina

Note that ganglion and bipolar cells are in front of the photoreceptors (rods and cones).

Source: Shier, Butler and Lewis, 2010.

need a well-lit environment to work properly. Their concentration is higher in the fovea, to the point that the surface of the fovea is mostly made of cones. There are three types of cone. The *S-cones* are sensitive to comparatively shorter wavelengths such as blue. The *M-cones* are more sensitive to medium wavelengths such as green. Finally, the *L-cones* are more sensitive to longer wavelengths such as red. It is important to stress that cones do not respond to a single colour but to a range of wavelengths.

Figure 16.2 shows the spectrum of sensitivity for each type of photoreceptor. It illustrates that a given type of photoreceptor is more sensitive to some wavelengths and less to others, but the receptors are still active when the radiation is outside the wavelength of maximum responsiveness. As photoreceptors are sensitive to a specific window of frequencies, they filter part of the information from the environment. For instance, if we humans had photoreceptors sensitive to higher frequencies, then we could see X-rays and thus scan the body of our relatives! The input selection of photoreceptors constitutes a first sampling of the available data and

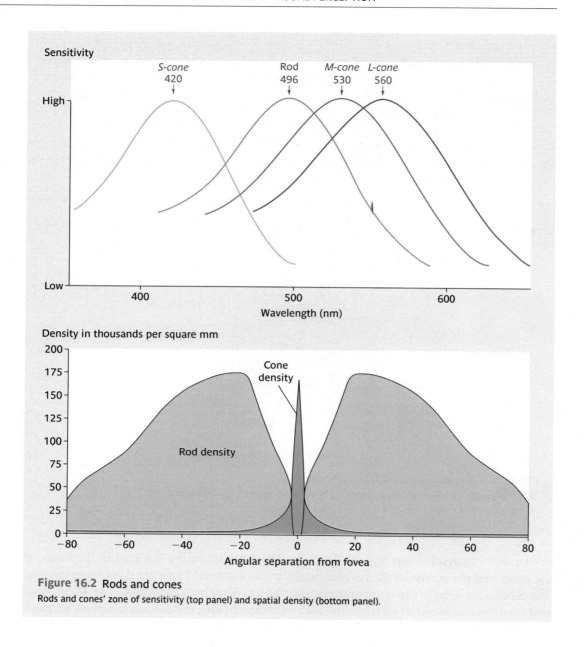

Figure 16.2 Rods and cones
Rods and cones' zone of sensitivity (top panel) and spatial density (bottom panel).

presents an initial impression of how we perceive the world. It is then the job of the visual system to deal with the messiness of the input.

We have already mentioned that ganglion cells are the last step before the neural signal exits the retina to reach other brain structures. Ganglion cells integrate the information received by the photoreceptors so that they respond to stimulations of small regions of the retina. The flow of information is modulated by cells operating transversally (e.g. amacrine cells). The two main kinds of ganglion cells in charge of forwarding the neural signal are the P cells and M cells. **P cells** show slow and sustained responses. Essentially they convey information about colour and fine details, and have high spatial resolution. **M cells**, which have low spatial resolution, show transient responses reaching a peak and falling off rapidly. This makes them very sensitive to the timing of stimulation and so ideal for detecting motion. P cells feed into the **parvocellular pathway** and M cells feed into the **magnocellular pathway**. From the nature of the ganglion cells, we can already draw the conclusion that the parvocellular pathway is mainly concerned with colour and form processing. The magnocellular pathway is concerned with motion processing and in the rapid representation of a scene, but in terms of contrast rather than colour. Let us follow how visual information is handled by the two paths of the visual system (see Figure 16.3).

Stop and Think Animal vision

Some animals, such as insects, have visual systems quite different to ours. Does it follow that their cognition must be different as well?

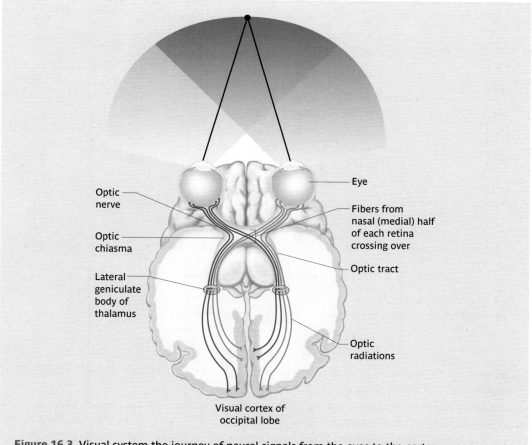

Figure 16.3 Visual system the journey of neural signals from the eyes to the cortex.
Source: Shier, Butler and Lewis, 2010.

The visual cortex

The axons of the M and P ganglion cells form the optic nerve and leave the retina at the *blind spot* (this location is so named because it contains no rods or cones, and therefore no vision is possible). After some of the axons cross at the optic chiasm, they travel to the lateral geniculate nucleus, where they are relayed by the optic radiations to the primary visual cortex at the back of the brain. As we have seen in Chapter 3, the **lateral geniculate nucleus** (LGN) is a structure in the thalamus. Most of its output is directed to the neocortex in the occipital lobe where visual information is analysed. The optic chiasm inverts the streams so that your left hemisphere will process information from the right hemi-field (i.e. the right half of the field of vision), and conversely. This allows the brain to combine information from both eyes, and possibly binocular vision. Processing in the visual system, like in other sensory systems, is both parallel and hierarchical. In this context, 'parallel' means that the information coming from the M and P pathways will be processed simultaneously at every stage, and 'hierarchical' means that information from both pathways will be processed with increasing specificity and complexity of representations. The modular structure of cortices concerned with vision is depicted in Figure 16.4.

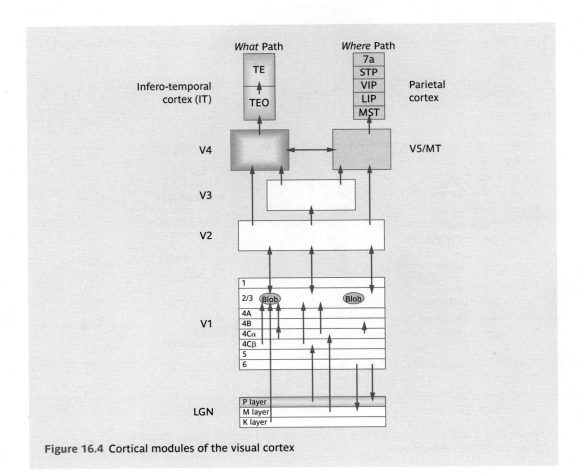

Figure 16.4 Cortical modules of the visual cortex

Neurons in visual area 1 (also known as **V1**) respond to stimuli that are presented in a specific region of the visual field. Any given neuron is responsible for one portion of the visual field. As long as light does not fall on this region, the neuron does not respond differentially. When light falls on the region, the neuron responds by emitting a signal. The region of the visual field to which a neuron is sensitive is termed the **receptive field** (see Box 16.1).

Neurons coding for neighbouring receptive fields are arranged next to one another. As a result, when a colorant is used to mark active V1 neurons while the brain perceives a pattern, the pattern that has been presented is reflected by the activity of neurons. This arrangement of neurons has the consequence that adjacent areas in V1 respond to light on adjacent areas on the retina. This one-to-one correspondence between regions of the retina and V1 neurons is called **retinotopic organisation**. Neurons concerned with the same receptive field are clustered together in a **hypercolumn** (a group of cortical columns that respond to lines of all orientations from a specific region in space), and neurons having the same orientation preference are close to each other. The structure of a hypercolumn is depicted in Figure 16.6.

A hypercolumn has three distinctive input-dependent active sectors. One sector, called *blob*, is highly responsive and concerned with colour processing. Another sector, called *inter-blob*, is concerned with shape. The third sector depends mainly on the input by M cells and is concerned with space and motion. The output of V1 is structured so as to forward two streams to the next visual area. One stream is concerned with form (interblob) and colour (blob) and the

Box 16.1 RESEARCH CLOSE-UP: **Receptive field – receptive fields in V1**

Neurons in V1 show a preference for bars of light at specific angles. While one neuron will respond optimally to a vertical bar of light in its receptive field, another neuron will display a preference to a horizontal bar of light (see Figure 16.5). This makes V1 neurons ideal for identifying edges and boundaries (a fundamental process in representing distinct objects in a scene). The intensity of the neuronal response decreases as a function of the angle with the preferred orientation and the tuning characteristics of the neuron. The only case when the neuron does not respond is when the bar of light is orthogonal to the preferred orientation. Finally, the third factor affecting the response of a neuron is ocular dominance. Some neurons will be more sensitive to the input of one eye rather than to the other.

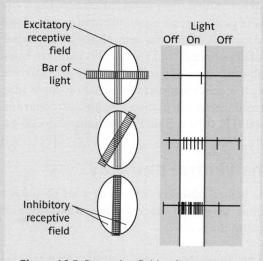

Figure 16.5 Receptive fields of V1 neurons
Source: Hubel, 1963.

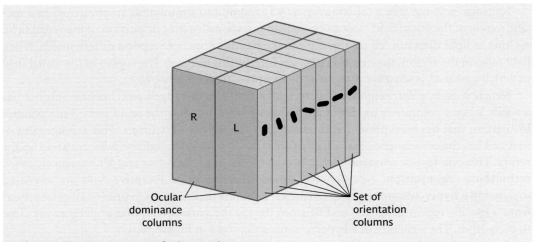

Figure 16.6 The structure of a hypercolumn

Orientation columns are columns of cells with receptive fields that monitor similar retinal position and have an identical axis of orientation. Ocular dominance columns are arrangements of cells that receive input from only the left eye or the right eye.

other stream is concerned with spatial and motion information. The process of building a representation of the world by analysing components has begun.

The signal from V1 is forwarded to visual area 2 (also known as **V2**), which looks like a traffic interchange. From V2, the information is forwarded to any of two output paths according to whether information concerns objects form and colour, or spatial location and motion. The **where pathway** processes information concerned with objects' motion, object location in space and control of actions with objects. The major stream of this pathway carries signals to the medial temporal (MT) area. This pathway is also called the *dorsal* (from Latin *dorsum*, back) pathway because it terminates in the parietal cortex. The other main stream is the **what pathway**, which is concerned with information about object form and colour. The *what* pathway is also termed the ventral pathway (from Latin *ventrum*, abdomen) and terminates in the inferior temporal (IT) cortex. Both the ventral and dorsal pathways are featured in Figure 16.7.

The ventral pathway

The ventral pathway consists of a set of visual areas that process shape or colour. Two areas within this stream – area 4 of the visual cortex and the infero-temporal cortex – are the focus of most of the research.

Colour

Visual area 4 (also known as **V4**) is concerned with colour processing, orientation and recognition of simple object features, such as geometric shapes. Let us consider the phenomenon of colour constancy as an example of the type of processing carried out in this brain area. Visible light is a compound of electromagnetic radiations of various wavelengths. The profile of various

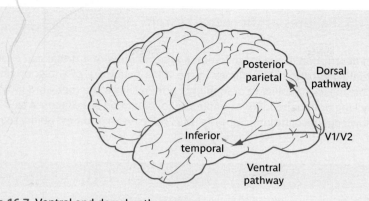

Figure 16.7 Ventral and dorsal pathways
The ventral pathway is in charge of object recognition, and the dorsal pathway is in charge of motion and spatial processing.
Source: Kandel *et al.*, 2000.

wavelengths in a given light is known as the spectrum. The light received by the retina comes from objects (e.g. a table or a chair) that reflect the light from a source (e.g. the sun or an electric bulb). The composition of light depends on the spectrum of the source and the colour of the object (e.g. material properties of the object). The visual system is able, within limits, to determine the colour of an object whatever the composition of the incident light. The receptors in early visual areas, such as cells in V1 blobs are responsive to *wavelengths*. By contrast, cells in V4 are not responsive to wavelengths, but to the *colour* of an object. Imagine a red coat under a white light (i.e. the incident light): photoreceptors capture the light reflected by a red object when lightened by a white incident light. The coat is perceived as red. If we put the coat under a yellow light, we still see it as red, even though the photoreceptors now capture a different spectrum because of the incident yellow light. This raises the question of how the visual system can eliminate the influence of the incident light. The answer lies in the integration of information with neurons concerned with the same object. The visual system compares how much neighbouring neurons are affected by a change in light to extract the real colour of an object.

Form and shape

The **infero-temporal cortex** (IT cortex) is concerned with processing form and shape. It has been known for a long time that damage to this region of the brain results in impaired perception. Specific failures to recognise and associate meaning with persons, objects, sounds, and so on, are collectively called **agnosia**. The ability to distinguish shape (picture copying) and identify components of the object is preserved differentially in different kinds of agnosia. Many forms of agnosia have been identified, many of them being related to damage of a subregion of the IT cortex (see Box 16.2). The most noticeable form of agnosia is the inability to recognise familiar faces (**prosopagnosia**) and appears when a region of the **fusiform gyrus,** located at the bottom of the IT cortex, is damaged. The current view is that a specific form of agnosia arises when a component of the recognition system is impaired. The IT cortex is of key interest and will be mentioned again later in this chapter in the section devoted to recognition processes.

Box 16.2 IN FOCUS: **Failures of the visual system**

We give here a brief description of the most common types of impairment that can arise as a result of a perceptual dysfunction. The names in the table below are of Greek origin. The letter 'a' is used to mean lack of ability to or inability to; then comes the root word indicating which function is lacking or impaired. For example, 'agnosia' can be de-composed as 'a' (lack of) and 'gnosis' (knowledge/recognition). 'Agnosia' thus refers to an impaired ability to recognise objects.

Name	Inability to
Apperceptive agnosia	recognise visual shapes
Associative agnosia	recognise objects (but visual shapes can be recognised)
Achromatopsia	recognise a colour (even though it is perceived)
Prosopagnosia	recognise familiar faces
Alexia	recognise text
Social emotional agnosia	interpret non-verbal behaviour of social content

The dorsal pathway

The dorsal pathway originates in the occipital cortex, including V1, and terminates its route in the parietal cortex. Processing in the parietal cortex is not limited to spatial information, and deals, among other things, with numerical cognition and the control of some motor actions. For the sake of brevity, the following discussion focuses on the motion aspects of the dorsal stream, but you should keep in mind that the parietal cortex is not exclusive to motion.

As noted above, the anatomy of the visual areas of the human brain is similar to that of non-human primates, given that we are evolutionarily close to them. Animals need to analyse motion in order to find resources and detect any threat in their environment as fast as possible. We have seen that visual information about motion is processed along the dorsal stream, and that motion perception is mainly dependent on the signals carried by M cells. Cells in V1 respond to simple stimulation: a neuron responding optimally to a vertical bar will respond to any motion that includes a vertical component. For instance, a motion from bottom left to top right will activate the vertical motion detector in V1.

In Figure 16.8, the two stripes (i.e. in A and B) are moving in different directions. Stripes A move towards north-east, whilst stripes B move towards south-east. When presented together, these two types of stripes are perceived as a single motion going eastwards. Neurons in visual area V1 are responsive to component motion: that is, they respond to either the component A or to the component B. By contrast, some neurons in the medial-temporal (MT) cortex respond to the compound of both motions. Area MT is a region that collects synapses from V1. Virtually all neurons in MT are direction-selective motion cells. Similar to what occurs for photorecep-

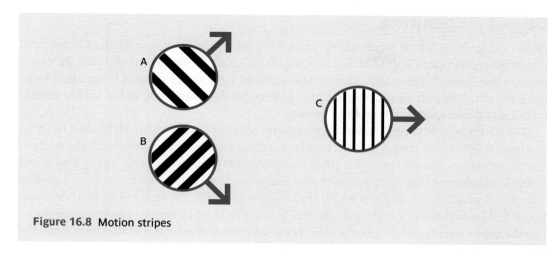

Figure 16.8 Motion stripes

tors, motion neurons fire robustly to a particular motion direction, but also respond to non-optimal directions. A motion neuron does not respond when the direction of motion is perpendicular to its preferred direction. For more about motion, see Box 16.3.

It is thought that neural signals from MT are forwarded to areas in subregions of the parietal cortex that are concerned with the processing of spatial information. Data from neuropsychological patients support this view. After lesions of the right posterior parietal cortex, patients fail to respond to visual stimuli presented in the left side of the visual field.

Stop and Think Ventral and dorsal pathways

Speculate about why evolution has led to a ventral pathway and a dorsal pathway in the primate brain in general and the human brain in particular, with different properties and functions.

Box 16.3 CLASSIC EXPERIMENT: **Motion coherence**

MT cells also respond to *motion coherence*. A key experiment conducted with monkeys illustrates this idea (Stoner and Albright, 1992). Animals were trained to identify the direction of dots moving in one of two opposite directions (either up vs down or left vs right). The activity of MT cells was recorded while monkeys were tested. The experimenters used multiple dots that were roaming randomly and they varied the percentage of dots moving in one direction. So, in one condition, 10 per cent of the dots were moving in a given direction; in another condition, 20 per cent of the dots were showing such a coherent motion, and in yet another condition 30 per cent of the dots were in coherent motion, and so on. Previous experiments had shown that coherent motion appears to a perceiver only if a high enough percentage of dots is moving. If this is not the case, no motion is detected. The results of the experiment were striking. There was a near-perfect correlation between the ability of the monkeys to point to the direction in which the dots were moving and the activity of the MT neurons. Such results suggest that, if MT neurons do not fire, then perception of motion cannot take place.

Object recognition

Object recognition, which requires only a few hundred milliseconds, constitutes a substantial part of perception (see Chapter 4). It allows the identification of almost any object in the environment and immediately points to its salient features. Interestingly, object recognition highlights the structure of high-order visual areas and reveals that specialisation has led some brain modules to detect specific categories of objects.

The relationship between neurons and property coding has been extensively studied recently, and has led to some exciting results. In monkeys, inferotemporal neurons respond selectively to specific categories (Booth and Rolls, 1998; Desimone, 1991; Miyashita *et al.*, 1993). Booth and Rolls (1998) showed that recognition, in some neurons, is **view-invariant**: that is, recognition does not depend on the angle at which the object is seen. On the strength of their findings, Booth and Rolls claimed that the pattern of response displayed by the recorded neurons shows that the neurons are responding to the *object* being seen rather than to its *visual features*. Recently, it has been shown that neurons can be surprisingly specific, as some neurons respond preferentially to particular items (Quiroga *et al.*, 2005). Neurons in the medial temporal lobe were recorded while human participants were looking at pictures of individuals, landmarks or objects. The results indicated that some neurons responded selectively and systematically to a given individual, such as Jennifer Aniston of *Friends* fame. These results, however, have to be interpreted cautiously as the medial temporal lobe is also a memory structure and information is likely to be under top-down influence. The expectations of the participants might modulate the activity of perception. Furthermore, these studies should not mislead you into believing that one neuron encodes one percept. This hypothesis, once popular, has been disconfirmed by the evidence showing that multiple neurons are necessary to code a percept (see Chapter 4).

On a larger scale, neuroimaging studies have shown that object recognition – that is, activation of the neural trace coding for a given object – involves at least one million neurons in the visual-related cortex (Levy *et al.*, 2004). Several studies support the view that recognition takes place in high, modality-specific cortical areas. This supports the so-called 'modular' organisation of the brain. When a specific constellation of neurons in several modules is activated, the corresponding object is recognised. This view implies that sub-parts of the visual cortex are particularly activated when a category of objects is presented, as all the objects belonging to the category share the same general physical features. This hypothesis is well supported by evidence collected recently. For instance, the 'face area' on the fusiform gyrus seems to respond preferentially to faces (Kanwisher *et al.*, 1997), while the lateral occipito-temporal cortex appears to be selective for human body parts (Downing *et al.*, 2001).

The fact that a brain region responds preferentially to a given category of objects does not imply that its activation is sufficient for object recognition. While recognition is performed, activation is not restricted to a single region. In fact, a distributed pattern of activation is observed in lateral and inferior temporal cortices. Confirming the findings of Booth and Rolls about stability and view independence, Spiridon and Kanwisher (2002) have shown that the neural networks that code target objects are viewpoint independent. These findings have been extended by Haxby *et al.* (2001), who showed that the activation patterns associated with different categories of objects are replicable both between and within subjects. The *between-subject replication* is an argument in favour of a general architecture, i.e. modularity of the brain. The *within-subject replication* suggests that an object is coded by a stable neural network. Another line of evidence in favour of the neural network hypothesis comes from neuroimaging studies involving bistable percepts. To test whether two images are coded by two different neural networks, Hasson *et al.* (2001) ran an experiment with an ambiguous image – Rubin's illusion (see Chapter 4). They found that the face area in the fusiform gyrus was more activated when the drawing was perceived as two faces than when it was perceived as a vase, suggesting that the pattern of activation covaries with subjective perception. What is fascinating in this study is that the physical stimulus does not change, while subjective perception and the corresponding neural activation do.

Stop and Think Hierarchies in the brain

In Chapter 3, we argued that the brain is organised hierarchically. Use the information about vision provided in the current chapter to support this view.

The binding problem

As pointed out earlier, dozens of visual areas are involved in vision. The distributed character of perception seems at odds with our subjective feeling that visual scenes are consciously perceived as wholes. For example, if you look at a moving car in the street, neither the colour of the car nor its motion are perceived separately from the car. The binding of perceptual events is even more striking if we consider multimodal perceptions. In spite of the fact that sound and light are analysed by two separated perceptual systems, the noise from a car is perceived as coming from it rather than coming from any other object. For perception to function, some mechanisms should bind together the building blocks of perception. This theoretical issue has long been known as the **binding problem**. In cognitive neuroscience, the problem is stated as follows: how do neurons belonging to different cortical areas combine to provide a single percept? Based on the fact that neurons fire at a regular pace – it is said that they oscillate – the answer lies in **synchrony firing** (Gray and Singer, 1989). Cells coding for a given object fire in synchrony at a given rate, even though they might belong to different regions of the brain. Support for this phenomenon comes from recordings of the electrical activity of visual areas with an EEG, which show that large populations of neurons display synchronised responses.

Early empirical evidence of synchrony firing was provided by Gray and Singer (1989), who showed that perception of objects in the visual cortex of cats emerges according to stimulus-specific neuronal oscillations. This study has spawned a considerable amount of research, which suggests that perceptual binding is processed in a typical frequency range, the gamma band (oscillations around 40 Hz, i.e. 40 times per second). An experiment conducted on humans by Tallon-Baudry *et al.* (1996) has found that visually searching for a dog in the Dalmatian picture (see Figure 4.9 in Chapter 4) induces gamma band oscillations in visual areas. In this experiment, the object to be matched induced the activation of the neural network coding its features and properties, and the neural network was oscillating at the gamma band frequency. Finally, strong evidence in favour of the view that synchronicity is stimulus specific was provided by Castelo-Branco *et al.* (2000), who have shown that synchrony occurs in cells coding for contours belonging to the same surface, but not in cells coding for contours belonging to different surfaces.

Stop and Think Synchrony
We saw in Chapter 4 that, contrary to the prediction of Gestalt psychology, interfering with the electrical field of the brain does not affect perception (the classic experiment of Lashley and colleagues, 1951). Shouldn't this experiment also count against the synchrony hypothesis, which involves electrical activity as well?

Chapter summary

In this chapter we have considered the series of operations that are applied to visual input, from the moment light hits the retina to the moment visual memories are retrieved and put into consciousness. Although we have presented a simplified picture, two key conclusions can be put forward with confidence: first, there are many processing steps, which are done partly in sequence and partly in parallel; and, second, processing can be described as hierarchical, starting from single cells on the retina and moving to increasingly complex representations, to culminate with the recognition of full objects. The low-level aspects of visual perception (e.g. how cones and rods process information in the retina, or how neurons in V1 code features) are fairly well understood, not least because of the contributions made through animal research. Our understanding of high-level aspects of visual processing (e.g. how different representations of the same object are put together, presumably by neural synchrony) is much weaker and is currently the topic of intense research. Some of the questions addressed go beyond perception per se and touch on memory and even consciousness, which will be the topic of the next chapter.

Further reading

Zeki (1993) offers a fascinating discussion of the biological basis of vision. The cognitive neuroscience of vision is also discussed by Farah (2000). General neuroscience texts, such as Bear *et al.* (2007) and Carlson (2007), also provide useful information on the visual system. Grill-Spector (Grill-Spector, 2003; Grill-Spector and Malach, 2004) has written two useful reviews of the neural basis of object perception.

Chapter # 17

Consciousness

CHAPTER PREVIEW

☑ We are aware of ourselves most of the time. We have a feeling that there is something special about us, something extra in addition to all cognitive processes that help us interact with the physical world. We can say that we feel conscious.

☑ Is it possible that there is another realm of reality besides the physical world? Or could it be that there is no physical world except in our mind? Or indeed, could our feeling of consciousness be produced by brain processes? These are the main views on consciousness, which are called dualism, idealism and materialism, respectively.

☑ If there is something extra in addition to the brain, we need to explain the interaction between the physical and non-physical worlds. If consciousness is just the product of the firing of neurons in the brain, it is necessary to explain how we have our subjective experiences.

☑ Some theories assume a kind of theatre in our mind where all processes come together and only those in the current spotlight become conscious. Others do not assume a single place but a network of brain regions that communicate with each other.

☑ There is a possibility that there really is no consciousness. It is just an illusion, a trick that our brains play on us.

Introduction

In the cult film *The Matrix*, the hero, Neo, whom we have already met in Chapter 4, believes that he lives a normal twentieth-century life where he has a job, falls in love and decides for himself. In reality it is the twenty-second century and he is held by evil machines that use the energy of human brains to control the world. Neo is connected to a super computer (The Matrix), which fills his brain with the necessary stimulations and maintains the illusion of a real life. There is no job, no love, and he certainly does not decide for himself. It is a horrendous scenario and it is no wonder

that Neo decides to fight the machines (in no fewer than three instalments). But what exactly is the difference between our current experience and that of our descendants in The Matrix two hundred years in the future? What feels so wrong in the film that makes us identify with the main hero? Underneath all the action in the film, a problem is hidden that has plagued human kind for centuries, the problem of ourselves, the problem of our **consciousness**.

Consciousness seems obvious and almost trivial at first sight. You are reading these printed words, you may even like what is written, and a few seconds ago you turned to this page. You were not only aware of those actions, but you also felt that you had initiated them. The concept of consciousness appears intuitively clear and one is tempted to paraphrase James's immortal words on attention and say that 'everybody knows what consciousness is'. We, do, however, need to explain how our subjective experience arises from the interaction with the material and objective world. Consciousness has a touch of subjectivity; it feels strongly like something extra, something that makes us so special. This feeling is what another American philosopher, Ned Block (2005), calls **phenomenal consciousness**. It is different from **access consciousness**, which refers to the elements for use in thinking, speech or action. While most of cognitive psychology deals with access consciousness, the real challenge, the so-called **hard problem** (Chalmers, 1995), is to explain phenomenal consciousness.

Historical perspective

The problem of consciousness is not a new one. It is a modern version of the notorious **mind–body problem**, with which philosophers have struggled for more than two thousand years. There seem to be two obvious realms – the physical world and subjective experience – as our whole civilisation, including religion, is based on the premises of some kind of **dualism**. Probably the most famous dualist theory is **Cartesian dualism** by the French philosopher René Descartes, who treated mind and brain as two different entities meeting in a small structure in the middle of the brain, the pineal gland.

Implicit in the notion of dualism is that the mind, a non-physical entity, can influence the brain, a physical entity. This somewhat unrealistic assumption represents the most worrying

Figure 17.1 What is it really like to be a bat?
To illustrate the difficulty of defining consciousness, American philosopher Thomas Nagel (1974) asked the above question. Bats use a cumbersome technique relying on highly pitched sounds for locating objects, and we really cannot imagine the life of a bat. Like bats, we do nothing more than perceive different wavelengths from the environment (see Chapter 4), but a juicy apple does not seem and feel like a bunch of light waves.
Source: © Philip Date/fotolia

Box 17.1 IN FOCUS: Neuropsychology and consciousness

Our life is meaningful and there is a sense of continuity about it. It seems that we would notice if something were missing. Yet, some patients with brain damage do not notice when something is awfully wrong. People with **neglect**, who have suffered damage to the right side of their brain, lose not only some cognitive abilities but also one half of the world. They cannot see the left side of a picture or a room. Neurologist Edoardo Bisiach (Bisiach and Luzzatti, 1978) asked neglect patients from Milan to imagine the Piazza del Duomo, a well-known square in the centre of the city. Their task was to describe what they saw when they arrived at the square from the north side. The patients described many shops, cafes and buildings, but they were all to their right. They completely ignored the buildings on the left side. When they were asked to imagine what they saw when they were coming from the opposite side, they mentioned the buildings they had just failed to describe and forgot all the buildings they had previously described. The most curious thing is that they did not think that something was wrong with their description. Surely, if their consciousness was unimpaired, they would have realised the inconsistencies in their descriptions.

We have seen in Chapter 7 that amnesic patients have an impaired ability to store new information, while their short-term memory is intact. Patient HM could learn a new skill but would always claim that he was doing it for the first time. Similarly, CW enjoyed music and even performed as a musician, but he did not remember any practice session nor anything else that had happened to him since the onset of his amnesia. These patients are obviously conscious in some way, as they are awake, take interest in the world around them, and can tell how they feel. And yet, there is something profoundly different in their experience. The continuous feeling of being and the perception of elapsing time are completely absent. However, just like people with neglect, they do not seem to notice the problem. If there is consciousness or some kind of non-physical property, how is this possible?

aspect of dualism for most philosophers and scientists. A radical solution to the problem is to assume that only the things that are in our mind really exist. This **idealist** view, pioneered by Irish philosopher George Berkeley, avoids the interaction problem by rendering the physical world redundant. Just as idealism presents an extreme reaction to dualism, half a century of behaviourism is a direct and extreme reaction to idealism. Idealism made the world completely subjective and impossible to investigate while, as we know from Chapter 2, behaviourists put the notion of consciousness away by denying the existence of the mental states.

Modern materialism and theories of consciousness

The days of behaviourism are long gone and in the previous chapters you witnessed the progress made by the study of cognitive processes. The study of complex processes, such as thinking and attention, undoubtedly leaves the door open for the investigation of consciousness. One could even argue that the question of consciousness is of immense importance for cognitive psychology. After all, cognitive psychologists often investigate mental processes relying on the phenomenal experience of participants. They also depend on participants' understanding of instructions, an obviously conscious act. It is not surprising, therefore, that we have already dealt with a number of conscious and unconscious processes in the previous chapters – change and inattentional blindness, subliminal priming, automatic processing, automatisation, implicit and explicit memory, declarative and procedural memory.

Attention in particular seems to be closely related to consciousness. In order to become aware of an event or stimulus, attention is necessary. Some researchers go even further, essentially equating consciousness with attention. The supervisory attentional system (SAS) in Norman and Shallice's (1986) model (see Chapter 5), for example, controls allocation of attention and practically decides which process will become conscious. The SAS component resembles a homunculus (little human) who is in charge of our behaviour. It is another version of a dualist trap where we have a place, sometimes called the **Cartesian theatre** (Dennett, 1991), where all the processes come together and some of them are chosen to become consciousness. This kind of scenario is hardly possible as there is no such thing as a central processor in the brain – not even the pineal gland.

There are several ways around this obstacle, one of which is the **Global Workspace Theory** by Bernard Baars (2002). Instead of a central processor such as working memory or SAS, we have a network of sub-systems. Each of these sub-systems is responsible for different cognitive processes (e.g. perception, attention) that are happening at the same time in our brain and of which we are mostly unaware. Which of these processes will enter consciousness depends on their access to the global workspace. The global workspace subsequently broadcasts information about the processes to other sub-systems. The conscious information is then used by these sub-systems for possible action. This way, consciousness represents a general availability and has a central communicative role.

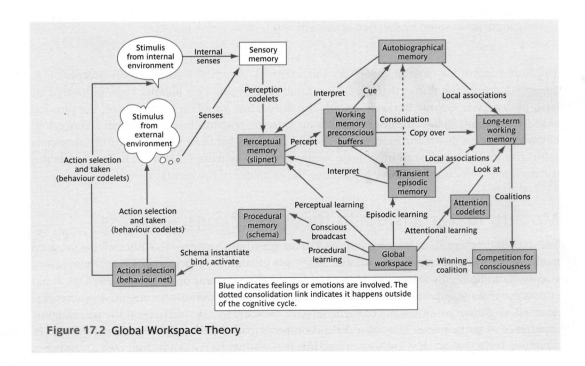

Figure 17.2 Global Workspace Theory

The theory clearly specifies which things will come into consciousness, but some claim that it is unclear why exactly the processes which are broadcast will become conscious and others not. Another problem is that describing information processing associated with consciousness does not answer the question of the nature and function of consciousness. This is a general problem with the modern view of equating the mind with physical brain processes called **materialism**. Materialism solves the problem of interaction by proposing that brain and mental states are one and the same thing. However, explaining the processes of perception and thinking completely, in the smallest detail, is one thing, but explaining how the physical processes of our brain give rise to our conscious subjective experience is another matter entirely.

A number of philosophers and scientists believe that this position is difficult to maintain. To illustrate the potential fallacy of materialism, they use a thought experiment about **zombies** (Chalmers, 1996). The zombies talked about by philosophers are not those that we are accustomed to in popular films, where they wander around mindlessly and painfully trying to sink their teeth into you. To philosophers, zombies are much more like a complete replica of humans, with all the accompanying processes but without consciousness. They behave just like their originals but they lack a certain something, what film-makers like to call 'soul' and what scientists and philosophers call 'consciousness'. Are such zombies possible? Materialists' answer to this question is that it is really not a question. If zombies are a true replica of humans with identical characteristics, just by definition they behave as conscious people do. But are the computers which carry out numerous computational simulations of cognitive processes we have encountered in this book conscious? The results are practically indistinguishable from actual behaviour (see, for example, Figure 15.1 in Chapter 15). Yet it is difficult to imagine someone positively answering this question, just as it is difficult to imagine that Neo is living it up in the vat.

Stop and Think Teleport thought experiment

In David Carpenter's cult film *The Fly*, the hero, played by Jeff Goldblum, builds a teleport that initially destroys the substance placed in it only to recreate it in a different place. The experiment goes awfully wrong when a fly sneaks into the teleport and is recreated together with Jeff Goldblum. Leaving aside science fiction for a moment, imagine that we have such a machine and that there are no flies around. The question is: would you allow yourself to be teleported – that is, to be completely destroyed initially and then identically reconstructed a few miles away at a desired place? It would be the same you, at least physically. Depending on your answer, what can you say about your take on consciousness – do you prefer materialism or dualism?

An illusion?

We have already seen that materialist theorists do not assume that consciousness is an independent force. In fact, many think it is completely powerless. A version of this view is **epiphenomenalism**, where consciousness is just a by-product of the cognitive processes. Consciousness could be described by the metaphor of the tin cans attached to a wedding car – although they make a lot of noise and remind us of their presence, they are good for nothing.

A similar view, albeit not as extreme as epiphenomenalism, is to consider consciousness as an illusion. This is another, at first sight, counter-intuitive view. We have, however, encountered numerous examples throughout this book of things that are not what they seem to be. Most prominently, in Chapters 4 and 5, we saw that our picture of the world is not as complete as it seems. The change blindness phenomenon teaches us that we carry out many inferences from the sensations we gain from the physical world. Could it be that we are also filling gaps with consciousness?

Stop and Think The purpose of consciousness

To think that consciousness is without actual power or is an illusion is one thing, but to say that it is completely useless may be taking an unnecessarily extreme position. Given that all our cognitive processes have been developed through evolution and are there for a reason, there is a good chance that it is the case with consciousness too. What do you think consciousness could be good for?

Daniel Wegner (2003) certainly thinks that the feeling that our thoughts influence our actions is just an illusion. To show that the feeling of consciousness is preceded by thoughts about the action, Wegner devised a clever experiment. Two participants, one of them a confederate, placed their fingertips on a board attached to the top of a computer mouse. They could move the cursor on the computer screen, which contained numerous objects, by applying pressure on the board. Their task was to move the cursor seemingly randomly and make a stop about every 30 seconds. Finally, they had to specify how strongly they intended to make the particular stop. They both had headphones through which they received, among other things, words describing the objects they could find on the screen. The words should initiate thoughts about objects. Unknown to the participant, the confederate was instructed long before the actual stop to steer the cursor towards a particular object. The participant received the name of the object on which the cursor would eventually stop, 30, 5 or 1 second(s) before the stop or one second after the stop. The idea was to see whether the participant would assume that they initiated the stopping of the cursor on the object they had heard before. When the word describing the object at which the cursor would eventually stop preceded the action (cursor stopping on the object) for five or even just a single second, participants thought that they initiated the action. If the word preceded the action for 30 seconds, or it came one second after the action, participants did not think they initiated the action. Wegner's experiment demonstrates that the

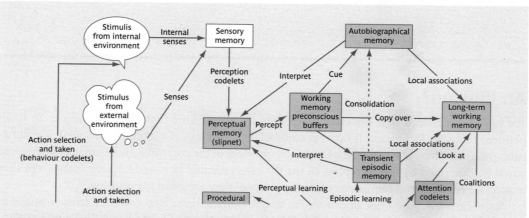

Figure 17.3 Wegner's theory, mouse board settings and results
Source: Wegner, 2003

Box 17.2 CLASSIC EXPERIMENT: Libet's clock and the question of free will

If you hold out your hand and flex your wrist, you will have a feeling that you did it in that particular moment because you wanted to do it in that particular moment. Our actions are the products of our own (free) will. Neuroscientist Benjamin Libet found an ingenious way to check whether it is the case, by timing free will. He placed electrodes on the wrists of the participants, who were supposed to voluntarily flex their wrists for dozens of trials. This way he measured the actual time of the action. To measure the start of brain activation, he placed electrodes on the scalp to measure the electrical activity of the brain (EEG; see Chapter 3). The most difficult part was to time consciousness, in this case (free) will. Obviously, if participants are asked to verbalise or press a button when they become aware of the action, we would get another time lag. Libet devised an instrument that was to become famous as **Libet's clock**. Participants were asked to watch a dot that was going round in a circle, like the hand of a clock. They had to remember the exact location of the dot when they decided to act, and report it after the action had been executed. This way, Libet could get exact timing of will, the brain activity that started the movement, and the actual movement. As expected, the will to act came before the actual action, some 200 ms before. But when did the brain initiate the action? It turned out that brain activity started some good 350 ms before the participants became aware of their desire to execute the action (and some 550 ms before the action). It seemed that our brain decides for us, and that, in terms of neuronal brain time, we are aware of the decision only much later!

Stop and Think Are Libet's findings really surprising?
Libet's findings are highly counter-intuitive, as we always have a feeling that *we* decide when to flex our wrist, and not some neurons in our motor and premotor cortex. What would be the implications if the awareness of the decision indeed comes before the brain activity: that is, (free) will causes brain activity?

Do Libet's findings mean that we do not have free will, that we are not responsible for our actions? This is a serious claim, with far-reaching repercussions. Libet noticed that the participants could sometimes abort the initiated action just before it happened. In another experiment he tested what happened when the planned action is aborted. It turns out that the initial brain activity is the same as in the normally executed movements, but this time the activity dies out at around 200 ms before the action was due to happen. It looks like we are aware of some kind of veto. This prompted some to say that we may not have 'free will', but we do have 'free won't'!

brain initiates the planning for an action, but at the same time it initiates the thoughts about the action. Once the action is executed, we jump to the conclusion that our thoughts caused the action. In other words, the feeling of control and planning is just an illusion.

Conclusion

As you have probably realised, consciousness is a notoriously difficult problem. William James's (1890, Vol. 1, p. 244) feeling that exploring consciousness is like 'trying to turn up the gas quickly enough to see how the darkness looks' is without any doubt shared by many modern scientists. Some believe that we simply lack the tools to pursue this topic scientifically and that the secret of consciousness will always remain hidden from us. The choice between these options is certainly not an easy one. On the one hand, we have mysterious processes and mental forces in dualism. On the other, we need to realise that what we feel and what we believe we are is possibly just an illusion. It is not unlike the choice Neo is facing at the end of the first instalment of *The Matrix* where he is offered a life in ignorance and potential bliss in The Matrix in the way of a blue pill, and a life full of struggle and search for reality, whatever it may be, in the red one.

Chapter summary

In spite of all the cognitive processes that are going on in our heads, we still do have a feeling that we somehow supervise them. The physical world seems one thing and we do need our senses to interact with it, but there seems to be something inside our head that differentiates us from other animals. Everything we do seems to be under our firm control. We have a feeling that we are aware of ourselves all the time (except when we sleep). The main problem in research on consciousness is to explain this feeling of our constant consciousness.

This is a modern-day version of the mind–body problem that has occupied philosophers' attention for centuries. How does the physical world map into our non-physical mind? The most common and highly intuitive answer, deeply rooted in all human civilisations, is to assume that mind and physical world are two distinct entities. This popular dualist view is difficult to defend, because it is hardly possible to explain how a non-physical entity such as the mind can cause anything in the physical world (leaving aside mysterious forces). An extreme reaction to this view is idealism where absolutely nothing exists besides the things that are currently in our minds. One can consider behaviourism an extreme reaction to idealism. While idealism considered the physical world redundant, behaviourism took the mind out of the equation.

Most modern scientists reject these views in favour of materialism. The main idea behind materialism is that our consciousness is actually our mental states. There is no interaction needed, as there are not two different entities. The new problem now is to explain our subjective experience of something that certainly does not look like a bunch of neurons firing. A popular metaphor is to see the mind as a theatre where all the processes come together. The processes are chosen to become consciousness by directing the spotlight on some of them. Given that there is probably no central place in the brain where all things come together, most theories involve a kind of network that is able to make information available to other parts.

Yet another possibility is that consciousness is just an *illusion*. We do feel in control all the time, but in reality our brain does the work for us while we wrongly attribute the control to our consciousness.

Further reading

In readable articles, Block (2005) elaborates on phenomenal and access consciousness and Baars (2002) on his workspace theory. Dehaene *et al.* (2006) discuss the link between consciousness and subliminal perception, which we encountered in Chapter 5. The papers by Wegner (2003; Wegner and Wheatley, 1999), elaborate on the tricks our minds play on us, and Libet (1985) considers in detail the timing of consciousness; these papers are already classics. Blackmore (2004) has a readable introductory book on consciousness.

Chapter **18**

Social cognition

CHAPTER PREVIEW

- ☑ Social cognition is the study of how we process information about the social world and ourselves. Limits in attention, memory and decision-making abilities mean that we have to minimise cognitive processing by using shortcuts and heuristics: we are 'cognitive misers'.

- ☑ Schemas are omnipresent in social cognition. They are useful because they make it possible to access a wealth of knowledge rapidly, thus allowing us to make quick decisions.

- ☑ When making social inferences, we do not behave optimally but use heuristics that sometimes lead to biases and errors.

- ☑ Three dimensions determine first impressions: evaluation (good–bad), activity (active–passive) and potency (strong–weak). Evaluation is the most important dimension, and if later impressions are not consistent with it, they are sometimes adjusted to remove any inconsistency.

- ☑ People scoring high on one trait (e.g. attractiveness) tend to receive high ratings on characteristics that are unrelated to this trait (e.g. intelligence). This general tendency of the perception of one trait to influence how we perceive other traits is called the 'halo effect'.

- ☑ We tend to evaluate other people positively (the person positivity bias) but attach more weight to negative information when present (negativity effect).

- ☑ Salience is an important factor in selecting cues when forming impressions. Salience affects perception of causality and makes evaluations more extreme.

Introduction

During the campaign leading up to the 2010 UK general election, one apparently uninformed voter said that she would vote for liberal democrat candidate Nick Clegg because 'he is cute'. In the same election, a poster of the Conservative leader David Cameron was digitally enhanced to make him more attractive. The poster was ridiculed and set off a wave of internet spoofs. But was the 'cute' voter so clueless and were the designers of Cameron's airbrushed poster so naïve? Does attractiveness really influence our first impressions and does it direct our later decisions? More generally, how do perception, memory and other cognitive processes influence our social life? This is one of the interesting questions that the field of social cognition tries to answer.

What is social cognition?

Before defining social cognition, we need to say a few words about social psychology. According to Allport's classic definition, social psychology is the part of psychology that attempts 'to understand and explain how the thoughts, feelings, and behavior of individuals are influenced by the actual, imagined, or implied presence of others' (Allport, 1985, p. 3). Social psychology studies relations between people, and standard topics of research include, among many others, attitudes, attributions, majority and minority influence, obedience, prejudice, close relationships and altruism. Social psychology always had an interest in cognition, and in particular in the representations that people draw on to interact socially. Thus, and somewhat paradoxically, when the use of cognitive concepts was banned from mainstream psychology by behaviourism

Figure 18.1 Clegg and Cameron
Did people vote for them because of their looks?
Source: © Alamy

in the first half of the twentieth century, social psychology routinely used concepts such as beliefs, attitudes, norms, etc. Thereafter, over the years, social psychology adopted much of the methodology of cognitive psychology. Social cognition is one area of social psychology where the use of cognitive methods is particularly prevalent.

Social cognition, the topic of this chapter, is therefore a field at the intersection between cognitive psychology and social psychology. Its emphasis is on the internal processes at play in social interactions, and it studies how we process information about the social world: how we perceive, form memories of, and make inferences about other people and about ourselves. Much of what we have covered in this book readily applies to social cognition. However, people are not just any kind of 'objects' that our cognition processes. People have beliefs and intentions, and they think about causality and reflect on their interactions with other people. All this makes dealing with them much more challenging than dealing with inanimate objects such as chairs or even with animals.

Given the complexity of the 'objects' dealt with by social cognition – people – the different cognitive processes we have discussed in the previous chapters tend to be intermeshed even more than with other stimuli. However, to simplify presentation, we organise the chapter along three main themes: social perception, social memory and social inferences.

Social perception

The way people perceive a social situation will to a large extent determine their behaviour, and this often happens automatically beyond awareness. Perceptual processes help to make sense of complex situations, to simplify them and to trigger appropriate behaviour. We have here a theme that we have met in other chapters of this book: the limits in attention and short-term memory capacity mean that people have to minimise cognitive processing and take shortcuts when making decisions. The use of perception together with prior long-term memory is one such shortcut. In the social cognition literature, this idea is captured by characterising people as **cognitive misers** (Fiske and Taylor, 1984).

One efficient shortcut is to categorise social situations and people spontaneously. In doing so, some of the basic principles we have discussed in Chapters 4 and 8 will also be essential here. When meeting new people, we rapidly form quite wide-ranging impressions using a very limited amount of information. If pressed, we can estimate new acquaintances' educational level, their intelligence, their age and so on. First of all, however, we evaluate whether we like them or not. It has been known since the work of Osgood *et al.* (1957) that first impressions are dominated by three dimensions, which are called **central traits**: evaluation (good–bad, warm–cold), potency (strong–weak) and activity (active–passive). Once we have established whether we like or dislike somebody, valuations along most of the other dimensions will follow.

Another important aspect of impression formation is that we tend to be consistent. In particular, we tend to perceive people as consistently good or bad, even in the presence of contradictory information, and even if we have to distort new information in order to avoid inconsistencies. For example, if our first impression of Donald is that he is nice and trustworthy, and hence likeable, we are likely to neglect additional information that is less positive, such as 'he is dishonest'. This tendency is called the **halo effect**. In a typical experiment supporting this effect, Dion *et al.* (1972) presented pictures of people of low, medium or high attractiveness

Figure 18.2 Halo effect
Is this adorable cat friendly, intelligent and sociable?
Source: C Peter Bregman/fotolia

(the level of attractiveness was estimated beforehand by ratings provided by a large sample of students). Participants were then asked to rate these people on a number of dimensions unrelated to attractiveness, such as social desirability, personality, occupational status and professional happiness. The results showed that attractive people tended to receive higher ratings than unattractive ones. The halo effect is not limited to physical beauty and has also been observed with other factors that produce a positive first impression, such as being famous, being rich and having a warm personality. And yes, as suggested in the introduction, we tend to vote for politicians who are more attractive (Efran and Patterson, 1974; Surawski and Ossoff, 2006).

If you feel a bit depressed by the key role played by attractiveness in forming impressions, as opposed to more reliable information such as abilities, we have good news for you. There is a tendency to evaluate other people positively, a phenomenon called the **person positivity bias** (Sears, 1983). For example, in a study with American college students, Sears found that 97 per cent of the professors were rated above average. Interestingly, this bias did not extend to the evaluation of courses: professors received higher ratings than the course they taught 74 per cent of the time. More recently, Willis and Todorov (2006) showed that the person positivity bias occurs extremely rapidly. They briefly presented unfamiliar faces to participants and found that the judgements that were made after an exposure of 100 milliseconds corresponded closely with the judgements made without time limitations.

Perhaps as a consequence of the person positivity bias, people tend to give more weight to negative evaluations than to positive ones, a phenomenon called the **negativity effect** (Fiske, 1980). The reason is that, because they are overused, positive evaluations do not bring much information. By contrast, because they are rare, negative evaluations have more information value. Because of this effect, extremely negative traits will have disproportional effects on impressions, irrespective of the presence of many positive traits. A striking illustration of this effect was provided by Lau (1982) in his study of US presidential and congressional elections from 1968 to 1980. He found that negative evaluations were a much stronger predictor of voters' intentions than positive ones. Thus, being characterised as dishonest weighed much more, in the negative direction, than several positive evaluations concerning energy, commitment and expertise.

We have seen in Chapter 4 that perception is active. The same applies to social perception. People strive to find meaning for the perceived object, and thus tend to perceive objects spontaneously as part of a known structure (an instance of **top-down processing**). Also, just as with perception in general, the context plays an important role in social perception. Several studies have shown convincingly that the same information has a totally different meaning in different contexts. For example, Hamilton and Zanna (1974) showed that a feature such as 'proud' had different connotations depending on the context. In a positive context, the connotation was of being 'confident'. In a negative context, the connotation was of being 'conceited'.

As noted earlier, some traits are more powerful than others in imposing a meaning about an individual or a group. Kelley (1950) invited a guest lecturer to lead a 20-minute discussion. Before the session, Kelley gave half of the students the description of the lecturer using the following traits: very warm, industrious, critical, practical and determined. The other half received a similar description, with the only difference that 'very warm' was replaced by 'rather cold'. This manipulation affected the impressions formed by the students. After the lecture, the lecturer was rated more negatively (e.g. more self-centred, more formal and more irritable) by the students who had received the description 'rather cold'. More strikingly, the manipulation also affected the students' behaviour: the students for whom the lecturer had been described as 'very warm' initiated more verbal interactions with the lecturer than the other students.

Stop and Think Central traits
Why are central traits so important in impression formation?

When forming impressions, some cues are more important than others. In particular, in line with the **figure-ground principle** that we discussed in Chapter 4, the **salience** of the cue is a key factor directing people's attention. Any cue that is unusual and novel in a given context will be salient. A politician with a punk hairstyle or a black person in a group of white people will stand out. As noted earlier, we tend to form impressions and reach decisions with minimal cognitive effort, and using salient cues is an efficient way to reach this goal.

In addition to directing attention, salience also influences impression formation in two important ways (Fiske and Taylor, 2010). It affects perception of causality: people who are salient are considered to be more in control of their social environment. It also makes evaluations more extreme. For example, consider a woman who is the only female member of a group. If she is pleasant, she will be evaluated more positively than women in a mixed group; but if she is unpleasant, she will be evaluated more negatively.

Social memory

Another way to act as a 'cognitive miser' is to categorise objects, so that knowledge in long-term memory can be rapidly accessed. Once an individual or a group has been categorised, we can access useful information, such as **schemas** (see Chapters 7 and 8). Research has indeed shown that schemas play an essential role in the way we handle social interactions. Schemas offer the advantage that they give access to a wealth of structured and organised knowledge, in this case about individuals and their relationships. Categorisation and the use of schemas simplify complex situations so that cognitive processing is more efficient, which enables us to act more quickly.

We have different types of social schemas: schemas about *the self* (known as 'self-schemas'), schemas about *specific individuals* (e.g. your parents or Michael Jackson) and schemas about *groups of people*, of which **group stereotypes** are particularly important for social cognition, as you can imagine. Another type of schema important for the way we behave in our daily lives is **role schema**. These schemas tell us how people occupying a specific role in an organisation or in society at large should behave. For example, we expect from medical doctors that they are diligent, care about people and have knowledge of medicine. The term **script**, which we have encountered earlier in this book, is used when the emphasis is on the *actions* carried out in a given situation.

Because schemas are learned, there will be large differences between individuals in the kind of schemas they have, even within the same culture. For example, university students have schemas for intelligence that emphasise academic performance, while non-students have schemas that highlight practical and social problem solving (Sternberg *et al.*, 1981). An obvious bias accompanying schemas is that they lead to stereotypes. For example, the stereotype of English people as being drunk, aggressive, loud hooligans is widespread, in spite of the fact that we know that this description obviously does not apply to most English people. In general, schemas suffer from being inflexible, directing attention away from information which might refute them towards information which supports them. For better or for worse, many of our actions reflect our culture and our previous experiences.

When using social schemas, we tend to show a confirmatory bias in that we seek evidence that supports the schema, rather than evidence that refutes it. As you will remember from Chapters 10 and 12, this is a pervasive feature of human cognition (see also Bilalić *et al.*, 2010). However, social schemas are uniquely powerful in the sense that they have an impact not only on the person who holds them, but on other people as well. This idea is discussed further in Box 18.1.

Social inferences

When we interact with people, we continuously make inferences about them. Why do they behave the way they do? What is their goal? Do they like me? If not, why? An important subfield of social cognition has investigated the processes that allow us to make these inferences. Two main approaches can be singled out. The first, called the **rational model of inference**, assumes that we use information optimally in order to make inferences. The second, based on the idea of cognitive misers, assumes that the limits of our cognition force us to take shortcuts and to use simple but fallible **heuristics**. You will notice that these two approaches parallel those used in the fields of reasoning and decision making.

Box 18.1 EVERYDAY APPLICATION: **Self-fulfilling prophecy, Pygmalion and the halo effect revisited**

It sometimes happens that false expectations elicited by a schema affect our interaction with other people to the point that they also change the behaviour and attitudes of these people in a manner consistent with our expectations. It is as if the other people have internalised our schema, which will of course reinforce our own schema. This phenomenon is called a **self-fulfilling prophecy**.

A classical example of this phenomenon is the **Pygmalion effect**, in which positive expectations placed upon people lead to an improvement in performance. The effect, documented in Rosenthal and Jacobson's (1968) classic book *Pygmalion in the classroom*, originates from George Bernard Shaw's play, which tells the story of the poor, uneducated Cockney girl metamorphosed into a society lady with refined speech and manners. After administering an IQ test to elementary schoolchildren, Rosenthal and Jacobson told teachers that the IQ scores reliably predicted which children (about one-fifth of their class) would 'bloom' – that is, would shortly show rapid intellectual growth. In reality, the names were selected randomly, with the constraint that there would not be any IQ difference between the bloomers and the non-bloomers. As predicted, the teachers developed expectations of both groups: for example, the bloomers were perceived as being more curious and interested. This led to changes in the teachers' behaviour such as providing more attention and feedback to the bloomers' group. IQ scores at the end of the first and second year reflected these expectations, with bloomers performing better than non-bloomers. The effect has been often replicated. In a **meta-analysis**, Rosenthal and Rubin (1978) analysed 345 follow-up studies and found that the effect was very robust.

Beyond the classroom, self-fulfilling prophecies can also be observed in the workplace and in everyday interactions. For example, Snyder *et al.* (1977) provided biographical information and the photograph of a woman (either attractive or unattractive) to male students. As expected from the halo effect, the students judged the women with attractive pictures to be more friendly and sociable than those with unattractive pictures. Then, the students telephoned the woman for a 10-minute conversation. As you would expect from this type of research, the pictures were randomly assigned and thus real attractiveness did not necessarily correspond to picture attractiveness. Consistent with their expectations, the students with an attractive picture found the woman they talked to more friendly and sociable. In addition, the students behaved in a friendlier manner. Remarkably, the students' expectations affected the women's behaviour. Women with unattractive pictures were judged as cool and aloof by a group of independent observers who rated the phone conversations, while those with attractive pictures were rated as friendly and sociable. It is possible that a similar mechanism explains the halo effect more generally: people who are attractive receive more attention and feedback, and thus *do* become more confident, friendly and sociable.

When we make social inferences, we first gather the relevant information, and then integrate it in some way. Rational models (Einhorn and Hogarth, 1981) assume that both steps occur seamlessly: we receive unbiased information from the external world, and the methods we use to integrate it are logical and take into account all the information we have. However, research has shown that we suffer from a number of biases in each of these two steps.

When we gather information, our attention is selective. We tend to be biased by prior expectations and focus on information that is consistent with these expectations. According to Nisbett and Ross (1980), this can be particularly detrimental in three cases: when the expectations are incorrect; when we are not aware that prior expectations might lead to biases; and when the expectations simply prevent us from gathering any information. Interestingly, making people aware that the information could be biased does not help much. In a study by Hamill *et al.* (1980), participants viewed a video depicting a prison guard either as a humane and compassionate individual or as an inhumane and cruel person. Before seeing the video, participants received different information. The first group was told that the prison guard in the video was typical of most guards, the second group was told that he was atypical, and the last group did not receive any information about typicality. The participants then answered questions about the criminal justice system. Hamil *et al.* thus had a 2 (humane vs inhumane) × 3 (typical, atypical, no information) design. Added to this, there was a control condition in which participants did not see any video and simply reported their views about various political and social issues.

In all three conditions, and regardless of the typicality information given at the outset, participants who viewed the positive depictions were more favourable than those who viewed the negative portrayal (see Figure 18.3). Critically, there was no interaction between typicality

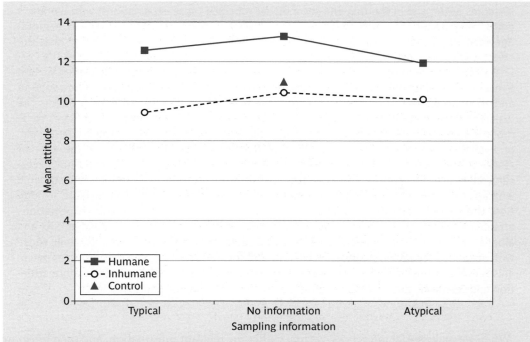

Figure 18.3 Mean level of attitude towards prison guards as a function of sampling information and guard humaneness. Higher means indicate more favourable attitudes.
Source: Hamil *et al.*, 1980.

and type of prison guard. Although participants could still remember the information about typicality given at the beginning of the experiment, there was no difference between the participants in the 'typical' group and those in the 'atypical' group. Thus, participants did not use information about typicality although they did use information provided by the guard depiction. The role of prior expectations with social inferences is also discussed in Box 18.2.

Box 18.2 CLASSIC EXPERIMENT: Obedience to authority: Milgram's experiments

When Adolf Eichmann, a former Nazi SS Lieutenant Colonel, stood trial in 1961 for his role in deporting over six millions Jews to concentration camps, his defence was the same as that of other Nazis: he was just following orders. A similar defence has since been used in a depressingly large number of crimes against humanity, from the Cambodian genocide to Abu Ghraib prison in Iraq. That obedience to authority could lead normal people to such odious acts worried Milgram, a psychologist at Yale University in the early 1960s. In a series of experiments that count among the most famous ever carried out in psychology (Milgram, 1963, 1974), he systematically explored this phenomenon.

In the basic version of the experiment, the participant, who responds to an advert promising $4 for taking part in a study, first meets the experimenter and another participant. The experimenter explains that the goal of the experiment is to find the optimal level of punishment in learning. The roles of 'teacher' and 'learner' are randomly assigned, and the first participant is selected as teacher. The learner is strapped to a chair and connected to electrodes, and the teacher and experimenter move to a different room. The teacher's task is to punish the learner every time he makes a mistake, by giving him an electric shock. The instructions also indicate that the level of voltage should be increased after each new mistake. An impressive-looking apparatus allows shocks of 30 different levels to be administered: from 15 to 450 volts, by steps of 15 volts. Above each button, a label indicates the severity of the shock, with information such as 'Slight' and 'Danger: severe shock'. The experimenter explains that, while painful, these shocks will not lead to permanent lesions. So that the teacher has a sense of the pain inflicted to the learner, he receives a 40-volt 'Slight' electric shock, which most people find quite painful.

The experiment then starts. Every time the learner makes a mistake, the teacher administers an electric shock. The teacher cannot see the learner, but he can hear him through an intercom. Starting from 75 volts, the learner grunts when receiving a shock. At 120 volts, he screams that the shocks are painful. At 150 volts, he screams that he cannot continue the experiment. As you can imagine, the situation is rather unpleasant for the teacher, and he becomes increasingly nervous and anxious, torn between following the instructions and inflicting increasing pain on the learner. When the teacher hesitates, the experimenter encourages him with a standard sequence of four injunctions, from 'Please continue' to 'You have no other choice, you must go on.' The experimenter also assures the participant that they will not be held responsible. At 300 volts, the learner starts banging on the wall. Above 315 volts, no sound is heard. The experimenter orders the teacher to keep going, as no response from the learner corresponds to an incorrect response.

▶

In fact, the learner is a confederate and no shock is ever given – except the sample shock to the teacher. The random assignment is fake, and the participant is always assigned the role of teacher. Finally, the realistic grunts, screams and banging at the wall are pre-recorded.

When asked to predict how far the teacher would go in increasing the voltage, a panel of 110 college students and adults, including 39 psychiatrists, estimated that 90 per cent would stop at 180 volts or before, and that nobody would inflict 450 volts, the maximum shock. To his surprise, Milgram found that *all* his 40 participants would go up to at least 300 volts. Twenty-six went to the maximum shock. Figure 18.4 shows both the predicted and the actual results.

In a series of 18 experiments, Milgram systematically explored the factors facilitating or hindering this extreme form of obedience to authority. He found that obedience diminished when the teacher and learner were close together, and even more so when they had physical

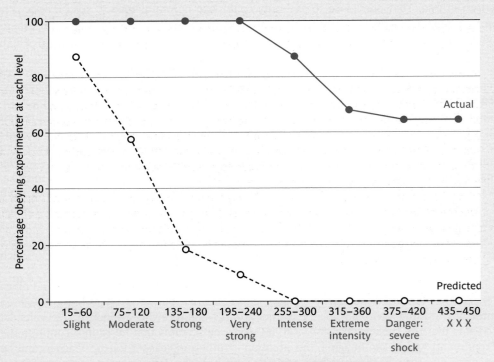

Figure 18.4 Results of Milgram's Experiments
Solid line: percentage of participants administering an electric shock at each level, as a function of voltage.
Dotted line: predicted levels.
Source: Data from Milgram, 1974.

contact. Obedience was stronger when the experimenter was present than when he gave instructions by telephone. By contrast, personality measures, the participants' gender and their professional occupation did not predict obedience.

The standard explanation for these disturbing results was provided by Milgram himself: 'The essence of obedience consists in the fact that a person comes to view himself as the instrument for carrying out another person's wishes, and he therefore no longer sees himself as responsible for his actions. Once this critical shift of viewpoint has occurred in the person, all of the essential features of obedience follow' (Milgram, 1974, p. xii).

However, other explanations have been proposed, such as politeness, awkwardness at withdrawing from the task, and anxiety. A particularly interesting explanation is Nissani's (1990), which relates to the difficulty we have in adopting new views. Rephrased in the language of schemas, the explanation is that participants came to the laboratory with a clear schema of what a scientific experiment was. In particular, an experiment carried out in a laboratory at Yale University, with impressive facilities, must be conducted by responsible scientists, they reasoned. Obviously, participants also know that university research is carried out under strict guidelines, and their schema for a scientific experiment does not include any form of barbarism. When confronted with evidence contrary to this schema (e.g. the pain of the learner), they find it difficult to give up this schema and adopt a new one – that is, to replace the view of a benevolent and moral experimenter with that of a malevolent and immoral one.

If this explanation is correct and explains at least part of the results, conditions that lead participants to reject or at least lessen their belief in the experimenter's morality should also weaken obedience to authority. As noted by Nissani, this is what Milgram found. In one variation of the experiment, participants were led to believe that the experiment was carried out by a private research firm, 'in a three-room office suite in a somewhat rundown commercial building located in the downtown shopping area' (Milgram, 1974, p. 69), rather than by a prestigious university. This difference in perceived scientific authority led to a decrease in obedience rate from 65 per cent to 48 per cent.

Nissani's explanation also accounts for why laypeople and psychiatrists could not predict the degree of obedience shown by the participants: both groups underestimated how difficult it is to give up a strongly held belief. If Nissani is correct, what these experiments do is not to tell us something about people's humanity, as argued by Milgram, but to illustrate how powerful preconceived views can be.

Stop and Think Eichmann's schemas

Obviously, Nissani's (1990) explanation does not apply to Adolf Eichmann arguing that he was just following orders. If not, what kind of schema do you think Eichmann was likely to hold?

Stop and Think Was Milgram right to carry out his experiments?

Milgram's experiments have caused considerable controversy in psychology and beyond. The issue is not whether the effect is real – several replications have shown that it is robust and that it can be found in different cultures. In fact, it has been 'replicated' in a 2010 French TV programme called *The Game of Death*, where only 16 out of 80 participants refused to administer extreme shocks. Rather, the issue is whether it is ethical to submit participants to such psychological torments in order to carry out scientific research. (See also Box 7.2 in Chapter 7.)

- Argue the pros and cons of Milgram's study.
- Slater et al. (2006) replicated one of Milgram's experiments within an immersive virtual environment. When the (female) virtual learner made a mistake, participants were invited to punish her with virtual electric shocks. The study concludes that 'our results show that in spite of the fact that all participants knew for sure that neither the stranger nor the shocks were real, the participants who saw and heard her tended to respond to the situation at the subjective, behavioural and physiological levels as if it were real' (Slater et al., 2006, p. 1). Does this methodology address the ethical issues associated with Milgram's original study?

The biases we have described in Chapter 10 apply equally to social inferences. In particular, people overestimate the value of case history information as opposed to statistical information. They also tend to neglect the fact that small samples can provide skewed information.

The second stage – putting information together – does not fare better with respect to rationality. A powerful example is offered by the selection of graduate students in the USA. Universities spend considerable amounts of money to select the best candidates possible; in addition to information about ability in mathematical and verbal intelligence, which is routinely collected in the USA, they obtain letters of recommendation and invite the best candidates for interview. There is thus a fair amount of information to integrate. Several studies have actually found that humans – even when they specialise in this type of selection process – perform poorly, and in particular perform worse than simple mathematical models (Camerer and Johnson, 1991; Meehl, 1954).

Chapter summary

This chapter has barely scratched the surface of research into social cognition. A key theme, echoing the conclusions of Chapter 10 on bounded rationality, is that we are 'cognitive misers'. As a consequence of strict limitations in attention, memory capacity and decision-making abilities, we are severely constrained in our cognitive processing and must use shortcuts and heuristics. When making social judgements and decisions, we tend to use simple and salient cues, such as attractiveness, and spontaneously generalise our evaluations to other dimensions (the halo effect). We also simplify our lives by judging other people positively by default (the positivity effect) and by using schemas when making social decisions. These heuristics have advantages: they are fast, often work, and do not necessitate much cognitive processing. However, they also have costs: they can lead us to use stereotypes, to infer incorrect links of causality when explaining the behaviour of others, and to fall prey of a number of biases such as uncritically accepting supporting evidence and neglecting evidence that is inconsistent with our strongly held views. These biases might have benign consequences when they are used to rate the performance of a lecturer or to decide whether to invite somebody out on a date, but the consequences are not so benign when they affect children's education or the decisions about national and international crises made by political leaders – political leaders who are elected not only because of their abilities but also, or even mainly, because of the way they look.

Stop and Think Coaching a politician
You are advisor to a local politician campaigning for parliamentary office. Using the information provided in this chapter, what advice would you give her?

Further reading

First published in 1984 and now in its third edition, Fiske and Taylor (2010) is the classic textbook on social cognition. Written for advanced students, it provides extensive coverage of past and current research, with a bibliography running to over 100 pages. Pennington (2000) offers an easier introduction to the field. Social psychology more generally is covered in Taylor *et al.* (2006) and Augustinos *et al.* (2006). Hewstone *et al.* (2007) also provide a broad introduction to social psychology, but with a focus on European research. Fine (2006) and Tavris and Aronson (2007) are instructive and entertaining popular science books about social cognition.

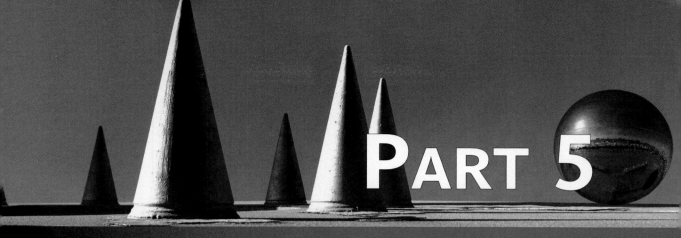

PART 5

Putting it all together

Part contents

Chapter 19

Putting it all together

This book has covered much ground and several challenging topics. However, at a certain level of abstraction, the picture is fairly simple and everything fits together. The aim of this concluding chapter is to revisit and discuss some of the key ideas addressed in the previous chapters, and to highlight how various concepts fit together. We will do so by first presenting a situation that will be of practical interest to you – the preparation of an exam, specifically an exam in cognitive psychology – and then by taking a more theoretical stance, showing how a fairly simple theory can in fact make correct predictions about many empirical phenomena. We will also discuss the extent to which current knowledge of cognitive psychology makes sense from an evolutionary point of view.

Preparing for an exam

What cognitive processes are engaged when you study to prepare for an exam? How can we explain them scientifically? Can we improve their efficiency? This section will answer these questions. Do not hesitate to flick back to previous chapters if aspects of the explanations are not clear.

Exam preparation can be seen as trying to solve a problem. Although you could consider problem solving as a sequence of trial and error, as behaviourists did, or as restructuring and insight, as Gestalt psychologists did, it is more helpful – and practically less risky – to see it as a search through a problem space. The starting state is what you currently know about the topic, the goal is to get a good grade, and the operators are study activities. Your planning then consists of deciding the order in which to study the topics, which study methods to use and how much time to allocate for each of them. Just as we did with the Tower of Hanoi in Chapter 11, we can draw a diagram of your search space (Figure 19.1).

Revising will obviously involve much reading. Reading taps into many of the basic processes we have discussed in this book. You have to recognise patterns (letters, words and even sentences), which makes use of perceptual mechanisms such as Gestalt principles and chunking.

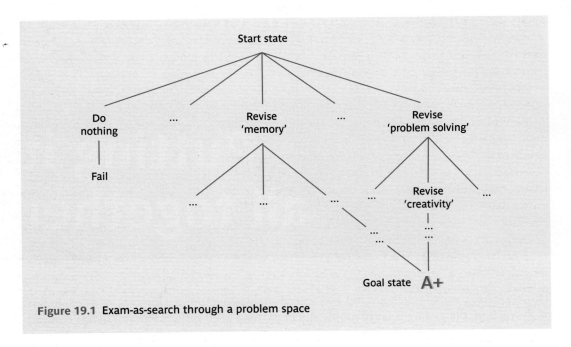

Figure 19.1 Exam-as-search through a problem space

At a lower level of analysis, you use the biological mechanisms described in Chapter 16, which in turn rely on the basic neuronal mechanisms discussed in Chapter 3. To do this, of course you have to move your eyes, and indeed a very large number of times – how many saccades are necessary to revise one chapter?

Just moving your eyes around will not be of much use if you do not direct your attention to what you are reading. We know that attention is serial (just one or only a few things can be heeded) and that its capacity is limited. You can test this assertion by seeing to what extent you can read a chapter when talking to friends or listening to an engaging radio programme at the same time. An important theme of Chapters 5 and 6 was that attention is closely linked to short-term memory (a.k.a. working memory). To test some predictions made by the leading theory in the field, Baddeley and Hitch's working memory model, try to study a chapter when at the same time (a) repeating a word such as 'taxi', (b) typing a sequence of keys on a keyboard and (c) generating random numbers. These of course are the standard interference tasks used to study working memory, and it will be interesting to see whether they affect your learning as predicted by the theory. (But if you are under time pressure, you had better skip this experiment and go back to the control condition where no interference is used!)

Language will also be continuously engaged when you read a chapter. You will have to parse sentences, and try to make sense of them by the mechanisms proposed by the theories of text comprehension, for example that of Kintsch. If Chomsky is correct, every time you read a sentence, you construct a parse tree for it. Next time you happen to be caught in a 'garden path', try to understand the factors in the written text that are likely to have caused the incorrect parsing.

The reason you are studying is, of course, to learn material. You know that short-term memory is hopelessly limited, so you will count on information being transferred to long-term memory. From the depth-of-processing theory, you also know that rehearsal is not enough for reliably storing information, and you are likely to use more meaningful ways to encode information (the so-called *elaborative encoding*). As you know, learning requires the acquisition of chunks and schemata, the creation of links that connect these chunks and schemata together, and the creation of retrieval cues. The activities you perform during studying should implement these mechanisms. As we saw in Chapter 1, the SQ3R method is a great way to do so.

A different way of looking at memory is to consider what is actually learned. You will acquire many concepts, and in general the type of knowledge you acquire will be declarative, explicit and semantic. Unless you reach a fairly high level of expertise, little of your knowledge will be procedural and implicit. For example, when applying Marr's theory of perception to explain how a specific object is recognised, you most likely have to go step by step through the facts you know about this theory, and you are not able to apply it in a smooth and automatic way. Similarly, your knowledge of cognitive psychology includes few episodic elements, although making links to memories of your own life will sometimes be a great way to enhance learning.

Sadly you will forget much of what you have learned. Obviously, given its limited capacity, forgetting from short-term memory will be rapid. But you will also forget from long-term memory, in spite of its theoretically unlimited capacity. Although this might not be much consolation, you even know that forgetting follows a power law: rapid at the beginning and slower at later stages. From the point of view of getting good grades in your exam, the only way to mitigate forgetting is by over-learning, repeatedly using the methods described above.

We have mentioned that preparing for an exam is a type of problem solving (and decision making), and you might be tempted to use a few heuristics as a way to simplify your problem space. You might decide that the same question(s) as last year will be asked. You might also decide that, given your limited time, it is best to study only one chapter in depth or, alternatively, to just learn an outline of all chapters. These are good examples of heuristics – rules of thumb that can sometimes lead to good enough results. You might actually try to compute the probability that using one or another heuristic will lead to a satisfactory mark. But we know from Chapter 10 that we are poor at using probabilities, so you might as well follow a risk-averse path and spend time studying the material thoroughly.

And creativity? Exams typically test for knowledge, which is almost antithetical to creativity. So, except for some freedom in the way you write your answer during the exam itself, we are afraid that there is not much room for creativity in exam preparation. That said, keep asking yourself questions and keep challenging the material you learn, as this leads to better encoding. Making unexpected connections between chapters also provides a modicum of creativity and enhances learning. Indeed, as we saw in Chapter 13, one view of creativity is that the more you know, the more you are likely to be creative. Finally, do not forget that emotions play an important role in cognition, and that one learns better when displaying positive emotions. So, be positive!

A simple theory of human cognition

Now that we have reviewed the main cognitive mechanisms engaged in exam preparation, we can present a simple, informal theory of cognition that weaves together many of the strands that we have discussed in this book. *Perception* is without doubt the most finely tuned component of cognition. This is not surprising, given that perception relies on relatively old parts of the cortex, and evolution has had a substantial amount of time to optimise it – just as with all primates. Even so, perception can be tricked, typically by two-dimensional images. But do not forget that the brain has evolved to deal with a three-dimensional, not a two-dimensional space.

Perception is a highly *parallel* system – think for example of the 120 million rods and 8 million cones processing the light impinging on the retina. As one moves to higher levels of perception, however, the tendency is clearly towards *serial processing* – only a few items can be processed at a time. This is particularly clear when one reaches what has often been called the *bottleneck of attention*. There, only a few items can be heeded, and most of the information that was provided by perception has to be discarded.

Why is attention limited? From an evolutionary point of view, this limit is adaptive and thus makes sense. It is better to pay attention to just a few relevant things than to allocate them to a mass of information, a lot of which is most probably irrelevant. If you see a potential predator in front of you, you want to be able to react quickly, rather than having to sieve through all the items encoded in a large attention span and rank-order them in order to select the most important. An abundance of information creates a poverty of attention! (A similar phenomenon can be found with the mass of information now available on the Internet.)

In addition, with a short attention span, it is easier to interrupt processing by directing attention to things (e.g. a sudden movement or noise) that are likely to indicate the presence of danger – at least this was the case in the type of environment in which our ancestors evolved. *Emotions* play an important role in channelling attention to important aspects of the environment, possibly forcing us to interrupt whatever activity we were engaged in. Capacity limitation is also a feature of *short-term memory*. Again, this is not surprising, as there is a close link between these two cognitive components. Both really go together.

Even with a powerful perceptual system, an organism with such severe limits in attention and short-term memory seems unlikely to dominate the planet, as humans have done. What is missing? The answer is simply the ability to *learn*, which is, in humans, essentially unlimited.

Low-level learning, such as conditioning, can be very fast. It takes just one exposure to learn to avoid food that makes you sick. By contrast, learning is relatively slow with declarative knowledge. Simon (1969) has estimated that it takes about ten seconds to learn a new chunk. If you believe that this time estimate is unreasonably slow, consider how little you can remember after attending a one-hour lecture or reading one chapter in a textbook. (We recommend that you actually carry out these 'experiments', by writing down everything you can remember in both cases.) Again, this makes sense from an evolutionary point of view, as conditioning relies on old parts of the brain, while declarative knowledge relies on parts that are more recent.

With dedication and patience, it is possible to learn just about anything, even with the relatively slow encoding times characteristic of declarative memory. In fact, learning and short-term memory encoding are much faster if one already possesses extensive knowledge about the topic one is learning. New things get stored easily in long-term memory by being associated with related material. You can learn dozens of languages, master complex disciplines such as cognitive psychology, or, if you are inclined to more exotic endeavours, you can learn 15 000 telephone numbers from the *Yellow Pages* of Blackpool (Wilding and Valentine, 1997) or the first 67 890 digits of the number π (3.1415...; but be patient for that one: it takes about 24 hours without any break just to recite these digits... (Glenday, 2009)).

This is a clear indication that the human mind (brain) is highly plastic, and this is in fact a key feature of the kind of human adaptations that evolution has produced. Note also that learning, and specifically chunking, plays a key role in the plasticity of the mind. While encoding can be slow, retrieval is quick – just a few hundredths of milliseconds. In the former case, you have to create a memory trace; in the latter, you just retrieve information. Also, note that retrieval is unconscious and, most of the time, automatic.

It is possible to consider *language* and *categorisation* as two (important) extensions of long-term memory. Language is of course essential for communication, but also for acquiring new declarative knowledge. As for concepts, they represent a fundamental way to simplify the world, by filtering out unnecessary detail to encode only the essential features – think of the similar role played by attention. Ultimately, they make it possible to rapidly predict how creatures might behave or other aspects of the world might change.

To a large extent, the basic cognitive components discussed in Part 2 of this book (Basic processes') constrain and determine the higher cognitive functions discussed in Part 3 ('Complex cognition'), such as *decision making* and *problem solving*. These high-level functions inherit, so to speak, the features of the low-level functions. For example, *creativity* will be particularly hard in domains where perception leads to strong internal representations that will have to be overcome, and in domains where a lot of information has to be kept in short-term memory.

Similarly, the use of *heuristics* naturally follows from limits in cognitive processing. Based on simple pattern recognition mechanisms, they make it possible to simplify problems and thus to reach rapid decisions while minimising the use of attentional and memory resources. In addition, relying on experience is adaptive, as long-term memory has an essentially unlimited capacity storage. Information learned from previous experiences will provide estimates of what action is most likely to work. These considerations readily explain several features of heuristics: they make it possible to reach rapid decisions, enable a highly selective search, particularly visible in the case of experts, but also sometimes lead to *Einstellung*-like effects (see Chapter 11) and suffer from the biases identified by Tversky and Kahneman, such as representativeness and neglect of base rates (see Chapter 10). The role of heuristics in alleviating the impact of human cognitive limitations was of course a central motivation behind Simon's theory of 'bounded rationality'.

The overall picture, then, is an organism with (a) a large-capacity perception, the output of which is filtered to a minimum by (b) capacity limits in attention and short-term memory, and with (c) essentially an unlimited capacity to learn. These capacities, discussed in Part 2 of this book, are (d) modulated by emotions and (e) augmented by language, which facilitates communication, makes it possible to use abstractions and enables considerable compression of information (e.g. 'house': a single word instead of a complex visual and auditory scene).

Some direct consequences of the theory

If we add a few assumptions about the kind of strategy humans typically use (e.g. they tend to focus on the beginning and end of sequences; they direct their attention to unexpected information) and parameters of capacity (e.g. four items in visual short-term memory, and 10 seconds to learn a new chunk), we can correctly predict a surprisingly large number of experimental results.

For example, we can predict that learning lists of nonsense syllables will take a long time (because many chunks need to be created), but that humans should be fast and fairly accurate in tasks requiring simple perceptual decisions (because they can then rely on a system that is essentially parallel). We can also predict that, as soon as they have to rely on short-term memory and attention, humans show poor performance in most experiments, unless they can supplement attention and short-term memory by either perceptual mechanisms and/or rapid retrieval from long-term memory.

As another prediction, consider perception. It is automatically used, and the prediction is that it will sometimes lead to unproductive mindsets. Examples of this are offered by the nine-dot problem (Figure 11.7 in Chapter 11) and of course by the visual illusions discussed in Chapter 4. Similarly, information from long-term memory is used whenever possible, even in cases where it is actually unhelpful. Maier's pendulum problem, Dunker's radiation problem and Luchins' *Einstellung* effect, all discussed in Chapter 11, are good instances of such negative mindsets. Several additional striking examples of this phenomenon were offered in Chapters 10 and 18 (e.g. biases and stereotypes).

It can also be predicted that, with domains where perception and knowledge are of limited use, problems will be hard and will cause many errors. In these cases, people will use heuristics to compensate for the limits of attention and short-term memory. In Chapters 10 and 11, we have seen several examples of how heuristics can help simplify problems and make reasonable decisions, even though they sometimes lead to incorrect solutions.

A final direct consequence of the theory is that learning, which might lead to expertise in the long term, will provide a central way of alleviating human cognitive limitations. By relying on long-term memory knowledge – declarative but particularly procedural knowledge – we can circumvent limits of attention and STM. Rather than storing one item in one short-term memory slot, we can store several items by using chunks and schemata. Rather than paying attention to a single action, we can carry out several actions in parallel if each of these actions has been sufficiently learned by proceduralisation. As a consequence, each action can be carried out automatically by a production, without needing attention.

A final chunk

Giving the importance we have attached to the mechanism of chunking, it is fitting to summarise the key ideas of the book using a mnemonic chunk:

CLASSIC MARBRE

Cognition is **L**imited **A**ttention, **S**elective **S**earch, **I**nformation-processing, **C**hunking, **M**emory, **A**daptation, **R**ecognition, **B**ounded **R**ationality and **E**motion.

Abelson, R. P. (1981). The psychological status of the script concept. *American Psychologist, 36,* 715–729.

Abernethy, B. and Russell, D. G. (1987). Expert–novice differences in an applied selective attention task. *Journal of Sport Psychology, 9,* 326–345.

Abernethy, B., Farrow, D. and Berry, J. (2003). Constraints and issues in the development of a general theory of expert perceptual-motor performance: A critique of the deliberate practice framework. In J. L. Starkes and K. A. Ericsson (eds), *Expert performance in sports: Advances in research on sport expertise* (pp. 349–370). Champaign, IL: Human Kinetics.

Abernethy, B., Gill, D. P., Parks, S. L. and Packer, S. T. (2001). Expertise and the perception of kinematic and situational probability information. *Perception, 30,* 233–252.

Adams, J. A. (1971). A closed-loop theory of motor learning. *Journal of Motor Behavior, 3,* 1 11–49.

Adams, L., Kasserman, J., Yearwood, A., Perfetto, G., Bransford, J. and Franks, J. (1988). The effects of facts versus problem-oriented acquisition. *Memory & Cognition, 16,* 167–175.

Allport, G. W. (1985). The historical background of social psychology. In G. Lindzey and E. Aronson (eds), *Handbook of social psychology* (3rd edn, Vol. 1, pp. 1–46). New York: Random House.

Amabile, T. M. (1996). *Creativity in context.* Boulder, CO: Westview Press.

Anderson, J. R. (1982). Acquisition of cognitive skill. *Psychological Review, 89,* 369–406.

Anderson, J. R. (1990). *Cognitive psychology and its implications* (3rd edn). New York: Freeman & Cie.

Anderson, J. R. (2005). Human symbol manipulation within an integrated cognitive architecture. *Cognitive Science, 29,* 313–341.

Anderson, J. R. (2007). *How can the human mind occur in the physical universe?* New York, NY: Oxford University Press.

Anderson, J. R., Bothell, D., Byrne, M. D., Douglass, S., Lebière, C. and Qin, Y. L. (2004). An integrated theory of the mind. *Psychological Review, 111,* 1036–1060.

Anderson, J. R., Corbett, A. T., Koedinger, K. R. and Pelletier, R. (1995). Cognitive tutors: Lessons learned. *Journal of the Learning Sciences, 4,* 167–207.

Anderson, J. R. and Lebière, C. (eds). (1998). *The atomic components of thought.* Mahwah, NJ: Erlbaum.

Armstrong, S. L., Gleitman, L. R. and Gleitman, H. (1983). What some concepts might not be. *Cognition, 13,* 263–308.

Arnheim, R. (2004). *Art and visual perception: A psychology of the creative eye.* Berkeley, CA: University of California Press.

Ashby, E. G. and Maddox, W. T. (2005). Human category learning. *Annual Review of Psychology, 56,* 149–178.

Atkinson, R. C. and Shiffrin, R. M. (1968). Human memory: A proposed system and its control processes. In K. W. Spence and J. T. Spence (eds), *The psychology of learning and motivation* (Vol. 2, pp. 89–195). London: Academic Press.

Augustinos, M., Walker, I., and Donaghue, N. (2006). *Social cognition: An integrated introduction* (2nd edn). London: Sage.

Baars, B. (2002). The conscious access hypothesis: Origins and recent evidence. *Trends in Cognitive Sciences, 6,* 47–52.

Baddeley, A. D. (1986). *Working memory.* Oxford: Clarendon Press.

Baddeley, A. D. (1997). *Human memory: Theory and practice.* Hove, UK: Psychology Press.

Baddeley, A. D. (2000). The episodic buffer: A new component of working memory? *Trends in Cognitive Sciences, 4,* 417–423.

Baddeley, A. D. (2003). Working memory: Looking back and looking forward. *Nature Reviews Neuroscience, 4,* 829–839.

Baddeley, A. D. and Hitch, G. J. (1974). Working memory. In G. Bower (ed.), *The psychology of learning and motivation: Advances in research and theory* (pp. 47–90). New York, NY: Academic Press.

Baddeley, A. D. and Longman, D. J. A. (1978). The influence of length and frequency on training sessions on the rate of learning to type. *Ergonomics, 21*, 627–635.

Baddeley, A. D., Thomson, N. and Buchanan, M. (1975). Word length and the structure of short-term memory. *Journal of Verbal Learning and Verbal Behavior, 14*, 575–589.

Bahrick, H. P. (1984). Semantic memory content in permastore: 50 years of memory for Spanish learned in school. *Journal of Experimental Psychology-General, 113*, 1–29.

Bahrick, H. P., Hall, L. K. and Da Costa, L. A. (2008). Fifty years of memory of college grades: Accuracy and distortions. *Emotion, 8*, 13–22.

Bar, M. and Biederman, I. (1998). Subliminal visual priming. *Psychological Science, 9*, 464–469.

Barnett, S. M. and Ceci, S. J. (2002). When and where do we apply what we learn? A taxonomy for far transfer. *Psychological Bulletin, 128*, 612–637.

Barron, F. and Harrington, D. M. (1981). Creativity, intelligence, and personality. *Annual Reviews in Psychology, 32*, 439–476.

Barsalou, L. W. (1983). Ad hoc categories. *Memory & Cognition, 11*, 211–227.

Bayley, J. (1998). *Iris: A memoir of Iris Murdoch.* London, UK: Abacus.

Bear, M. F., Connors, B. W. and Paradiso, M. A. (2007). *Neuroscience: Exploring the brain* (3rd edn). Baltimore, MD: Lippincott Williams & Wilkins.

Bechara, A., Damasio, A. R., Damasio, H. and Anderson, S. W. (1994). Insensitivity to future consequences following damage to human prefrontal cortex. *Cognition, 50*, 7–15.

Bechara, A., Tranel, D., Damasio, H. and Damasio, A. R. (1996). Failure to respond autonomically to anticipated future outcomes following damage to prefrontalcortex. *Cerebral Cortex, 6*, 215–225.

Bechtel, W. and Abrahamsen, A. (1991). *Connectionism and the mind. An introduction to parallel processing in networks.* Cambridge, MA: Blackwell.

Beck, A. T. (1975). *Cognitive therapy and the emotional disorders.* New York, NY: International Universities Press.

Beck, A. T. (1978). *Depressive inventory.* Philadelphia, PA: Center for Cognitive Therapy.

Beck, A. T., Rush, A. J., Shaw, B. F. and Emery, G. (1979). *Cognitive therapy of depression.* New York: The Guilford Press.

Beggs, W. D. A. and Howarth, C. I. (1970). Movement control in a repetitive motor task. *Nature, 225*, 752–753.

Berlin, B. (1992). *Ethnobiological classification: Principles of categorization of plants and animals in traditional societies.* Princeton, NJ: Princeton University Press.

Biederman, I. (1987). Recognition-by-components: A theory of human image understanding. *Psychological Review, 2*, 115–147.

Bilalić, M., McLeod, P. and Gobet, F. (2008a). Why good thoughts block better ones: The mechanism of the pernicious *Einstellung* (set) effect. *Cognition, 108*, 652–661.

Bilalić, M., McLeod, P. and Gobet, F. (2008b). Inflexibility of experts – Reality or myth? Quantifying the *Einstellung* effect in chess masters. *Cognitive Psychology, 56*, 73–102.

Bilalić, M., McLeod, P. and Gobet, F. (2010). The mechanism of the *Einstellung* (set) effect: A pervasive source of cognitive bias. *Current Directions in Psychological Science, 19*, 111–115.

Birch, H. and Rabinowitz, H. (1951). The negative effect of previous experience on productive thinking. *Journal of Experimental Psychology, 41*, 121–125.

Bisiach, E. and Luzzatti, C. (1978). Unilateral neglect of representational space. *Cortex, 14*, 129–133.

Blackmore, S. J. (2004). *Consciousness: An introduction.* New York, NY: Oxford University Press.

Blake, R. and Sekuler, R. (2005). *Perception* (5th edn). New York, NY: McGraw-Hill.

Block, N. (2005). Two neural correlates of consciousness. *Trends in Cognitive Sciences, 9*, 46–52.

Bloom, B. S. and Sosniak, L. A. (1985). *Developing talent in young people.* New York, NY: Ballantine Books.

Bock, B. and Ackrill, K. (1993). *The origins and development of high ability – CIBA Foundation Symposium – No. 178.* New York, NY: Wiley.

Boden, M. (1990). *The creative mind.* New York, NY: Basic Books.

Booth, M. C. A. and Rolls, E. T. (1998). View-invariant representations of familiar objects by neurons in the inferior temporal visual cortex. *Cerebral Cortex, 8*, 510–523.

Borges, J. L. (1962). *Ficciones.* New York, NY: Grove Press.

Bower, G. H. (1981). Mood and memory. *American Psychologist, 36,* 129–148.

Brewer, M. B. and Hewstone, M. (eds) (2004). *Social cognition.* Oxford, UK: Blackwell.

Brewer, W. F. (1992). The theoretical and empirical status of the flashbulb memory hypothesis. In E. Winograd and U. Neisser (eds), *Affect and accuracy in recall: Studies of 'flashbulb' memories* (Vol. 4, pp. 274–305). New York: Cambridge University Press.

Brewer, W. F. and Treyens, J. C. (1981). Role of schemata in memory for places. *Cognitive Psychology, 13,* 207–230.

Broadbent, D. E. (1958). *Perception and communication.* New York, NY: Pergamon.

Brown, J. (1958). Some test of decay theory of immediate memory. *Quarterly Journal of Experimental Psychology, 10,* 12–21.

Brown, R. (1973). *A first language.* Boston, MA: Harvard University Press.

Brown, R. and Kulik, J. (1977). Flashbulb memories. *Cognition and Emotion, 5,* 73–99.

Brown, R. T. (1989). Creativity: What are we to measure? In J. A. Glover, R. R. Ronning and C. R. Reynolds (eds), *Handbook of creativity* (pp. 3–32). New York, NY: Plenum.

Bruner, J. S., Goodnow, J. J. and Austin, G. A. (1956). *A study of thinking. An analysis of strategies in the utilizing of information for thinking and problem solving.* New York, NY: Wiley & Sons.

Camerer, C. F. and Johnson, E. J. (1991). The process-performance paradox in expert judgment: How can experts know so much and predict so badly? In K. A. Ericsson and J. Smith (eds), *Studies of expertise: Prospects and limits* (pp. 195–217). Cambridge: Cambridge University Press.

Campitelli, G. and Gobet, F. (2004). Adaptive expert decision making: Skilled chessplayers search more and deeper. *Journal of the International Computer Games Association, 27,* 209–216.

Campitelli, G. and Gobet, F. (2007). The role of practice in chess: A longitudinal study. *Learning and Individual Differences, 18,* 446–458.

Carlson, N. R. (2007). *Physiology of behavior* (9th edn). Boston: Allyn and Bacon.

Carreiras, M. and Clifton, C. (1993). Relative clause interpretation preferences in Spanish and English. *Language & Speech, 36,* 353–372.

Casey, B. J., Tottenham, N., Liston, C. and Durston, S. (2005). Imaging the developing brain: What have we learned about cognitive development? *Trends in Cognitive Sciences, 9,* 104–110.

Castelo-Branco, M., Goebel, R., Neuenschwander, S. and Singer, W. (2000). Neural synchrony correlates with surface segregation rules. *Nature, 405,* 685–689.

Chalmers, D. J. (1995). Facing up to the problem of consciousness. *Journal of Consciousness Studies 2,* 200–219.

Chalmers, D. J. (1996). *The conscious mind.* New York, NY: Oxford University Press.

Charness, N. (1976). Memory for chess positions: Resistance to interference. *Journal of Experimental Psychology: Human Learning and Memory, 2,* 641–53.

Charness, N., Tuffiash, M., Krampe, R., Reingold, E. and Vasyukova, E. (2005). The role of deliberate practice in chess expertise. *Applied Cognitive Psychology, 19,* 151–165.

Chase, W. G. and Simon, H. A. (1973a). Perception in chess. *Cognitive Psychology, 4,* 55–81.

Chase, W. G. and Simon, H. A. (1973b). The mind's eye in chess. In W. G. Chase (ed.), *Visual information processing* (pp. 215–281). New York, NY: Academic Press.

Chassy, P. and Gobet, F. (2010). Speed of expertise acquisition depends upon inherited factors. *Talent Development and Excellence, 2,* 17–27.

Cheng, P. W. and Holyoak, K. J. (1985). Pragmatic reasoning schemas. *Cognitive Psychology, 17,* 391–416.

Cherry, E. C. (1953). Some experiments upon the recognition of speech, with one and with two ears. *Journal of the Acoustical Society of America, 25,* 975–979.

Chi, M. T. H. (1978). Knowledge structures and memory development. In R. Siegler (ed.), *Children's thinking: What develops* (pp. 73–96). Hillsdale, NJ: Lawrence Erlbaum Associates.

Chomsky, N. (1957). *Syntactic structures.* The Hague: Mouton.

Chomsky, N. (1959). A review of B. F. Skinner's 'Verbal behavior'. *Language, 35,* 26–58.

Churchland, P. M. and Churchland, P. S. (1998). *On the contrary: Critical essays 1987–1997.* Cambridge, MA: The MIT Press.

Clancy, S. A. (2005). *Abducted: How people come to believe they were kidnapped by aliens.* Cambridge, MA: Harvard University Press.

Clark, H. and Clark, E. (1977). *Psychology and*

language: An introduction to psycholinguistics. New York: Harcourt, Brace, and Jovanovich.

Cohen, H. (1981). *On the modelling of creative behavior* (RAND Paper No. P-6681). Santa Monica, CA: RAND Corporation.

Collet, C., Vernet-Maury, E., Delhomme, G. and Dittmar, A. (1997). Autonomic nervous system response patterns specificity to basic emotions. *Journal of the Autonomic Nervous System, 62,* 45–57.

Collins, A. M. and Loftus, E. F. (1975). A spreading-activation theory of semantic memory. *Psychological Review, 82,* 407–428.

Collins, A. M. and Quillian, M. R. (1969). Retrieval time from semantic memory. *Journal of Verbal Learning and Verbal Behavior, 9,* 240–247.

Coltheart, M. (1978). Lexical access in simple reading tasks. In G. Underwood (ed.), *Strategies of information processing* (pp. 151–216). London: Academic Press.

Coltheart, M., Rastle, K., Perry, C., Langdon, R. and Ziegler, J. (2001). The DRC Model: A model of visual word recognition and reading aloud. *Psychological Review, 108,* 204–256.

Conrad, R. (1964). Acoustic confusion in immediate memory. *British Journal of Psychology, 55,* 75–84.

Conway, M. A., Cohen, G. and Stanhope, N. (1991). On the very long-term retention of knowledge acquired through formal education: 12 years of cognitive psychology. *Journal of Experimental Psychology-General, 120,* 395–409.

Cooper, R., Fox, J., Farringdon, J. and Shallice, T. (1996). A systematic methodology for cognitive modelling. *Artificial Intelligence, 85,* 3–44.

Cowan, N. (1988). Evolving conceptions of memory storage, selective attention, and their mutual constraints within the human information-processing system. *Psychological Review, 104,* 163–191.

Craik, F. I. M. and Lockhart, R. S. (1972). Levels of processing: A framework for memory research. *Journal of Verbal Learning and Verbal Behavior, 11,* 671–684.

Craik, F. I. M. and Tulving, E. (1975). Depth of processing and the retention of words in episodic memory. *Journal of Experimental Psychology: General, 104,* 268–294.

Craik, F. I. M. and Watkins, M. J. (1973). The role of rehearsal in short-term memory. *Journal of Verbal Learning and Verbal Behaviour, 12,* 599–6070.

Crundall, D., Bains, M., Chapman, P. and Underwood, G. (2005). Regulating conversation during driving: A problem for mobile telephones? *Transportation Research, Part F: Traffic Psychology and Behaviour, 8F,* 197–211.

Csikszentmihalyi, M. (1988). Society, culture, and person: A systems view of creativity. In R. J. Sternberg (ed.), *The nature of creativity* (pp. 325–339). Cambridge, MA: Cambridge University Press.

Csikszentmihalyi, M. (1996). *Creativity: Flow and the psychology of discovery and invention*. New York, NY: HarperCollins.

Csikszentmihalyi, M. and Sawyer, K. (1995). Creative insight: The social dimension of a solitary moment. In R. J. Sternberg, and J. Davidson (eds), *The nature of insight* (pp. 329–363). Bradford, MA: MIT Press.

Cutler, A., Mehler, J., Norris, D. and Segui, J. (1987). Phoneme identification and the lexicon. *Cognitive Psychology, 19,* 141–177.

Daneman, M. and Carpenter, P. A. (1980). Individual differences in working memory and reading. *Journal of Verbal Learning and Verbal Behavior, 19,* 450–466.

Darwin, C. J., Turvey, M. T. and Crowder, R. G. (1972). The auditory analogue of the Sperling partial report procedure: Evidence from auditory storage. *Cognitive Psychology, 3,* 255–267.

De Bono, E. (1973). *Lateral thinking: Creativity step by step*. New York, NY: Harper and Row.

De Groot, A. D. (1978). *Thought and choice in chess (first Dutch edition in 1946)*. The Hague: Mouton Publishers.

Debner, J. A. and Jacoby, L. L. (1994). Unconscious perception: Attention, awareness, and control. *Journal of Experimental Psychology: Learning, Memory, and Cognition, 20,* 304–317.

Dehaene, S., Changeux, J., Naccache, L., Sackur, J. and Sergent, C. (2006). Conscious, preconscious, and subliminal processing: A testable taxonomy. *Trends in Cognitive Sciences, 10,* 204–211.

Dehaene, S., Naccache, L., LeClec'h, G., Koechlin, E., Mueller, M., Dehaene-Lambertz, G., van de Moortele, P. and Le Bihan, D. (1998). Imaging unconscious semantic priming, *Nature, 395,* 597–600.

Dempster, F. N. (1981). Memory span: Sources of individual and developmental differences. *Psychological Bulletin, 89,* 63–100.

Dennett, D. C. (1991). *Consciousness explained*. Boston. MA: Little, Brown.

Desimone, R. (1991). Face-selective cells in the temporal cortex of monkeys. *Journal of Cognitive Neuroscience, 3*, 1–8.

Deutsch, J. A. and Deutsch, D. (1963). Attention: Some theoretical considerations. *Psychological Review, 70*, 80–90.

Dijksterhuis, A., Bos, M. W., Nordgren, L. F. and van Baaren, R. B. (2006). On making the right choice: The deliberation-without-attention effect. *Science, 311*, 1005–1007.

Dion, K., Berscheid, E. and Walster, E. (1972). What is beautiful is good. *Journal of Personality and Social Psychology, 24*, 85–290.

Dodds, R. A., Ward, T. B. and Smith, S. M. (2003). A review of the experimental literature on incubation in problem solving and creativity. in M. A. Runco (ed.), *Creativity research handbook Vol. 3.* Cresskill, NJ: Hampton Press.

Downing, P. E., Jiang, Y., Shuman, M. and Kanwisher, N. (2001). A cortical area selective for visual processing of the human body. *Science, 293*, 2470–2473.

Dromey, C. and Sanders, M. (2009). Intra-speaker variability in palatometric measures of consonant articulation. *Journal of Communication Disorders, 42*, 397–407.

Dunbar, K. (1993). Concept discovery in a scientific domain. *Cognitive Science, 17*, 397–434.

Dunbar, K. (1997). How scientists think: On-line creativity and conceptual change in science. In T. B. Ward, S. M. Smith and S. Vaid (eds), *Conceptual structures and processes: Emergence, discovery and change* (pp. 461–493). Washington DC: APA Press.

Duncker, K. (1945). On problem-solving (L.S. Lees, trans.). *Psychological Monographs, 58* (whole No. 270).

Dyer, E. N. (1971). Color-naming interference in monolinguals and bilinguals. *Journal of Verbal Learning and Verbal Behavior, 10*, 297–302.

Ebbinghaus, H. (1913). *Memory: A contribution to experimental psychology.* New York, NY: Teachers College, Columbia University.

Efran, M. G. and Patterson, E. (1974). Voters vote beautiful – Effect of physical appearance on a national election. *Canadian Journal of Behavioural Science, 6*, 352–356.

Ehri, L. C., Nunes, S. R., Willows, D. M., Schuster, B. V., Yaghoub-Zadeh, Z. and Shanahan, T. (2001). Phonemic awareness instruction helps children learn to read: Evidence from a National Reading Panel's meta-analysis. *Reading Research Quarterly, 36*, 250–287.

Eichenbaum, H. (2008). *Learning and memory.* New York, NY: Norton.

Einhorn, H. J. and Hogarth, R. M. (1981). Behavioral decision theory: Processes of judgment and choice. *Annual Review of Psychology, 32*, 53–88.

Ekman, P. (1999). Basic emotions. In T. Dalgleish and M. Power (eds), *Handbook of cognition and emotion.* Sussex: John Wiley & Sons Ltd.

Ekman, P., Levenson, R. W. and Friesen, W. V. (1983). Autonomic nervous system activity distinguishes among emotions. *Science, 221*, 1208–1210.

Ellis, A. W. and Young, A. W. (1988). *Human cognitive neuropsychology.* Hove, UK: Psychology Press.

Ellis, N. C. and Hennelly, R. A. (1980). A bilingual word-length effect: Implications for intelligence testing and the relative ease of mental calculation in Welsh and English. *British Journal of Psychology, 71*, 43–52.

Ellis, R. and Humphreys, G. W. (1999). *Connectionist psychology: A text with readings.* Hove, UK: Psychology Press.

Emery, N. J. (2006). Cognitive ornithology: The evolution of avian intelligence. *Philosophical Transactions of the Royal Society B: Biological Sciences, 361*, 23–43.

Ericsson, K. A. (1998). The scientific study of expert levels of performance: General implications for optimal learning and creativity. *High Ability Studies, 9*, 75–100.

Ericsson, K. A. (2006). The influence of experience and deliberate practice on the development of superior expert performance. In K. A. Ericsson, N. Charness, P. Feltovich and R. R. Hoffman (eds), *The Cambridge handbook of expertise and expert performance* (pp. 223–241). Cambridge: Cambridge University Press.

Ericsson, K. A. and Charness, N. (1994). Expert performance: Its structure and acquisition. *American Psychologist, 49*, 725–747.

Ericsson, K. A., Charness, N., Feltovich, P. J. and Hoffman, R. P. (eds) (2006). *The Cambridge handbook of expertise and expert performance.* Cambridge: Cambridge University Press.

Ericsson, K. A. and Kintsch, W. (1995). Long-term working memory. *Psychological Review, 102*, 211–245.

Ericsson, K. A. and Kintsch, W. (2000). Shortcomings

of generic retrieval structures with slots of the type that Gobet (1993) proposed and modelled. *British Journal of Psychology, 91,* 571–590.

Ericsson, K. A., Krampe, R. T. and Tesch-Roemer, C. (1993). The role of deliberate practice in the acquisition of expert performance. *Psychological Review, 100,* 363–406.

Ericsson, K. A. and Lehmann, A. C. (1996). Expert and exceptional performance: evidence of maximal adaptation to task constraints. *Annual Reviews in Psychology, 47,* 273–305.

Ericsson, K. A. and Smith, J. (1991). Prospects and limits of the empirical study of expertise: an introduction. In K. A. Ericsson and J. Smith (eds), *Toward a general theory of expertise: Prospects and limits* (pp. 1–38). Cambridge: Cambridge University Press.

Farah, M. J. (2000). *The cognitive neuroscience of vision.* Oxford, UK: Blackwell Publishers.

Fazey, J. A. and Marton, F. (2002). Understanding the space of experiential variation. *Active Learning in Higher Education, 3,* 234–250.

Fechner, G. T. (1860/1966). *Elements of psychophysics (Vol. 1; original work published in 1860)* (H. E. Adler, trans. ed.). New York: Holt, Rinehart & Winston.

Fernández, E. M. (2002). Are bilinguals like two monolinguals in one person? Evidence from research in sentence processing. *Paper presented at the CUNY Academy Junior Faculty Series, Queens College (CUNY), Flushing, NY.*

Fine, C. (2006). *A mind of its own: How your brain distorts and deceives.* Cambridge, UK: Icon Books.

Finkbeiner, M. and Forster K. I. (2008). Attention, intention and domain-specific processing. *Trends in Cognitive Sciences, 12,* 59–64.

Fiske, S. T. (1980). Attention and weight in person perception: The impact of negative and extreme behavior. *Journal of Personality & Social Psychology, 38,* 889–906.

Fiske, S. T. and Taylor, S. E. (1984). *Social cognition* (2nd edn). Reading, MA: Addison-Wesley.

Fiske, S. T. and Taylor, S. E. (2010). *Social cognition: From brains to culture* (3rd edn). New York, NY: McGraw-Hill

Flavell, J. H. (1963). *The developmental psychology of Jean Piaget.* Princeton, NJ: Van Nostrand Company.

Fleck, J. I. and Weisberg, R. W. (2004). The use of verbal protocols as data: An analysis of insight in the candle problem. *Memory & Cognition, 32,* 990–1006.

Forer, B. R. (1949). The fallacy of personal validation: A classroom demonstration of gullibility. *Journal of Abnormal and Social Psychology, 44,* 23.

Foulke, E. and Sticht, T. (1969). A review of research on the intelligibility of accelerated speech. *Psychological Bulletin, 72,* 50–62.

Fournier, E. A., Mazzarella, M. M., Ricciardi, M. M. and Fingeret, A. L. (1975). Reading level and locus of interference in the Stroop colorword task. *Perceptual and Motor Skills, 41,* 239–242.

Frauenfelder, U. H., Segui, J. and Dijkstra, T. (1990). Lexical effects in phonemic processing: Facilitatory or inhibitory? *Journal of Experimental Psychology: Human Perception and Performance, 16,* 77–91.

Frazier, L. (1987). Sentence processing: A tutorial review. In M. Coltheart (ed.), *Attention and performance* (Vol. 12, pp. 601–681). London, UK: Erlbaum.

Frazier, L. and Rayner, K. (1982). Making and correcting errors during sentence comprehension: Eye-movements in the analysis of structurally ambiguous sentences. *Cognitive Psychology, 14,* 178–210.

Fredrickson, B. L. and Levenson, R. W. (1998). Positive emotions speed recovery from the cardiovascular sequelae of negative emotions. *Cognition and Emotion, 12,* 191–220.

Frege, G. (1984). On sense and meaning. In B. McGuinness (ed.), *Gottlob Frege's collected papers on mathematics, logic, and philosophy* (pp. 157–177). Oxford: Basil Blackwell.

Frensch, P. A. and Sternberg, R. J. (1989). Expertise and intelligent thinking: When is it worse to know better. In R. J. Sternberg (ed.), *Advances in the psychology of human intelligence: Vol. 5* (pp. 157–188). Hillsdale, NJ: Erlbaum.

Freudenthal, D., Pine, J. M. and Gobet, F. (2009). Simulating the referential properties of Dutch, German and English root infinitives in MOSAIC. *Language Learning and Development, 5,* 1–29.

Freudenthal, D., Pine, J. M., Aguado-Orea, J. and Gobet, F. (2007). Modelling the developmental patterning of finiteness marking in English, Dutch, German and Spanish using MOSAIC. *Cognitive Science, 31,* 311–341.

Frey, P. W. and Adesman, P. (1976). Recall memory for visually presented chess positions. *Memory & Cognition, 4,* 541–547.

Frijda, N. H. (1993). Moods, emotion episodes and emotions. In H. Lewis and J. H. Haviland (eds), *Handbook of emotions* (pp. 381–403). New York: The Guilford Press.

Frijda, N. H. (2006). *The laws of emotions*. Mahwah, NJ: Erlbaum.

Frisoni, G. B., Fox, N. C., Clifford, R. J., Scheltens, P. and Thompson, P. M. (2010). The clinical use of structural MRI in Alzheimer disease. *Nature Reviews Neurology, 6*, 67–77.

Gabrielsson, A. and Juslin, P. (1996). Emotional expression in music performance. *Psychology of Music, 24*, 68–91.

Gardner, H. (1987). *The mind's new science: A history of the cognitive revolution*. New York, NY: Basic Books.

Garrard, P., Maloney, L. M., Hodges, J. R. and Patterson, K. (2005). The effects of very early Alzheimer's disease on the characteristics of writing by a renowned author. *Brain, 128*, 250–260.

Gauthier, I., Tarr, M. J., Anderson, A. W., Skudlarski, P. and Gore, J. C. (1999). Activation of the middle fusiform 'face area' increases with expertise in recognizing novel objects. *Nature Neuroscience, 2*, 568–573.

Gazzaniga, M. S., Ivry, R. B. and Mangun, G. R. (2009). *Cognitive neuroscience: The biology of the mind* (3rd edn). New York, NY: Norton.

Geraerts, E., Bernstein, D. M., Merckelbach, H., Linders, C., Raymaekers, L. and Loftus, E. F. (2008). Lasting false beliefs and their behavioral consequences. *Psychological Science, 19*, 749–753.

Ghiselin, B. (1952). *The creative process*. New York, NY: Mentor.

Giannakopoulou, A. (2003). Prototype theory: An evaluation, *Ecloga*: http://www.strath.ac.uk/ecloga/archive/2003/ecloga2003contents/.

Gick, M. L. and Holyoak, K. J. (1980). Analogical problem solving. *Cognitive Psychology, 12*, 306–355.

Gick, M. L. and Holyoak, K. J. (1983). Schema induction and analogical transfer. *Cognitive Psychology, 15*, 1–38.

Gigerenzer, G. (2003). *Reckoning with risk: Learning to live with uncertainty*. London: Penguin Books.

Gigerenzer, G. (2004). Dread risk, September 11, and fatal traffic accidents. *Psychological Science, 15*, 286–287.

Gigerenzer, G., Todd, P. M. and the ABC Group (eds) (1999). *Simple heuristics that make us smart*. New York: Oxford University Press.

Glenberg, A. M., Smith, S. M. and Green, C. (1977). Type I rehearsal: Maintenance and more. *Journal of Verbal Learning and Verbal Behavior, 16*, 339–352.

Glenday, C. (2009). *Guinness World Records 2010*. London, UK: Guinness World Records Limited.

Glushko, R. J. (1979). Organization and activation of orthographic knowledge in reading aloud. *Journal of Experimental Psychology – Human Perception and Performance, 5*, 674–691.

Gobet, F. and Clarkson, G. (2004). Chunks in expert memory: Evidence for the magical number four … or is it two? *Memory, 12*, 732–747.

Gobet, F. and Lane, P. C. R. (forthcoming). *Simulating cognitive behaviour: CHREST models of perception, learning and expertise*. New York, NY: Oxford University Press.

Gobet, F., Lane, P. C. R., Croker, S., Cheng, P. C. H., Jones, G., Oliver, I. and Pine, J. M. (2001). Chunking mechanisms in human learning. *Trends in Cognitive Sciences, 5*, 236–243.

Gobet, F., Richman, H. B., Staszewski, J. J. and Simon, H. A. (1997). Goals, representations, and strategies in a concept attainment task: The EPAM model. *The Psychology of Learning and Motivation, 37*, 265–290.

Gobet, F. and Simon, H. A. (1996). Recall of random and distorted positions. Implications for the theory of expertise. *Memory & Cognition, 24*, 493–503.

Gobet, F. and Simon, H. A. (1996). Templates in chess memory: A mechanism for recalling several boards. *Cognitive Psychology, 31*, 1–40.

Gobet, F. and Simon, H. A. (2000). Five seconds or sixty? Presentation time in expert memory. *Cognitive Science, 24*, 651–682.

Gobet, F., de Voogt, A. and Retschitzki, J. (2004). *Moves in mind: The psychology of board games*. London: Psychology Press.

Goldstein, D. G. and Gigerenzer, G. (2002). Models of ecological rationality: The recognition heuristic. *Psychological Review, 109*, 75–90.

Gray, J. A. and Singer, W. (1989). Stimulus-specific neuronal oscillations in orientation columns of cat visual cortex. *Proceedings of the National Academy of Sciences, 86*, 1698–1702.

Gregory, R. L. (1980). Perceptions as hypotheses. *Philosophical Transactions of the Royal Society of*

London – Series B: Biological Sciences, 290, 181–197.

Grice, H. P. (1975). Logic and conversation. In D. Davidson and G. Harman (eds), *The logic of grammar* (pp. 64–75). Encino, CA: Dickenson.

Griggs, R. A. and Cox, J. R. (1982). The elusive thematic-materials effect in Wason's selection task. *British Journal of Psychology, 73,* 407–420.

Grill-Spector, K. (2003). The neural basis of object perception. *Current Opinion in Neurobiology, 13,* 159–166.

Grill-Spector, K. and Malach, R. (2004). The human visual cortex. *Annual Review of Neuroscience, 27,* 649–677.

Gross, C. G. (2002). Genealogy of the 'grandmother cell'. *The Neuroscientist, 8,* 512–518.

Guilford, J. (1950). Creativity. *American Psychologist, 5,* 444–454.

Guilford, J. P. (1967). *The nature of human intelligence.* New York, NY: McGraw-Hill.

Hamann, S. B. and Squire, L. R. (1997). Intact perceptual memory in the absence of conscious memory. *Behavioral Neuroscience, 111,* 850–885.

Hamill, R., Wilson, T. D. and Nisbett, R. E. (1980). Insensitivity to sample bias: Generalizing from atypical cases. *Journal of Personality and Social Psychology, 39,* 578–589.

Hamilton, D. L. and Zanna, M. P. (1974). Context effects in impression formation: Changes in connotative meaning. *Journal of Personality and Social Psychology, 29,* 649–654.

Hampton, J. A. (1982). A demonstration of intransitivity in natural categories. *Cognition, 12,* 151–164.

Harley, T. (2008). *The psychology of language* (3rd edn). Hove, UK: Psychology Press.

Harris, J. A., Miniussi, C., Harris, I. M. and Diamond, M. E. (2002). Transient storage of a tactile memory trace in primary somatosensory cortex. *Journal of Neuroscience, 22,* 8720–8725.

Hasson, U., Hendler, T., Ben Bashat, D. and Malach, R. (2001). Vase or face? A neural correlate of shape-selective grouping processes in the human brain. *Journal of Cognitive Neuroscience, 13,* 744–753.

Haxby, J. V., Gobbini, M. I., Furey, M. L., Ishai, A., Schouten, J. L. and Pietrini, P. (2001). Distributed and overlapping representations of faces and objects in ventral temporal cortex. *Science, 293,* 2425–2430.

Hayes, J. R. (1978). *Cognitive psychology: Thinking and creating.* Homewood, IL: Dorsley.

Hayes, J. R. (1989a). Cognitive processes in creativity. In J. A. Glover, R. R. Ronning and C. R. Reynolds (eds), *Handbook of creativity* (pp. 135–145). New York, NY: Plenum.

Hayes, J. R. (1989b). Writing research: The analysis of a very complex task. In D. Klahr and K. Kotovsky (eds), *Complex information processing: The impact of Herbert A. Simon* (pp. 209–234). Hillsdale, NJ: Erlbaum.

Hayworth, K. J. and Biederman, I. (2006). Neural evidence for intermediate representations in object recognition. *Vision Research, 46,* 4024–4031.

Hebb, D. O. (1949). *Organization of behavior.* New Jersey: Wiley and Sons.

Hewstone, M., Stroebe, W. and Jonas, C. (eds) (2007). *Introduction to social psychology: A European perspective* (4th edn). Oxford: Blackwell.

Hirono, N., Mori, E., Ikejiri, Y., Imamura, T., Shimomura, T., Ikeda, M., *et al.* (1997). Procedural memory in patients with mild Alzheimer's disease. *Dementia and Geriatric Cognitive Disorders, 8,* 210–216.

Holyoak, K. J. and Thagard, P. (1995). *Mental leaps: Analogy in creative thought.* Cambridge, MA: MIT Press.

Howe, M. J. A., Davidson, J. W. and Sloboda, J. A. (1998). Innate talents: Reality or myth? *Behavioral and Brain Sciences, 21,* 399–407.

Hubel, D. H. (1963). The visual cortex of the brain. *Scientific American, 209,* 54–62.

Huettel, S. A., Song, A. W. and McCarthy, G. (2004). *Functional magnetic resonance imaging.* Sunderland, MA: Sinauer.

Isen, A. M. and Means, B. (1983). The influence of positive affect on decision-making strategy. *Social Cognition, 2,* 18–31.

Isen, A. M., Daubman, K. A. and Nowicki, G. P. (1987). Positive affect facilitates creative problem solving. *Journal of Personality and Social Psychology, 52,* 1122–1131.

James, W. (1890). *Principles of psychology* (Vols 1 and 2). New York, NY: Holt.

Jamison, K. R. (1993). *Touched with fire.* New York, NY: Simon & Schuster.

Johnson-Laird, P. N. (1981). Mental models in cognitive science. *Cognitive Science, 4,* 71–115.

Johnson-Laird, P. N. (2001). Mental models and

deduction. *Trends in Cognitive Sciences, 5,* 434–442.

Johnson-Laird, P. and Byrne, R. (1992). Modal reasoning, models, and Manktelow and Over. *Cognition, 43,* 173–182.

Jones, C. M. and Miles, T. R. (1978). Use of advance cues in predicting the flight of a lawn tennis ball. *Journal of Human Movement Studies, 4,* 231–235.

Jones, D. M., Macken, W. J. and Nicholls, A. P. (2004). The phonological store of working memory: Is it phonological and is it a store? *Journal of Experimental Psychology: Learning, Memory, and Cognition, 30,* 656–674.

Jones, G., Gobet, F. and Pine, J. M. (2007). Linking working memory and long-term memory: A computational model of the learning of new words. *Developmental Science, 10,* 853–873.

Juola, J. F. and Atkinson, R. C. (1971). Memory scanning for words versus categories. *Journal of Verbal Learning and Verbal Behavior, 10,* 522–527.

Just, M. A. and Carpenter, P. A. (1992). A capacity theory of comprehension: Individual differences in working memory. *Psychological Review, 99,* 122–149.

Kahneman, D. and Tversky, A. (1972). Subjective probability: A judgment of representativeness. *Cognitive Psychology, 3,* 430–454.

Kahneman, D. and Tversky, A. (1973a). Availability: A heuristic for judging frequency and probability. *Cognitive Psychology, 5,* 207–232.

Kahneman, D. and Tversky, A. (1973b). On the psychology of prediction. *Psychological Review, 80,* 237–51.

Kandel, E. R. (1976). *Cellular basis of behavior: An introduction to behavioral neurobiology.* San Francisco, CA: W. H. Freeman.

Kandel, E. R. (2001). The molecular biology of memory storage: A dialogue between genes and synapses. *Science, 294,* 1030–1038.

Kandel, E. R. (2006). *In search of memory: The emergence of a new science of mind.* New York: Norton.

Kandel, E. R., Schwartz, J. H. and Jessell, T. M. (2000). *Principles of neural science* (4th edn). New York: McGraw-Hill.

Kanwisher, N., McDermott, J. and Chun, M. M. (1997). The fusiform face area: A module in human extrastriate cortex specialized for face perception. *Journal of Neuroscience, 17,* 4302–4311.

Kaplan, C. A. and Simon, H. A. (1990). In search of insight. *Cognitive Psychology, 22,* 374–419.

Karni, A. and Sagi, D. (1991). Where practice makes perfect in texture discrimination: Evidence for primary visual cortex plasticity. *Proceedings of the National Academy of Sciences, USA, 88,* 4966–4970.

Katz, J. J. and Fodor, J. A. (1963). The structure of a semantic theory. *Language, 39,* 170–210.

Kay, J. and Marcel, A. (1981). One process, not two, in reading aloud: Lexical analogies do the work of non-lexical rules. *Quarterly Journal of Experimental Psychology Section a – Human Experimental Psychology, 33,* 397–413.

Keele, S. W. and Posner, M. I. (1968). Processing of visual feedback in rapid movements. *Journal of Experimental Psychology, 77,* 155–158.

Kelley, H. H. (1950). The warm–cold variable in first impressions of persons. *Journal of Personality, 18,* 431–439.

Kintsch, W. (1988). The role of knowledge in discourse comprehension: A construction integration model. *Psychological Review, 95,* 163–182.

Kintsch, W. (1998). *Comprehension: A paradigm for cognition.* Cambridge: Cambridge University Press.

Kintsch, W. and Van Dijk, T. A. (1978). Toward a model of text comprehension and production. *Psychological Review, 85,* 363–394.

Kintsch, W., Welsch, D., Schmalhofer, F. and Zimny, S. (1990). Sentence memory: A theoretical analysis. *Journal of Memory and Language, 29,* 133–159.

Klahr, D. and Simon, H. A. (1999). Studies of scientific discovery: Complementary approaches and convergent findings. *Psychological Bulletin, 125,* 524–543.

Klahr, D., Langley, P. and Neches, R. (1987). *Production system models of learning and development.* Cambridge, MA: MIT Press.

Klein, G. A. (1970). Temporal changes in acoustic and semantic confusion effects. *Journal of Experimental Psychology, 86,* 236–240.

Knoblich, G., Ohlsson, S., Haider, H. and Rhenius, D. (1999). Constraint relaxation and chunk decomposition in insight problem solving. *Journal of Experimental Psychology: Learning, Memory, and Cognition, 25,* 1534–1555.

Knoblich, G., Ohlsson, S. and Raney, G. E. (2001). An eye movement study of insight problem solving. *Memory & Cognition, 29,* 1000–1009.

Koedinger, K. R. and Corbett, A. T. (2006). Cognitive tutors: Technology bringing learning science to the classroom. In K. Sawyer (ed.), *The Cambridge handbook of the learning sciences* (pp. 61–78). Cambridge, MA: Cambridge University Press.

Koestler, A. (1964). *The art of creation*. New York, NY: Dell.

Köhler, W. (1921). *Intelligenzprüfungen an Menschenaffen*. Berlin: J. Springer.

Kosslyn, S. M., Ball, T. M. and Reiser, B. J. (1978). Visual images preserve metric spatial information: Evidence from studies of image scanning. *Journal of Experimental Psychology: Human Perception and Performance, 4*, 47–60.

Kuhn, G. and Land, M. F. (2006). There's more to magic than meets the eye! *Current Biology, 16*, 950–951.

Kuhn, G. and Tatler, B. W. (2005). Magic and fixation: Now you don't see it, now you do. *Perception, 34*, 1153–1161.

Kulkarni, D. and Simon, H. A. (1988). The processes of scientific discovery: The strategy of experimentation. *Cognitive Science, 12*, 139–176.

LaBar, K. S., Gatenby, J. C., Gore, J. C., LeDoux, J. E. and Phelps, E. A. (1998). Human amygdala activation during conditioned fear acquisition and extinction: A mixed-trial fMRI study. *Neuron, 20*, 937–945.

Lachman, R., Lachman, J. L. and Butterfield, E. C. (1979). *Cognitive psychology and information processing: An introduction*. Hillsdale, NJ: Erlbaum.

Lane, P. C. R. and Gobet, F. (2001). Simple environments fail as illustrations of intelligence: A review of R. Pfeifer and C. Scheier: 'Understanding Intelligence'. *Artificial Intelligence, 127*, 261–267.

Lane, P. C. R. and Gobet, F. (2003). Developing reproducible and comprehensible computational models. *Artificial Intelligence, 144*, 251–263.

Lane, P. C. R., Gobet, F. and Cheng, P. C. H. (2000). Learning-based constraints on schemata. In *Proceedings of the Twenty Second Annual Meeting of the Cognitive Science Society* (pp. 776–781). Philadelphia, USA: Erlbaum.

Langley, P., Simon, H. A., Bradshaw, G. L. and Zytkow, J. M. (1987). *Scientific discovery: Computational explorations of the creative processes*. Cambridge, MA: MIT Press.

Lashley, K. S., Chow, K. L. and Semmes, J. (1951). An examination of the electric field theory of cerebral integration. *Psychological Review, 58*, 123–136.

Lau, R. R. (1982). Negativity in political perception. *Political Behavior, 4*, 353–378.

Lavie, N. (1995). Perceptual load as a necessary condition for selective attention. *Journal of Experimental Psychology: Human Perception and Performance, 21*, 451–468.

Lavie, N. (2000). Selective attention and cognitive control: Dissociating attentional functions through different types of load. In S. Monsell and J. Driver (eds), *Control of cognitive processes: Attention and performance XVIII* (pp. 175–194). Cambridge, MA: MIT Press.

Lazarus, R. S. (1982). Thoughts on the relations between emotions and cognition. *American Physiologist, 37*, 1019–1024.

LeDoux, J. E. (1998). Fear and the brain: Where have we been, and where are we going? *Biological Psychiatry, 44*, 1229–1238.

LeDoux, J. E. (1999). *The emotional brain*. London, UK: Phoenix.

Lépine, R. and Barrouillet, P. (2005). What makes working memory spans so predictive of high-level cognition? *Psychonomic Bulletin & Review, 12*, 165–170.

Lerner, J. S. and Keltner, D. (2000). Beyond valence: Toward a model of emotion-specific influences on judgement and choice. *Cognition & Emotion, 14*, 473–493.

Lerner, J. S. and Keltner, D. (2001). Fear, anger, and risk. *Journal of Personality and Social Psychology, 81*, 146–159.

Levy, I., Hasson, U. and Malach, R. (2004). One picture is worth at least a million neurons. *Current Biology, 14*, 996–1001.

Liberman, A. M. and Mattingly, I. G. (1985). The motor theory of speech perception revised. *Cognition, 21*, 1–36.

Liberman, A. M., Cooper, F. S., Shankweiler, D. P. and Studdert-Kennedy, M. (1967). Perception of the speech code. *Psychological Review, 74*, 431–461.

Libet, B. (1985). Unconscious cerebral initiative and the role of conscious will in voluntary action. *Behavioral and Brain Sciences, 8*, 529–566.

Liu, J., Harris, A. and Kanwisher, N. (2002). Stages of processing in face perception: An MEG study. *Nature Neuroscience, 5*, 910–916.

Lockhart, R. S. and Craik, F. I. M. (1990). Levels of processing: A retrospective commentary on a framework for memory research. *Canadian Journal of Psychology, 44*, 87–112.

Loftus, E. F., Miller, D. G. and Burns, H. J. (1978). Semantic integration of verbal information into a visual memory. *Human Learning and Memory, 4,* 19–31.

Loftus, E. F. and Palmer, J. C. (1974). Reconstruction of automobile destruction: An example of the interaction between language and memory. *Journal of Verbal Learning and Verbal Behavior, 13,* 585–589.

Loftus, E. F. and Pickrell, J. E. (1995). The formation of false memories. *Psychiatric Annals, 25,* 720–725.

Loftus, E. F. and Zanni, G. (1975). Eyewitness testimony: The influence of the wording of a question. *Bulletin of the Psychonomic Society, 5,* 86–88.

Logan, G. D. (1988). Toward an instance theory of automatization. *Psychological Review, 95,* 492–527.

Logie, R. H. (1995). *Visuo-spatial working memory.* Hove, UK: Erlbaum.

Logie, R. H., Maylor, E. A., Della Sala, S. and Smith, G. (2004). Working memory in event- and time-based prospective memory tasks: Effect of secondary demand and age. *European Journal of Cognitive Psychology, 16,* 441–456.

Lord, C. G., Ross, L. and Lepper, M. R. (1979). Biased assimilation and attitude polarization: The effects of prior theories on subsequently considered evidence. *Journal of Personality and Social Psychology, 37,* 2098–2109.

Lotto, A. J., Hickok, G. S. and Holt, L. L. (2009). Reflections on mirror neurons and speech perception. *Trends in Cognitive Sciences, 13,* 110–114.

Luchins, A. S. (1942). Mechanisation in problem solving. *Psychological Monographs, 54,* 1–95.

Luck, S. J. (2005). *An introduction to the event-related potential technique.* Cambridge, MA: The MIT Press.

Luria, A. R. (1968). *The mind of a mnemonist.* New York: Avon.

MacDonald, M. C., Pearlmutter, N. J. and Seidenberg, M. S. (1994). The lexical nature of syntactic ambiguity resolution. *Psychological Review, 101,* 676–703.

MacGregor, J. N., Ormerod, T. C. and Chronicle, E. P. (2001). Information processing and insight: A process model of performance on the nine-dot and related problems. *Journal of Experimental Psychology: Learning Memory and Cognition, 27,* 176–201.

Mackay, D. G. (1973). Aspects of the theory of comprehension, memory and attention. *Quarterly Journal of Experimental Psychology, 25,* 22–40.

MacLean, P. D. (1990). *The triune brain in evolution: Role in paleocerebral functions.* New York: Plenum Press.

MacLeod, C. M. (1991). Half a century of research on the Stroop effect: an integrative review. *Psychological Bulletin, 109,* 163–203.

MacLeod, C. M. and MacDonald, P. A. (2000). Interdimensional interference in the Stroop effect: Uncovering the cognitive and neural anatomy of attention. *Trends in Cognitive Science, 4,* 383–391.

Maddieson, I. (1984). *Patterns of sounds.* New York: Cambridge University Press.

Mägiste, E. (1984). Stroop tasks and dichotic translation: The development of interference patterns in bilinguals. *Journal of Experimental Psychology: Learning, Memory, and Cognition, 10,* 304–315.

Mägiste, E. (1985). Development of intra and inter lingual interference in bilinguals. *Journal of Psycholinguistic Research, 14,* 137–154.

Maier, N. R. F. (1931). Reasoning in humans: II. The solution of a problem and its appearance in consciousness. *Journal of Comparative Psychology, 12,* 181–194.

Malt, B. C. (1995). Category coherence in cross-cultural perspective. *Cognitive Psychology, 29,* 85–148.

Manktelow, K. I. and Over, D. E. (1991). Social roles and utilities in reasoning with deontic conditionals. *Cognition, 39,* 85–105.

Markman, A. B. and Gentner, D. (2001). Thinking. *Annual Reviews in Psychology, 52,* 223–247.

Markman, A. B. and Ross, B. H. (2003). Category use and category learning. *Psychological Bulletin, 129,* 592–613.

Marr, D. (1982). *Vision: A computational investigation into the human representation and processing of visual information.* San Francisco, CA: Freeman.

Marslen-Wilson, W. D. and Tyler, L. K. (1980). The temporal structure of spoken language understanding. *Cognition, 8,* 1–71.

Marslen-Wilson, W. D. and Warren, P. (1994). Levels of perceptual representation and process in lexical access: Words, phonemes, and features. *Psychological Review, 101,* 653–675.

McClelland, J. L. and Elman, J. L. (1986). The TRACE model of speech perception. *Cognitive Psychology, 18,* 1–86.

McClelland, J. L. and Rumelhart, D. E. (1981). An interactive activation model of context effects in letter perception: Part 1. An account of basic findings. *Psychological Review, 88*, 375–407.

McClelland, J. L. and Rumelhart, D. E. (eds) (1986). *Parallel distributed processing: Explorations in the microstructure of cognition.* Cambridge, MA: The MIT Press.

McCloskey, M. E. and Glucksberg, S. (1978). Natural categories: Well-defined or fuzzy sets? *Memory & Cognition, 6*, 462–472.

McConnell, J. V., Cutler, R. I. and McNeil, E. B. (1958). Subliminal stimulation: An overview. *American Psychologist, 13*, 229–242.

McCorduck, P. (1979). *Machines who think.* San Francisco, CA: Freeman.

McDaniel, M. A. and Einstein, G. O. (2000). Strategic and automatic processes in prospective memory retrieval. *Applied Cognitive Psychology, 14*, S127–S144.

McGeoch, J. A. and McDonald, W. T. (1931). Meaningful relation and retroactive inhibition. *American Journal of Psychology, 43*, 579–588.

McGuire, W. J. (1997). Creative hypothesis generating in psychology: Some useful heuristics. *Annual Review of Psychology, 48*, 1–30

McGurk, H. and MacDonald, J. (1976). Hearing lips and seeing voices. *Nature, 264*, 746–748.

McLeod, P. (1987). Visual reaction time and high-speed ball games. *Perception, 16*, 49–59.

McLeod, P., Plunkett, K. and Rolls, E. T. (1998). *Introduction to connectionist modelling of cognitive processes.* Oxford, UK: Oxford University Press.

McNeil, D. (1966). Developmental psycholinguistics. In F. Smith and G. A. Miller (eds), *The genesis of language: A psycholinguistic approach* (pp. 15–84). Cambridge, MA: The MIT Press.

Medin, D. L. and Smith, E. E. (1981). Strategies and classification learning. *Journal of Experimental Psychology: Human Learning and Memory, 7*, 241–253.

Mednick, S. (1962). The associative basis of the creative process. *Psychological Review, 69*, 220–232.

Meehl, P. E. (1954). *Clinical versus statistical prediction: A theoretical analysis and a review of the evidence.* Minneapolis, MN: University of Minneapolis Press.

Memmert, D. (2006). The effects of eye movements, age, and expertise on inattentional blindness. *Consciousness and Cognition, 15*, 620–627.

Merikle, P. M. and Smith, S. D. (2005). Memory for information perceived without awareness. In B. Uttl, N. Ohta and C. M. MacLeod (eds), *Dynamic cognitive processes* (pp. 79–99). Tokyo: Springer.

Mervis, C. B., Catlin, J. and Rosch, E. H. (1976). Relationships among goodness-of-example, category norms and word frequency. *Bulletin of the Psychonomic Society, 7*, 268–284.

Meyer, D. E. and Schvaneveldt, R. W. (1971). Facilitation in recognizing pairs of words: Evidence of a dependence between retrieval operations. *Journal of Experimental Psychology, 90*, 227–234.

Milgram, S. (1963). Behavioral study of obedience. *Journal of Abnormal and Social Psychology, 67*, 371–378.

Milgram, S. (1974). *Obedience to authority.* New York: Harper & Row.

Mill, J. S. (1843). *A system of logic.* London: Parker.

Miller, G. A. (1956). The magical number seven, plus or minus two: Some limits on our capacity for processing information. *Psychological Review, 63*, 81–97.

Minsky, M. and Papert, S. (1969). *Perceptrons.* Cambridge, MA: The MIT Press.

Miyake, A. and Shah, P. (eds). (1999). *Models of working memory. Mechanisms of active maintenance and executive control.* Cambridge: Cambridge University Press.

Miyashita, Y., Date, A. and Okuno, H. (1993). Configural encoding of complex visual forms by single neurons of monkey temporal cortex. *Neuropsychologia, 31*, 1119–1131.

Moore, T. E. (1982). Subliminal advertising: What you see is what you get. *Journal of Marketing, 46*, 38–47.

Moore, T. E. (1988). The case against subliminal manipulation. *Psychology & Marketing, 5*, 297–316.

Moore, T. E. (1996). Scientific consensus and expert testimony: Lessons from the Judas Priest trial. *Skeptical Inquirer, 20*, 32–38.

Moray, N. (1959). Attention in dichotic listening: Affective cues and the influence of instructions. *Quarterly Journal of Experimental Psychology, 11*, 56–60.

Müller, S., Abernethy, B. and Farrow, D. (2006). How do world-class cricket batsmen anticipate a bowler's intention? *Quarterly Journal of Experimental Psychology, 59*, 2162–2186.

Murdock, B. B. (1961). The retention of individual

items. *Journal of Experimental Psychology, 62,* 618–625.

Murdock, B. B. (1962). The serial position effect of free recall. *Journal of Experimental Psychology, 5,* 482–488.

Murphy, G. L. (2002). *The big book of concepts.* Cambridge, MA: The MIT Press.

Murphy, G. L. and Medin, D. L. (1985). The role of theories in conceptual coherence. *Psychological Review, 92,* 289–316.

Nagel, T. (1974). What is it like to be a bat? *Philosophical Review, 83,* 435–450.

Needham, D. R. and Begg, I. M. (1991). Problem-oriented training promotes spontaneous analogical transfer: Memory-oriented training promotes memory for training. *Memory & Cognition, 19,* 543–557.

Neely, J. H. (1977). Semantic priming and retrieval from lexical memory: Roles of inhibitionless spreading activation and limited-capacity attention. *Journal of Experimental Psychology: General, 106,* 226–254.

Neisser, U. (1967). *Cognitive psychology.* New York, NY: Appleton-Century-Crofts.

Newell, A. (1990). *Unified theories of cognition.* Cambridge, MA: Harvard University Press.

Newell, A. and Rosenbloom, P. S. (1981). Mechanisms of skill acquisition and the law of practice. In J. R. Anderson (ed.), *Cognitive skills and their acquisition.* Hillsdale, NJ: Erlbaum.

Newell, A. and Simon, H. A. (1972). *Human problem solving.* Englewood Cliffs, NJ: Prentice-Hall.

Newell, A., Shaw, J. C. and Simon, H. A. (1958). Elements of a theory of human problem solving. *Psychological Review, 65,* 151–166.

Newell, A., Shaw, J., Simon, H., Ginber, H., Terrell, G. and Wertheimer, M. (1962). *Contemporary approaches to creative thinking.* New York, NY: Atherton Press.

Newell, K. M. (1991). Motor skill acquisition. *Annual Reviews in Psychology, 42,* 213–237.

Nisbett, R. and Ross, L. (1980). *Human inference strategies and shortcomings of social judgment.* Englewood Cliffs, NJ: Prentice Hall.

Nissani, M. (1990). A cognitive reinterpretation of Stanley Milgram's observations on obedience to authority. *American Psychologist, 45,* 1384–1385.

Norman, D. A. (1968). Towards a theory of memory and attention. *Psychological Review, 75,* 522–536.

Norman, D. A. and Shallice, T. (1986). Attention to action: willed and automatic control of behaviour. In R. J. Davidson, G. E. Schwarts and D. Shapiro (eds), *Consciousness and self-regulation. Advances in research and theory Vol. 4* (pp. 1–18). New York, NY: Plenum.

Oakhill, J., Yuill, N. and Parkin, A. (1986). On the nature of the difference between skilled and less skilled comprehenders. *Journal of Research in Reading, 9,* 80–91.

Ohlsson, S. (1992). Information-processing explanations of insight and related phenomena. *Advances in the Psychology of Thinking, 1,* 1–44.

Öhman, A., Flykt, A. and Esteves, F. (2001). Emotion drives attention: Detecting the snake in the grass. *Journal of Experimental Psychology: General, 130,* 466–478.

O'Reilly, R. C. (1998). Six principles for biologically based computational models of cortical cognition. *Trends in Cognitive Sciences, 2,* 455–462.

Osborn, A. (1953). *Applied imagination: Principles and procedures of creative problem solving.* New York, NY: Charles Scribner's Sons.

Osgood, C. E., Suci, G. and Tannenbaum, P. (1957). *The measurement of meaning.* Urbana, IL: University of Illinois Press.

Panksepp, J. (2004). *Affective neuroscience: The foundations of human and animal emotions.* Oxford, UK: Oxford University Press.

Pashler, H. (1998). *The psychology of attention,* Cambridge, MA: MIT Press.

Pashler, H. (ed.) (2002). *Stevens' handbook of experimental psychology* (3rd edn). New York, NY: Wiley.

Pavlov, I. P. (1927). *Conditioned reflexes: An investigation of the physiological activity of the cerebral cortex* (G. V. Anrep, trans.). London: Oxford University Press.

Pennington, D. C. (2000). *Social cognition.* London, UK: Routledge.

Perfetto, G. A., Bransford, J. D. and Franks, J. J. (1983). Constraints on access in a problem solving context. *Memory & Cognition, 11,* 24–31.

Perkins, D. N. (1981). *The mind's best work.* Cambridge, MA: Harvard University Press.

Peterson, L. R. and Peterson, M. (1959). Short-term retention of individual verbal items. *Journal of Experimental Psychology, 58,* 193–198.

Pew, R. W. and Mavor, A. S. (eds) (1998). *Modeling human and organizational behavior. Applications to military simulations.* Washington, DC: National Academy Press.

Pezdek, K., Deffenbacher, K. A., Lam, S. and Hoffman, R. R. (2006). Cognitive psychology: Applications and careers. In S. Donaldson, D. Berger and K. Pezdek (eds), *Applied psychology: New frontiers and rewarding careers.* Mahwah, NJ: Erlbaum.

Pfeifer, R. and Scheier, C. (1999). *Understanding intelligence.* Cambridge, MA: MIT Press.

Pfungst, O. (1965). *Clever Hans, the horse of Mr. von Osten.* New York, NY: Holt, Rinehart & Winston.

Phillips, M. L., Drevets, W. C., Rauch, S. L. and Lane, R. (2003). Neurobiology of emotion perception I: the neural basis of normal emotion perception. *Biological Psychiatry, 54,* 504–514.

Piattelli-Palmarini, M. (1996). *Inevitable illusions: How mistakes of reason rule our minds.* New York, NY: Wiley.

Pinker, S. (1994). *The language instinct.* New York: Morrow.

Pinker, S. and Mehler, J. (eds) (1988). *Connections and symbols.* Cambridge, MA: MIT Press.

Pitt, D. (1999). In defense of definitions. *Philosophical Psychology, 12,* 139–156.

Pitz, G. F., Downing, L. and Reinhold, H. (1967). Sequential effects in the revision of subjective probabilities. *Canadian Journal of Psychology, 21,* 381–393.

Plaut, D. C. and Shallice, T. (1994). *Connectionist modelling in cognitive neuropsychology: A case study.* Mahwah, NJ: Erlbaum.

Plaut, D. C., McClelland, J. L., Seidenberg, M. S. and Patterson, K. (1996). Understanding normal and impaired word reading: Computational principles in quasi-regular domains. *Psychological Review, 103,* 56–115.

Poincaré, H. (1913). *The foundations of science* (G. H. Halstead, trans.). New York, NY: Science Press.

Pollack, I. and Pickett, J. M. (1964). Intelligibility of excerpts from fluent speech: Auditory vs structural context. *Journal of Verbal Learning and Verbal Behavior, 3,* 79–84.

Popper, K. (1959). *The logic of scientific discovery.* New York, NY: Basic Books.

Popper, K. R. (1968). *The logic of scientific discovery.* London: Hutchinson.

Postman, L. and Phillips, L. W. (1965). Short-term temporal changes in free recall. *Quarterly Journal of Experimental Psychology, 17,* 132–138.

Povinelli, D. J., Reaux, J. E., Theall, L. A. and Giambrone, S. (2000). *Folk physics for apes: The chimpanzee's theory of how the world works.* New York, NY: Oxford University Press.

Pratkanis, A. (1992). The cargo cult science of subliminal persuasion. *Skeptical Inquirer, 16,* 260–272.

Qin, Y. and Simon, H. A. (1990). Laboratory replication of scientific discovery processes. *Cognitive Science, 14,* 281–312.

Quiroga, R. Q., Reddy, L., Kreiman, G., Koch, C. and Fried, I. (2005). Invariant visual representation by single neurons in human brain. *Nature, 435,* 1102–1107.

Rayner, K. (1998). Eye movements in reading and information processing: 20 years of research. *Psychological Bulletin, 124,* 372–422.

Redington, M., Chater, N. and Finch, S. (1998). Distributional information: A powerful cue for acquiring syntactic categories. *Cognitive Science, 22,* 425–469.

Reicher, G. M. (1969). Perceptual recognition as a function of meaningfulness of stimulus material. *Journal of Experimental Psychology, 81,* 275–280.

Rensink, A. R. (2000). When good observers go bad: Change blindness, inattentional blindness, and visual experience. *Psyche, 6,* http://psyche. cs.monash.edu.au/v6/psyche-6-09-rensink.html.

Rensink, R.A., O'Regan, K. and Clark, J. (1997). To see or not to see: The need for attention to perceive changes in scenes. *Psychological Science, 8,* 368–373.

Rhodes, G. (2006). The evolutionary psychology of facial beauty. *Annual Review of Psychology, 57,* 199–226.

Richman, H. B. and Simon, H. A. (1989). Context effects in letter perception: Comparison of two theories. *Psychological Review, 3,* 417–432.

Richman, H. B., Staszewski, J. J. and Simon, H. A. (1995). Simulation of expert memory with EPAM IV. *Psychological Review, 102,* 305–330.

Rips, L. J. (1994). *The psychology of proof.* Cambridge, MA: MIT Press.

Rips, L. J. and Collins, A. (1993). Categories and resemblance. *Journal of Experimental Psychology-General, 122,* 468–486.

Rips, L. J., Shoben, E. J. and Smith, E. E. (1973). Semantic distance and the verification of semantic relations. *Journal of Verbal Learning and Verbal Behavior, 12,* 1–20.

Ritter, F. E., Shadbolt, N. R., Elliman, D., Young, R. M., Gobet, F. and Baxter, G. D. (2003). *Techniques for modelling human performance in synthetic environments: A supplementary review.* Wright-Patterson Air Force Base, OH: Human Systems Information Analysis Center.

Rizzolatti, G. and Craighero, L. (2004). The mirror-neuron system. *Annual Review of Neuroscience, 27,* 169–192.

Roberts, R. M. (1989). *Serendipity: Accidental discoveries in science.* New York, NY: Wiley.

Roberts, S. and Pashler, H. (2000). How persuasive is a good fit? A comment on theory testing. *Psychological Review, 107,* 358–367.

Rosch, E. H. (1973). On the internal structure of perceptual and semantic categories. In T. E. Moore (ed.), *Cognitive development and the acquisition of language* (pp. 111–144). New York: Academic Press.

Rosch, E. H. (1975). Cognitive representations of semantic categories. *Journal of Experimental Psychology: General, 104,* 192–233.

Rosch, E. H. and Mervis, C. B. (1975). Family resemblances: Studies in the internal structure of categories. *Cognitive Psychology, 7,* 573–605.

Rosch, E. H., Mervis, C. B., Gray, W. D., Johnson, D. M. and Boyes-Graem, P. (1976). Basic objects in natural categories. *Cognitive Psychology, 8,* 382–439.

Roseman, I. J. (1991). Appraisal determinants of discrete emotions? *Cognition and Emotion, 5,* 161–200.

Rosenblatt, F. (1958). The perceptron: A probabilistic model for information storage. *Psychological Review, 65,* 386–408.

Rosenthal, R. and Jacobson, L. (1968). *Pygmalion in the classroom.* New York: Holt, Rinehart & Winston.

Rosenthal, R. and Rubin, D. B. (1978). Interpersonal expectancy effects: The first 345 studies. *The Behavioral and Brain Sciences, 1,* 377–415.

Roth, E. M. and Shoben, E. J. (1983). The effect of context on the structure of categories. *Cognitive Psychology, 16,* 346–378.

Rumelhart, D. E. and McClelland, J. L. (1986). *Parallel distributed processing: Explorations in the microstructure of cognition.* Cambridge, MA: The MIT Press.

Rumelhart, D. E., Hinton, G. E. and Williams, R. J. (1986). Learning representations by back-propagating errors. *Nature, 323,* 533–536.

Runco, M. A. (2004). Creativity. *Annual Review of Psychology, 55,* 657–687.

Runco, M. A. (2006). *Creativity: Theories and themes: Research, development, and practice.* London: Elsevier.

Sacks, O. (1986). *The man who mistook his wife for a hat.* London: Duckworth.

Sagan, C. (1996). *The demon-haunted world: Science as a candle in the dark.* New York: Ballantine.

Salthouse, T. A. (1986). Effects of practice on a typing-like keying task. *Acta Psychologica, 62,* 189–198.

Salvucci, D. D. and Macuga, K. L. (2002). Predicting the effects of cellular-phone dialing on driver performance. *Cognitive Systems Research, 3,* 95–102.

Samuel, A. G. (1981). Phonemic restoration: Insights from a new methodology. *Journal of Experimental Psychology: General, 110,* 474–494.

Samuels, S. J. (1999). Developing reading fluency in learning-disabled students. In R. J. Sternberg and L. Spear-Swerling (eds), *Perspectives on learning disabilities: Biological, cognitive, contextual* (pp. 176–189). Boulder, CO: Westview.

Schank, R. C. (1975). *Conceptual information processing.* Amsterdam: North Holland.

Schiller, P. H. (1966). Developmental study of color-word interference. *Journal of Experimental Psychology, 72,* 105–108.

Schmidt, R. A. (1975). A schema theory of discrete motor skill learning. *Psychological Review, 82,* 225–60.

Schneider, E. W. (1966). *Coleridge, opium, and Kubla Khan.* Chicago, IL: University of Chicago Press.

Schneider, W. and Shiffrin, R. M. (1977). Controlled and automatic human information processing. Detection, search, and attention. *Psychological Review, 84,* 1–66.

Schweinberger, S. R. and Burton, A. M. (2003). Covert recognition and the neural system for face processing. *Cortex, 39,* 9–30.

Scoville, W. B. and Milner, B. (1957). Loss of recent memory after bilateral hippocampal lesions. *Journal of Neurology, Neurosurgery and Psychiatry, 20,* 11–21.

Sears, D. O. (1983). The person-positivity bias. *Journal of Personality and Social Psychology, 44,* 233–250.

Seidenberg, M. S. and McClelland, J. L. (1989). A distributed, developmental model of word recognition and naming. *Psychological Review, 96,* 523–568.

Shallice, T. (1982). Specific impairments of planning. *Royal Society of London Philosophical Transactions Series B, 298,* 199–209.

Shea, J. B. and Morgan, R. L. (1979). Contextual interference effects on the acquisition, retention, and transfer of a motor skill. *Journal of Experimental Psychology: Human Learning and Memory, 5,* 179–187.

Shepard, R. N. and Metzler, J. (1971). Mental rotation of three-dimensional objects. *Science, 171,* 701–703.

Shepherd, G. M. (1994). *Neurobiology* (3rd edn). Oxford, UK: Oxford University Press.

Shermer, M. (2002). *Why people believe weird things: Pseudoscience, superstition, and other confusions of our time.* New York, NY: Owl Books.

Shier, D., Butler, J. and Lewis, R. (2010). *Hole's human anatomy & physiology* (12th edn). Boston, MA: McGraw-Hill.

Shiffman, H. R. (2002). *Sensation and perception: An integrated view* (5th edn). New York, NY: Wiley & Sons.

Shiffrin, R. M. and Atkinson, R. C. (1969). Storage and retrieval processes in long-term memory. *Psychological Review, 76,* 179–193.

Shiffrin, R. M. and Schneider, W. (1977). Controlled and automatic information processing. II. Perceptual learning, automatic attending, and a general theory. *Psychological Review, 84,* 127–190.

Sides, A., Osherson, D., Bonini, N. and Viale, R. (2002). On the reality of the conjunction fallacy. *Memory & Cognition, 30,* 191–198.

Siegler, R. S. (1986). *Children's thinking.* Englewood Cliffs, NJ: Prentice-Hall.

Simon, H. A. (1957). *Models of man.* New York, NY: Wiley.

Simon, H. A. (1966). Scientific discovery and the psychology of problem solving. In R. Colodny (ed.), *Mind and cosmos* (pp. 22–40). Pittsburgh, PA: University of Pittburgh Press.

Simon, H. A. (1969). *The sciences of the artificial.* Cambridge, MA: The MIT Press.

Simon, H. A. (1974). How big is a chunk? *Science, 183,* 482–488.

Simon, H. A. (1992). What is an 'explanation' of behavior? *Psychological Science, 3,* 150–161.

Simon, H. A. (1996). *The sciences of the artificial* (3rd edn). Cambridge: The MIT Press.

Simon, H. A. and Chase, W. G. (1973). Skill in chess. *American Scientist, 61,* 393–403.

Simon, H. A. and Newell, A. (1976). Computer science as empirical inquiry: Symbols and search. *Communications of the Association for Computing Machinery, 19,* 113–126.

Simons, D. J. and Chabris, C. F. (1999). Gorillas in our midst: Sustained inattentional blindness for dynamic events. *Perception, 28,* 1059–1074.

Simons, D. J. and Rensink, R. A. (2005). Change blindness: Past, present, and future. *Trends in Cognitive Sciences, 9,* 16–20.

Simonton, D. K. (1999). *Origins of genius: Darwinian perspectives on creativity.* New York, NY: Oxford University Press.

Skinner, B. F. (1957). *Verbal behavior.* New York, NY: Appleton-Century-Crofts.

Slamecka, N. J. and Graf, P. (1978). The generation effect: Delineation of a phenomenon. *Journal of Experimental Psychology: Human Learning and Memory, 4,* 592–604.

Slater, M., Antley, A., Davison, A., Swapp, D., Guger, C., Barker, C. *et al.* (2006). A virtual reprise of the Stanley Milgram obedience experiments. *Plos One, 1.*

Sloboda, J. A. (1991). Music structure and emotional response: Some empirical findings. *Psychology of Music, 19,* 110–120.

Sloboda, J. A. (2005). *Exploring the musical mind: Cognition, emotion, ability, function.* New York, NY: Oxford University Press.

Smith, E. E., Shoben, E. J. and Rips, L. J. (1974). Structure and process in semantic memory: A featural model for semantic decisions. *Psychological Review, 81,* 214–241.

Smith, J. D. and Minda, J. P. (2000). Thirty categorization results in search of a model. *Journal of Experimental Psychology: Learning, Memory and Cognition, 26,* 3–27.

Snyder, M., Tanke, E. D. and Berscheid, E. (1977). Social perception and interpersonal behavior: On the self-fulfilling nature of social stereotypes. *Journal of Personality and Social Psychology, 35,* 656–666.

Sperling, G. (1960). The information available in brief visual presentations. *Psychological Monographs: General and Applied, 74,* 1–29.

Spiridon, M. and Kanwisher, N. (2002). How

distributed is visual category information in human occipito-temporal cortex? An fMRI study. *Neuron, 35,* 1157–1165.

Sporer, S. L. (1991). Deep-deeper-deepest? Encoding strategies and the recognition of human faces. *Journal of Experimental Psychology: Learning, Memory, and Cognition, 17,* 323–333.

Squire, L. R. (2004). Memory systems of the brain: A brief history and current perspectives. *Neurobiology of Learning and Memory, 82,* 171–177.

Squire, L. R. and Kandel, E. R. (1999). *Memory. From mind to molecules.* New York: W. H. Freeman & Company.

Sternberg, R. J. (1986). A triangular theory of love. *Psychological Review, 93,* 119–135.

Sternberg, R. J. (1999). *Handbook of creativity.* New York, NY: Cambridge University Press.

Sternberg, R. J., Conway, B. E., Ketron, J. L. and Bernstein, M. (1981). People's conceptions of intelligence. *Journal of Personality and Social Psychology, 41,* 37–55.

Sternberg, R. J. and Lubart, T. I. (1995). *Defying the crowd: Cultivating creativity in a culture of conformity.* New York, NY: Free Press.

Sternberg, S. S. (1966). High speed scanning in human memory. *Science, 153,* 652–654.

Stevens, S. S. (1957). On the psychophysical law. *Psychological Review, 64,* 153–181.

Stoker, B. (2000). *Dracula* (original edition, 1897). Ware, UK: Wordsworth.

Stoner, G. R. and Albright, T. D. (1992). Neural correlates of perceptual motion coherence. *Nature, 358,* 412–414.

Strayer, D. L., Drews, F. A. and Johnston, W. A. (2003). Cell phone-induced failures of visual attention during simulated driving. *Journal of Experimental Psychology: Applied, 9,* 23–32.

Stroop, J. R. (1935). Studies of interference in serial verbal reactions. *Journal of Experimental Psychology, 18,* 643–662.

Stroud, N. (2006). Accommodating language difference: A collaborative approach to justice in the Koori Court of Victoria. In K. Allan (ed.), *Selected papers from the 2005 Conference of the Australian Linguistic Society,* http://www.als.asn.au.

Styles, E. (2006). *The psychology of attention* (2nd edn). London: Psychology Press.

Surawski, M. K. and Ossoff, E. P. (2006). The effects of physical and vocal attractiveness on impression formation of politicians. *Current Psychology, 25,* 15–27.

Sutherland, S. (2007). *Irrationality* (2nd edn). London: Pinter & Martin.

Tadlock, D. F. (1978). SQ3R – Why it works, based on an information-processing theory of learning. *Journal of Reading, 22,* 110–112.

Talarico, J. M. and Rubin, D. C. (2003). Confidence, not consistency, characterizes flashbulb memories. *Psychological Science, 14,* 455–461.

Tallon-Baudry, C., Bertrand, O., Delpuech, C. and Pernier, J. (1996). Stimulus specificity of phase-locked and non-phase-locked 40 Hz visual responses in human. *Journal of Neurosciences, 16,* 4240–4249.

Tanaka, J. M. and Taylor, M. (1991). Object categories and expertise: Is the basic level in the eye of the beholder? *Cognitive Psychology, 23,* 457–482.

Tatler, B. W. and Kuhn, G. (2007). Don't look now: The magic of misdirection. In R. van Gompel, M. Fischer, W. Murray and R. Hill (eds), *Eye movement research: Insights on mind and brain* (pp. 697–714). London: Elsevier.

Tavris, C. and Aronson, E. (2007). *Mistakes were made (but not by me).* New York: Harcourt.

Taylor, I. and Taylor, M. (1990). *Psycholinguistics: Learning and using language.* Englewood Cliffs, NJ: Prentice Hall.

Taylor, S. E., Peplau, L. A. and Sears, D. O. (2006). *Social psychology* (12th edn). Upper Saddle River, NJ: Prentice-Hall.

Thorndike, E. L. (1898). *Animal intelligence. An experimental study of the associative processes in animals (Psychological Monographs 2).* New York, NY: Macmillan. (Reprint, New Brunswick, NJ, Transaction Publishing, 1999.)

Toates, F. (2007). *Biological psychology* (2nd edn). London: Prentice Hall.

Torrance, E. P. (1974). *The Torrance tests of creative thinking: Technical-norms manual.* Lexington, KY: Ginn.

Tovée, M. J. (2008). *An introduction to the visual system* (2nd edn). Cambridge: Cambridge University Press.

Treisman, A. (1964). Monitoring and storage of irrelevant messages in selective attention. *Journal of Verbal Learning and Verbal Behavior, 3,* 449–459.

Treisman, A. and Riley, J. G. A. (1969). Is selective attention selective perception or selective response? A further test. *Journal of Experimental Psychology, 79,* 27–34.

Treisman, A. M. and Geffen, G. (1967). Selective attention: Perception and response? *Quarterly Journal of Experimental Psychology, 19,* 1–18.

Tsao, F. M., Liu, H. M. and Kuhl, P. K. (2004). Speech perception in infancy predicts language development in the second year of life: A longitudinal study. *Child Development, 75,* 1067–1084.

Tschirgi, J. E. (1980). Sensible reasoning: A hypothesis about hypotheses. *Child Development, 51,* 1–10.

Turner, M. L. and Engle, R. W. (1989). Is working memory capacity task dependent? *Journal of Memory and Language, 28,* 127–154.

Tversky, A. and Kahneman, D. (1974). Judgment under uncertainty: Heuristics and biases. *Science, 185,* 1124–1131.

Underwood, G. (1974). Moray vs the rest: The effects of extended shadowing practice. *Quarterly Journal of Experimental Psychology, 26,* 368–372.

Vicente, K. and Wang, J. (1998). An ecological theory of expertise effects in memory recall. *Psychological Review, 105,* 33–57.

Vicente, K. J. and de Groot, A. D. (1990). The memory recall paradigm: Straightening out the historical record. *American Psychologist, 45,* 285–287.

Wade, K., Garry, M., Read, J. D. and Lindsay, D. S. (2002). A picture is worth a thousand lies: Using false photographs to create false childhood memories. *Psychonomic Bulletin & Review, 9,* 597–603.

Waldrop, M. M. (1988). A landmark in speech recognition. *Science, 240,* 1615.

Wallas, G. (1926). *The art of thought.* London: Cape.

Walsh, M. (1994). Interactional styles in the courtroom: An example from northern Australia. In J. Gibbons (ed.), *Language and the law* (pp. 217–233). Harlow, UK: Longman.

Ward, P., Hodges, N. J., Williams, A. M. and Starkes, J. L. (2004). Deliberate practice and expert performance: Defining the path to excellence. In A. M. Williams and N. J. Hodges (eds), *Skill acquisition in sport: Research, theory and practice* (pp. 231–258). London: Routledge.

Warren, R. M. and Warren, R. P. (1970). Auditory illusions and confusions. *Scientific American, 223,* 30–36.

Wason, P. C. (1960). On the failure to eliminate hypotheses in a conceptual task. *Quarterly Journal of Experimental Psychology, 12,* 129–140.

Wason, P. C. (1966). Reasoning. *New Horizons in Psychology, 1,* 135–151.

Wason, P. C. (1968). Reasoning about a rule. *Quarterly Journal of Experimental Psychology, 20,* 273–281.

Watson, D. and Tellegen, A. (1985). Toward a consensual structure of mood? *Psychological Bulletin, 98,* 219–235.

Watson, J. B. (1913). Psychology as the behaviorist views it. *Psychological Review, 20,* 158–177.

Waugh, N. C. and Norman, D. A. (1965). Primary memory. *Psychological Review, 72,* 89–104.

Wegner, D. (2003). The mind's best trick: How we experience conscious will. *Trends in Cognitive Sciences, 7,* 65–69.

Wegner, D. M. and Wheatley, T. (1999). Apparent mental causation. Sources of the experience of will. *American Psychologist, 54,* 480–492.

Weir, A. A. S., Chappell, J. and Kacelnik, A. (2002). Shaping of hooks in New Caledonian crows. *Science, 297,* 981–981.

Weisberg, R. W. (1999). Creativity and knowledge: A challenge to theories. In R. J. Sternberg (ed.), *Handbook of creativity* (pp. 226–250). New York, NY: Cambridge University Press.

Weisberg, R. W. (2006). *Creativity: Understanding innovation in problem solving, science, invention, and the arts.* New York, NY: Wiley.

Weisberg, R. W. and Alba, J. W. (1981). An examination of the alleged role of 'fixation' in the solution of several 'insight' problems. *Journal of Experimental Psychology: General, 110,* 169–192.

Wells, G. L. and Olson, E. A. (2003). Eyewitness testimony. *Annual Review of Psychology, 54,* 277–295.

Whiting, H. T. A. (1969). *Acquiring ball skill: A psychological interpretation.* Philadelphia, PA: Lea & Febiger.

Wilding, J. and Valentine, E. (1997). *Superior memory.* Hove, UK: Psychology Press.

Wilhelm, P. and Beishuizen, J.J. (2003). Content effects in self-directed inductive learning. *Learning and Instruction, 13,* 381–402.

Williams, A. M. and Davids, K. (1995). Declarative knowledge in sport: A by-product of experience or a characteristic of expertise? *Journal of Sport and Exercise Psychology, 17,* 259–275.

Williams, A. M. and Hodges, N. J. (2004). *Skill acquisition in sport: Research, theory and practice.* London: Routledge.

Williams, A. M., Davids, K. and Williams, J. G. (1999). *Visual perception and action in sport.* London: Routledge.

Willis, J. and Todorov, A. (2006). First impressions:

Making up your mind after a 100-ms exposure to a face. *Psychological Science, 17*, 592–598.

Winningham, R. G., Hyman, I. E. and Dinnel, D. L. (2000). Flashbulb memories? The effects of when the initial memory report was obtained. *Memory & Cognition, 8*, 209–216.

Wittgenstein, L. (1953). *Philosophical investigations* (G. E. M. Anscombe, trans.). Oxford, UK: Blackwell.

Wundt, W. (1874). *Grundzüge der physiologischen Psychologie (Principles of physiological psychology).* Leipzig, Germany: Engelmann.

Young, R. M. and O'Shea, T. (1981). Errors in children's subtraction. *Cognitive Science, 5*, 153–177.

Yuille, J. C. and Cutshall, J. L. (1986). A case study of eyewitness memory of a crime. *Journal of Applied Psychology, 71*, 291–301.

Zeki, S. (1993). *A vision of the brain.* Oxford: Blackwell.

Zhang, G. and Simon, H. A. (1985). STM capacity for Chinese words and idioms: Chunking and acoustical loop hypothesis. *Memory and Cognition, 13*, 193–201.

Zwitserlood, P. (1989). The locus of the effects of sentential-semantic context in spoken-word processing. *Cognition, 32*, 25–64.

Glossary

2 4 6 problem: Reasoning problem that underlines people's tendency for confirmation rather than falsification.

A

access consciousness: Elements of information in our mind that we can verbalise and describe.

acoustic confusion: The phenomenon where sounds that resemble each other tend to be confused in memory tasks.

acquired dyslexia: Difficulty in reading and writing, due to brain damage.

action potential: A brief electrical impulse used for transmitting information along an axon.

ad hoc hypothesis: A hypothesis that is specifically developed to explain a set of data.

Adaptive Control of Thought (ACT): Theory explaining expertise and skill acquisition as the progression from the application of isolated factual information to the application of complex procedures.

agnosia: Failure, due to brain damage, to recognise and associate meaning with persons, objects, sounds, and so on.

'a-ha' experience: The feeling that comes with the sudden realisation of a solution.

algorithm: A set of instructions (e.g. for specifying a computer program).

allocentric representation: Representation without a particular point of reference.

amnesia: Pathological loss of the ability to remember, either because information has been deleted or because one is unable to retrieve it. Amnesia can refer to the loss of past memories (retrograde amnesia) or the inability to store new memories (anterograde amnesia). Normal loss of information in long-term memory is referred to as forgetting.

amygdala: An almond-shaped group of nuclei located at the front and at the base of the temporal lobe. It is part of the limbic system, and is implicated in emotion (in particular, fear), learning and memory.

analogical problem solving: Method of solving a problem where one uses the solution known from another problem.

analogue format: Format where information is represented in a way that mirrors reality. For example, representing a map in an analogue format implies that the time to travel mentally from one point to another is proportional to the distance on the map.

anterograde amnesia: Inability to encode new information in LTM.

aphasia: A generic term covering a wide range of language impairments resulting from brain damage.

appraisal: The evaluative process that will serve as a base to determine an emotion.

approach (symbolic approach): The school of cognitive psychology which considers that cognition consists of the manipulation of symbols and which uses the computer analogy of the mind.

argument: In Kintsch and van Dijk's theory, the meaning of a word.

arousal: Level of activity of the automatic nervous system.

artefact category: A category consisting of human-made objects.

attention: Basic cognitive process that enables us to focus on a particular stimulus at the expense of others.

attenuator model: An early selection model of attention, which features an attenuator that may process information to various degrees.

autobiographical memory: Memory structure encoding sequences of events. For example, the 'doctor script' lists the time-dependent actions that typically occur when you go to your doctor.

automatic processing: Processing of information that is effortless, fast and outside consciousness; as a consequence, it is difficult to control.

automaticity: Notion that a cognitive process can be executed without attention.

availability heuristic: Heuristic consisting of assessing the frequency of an event based on how accessible the information is from memory.

axon: (Also called nerve fibre.) A long and thin projection of a neuron, which transmits action potentials from the neuron's body to the terminal buttons.

B

back-propagation: Learning algorithm used by some connectionist models, where information about errors is used to change the weight of the connections between nodes.

Barnum statement: Ambiguous statement that normally contains contradictory information and therefore applies to many people.

basal ganglia: A group of subcortical nuclei, including the caudate nucleus, the putamen and the globus pallidus. They play an important role in learning skills and controlling movement.

base rate information: Frequency of an event in the whole population.

behaviourism: The school of thought that dominated psychology from 1900 to 1960. It argued that psychology should study the relation between observable behaviour and observable stimuli in the environment, and avoided the use of 'mentalistic' terms such as memory and thinking.

binding problem: The question as to how the information in different parts of the brain is combined to form a unified representation.

binocular: Relating to two eyes.

binocular disparity: The fact that each retina receives a slightly different image of a scene.

bipolar cell: A cell in the retina, located between photoreceptors and ganglion cells, and transmitting signals from the former to the latter.

bistable percept: Stimulus that may be perceived in two different ways.

bottom-up: In a hierarchical system, a flow of information from a lower level to a higher level (a.k.a. stimulus-driven). Lower-level processes influence higher-level processes.

bounded rationality: Idea that people are rational within the limits imposed by the limited capacities of their cognitive processes.

brain imaging: A set of techniques that allow brain activity to be measured in real time.

brain stem: The lower part of the brain that connects to the spinal cord.

Broca's area: Area of the left posterior frontal lobe linked with speech production.

buffer: A memory structure where information is held temporarily.

C

Cartesian dualism: Prominent theory by René Descartes that assumes different entities for mind and body; these entities are supposed to interact in the pineal gland.

Cartesian theatre: A metaphor for the theories that assume that there must be a single place where all brain processes come together to produce consciousness.

case study approach: Method of investigating a phenomenon (e.g. creativity) that uses archival data (e.g. biographical reports of a specific and well-known discovery).

categorical speech perception: The phenomenon by which different sounds (called phones) are perceived as the same phoneme, in spite of small physical differences in the way they are pronounced.

category: A class of concepts that share some common properties.

cell assembly: A dynamically linked set of neurons that code for a chunk.

central executive: A theoretical concept encapsulating all the processes that regulate the flow of information within working memory, and between working memory and the other cognitive components.

central traits: Traits that are particularly important in forming an impression of a person or of a group (e.g. warm vs cold).

cerebellum: A large part of the brain (about 10% of the volume of the brain) attached to the brain stem, which is engaged in classical conditioning, motor control and language production.

cerebral cortex: The outermost layer of grey matter of the cerebral hemispheres, consisting of sulci and gyri.

cerebrum: (Also called telencephalon.) The most superior region of the brain, which consists of the cerebral cortex, the basal ganglia and the limbic system.

change blindness: Attention-related phenomenon in which it is difficult to spot a change in a scene after a blink (or a flicker) despite the subjective feeling of complete perception of the scene.

characteristic feature: A feature that is part of the best description of a prototype. Unlike defining features, such features are not necessary.

chunk: Meaningful unit of information formed from smaller pieces of information.

Chunks can be of different sizes. Used by the memory system and by extension by the cognitive system in general. Chunking: the process of creating new chunks.

chunking: See chunk.

chunking theory: Theory explaining how experts circumvent the limitations of cognitive processes through the acquisition of domain-specific knowledge, in particular small meaningful units of inter-connected elements (chunks).

cingulate cortex: A large piece of cortex, located within the hemispheres above the corpus callousum. It is part of the limbic system.

classical conditioning: Ch. 7.

classical conditioning: Process by which a stimulus neutral to an organism (animal or human) becomes associated with an automatic response.

co-articulation: The fact that sounds are not articulated individually and independently, but are affected by the articulation of adjacent sounds.

cocktail party phenomenon: Ability to concentrate on a single stimulus while disregarding others; often used to illustrate selectivity of attention.

code: A specific type of representation.

cognitive architecture: The structure and related processes of the cognitive system, within which information is manipulated. More specifically, refers to computer programs embodying this structure.

cognitive misers: The assumption that people process only a small amount of information when making decisions, and that they use heuristics to minimise

processing load. A variation of the idea of bounded rationality.

cognitive neuropsychology: The subfield of cognitive psychology studying patients with brain damage to understand human cognition.

cognitive neuroscience: The field studying cognition using the methods of neuroscience, including brain imaging.

competence: The abstract linguistic knowledge that native speakers have, irrespective of the errors they might make (cf. performance).

composition: Processes of making increasingly sophisticated sequences of actions by collapsing smaller sequences of actions (productions).

computational theory: A theory expressed as a computer program.

computer model: A theory expressed as one or several computer programs. The advantage of computer programs is that they can carry out the behaviour under study.

computer–mind analogy: The key assumption of the information-processing approach that, at some level of abstraction, the human mind functions in the same way as a computer.

concept: The building block of semantic knowledge.

concept-driven: See top-down processing.

conditional problem: Problem involving an if–then structure.

cone: A light-sensitive photoreceptor specialised in colour processing.

confirmation bias: Tendency to look for evidence that confirms a belief held rather than for evidence that may disconfirm it.

conjunctive concept: A concept defined by the joint presence of several attributes.

connectionism: Same as neural modelling.

consciousness: Awareness of experiencing perceptions and thoughts.

consolidation: Process by which memory traces are progressively strengthened. In theory, the process ends when the memory trace is stable.

controlled processing: Processing of information that is effortful, error prone and attention demanding.

convergence: The simultaneous and inward movement made by the two eyes to focus on a near object in order to maintain binocular vision.

convergent thinking: Mode of thinking that aims to find a single standard solution.

core: The fixed part of a schema.

covert attention: Attention to a stimulus without explicit movements of sense organs (e.g. eye).

creative person: A person who produces original and useful products.

Creative problem solving/ thinking out of the box: Assumption that, for finding a truly creative solution to a problem, we need to leave our knowledge behind and try to look at the problem from a fresh perspective.

creative process: Cognitive mechanisms that lead to original, novel and useful products.

creative product: A novel and useful creation that goes beyond the known.

creativity: Field of psychology investigating the cognitive processes leading to original creations or ideas.

D

decision making: Field of psychology that investigates how people reach decisions.

declarative memory: Component of memory containing verbalisable information about particular facts and events.

deductive reasoning: Type of reasoning consisting of coming to a necessary conclusion using a set of statements, also called premises.

defining feature (or defining attribute): A feature (or attribute) that is part of the definition of a concept.

definition: In the context of concepts, a rule making it possible to decide whether an object belongs or does not belong to a given category.

deliberate practice: Theory proposing that focused, effortful and inherently not enjoyable practice is the main engine behind the acquisition of domain-related knowledge and thus exceptional performance.

dendrite: A tree-like projection of the neuron's body that receives synaptic information from other neurons.

dependent variable: In an experiment, the variable that is being measured (e.g. response time).

detection threshold: The minimum intensity necessary for a sensory modality to respond.

developmental dyslexia: Difficulty in reading and writing, due to developmental factors.

dichotic listening: Method of investigating attention where participants get different auditory messages presented to each ear simultaneously.

disjunctive concept: A concept defined by the presence of at least one of several attributes.

divergent thinking: Mode of thinking that aims to find as many uncommon solutions as possible.

dorsal pathway: See where pathway.

dual-route model: Model proposing that reading out loud is made possible by two modules. The first contains rules translating written letters or groups of letters into sounds, and the second contains a lexicon providing pronunciation for entire written words.

dualism: The view that physical world and mental states are independent entities.

E

early selection models: Models of attention that propose that stimuli get selected at an early stage for later processing.

echoic memory: A memory buffer that holds information in sound format for a very brief period of time (similar to iconic memory).

ecological validity: The degree to which laboratory findings have relevance for everyday life.

EEG: Brain imaging technique recording electrical activity.

effective field of view: Same as perceptual span.

egocentric representation: Representation where the reference point is the position of the perceiver.

Einstellung **(mental set) effect:** The phenomenon where a well-known solution that comes first to the mind in a familiar situation blocks access to less-known, but possibly better, solutions.

Elaborative rehearsal: Repetition of items in short-term memory that includes semantic processing and thus leads to more durable memory traces.

embodied cognition: An approach at the intersection of cognitive psychology, computer science and robotics, which proposes that cognitive theories should take the body into account. This is typically done by carrying out simulations with robots.

emotion: An automatic response reflecting the evaluation of a stimulus or a situation.

emotional experience: The subjective feeling that emerges when we become conscious of an emotional response.

emotional response: Set of changes taking place in the brain and the body as a result of the evaluation of an item by the emotional system.

encoding: The process by which information in one type of representation is converted in a different type of representation.

epiphenomenalism: The view that our subjective feelings are not the product of an extra process but rather a by-product, sometimes even an illusion, of our cognitive processes.

episodic buffer: In Baddeley's theory, the memory store where information coming from the other components of working memory and from long-term memory are integrated to form a unified representation.

episodic memory: Memory system in charge of storing the memories of one's life.

event-related potential: Brain imaging technique recording electrical activity during the repeated presentation of stimuli.

exemplar: According to exemplar theory, one of the many representations that long-term memory holds about a given category.

expected utility: Subjective quality of a solution based on its desirability and probability.

experiment: A method for collecting empirical data in order to test a hypothesis or to understand the causal relationship between variables. In an experiment, one or several independent variables are manipulated, and one or several dependent variables are measured. Experiments are key to the scientific approach.

expertise: The field of psychology that investigates the cognitive processes behind exceptional performances.

exteroception: Sensory modalities in charge of detecting changes outside the body.

eyewitness testimony: The field of research concerned with the mechanisms underlying people's ability to testify what they have seen. Most of the research aims to uncover the biases in human testimony.

F

falsification: Deliberate and direct search for evidence that may run counter to the hypothesis or belief currently held.

family resemblance: The notion, proposed by the Austrian philosopher Ludwig Wittgenstein, that different members of a category resemble each other in different ways, thus making it impossible to infer defining features.

figure-ground principle: The principle that, in perception in general and in social perception in particular, a few things stand out while other things remain in the background.

filter model: Historically one of the first cognitive theories. Developed by Donald Broadbent, it proposes that information selection happens at an early stage through a filter that selects relevant information.

fixation: Pause between two saccades, when the visual gaze remains on the same location.

fixed parameter: A parameter the value of which cannot be changed.

flashbulb memory: Type of episodic memory that has strong emotional content, typically dramatic news.

flowchart: A diagram specifying the order with which information is processed in a model.

fMRI: Brain imaging technique recording change in blood flow related to neutral activity.

forgetting: The process(es) by which we lose information we once knew. Forgetting happens either because information has been deleted or it is not possible to retrieve it from long-term memory. Forgetting can be normal or pathological (see amnesia).

formal theory: A theory expressed using a formal language such as mathematics.

formalism: An abstract language or notation (e.g. mathematics, logic, computer programs) that is being used to express scientific theories.

fovea: Central part of the retina where visual acuity is the highest.

framework: A loose set of theoretical constructs, which can be used to develop more precise theories and models.

free parameter: A parameter in a model that is free to vary, and that is usually estimated using the empirical data that the model is supposed to explain. Models with many free parameters can explain any data, and are thus of limited scientific interest.

free recall: Experimental paradigm where participants are asked to reproduce briefly presented material (e.g. list of words) without particular order.

functional fixedness: Tendency to consider only the common functions of human-made objects when they could be used for other purposes.

fusiform gyrus: Cortex located at the bottom of the temporal lobe, engaged among other things with face recognition.

G

gambler's fallacy: False belief that an event (e.g. tails if a fair coin is tossed) will soon happen only because it has not happened in the few previous trials.

ganglion cell: A type of neuron in the retina receiving information from photoreceptors through bipolar cells and amacrine cells. The long axons of ganglion cells form the optic nerve.

garden-path model: A model proposed by Frazier and Rayner that assumes that syntactic processing whilst reading is done serially.

geons: Stands for geometric ion. Basic perceptual units used to mentally reconstruct objects in Biederman's recognition-by-components theory. Geons act as a kind of visual alphabet.

Gestalt laws: The laws with which we organise elements in a two-dimensional display.

Gestalt psychology: A school of thought that flourished in the first half of the twentieth century. It was based on the principle that 'The whole is greater than the sum of the parts' and that reorganisation is a key mechanism for perception and problem solving.

glial cell: A supportive cell in the central nervous system that produces myelin, and provides support, nutrition and protection to neurons.

global workspace theory: The theory that consciousness is achieved through the connectivity of various brain subsystems and is a consequence of the information exchanged between them.

goal state: The desired end situation of a problem.

grammatical morpheme: Function words (e.g. 'for', 'a') and inflectional endings (e.g. -ed or -s to indicate past tense and plural, respectively) that are used for syntactic reasons.

grapheme: A basic unit of a written language.

group stereotype: A simplified and commonly held schema about a group of people, typically not based on objective information.

gyrus: A bump in the cortex separated by sulci.

H

habit: A learned pattern of behaviour that is regularly repeated. Habits lead to actions that occur automatically, require little or no attention.

habituation: The decrease of sensitivity to a harmless and repeated stimulus.

halo effect: A cognitive bias where the first impression affects the perception of others characteristics, so that one can form a consistent representation of other people (e.g., as consistently good or bad).

hard problem: Problem of how to explain the feeling of existence (phenomenal consciousness) using material neural processes.

heuristic: Rule of thumb used to solve a problem or make a decision, which leads to a solution that is usually good enough, although it might not be best one.

hierarchy of inclusion relations: Nested organisation of categories, with some categories being included in others (e.g. the category 'birds' is a subset of the category 'animals').

hill climbing: The heuristic consisting in choosing an action that brings one closer to a goal state.

hippocampus: Part of the limbic system located in the medial temporal lobe that is essential for learning, memory and spatial navigation.

hybrid architecture: A cognitive theory that combines symbolic processing with neural modelling.

hypercolumn: A small processing module in the brain, where neurons processing the same receptive field are grouped together.

I

iconic memory: A memory buffer that holds information in visual format for a very brief period of time. This buffer does not allow any form of control over the information it holds.

idealism: The view that only our subjective experience exists; a reaction to dualism.

ill-defined problem: A problem where some aspects (e.g. the goal or the operators) are not specified; most everyday problems are ill-defined.

illumination: Stage in the creative process characterised by a sudden discovery of the solution.

illusion: A percept that does not reflect reality.

inattentional blindness: Attention-related phenomenon in which it is difficult to notice a seemingly obvious and constantly present feature in a complex scene because our attention is directed to a different aspect of the scene.

incubation: Stage in the creative process that follows active attempts to find a solution. This stage is characterised by little conscious problem-related activity, but insightful solutions are sometimes found.

independent variable: In an experiment, the variable that is under the control of the experimenter and that is varied to answer theoretical questions.

inductive reasoning: Type of reasoning consisting of obtaining a general conclusion based on specific facts. The conclusion is not necessarily true, but is likely to be true.

infero-temporal cortex: The lower part of the temporal lobe, essential for visual object recognition.

informal theory: A theory expressed only using a natural language such as English.

information flow: The path followed by information during its processing by the cognitive system, from input to output.

information-processing approach: A very influential approach in cognitive psychology where an analogy is made between the human mind and the way computers work.

initial state: The original situation of a problem.

inner scribe: In Logie's theory of working memory, the component in charge of carrying cognitive operations on visuo-spatial information.

input: The information that is accessed by a cognitive module. For the perceptual system, the input is the information captured by the senses. For short-term memory, the input is the information either forwarded by the perceptual system or retrieved from long-term memory.

insight: Sudden realisation of a solution, often after several unsuccessful trials. Sometimes happens when one does not think about the problem.

instance theory: Theory describing automaticity as a shift from effortful and general calculations to the fast retrieval of previous instances or memory traces.

instrumental (or operant) conditioning: Process by which a given behaviour sees its probability of occurring changed by a response in the environment.

interference: The phenomenon whereby a piece of information perturbs the processing of another piece of information.

interference theory: Theory dealing with the influence of various factors on how irrelevant information alters the processing of relevant, target information.

introspection: The method consisting of observing one's own thoughts and sensations to understand cognition. This method, used by Wundt at the beginning of scientific psychology, is now rarely used because of its limitations.

J

just-noticeable difference: The minimal difference between two stimulations that a sensory modality can detect.

K

knowledge compilation: Process of integrating simple isolated information into complex if–then procedures (productions). This corresponds to a shift from declarative to procedural knowledge.

knowledge-lean domains: Activities that can be executed without any prior specialised knowledge; usually puzzles.

knowledge-rich domains: Activities that require specific prior knowledge for successful performance; usually activities found in everyday life.

L

late selection models: Models of attention proposing that processing and selection of stimuli happen at a later stage.

lateral geniculate nucleus: A nucleus in the thalamus that relays information from the retina of the eye to the primary visual cortex.

law of large numbers: In statistics, the fact that many instances of an observation (e.g. measurement, experiment) are more likely to provide a correct estimate than just a few instances.

Libet's clock: An experimental method, using a simple clock, for disentangling the subjective feelings of will and the objective brain processes underpinning it.

limbic system: A set of interconnected brain structures thought to be important for emotion, learning and memory.

linguistics: The field concerned with the scientific study of language.

long-term memory (or long-term store): Structure and mechanisms storing the permanent knowledge we have acquired over our lifetime. This knowledge is not directly accessible to consciousness, unless it is placed in short-term memory.

long-term potentiation (LTP): Long-lasting synaptic change that increases the responsiveness of a neuron and leads to learning.

M

M cell: A type of ganglion cell with low spatial resolution transmitting information about motion and edges.

macro-structure: A reduced version of the micro-structure, to which schematic knowledge has been added. The global meaning of a text.

mad genius hypothesis: Assumption that highly creative people share uncommon characteristics of thinking with people who are mentally ill.

magnocellular pathway: A pathway from the retina to the lateral geniculate nucleus, which conveys information about motion and coarse representation of a scene.

maintenance rehearsal: Mere repetition of one or more items in short-term memory so that the memory trace is kept active.

materialism: The view that our subjective feelings are the product of material brain processes.

mathematical model: A theory expressed in mathematical terms. For example, a model could be expressed as a set of equations.

maximiser: An individual that tries to find the most desirable and optimal solution.

means–ends analysis: The heuristic consisting in finding the difference between the current state and the goal state, and then creating a subgoal that aims to remove this difference.

memory span: The maximum amount of information that one can hold in short-term memory at a given time.

memory trace: The physical substrate supporting the existence of a memory.

mental model theory: Theory according to which we build an internal representation of every statement when trying to reason.

meta-analysis: A statistical method to summarise the results of many different empirical studies on the same topic. One of the first meta-analyses was on the Pygmalion effect.

micro-structure: Propositions taken from a text and connected together. The local meaning of a text.

midbrain (also called the mesencephalon): The brain structure above the brain stem. It includes two main structures – the tegmentum and the tectum.

mind–body problem: Old philosophical problem about the dependence and interaction between the objective physical world and subjective non-material mental states.

model: A theory where all mechanisms and parameters have been specified in detail.

modulation: Process by which a cognitive operation is influenced by another operation.

monocular: Relating to one eye.

mood: The baseline level of activity of the emotional system when it is not solicited.

motion parallax: The fact that close objects seem to move faster than far-away objects when the perceiver is in motion.

motivation: The drive to attain (or avoid) a goal.

myelin: A fatty substance produced by glial cells that insulates and thus improves the electrical conductivity of certain axons.

N

natural category (or natural kind): A category that exists in the natural world.

nature versus nurture controversy: Debate about the relative importance of innate characteristics versus experience in determining the cause of individual differences in behaviour and traits.

negative emotions: Emotions indicating that a potentially harmful item is in the environment. Elaborated negative emotions such as shame are ontologically dependent on basic negative emotions and refer more to cognitions than to response reactions to a stimulus.

negativity effect: Tendency to attach more importance to negative evaluations than to positive evaluations.

neglect: Neuropsychological condition in which damage to one side of the brain (usually the right) results in ignoring one side of a scene (usually the left).

neural modelling: A type of computational modelling that is loosely inspired by the way neurons process information in the brain.

neuron: A brain cell that processes and transmits information.

neurotransmitter: A chemical substance released in a synapse to transmit information between two neurons.

node: An element of a network (e.g. a semantic network or a neural network).

node of Ranvier: A gap in the myelin sheath of an axon.

nominal category (or nominal kind): A category consisting of entities grouped together based on arbitrary characteristics.

non-computational theory: A formal theory expressed with a formalism other than a computer program (e.g. logic).

non-declarative memory: All forms of memories that cannot be verbalised.

O

occipital lobe: The most posterior region of the cerebral cortex, which processes visual input.

occlusion: When an object or part of an object is hidden by the presence of another object.

occlusion paradigm: Technique for investigating expert performance by disabling particular information in a complex dynamic stimulus.

operator: In problem solving, an action or a move that leads to a new state.

optic nerve: The bundle of nervous fibres made by the axons of retinal ganglion cells, and going from the eye to lateral geniculate nucleus.

output: The information that is provided by a cognitive module. For example, perception takes a set of signals from various modalities as input and outputs a unified piece of information of the reality: the percept.

overfitting: In modelling, the use of many free parameters to obtain a nearly perfect fit to the data.

overt attention: Attention to a stimulus with explicit movements of sense organs (e.g. the eye) towards the stimulus.

P

P cell: A type of ganglion cell with high spatial resolution, and transmitting information about colour and fine details.

parietal lobe: Region of cerebral cortex located above the temporal lobe and behind the frontal lobe.

parvocellular pathway: A pathway from the retina to the lateral geniculate nucleus, which conveys information about colour and form processing.

percept: The output of perceptual processing. Usually a chunk of information reflecting an aspect of reality.

perception: A set of systems that aim to inform the brain about all the events occurring inside and outside the body.

perceptual priming: See priming.

perceptual span: The amount of information that can be held in one fixation. This varies with the difficulty of the input (e.g. in reading, complexity of text) and the level of expertise of the perceiver. Also called effective field of view.

performance: The actual behaviour shown by the speakers of a given language, possibly marred by hesitations, errors and repetitions (cf. competence).

person positivity bias: Tendency to evaluate other people positively.

PET: Imaging technique producing a three-dimensional picture of the brain.

phenomenal consciousness: Subjective experience of ourselves, subjective feeling of self.

phoneme: The smallest sound unit that forms a meaningful contrast in a given language. Note that different languages typically use different sets of phonemes.

phonological loop: In Baddeley's theory of working memory, the process that constantly rehearses speech-based information so that it is not lost due to normal forgetting.

phonological store: In Baddeley's theory of working memory, the passive store in which speech-based information is held.

phonology: The subfield of linguistics studying the way sounds are produced and perceived in human languages.

photoreceptor: A cell transforming light energy into a neural signal. In the human eye, photoreceptors consist of rods and cones.

positive emotions: Emotions indicating either the absence of issue or positive prospects.

poverty of the stimulus argument: The argument, defended by Chomsky, that there is not enough information in the speech received by children for them to learn the syntax of their language. Therefore, there must exist some innate knowledge of language (see Universal Grammar).

power law of practice: The phenomenon that performance typically improves rapidly at the beginning, and increasingly more slowly later. The term comes from the fact that the best way to fit the learning data is typically obtained with a power function: $P = aT^b$, where P is performance, T is time devoted to practice, and a and b are free parameters.

practice view: The view that dedication and practice are the main reasons for exceptional performance.

pragmatic reasoning schema theory: Theory according to which people reason about permission, obligation and causation using context-sensitive schemata.

pragmatics: The subfield of linguistics studying how intended meaning is conveyed in languages.

premise: Fact or statement used to arrive at a conclusion.

preparation: First stage in the creative process where one is familiarised with the situation at hand.

primacy effect: The fact that people have better memory for the first items in a list. This effect is not eliminated when another task is interpolated between presentation and recall.

primary memory: William James's term for short-term memory.

priming: The phenomenon where a previously experienced stimulus influences perception/ performance of the subsequent stimuli of a similar kind.

problem constraints: The rules of the problem at hand.

problem solving: The field of psychology that investigates the strategies people employ when they are faced with an unknown situation.

problem space: All possible situations (states) in a problem.

procedural memory/procedural knowledge: Component of memory containing actions and sequences of actions (productions), which are applicable in various situations and constitute the core of skilful behaviour. Procedural knowledge cannot be verbalised.

processing: Operations that are applied to a piece of information.

production rules (a.k.a. IF–THEN rules, or simply productions): Specific actions, or sequences of actions, which are executed if a situation is recognised as a familiar one. A production system is a model consisting of a set of productions.

proposition: Refers to the minimal combination of words of which one can say whether it is true or false (typically, a phrase or clause).

propositional format: Language-like format where there is no direct correspondence between mental representations and what is being represented. For example, a map could be represented with a statement such as 'the tree is next to the house'. In this case, mentally travelling from one point to another is not proportional to the distance on the map.

proprioception: Sensory modalities in charge of detecting changes inside the body.

prosopagnosia: Specific failure to recognise and associate meaning with faces.

prospective memory: A memory aimed at reminding people to undertake an action at some point in the future.

protocol analysis: Technique that analyses and quantifies the think-aloud statements collected during problem solving.

prototype: The most typical member of a category.

pseudo-word superiority effect: The phenomenon where a letter is recognised more rapidly when it is presented as part of a pronounceable non-word than a non-pronounceable non-word.

Pygmalion effect: The phenomenon where placing positive expectations on somebody causes an improvement in performance.

R

rational model of inference: A class of models postulating that people draw conclusions and make decisions using a logical and optimal way of thinking.

rationality: The assumption that humans act optimally when trying to achieve their goals.

reasoning: Field of psychology that investigates how people come to conclusions.

recall task: See free recall.

recency effect: The fact that people have better memory for the last items in a list. This effect is sensitive to interferences. If participants carry out a demanding task, such as counting backwards by 3s, between presentation and recall, then recall performance with the last items drops.

receptive field: The region of the visual field where the presence of a stimulus affects the firing rate of a neuron.

receptors: When referring to sensory modalities, the cells at the interface between the body and external world. When referring to neurons, the elements on the surface that detect the presence of specific compounds (e.g. neurotransmitters).

recognition by components: A theory of object recognition developed by Biederman. It posits that we recognise objects by using basic geometrical building blocks (the geons).

recognition heuristic: Use of a single piece of knowledge available through familiarity to make decisions about complex issues.

recognition task: An experimental paradigm consisting of two stages. In the first stage, participants are presented with a list of items. In the second stage, these items are mixed with new items; participants have to indicate whether each item was presented in the first stage.

reductionism: Philosophical position that aims to describe and understand complex phenomena in terms of simple constituents.

regression: Eye movement to a point of the display that had previously been fixated on.

representation: A mental unit with which we understand the world. It can be processed, stored, transformed.

representational change theory: Theory explaining insight as the consequence of a different problem representation.

representativeness heuristic: Heuristic where membership of a category is judged based on similarity with the typical member of the category, and where base rate information is ignored.

restructuring: Process by which the representation of a problem is changed in order to find the appropriate solution.

retina: A 0.5 mm layer of cells at the back of the eye, consisting of photoreceptors, bipolar cells and ganglion cells.

retinotopic map: The fact that the spatial arrangement of information on the retina is maintained in a given brain region.

retinotopic organisation: One-to-one correspondence between regions of the retina and the organisation of neurons in a specific part of the brain.

retrograde amnesia: Loss of information that preceded a trauma.

rod: A cylinder-like photoreceptor requiring less light intensity than a cone, and providing information about shades of grey.

role schema: Schema about how people in particular roles should behave (e.g. 'good citizen' or 'university student'). Role schemas tend to be unrealistic.

rule of agreement: Reasoning rule for drawing conclusions about causality. Specifically, it states that if X is followed by Y, then X is sufficient to Y, thus X might be the cause of Y although it might not.

rule of difference: Reasoning rule for drawing conclusions about causality. Specifically, it states that if Y does not occur when X does not occur, then X is necessary for Y to occur.

S

saccade: Type of eye movement characterised by a sudden move from one point of the display to another point.

salience: What makes a stimulus stand out (e.g. brightness, colour, novelty).

satisficer: An individual that uses solutions that are good enough, but that may not be the best.

scaling: A quantification of the relation between the objective intensity of a physical stimulus and its subjective perception.

schema: Information about a particular situation acquired through experience, with ways of dealing with that situation. A schema typically consists of a core (fixed information) and slots (variable information).

scientific law: A statement summarising a large number of empirical phenomena. Some scientific laws can be expressed mathematically. In cognitive psychology, a classic scientific law is the power law of learning.

script: Long-term memory structure encoding sequences of events. For example, the script of 'visit to the doctor' lists the time-dependent actions that typically occur when you go to your physician.

secondary memory: William James's term for long-term memory.

selection task: Reasoning problem that underlines people's tendency for confirmation rather than falsification.

self-fulfilling prophecy: The phenomenon where false expectations influence interactions with people to the point that these people change their behaviour and attitudes in

a way that is consistent with those expectations.

semantic memory: Part of long-term memory dedicated to items that carry meaning.

semantic network: Network of semantically related items, in which the activation of one item spreads to other items. A semantic network reflects not only what a person knows but also how knowledge is organised.

semantics: The subfield of linguistics studying how meaning is conveyed in languages.

sensation: Simple input data in the first stage of processing external stimuli by the senses, which are the building blocks for percepts.

sensitisation: The increased sensitivity following the repeated presentation of a noxious stimulus.

sensors: In biology, the cells that transform the physical dimension being detected into a neural signal.

sensory modality: A system dedicated to detect the values or variations in one or more physical dimension(s). For example, audition detects variation in air pressure, and smell detects (and quantifies) the presence of molecules.

sensory registers: Short-lasting memory buffers that store perceptual information for a few hundred milliseconds. This information is not accessible to conscious control.

serial position curve: The curve formed when recall performance is plotted as a function of the order of presentation of the items. This curve typically forms a 'U' as the first and last items tend to be remembered better than those that were presented in between.

shadowing: Technique in dichotic listening that requires participants to repeat the sentences heard in one ear, in order to direct their attention.

short-term memory (or short-term store): A temporary memory buffer in which we put the information we need to process. This information is accessible to consciousness.

simple concept: A concept defined by a single attribute.

slot: The variable part of a schema.

social cognition: Field of psychology between cognitive psychology and social psychology, which studies how people process information about the social world.

spelling-to-sound rule: A rule indicating how a grapheme should be pronounced. For example, 'ph' should be read with the /f/ sound.

spillover effect: Phenomenon where the reading difficulty of a word affects the fixation time of a following word.

spreading of activation: The fact that the activation of one node in a network spreads to all nodes that are linked.

stimulus-driven: See bottom-up.

Stroop effect: When asked to name the colour in which words are written, it takes longer to name words referring to a colour incongruent with the name than to name words that are congruent or neutral. Classic evidence for automatic processing, as participants cannot help reading words.

structuralism: The school of thought proposing that the content of mind can be broken down into elementary parts. This approach fell into

disrepute because of its association with introspection.

subliminal persuasion: Claim that people's behaviour could be influenced by previously experienced stimuli or messages that had not been consciously processed.

subliminal priming: The phenomenon where an unconsciously perceived stimulus influences conscious perception and performance on the subsequent stimuli.

sulcus: A groove on the surface of the cortex.

supervisory activating system: System responsible for suppressing automated behaviour and resolving conflicts when necessary.

symbol: A pattern standing for, or representing, something else.

symbolic modelling: A type of computational modelling, popularised by Newell and Simon, which proposes that the manipulation of symbols is central to cognition. A symbol is defined as a pattern standing for something else.

synapse: The junction point between two neurons, which allows electrical (rare in adult mammals) or chemical communication. With chemical synapses: the tiny gap between two neurons (typically between an axon and a dendrite) where neurotransmitters are released.

synchrony firing: The phenomenon where cells fire at the same rhythm to code an object. A possible answer to the binding problem.

syntax: The subfield of linguistics studying the relation between words in a sentence.

system: A set of components and their relationships.

T

talent view: The view that exceptional performance is primarily due to innate abilities.

template: A complex schematic structure made out of smaller chunks, stored in memory and connected to characteristic actions/solutions.

template theory: Theory of expertise building on chunking theory and proposing that well-elaborated chunks lead to larger meaningful units (templates).

temporal lobe: Region of cerebral cortex located beneath the frontal and parietal lobes. Involved in auditory perception and stores perceptual information.

texture gradient: The fact that the apparent texture of an object changes with distance.

thalamus: A structure near the centre of the brain, which relays sensory information towards the cerebral cortex.

theory: A set of statements aimed at summarising and explaining a body of empirical phenomena and at making new predictions.

theory of (perceptual) load: Theory proposing that attention is a cognitive process with limited resources, based on which early or late selection occurs.

think-aloud technique: A technique where participants are asked to verbalise their thoughts while solving a problem.

top-down processing: In a hierarchical system, a flow of information from a higher level to a lower level. Higher-level processes influence lower-level processes.

transduction: Cellular mechanism by which an

external stimulus (e.g. molecule or pressure) is converted into a specific neural response.

transfer: Phenomenon where knowledge acquired in one situation is applied in another, possibly similar, situation.

trial and error learning: Learning without a general plan, where people (and animals) painstakingly learn to solve a problem by trying out various solutions, usually without success.

typicality gradient: Ordering of the members of a category as a function of the extent to which they resemble the prototype.

U

unified theory of cognition: A theory aiming to explain not only one aspect of cognition, but all aspects. Usually implemented as a computer program.

Universal Grammar: The theory, put forward by Chomsky, that the key elements of syntax are the same in all human languages and that they are innate.

V

V1: Another name for the primary visual cortex, which is located at the back of the occipital cortex. It processes simple visual features and joins them into more complex ones.

v4: Visual area 4, one of the components of the visual cortex. It is concerned with colour processing, orientation and recognition of visual features of intermediate complexity.

valence: The positive or negative character of an emotional experience.

ventral pathway: See what pathway.

verbal protocols: The protocols obtained when participants are asked to verbalise their thoughts.

verification: Last stage in the creative process, during which the feasibility of the solution is tested.

view-invariant: Not depending on the angle of vision with which an object is perceived.

visual cache: In Logie's theory of working memory, the passive memory store used to transiently store visual information.

visual search: An often-used paradigm where participants look for the presence of specific stimuli among other elements.

W

well-defined problem: A problem where all aspects are clearly specified; refers mostly to artificial laboratory puzzles.

Wernicke's area: A region of the posterior part of the left temporal lobe involved with language comprehension.

what pathway: The route of visual processing leading to the inferior temporal cortex and concerned with object form and colour. Also called ventral pathway.

where pathway: The route of visual processing leading to the parietal cortex and concerned with motion, object location in space and control of actions with objects. Also called the dorsal pathway.

word length effect: The phenomenon where short words are better recalled than long words.

word segmentation: The process by which speech, which is continuous, is perceived as distinct words.

word superiority effect: The phenomenon where a letter is recognised more rapidly when it is presented as part of a word than when it is presented individually or as part of a non-word.

working memory: See short-term memory.

Würzburg School: A school of thought active before the Second World War that was interested in high-level thinking.

Z

zombie thought experiment: An argument often used to question the validity of the materialist view according to which objective brain processes can be equated to subjective feelings.

Index